THE FIRST ADMINISTRATION

OF

JAMES MADISON

1809—1813

HISTORY OF THE UNITED STATES.

BY

HENRY ADAMS.

Vols. I. and II.—The First Administration of Jefferson. 1801–1805.

Vols. III. and IV.—The Second Administration of Jefferson. 1805–1809.

Vols. V. and VI.—The First Administration of Madison. 1809–1813.

Vols. VII., VIII., and IX.—The Second Administration of Madison. 1813–1817. With an Index to the Entire Work.

HISTORY

OF THE

UNITED STATES OF AMERICA

DURING THE FIRST ADMINISTRATION OF

JAMES MADISON

BY HENRY ADAMS

VOL. II.

ANTIQUARIAN PRESS LTD.
New York
1962

First Published
1891-1896
by
Charles Scribner's Sons

———

Reprinted 1962
by
Antiquarian Press, Ltd.
New York, N.Y.

Edition Limited to 750 Sets

Library of Congress Catalog Card Number: 61-8054

Printed in the U.S.A.
———
NOBLE OFFSET PRINTERS, INC.
NEW YORK 3, N.Y.

CONTENTS OF VOL. II.

CHAPTER   PAGE

I. PINKNEY'S INAMICABLE LEAVE 1

II. THE "LITTLE BELT" 25

III. MADISON TRIUMPHANT 46

IV. HARRISON AND TECUMTHE 67

V. TIPPECANOE 90

VI. MEETING OF THE TWELFTH CONGRESS . . . 113

VII. WAR DEBATES 133

VIII. WAR LEGISLATION 154

IX. MADISON AS MINERVA 176

X. HESITATIONS 199

XI. WAR 220

XII. JOEL BARLOW 245

XIII. REPEAL OF THE ORDERS IN COUNCIL . . . 267

XIV. INVASION OF CANADA 289

XV. HULL'S SURRENDER 312

XVI. THE NIAGARA CAMPAIGN 336

XVII. NAVAL BATTLES 362

XVIII. DISCORD 388

XIX. EXECUTIVE EMBARRASSMENTS 412

XX. WAR LEGISLATION 435

INDEX 459

HISTORY OF THE UNITED STATES.

CHAPTER I.

RARELY had a great nation approached nearer than
England to ruin without showing consciousness of
danger. Napoleon's boast to his Chamber of Commerce, that within ten years he would subject his
rival, was not ill-founded. The conquest of Russia,
which Napoleon meant to make certain, combined
with a war between the United States and Great
Britain, coming immediately upon the destruction of
private credit and enterprise in 1810, could hardly
fail to shake the British empire to its foundation;
and perhaps the worst sign of danger was the absence
of popular alarm. The intelligence of all England
with feelings equally strong, whether mute or voci-
ferous, was united in contempt for the stolid incompetence of the Tory faction beyond anything known
in England since the Stuarts; but both Houses of
Parliament, as well as the Crown, were conscious of
needing no better representatives than Perceval and

Eldon, and convulsions that shook the world never stirred the composure of these men. The capital and credit on which England's power rested were swept away; the poorer classes were thrown out of employment; the price of wheat,[1] which averaged in 1807 seventy-eight shillings per quarter of eight bushels, in 1808 eighty-five shillings, and in 1809 one hundred and six shillings, in 1810 rose to one hundred and twelve shillings, or about three dollars and a half a bushel, and remained at or above this rate until the autumn of 1813; while abroad, the Spanish peninsula was subdued by Napoleon, whose armies occupied every part of Spain and Portugal except Cadiz and Lisbon. Sweden, the last neutral in Europe, elected a French general of Bonaparte's family as king, and immediately afterward declared war on England; and the United States closed their ports to British commerce, and menaced a declaration of war. The exports of Great Britain fell off one third in the year 1811. The sources of England's strength showed exhaustion.

Neither these arguments nor even the supreme argument of war shook the steadfast mind of Spencer Perceval. Responsibilities that might have driven him to insanity took the form of religious duties; and with the support of religious or patriotic formulas statesmen could sleep in peace amidst the wreck of nations. After the insanity of King George was admitted, at the beginning of November, 1810, Spencer

[1] Tooke's Prices, ii. 389, 390.

Perceval became for a time the King of England, but a king without title. The Prince of Wales, the future regent, was obliged to wait for an Act of Parliament authorizing him to assume power. The Prince of Wales had all his life detested the Tory influence that surrounded the throne, and had associated with Whigs and liberals, like Sheridan and Fox. Perceval expected to retire; the prince could not yet take control, and this dead-lock put a stop to serious government. Nothing but business of routine could be undertaken.

If the United States could wait till spring, their friends were likely to be once more in power, or the Tory influence would be so far shaken that the danger of war might pass. For this possible revolution both Madison and Pinkney twelve months before would have waited with confidence and pleasure; but repeated disappointments had convinced them that their patience was useless. Pinkney had asked and received instructions to require a decision or to quit England. When November arrived, the day on which Napoleon's Decrees stood revoked according to the Duc de Cadore, Pinkney acted in London on his own responsibility, as Madison acted at Washington, and sent to Lord Wellesley a note, dated November 3, asking for an immediate repeal of the British Orders in Council, on the ground that Napoleon's revocation had taken effect. "That it has taken effect cannot be doubted," he said; [1] but he offered no evidence

[1] State Papers, iii. 373.

to support his assertion.   He also assumed that
England was bound to withdraw Fox's blockade of
the French coast from Brest to the Elbe, as well as
Spencer Perceval's subsequent measures which were
called into existence by Napoleon's Continental system, and were to cease with it.   Both these demands were made without instructions founded on
the knowledge of Cadore's letter.

At that moment Lord Wellesley was full of hope
that at last he should remove Spencer Perceval from
his path.   Every one supposed, and had good ground
for believing, that the Prince of Wales would at once
form a new Government, with Wellesley and the
Whigs for its support.   At such a crisis Wellesley
could not expect or indeed wish to effect a partial
and sudden change of foreign policy.   He waited a
month before taking official notice of Pinkney's letter,
and when he replied,[1] December 4, said only that
" after the most accurate inquiry " he had been unable to obtain any authentic intelligence of the French
repeal, and begged the American minister to furnish
whatever information he possessed on the subject.

The American minister possessed no information
on the subject, but he received, December 11, news of
the President's proclamation founded on the French
repeal, and was the more decided to insist on his
ground.   Finding that conversations produced no
effect, Pinkney took his pen once more, — and then
began another of the diplomatic duels which had oc-

[1] State Papers, iii. 376.

curred so often in the course of the last six years;
but for the first time the American champion with
weak arguments and indifferent temper used the kind
of logic likely to produce conviction in the end.

Pinkney maintained that the French Decrees were
revoked and that Fox's blockade was illegal. Neither
position was beyond attack. The American doctrine
of blockade was by no means clear. The British
government never attempted to defend its sweeping
Orders of 1807 and 1809 on the ground of legality;
these were admittedly illegal, and a proper *casus belli*
if America chose to make war on their account.
England claimed only that the United States were
bound to make war on France for the Berlin Decree
of Nov. 21, 1806, before making war on England for
her retaliatory Orders of 1807. In order to evade
this difficulty, France declared that her Decree of
November, 1806, was retaliatory on Fox's blockade of
May, 1806. America began by maintaining that as
far as concerned neutral commerce both belligerents
used retaliation for illegitimate objects, and that the
United States might rightfully declare war against
either or both. The position was easily understood,
and had the advantage of being historically true; but
the United States stood on less certain ground when
they were drawn into discussion of the legal theory
involved in Fox's blockade.

England held [1] that Fox's blockade of May, 1806,

[1] Instructions of Wellesley to Foster, April 10, 1811; Papers
presented to Parliament, February, 1813.

covering the French coast from the Elbe to Brest, was a lawful blockade, supported by a particular naval force detached for that special purpose and sufficient for its object, until the blockade itself was merged in the avowedly extra-legal paper-blockades of 1809; and that if the paper-blockades were withdrawn, Great Britain had the right to re-establish Fox's blockade with an efficient naval force to execute it.

President Madison held a different opinion. He insisted,[1] and ordered Pinkney to insist, that a particular port must be invested by a particular naval force; and that Great Britain ought not to contend that her naval force was adequate to blockade a coast a thousand miles long. On this ground the President, July 5, 1810,[2] instructed Pinkney to require the annulment of Fox's blockade as "palpably at variance with the law of nations." In order to prove the impartiality of this demand, the President promised to insist that the repeal required from France as its counterpart should "embrace every part of the French Decrees which violate the neutral rights guaranteed to us by the law of nations."

No worse ground could have been found for Pinkney to stand upon. He was obliged to begin by asserting, what every public man in Europe knew to be untrue, that "every part of the French Decrees which

[1] Robert Smith to Pinkney, July 2, 1810; State Papers, iii. 360.

[2] Smith to Pinkney, July 5, 1810; State Papers, iii. 362.

violated the neutral rights " of America had been
repealed by Cadore's letter of August 5. His next
contention, that coasts could not be blockaded, was
at least open to dispute when the coast was that of
the British Channel. Pinkney's arguments became
necessarily technical, and although technical reasoning might be easily understood in a Court of Admiralty, the attempt to treat politics as a branch of the
profession of the law had the disadvantage of refining
issues to a point which no large society could com-
prehend. When Wellesley, Dec. 4, 1810, asked for
evidence that Napoleon's Decrees were repealed, Pinkney replied, in a long note dated December 10,[1] that
Cadore's letter of August 5 stated two disjunctive
conditions of repeal, — the first depending on Great
Britain, the last on the United States ; that although
Great Britain had not satisfied the first condition,
the United States would undoubtedly satisfy the last ;
therefore the French Decrees stood repealed. This
proposition, not even easy to understand, was supported by a long argument showing that Cadore could
not without absurdity have meant anything else. As
for further proof, not only had Pinkney none to
offer, but he gravely offered his want of evidence as
evidence : —

" On such an occasion it is no paradox to say that the
want of evidence is itself evidence. That certain decrees
are not in force is proved by the absence of such facts
as would appear if they were in force. Every motive

[1] Pinkney to Wellesley, Dec. 10, 1810; State Papers, iii. 376.

which can be conjectured to have led to the repeal of the
edicts invites to the full execution of that repeal, and no
motive can be imagined for a different course.   These
considerations are alone conclusive."

The argument might have escaped ridicule had not
Jonathan Russell been engaged at the same moment [1]
in remonstrating with the Duc de Cadore because the
"New Orleans Packet" had been seized at Bordeaux
under the Berlin and Milan Decrees ; and had not the
"Moniteur," within a week, published Cadore's official
Report, declaring that the decrees would never be
repealed as long as England maintained her blockades ; and had not the Comte de Semonville, within
another week, announced in the French Senate that
the decrees were the palladium of the seas.

Wellesley answered Pinkney, December 29, in a
note [2] comparatively short, and more courteous than
any important State paper that had come from the
British government since Fox's death.

" If nothing more had been required from Great Britain
than the repeal of our Orders in Council," he said, " I
should not have hesitated to declare the perfect readiness
of this Government to fulfil that condition.   On these
terms the Government has always been sincerely disposed
to repeal the Orders in Council.   It appears, however,
not only by the letter of the French minister, but by your
explanation, that the repeal of the Orders in Council will
not satisfy either the French or the American govern-

[1] Russell to Cadore, Dec. 10, 1810; State Papers, iii. 391.
[2] Wellesley to Pinkney, Dec. 29, 1810; State Papers, iii. 408.

ment.   The British government is further required by the letter of the French minister to renounce those principles of blockade which the French government alleges to be new. . . . On the part of the American government, I understand you to require that Great Britain shall revoke her Order of Blockade of May, 1806."

Wellesley declined to entertain this demand.   He appealed to the justice of America not to force an issue on such ground, and he protested that the Government retained an anxious solicitude to revoke the Orders in Council as soon as the Berlin and Milan Decrees should be effectually repealed, without conditions injurious to the maritime rights of Great Britain.

To this declaration Pinkney replied, Jan. 14, 1811, in a letter [1] defending his own position and attacking the good faith of the British government.   He began by defending the temper of his late remonstrances : —

" It would not have been very surprising nor very culpable, perhaps, if I had wholly forgotten to address myself to a spirit of conciliation which had met the most equitable claims with steady and unceasing repulsion ; which had yielded nothing that could be denied, and had answered complaints of injury by multiplying their causes.   With this forgetfulness, however, I am not chargeable ; for against all the discouragements suggested by the past, I have acted still upon a presumption that the disposition to conciliate, so often professed,

[1] Pinkney to Wellesley, Jan. 14, 1811 ; State Papers, iii. 409.

would finally be proved by some better evidence than a perseverance in oppressive novelties, as obviously incompatible with such a disposition in those who enforce them as in those whose patience they continue to exercise."

America, continued Pinkney, was not a party, either openly or covertly, to the French requisition. "What I have to request of your Lordship is that you will take our views and principles from our own mouths." The rejoinder was not so convincing as it would have been had Pinkney wholly discarded French views ; but on the point of Fox's blockade, the American and the French demand was the same. Pinkney was obliged to show that the two identical conditions rested on different grounds. At some length he laid down the law as the United States understood it.

"It is by no means clear," he began, "that it may not be fairly contended, on principle and early usage, that a maritime blockade is incomplete with regard to States at peace unless the place which it would affect is invested by land as well as by sea. The United States, however, have called for the recognition of no such rule. They appear to have contented themselves with urging in substance that ports not actually blockaded by a present, adequate, stationary force employed by the Power which attacks them shall not be considered as shut to neutral trade in articles not contraband of war ; . . . that a vessel cleared or bound to a blockaded port shall not be considered as violating in any manner the blockade unless on her approach to such port she shall have been previously warned not to enter it ; . . . that whole coasts and countries shall not be declared (for they can never be more than *declared*) to be in a state of blockade ; . . . and lastly, that every blockade shall be impartial in its operation."

On these definitions of law, and not to satisfy Napoleon's requirement, the President insisted on the abandonment of Fox's blockade.

The withdrawal of the Orders in Council, on the other hand, was required on the ground that England had pledged her faith to withdraw them whenever France revoked her decrees. France had revoked her decrees, and England could not honorably refuse to withdraw the orders.

" As to the Orders in Council which professed to be a reluctant departure from all ordinary rules, and to be justified only as a system of retaliation for a pre-existing measure of France, their foundation, such as it was, is gone the moment that measure is no longer in operation. But the Berlin Decree is repealed, and even the Milan Decree, the successor of your Orders in Council, is repealed also. Why is it, then, that your orders have outlived those edicts?"

In both instances the American position lost character by connection with Napoleon's acts.   Pinkney repudiated such a connection in the first case, and his argument would have been stronger could he have repudiated it in the second.   Unable or unwilling to do this, he had no resource but to lose his temper, which he did with proper self-control.   The correctness of his reasoning or of his facts became less important from the moment he showed himself

in earnest ; for then the controversy entered a new
phase.

In making an issue of war, President Madison
needed to exercise extreme caution not to shock the
sentiment of New England, but he needed to observe
no such delicacy in regard to the feelings of the British Tories.   In respect to the British government,
the nature of the issue mattered little, provided an
issue were made ; and Pinkney might reasonably
think that the more paradoxical his arguments the
more impression they would produce.   Centuries of
study at Oxford and Edinburgh, and generations devoted to the logic or rhetoric of Aristotle, Cicero, and
Quintilian, had left the most educated classes of Great
Britain still in the stage of culture where reasoning,
in order to convince, must cease to be reasonable.
As Pinkney became positive and arrogant, Wellesley
became conciliatory and almost yielding.   The American note of January 14, written in a tone that
had not hitherto been taken in London, was coupled
with a notice that brought the two governments in
presence of the long-threatened rupture.   Pinkney
informed Lord Wellesley that as the British government, after a lapse of many months, had taken no
steps to carry out the assurance of sending a new
minister to Washington, the United States government could not retain a minister at London.   Therewith Pinkney requested an audience of leave.

Although Wellesley had never avowed a political
motive for his systematic delays, no one could doubt

that he intentionally postponed not only concession
on the Orders in Council, but also a settlement of the
" Chesapeake " affair and the appointment of a new
minister at Washington, because his colleagues, as he
hinted [1] to Pinkney, were persuaded " that the British
interest in America would be completely destroyed by
sending thither at this time a minister plenipoten-
tiary," and of course by any other frank advance.
The influence of F. J. Jackson with the Government
was perhaps strong enough to check action that
would have amounted to a censure on his own conduct ; and although the American elections showed
that Jackson had for the time so much reduced British influence in America as to make some change
of policy necessary if it were to be revived, Jackson, in daily intercourse with the Foreign Office and
with ministers, was exerting every effort to maintain
his credit.   Nothing less than Pinkney's request for
an audience of leave was likely to end these minis-
terial hesitations.

For the moment, as Pinkney knew, his request
could not be granted, because the King was insane
and could give audience to no one.   Since Nov. 1,
1810, Parliament had done no other business than
such as related to the regency ; yet on Jan. 14, 1811,
when Pinkney's two notes were written, the Regency
Bill had not been brought before the Commons.   Introduced on the following day, Parliament showed

[1] Pinkney to Madison, Dec. 17, 1810 ; Wheaton's Pinkney,
p. 452.

extraordinary energy by making it law in little more than a fortnight; yet the Prince Regent, who took the oaths February 6, still required time to settle his government.

Everything depended on the Prince Regent's action. Had he followed the expected course, — had he dismissed Spencer Perceval, and put himself in the hands of Wellesley, Grenville, Grey, and Holland, — the danger of an American war might possibly have vanished. The Orders in Council might have been withdrawn, the "Chesapeake" affair might have been settled, a friendly minister would have been sent to Washington, and the war party in the Twelfth Congress would have been thrown into a minority. After much manœuvring, the Prince of Wales at last avowed his decision. February 4 he wrote to Spencer Perceval, announcing the wish, wholly in deference to the King's feelings, that the late ministers should remain in charge of the government. The Whigs were once more prostrated by this desertion, and the Marquess Wellesley abandoned his last hope of saving the government from Perceval's control.

The effect of the Prince Regent's course was instantly felt. His letter to Perceval was written February 4; he assumed the royal office February 6; and February 11 Wellesley was able to answer [1] Pinkney's note on blockades.

"France requires," said he, "that Great Britain shall not only repeal the Orders in Council, but renounce those

[1] Wellesley to Pinkney, Feb. 11, 1811; State Papers, iii. 412.

principles of blockade which are alleged in the same letter to be new, — an allegation which must be understood
to refer to the introductory part of the Berlin Decree.
If Great Britain shall not submit to those terms, it is
plainly intimated in the same letter that France requires
America to enforce them.   To these conditions his Royal
Highness, on behalf of his Majesty, cannot accede.   No
principles of blockade have been promulgated or acted
upon by Great Britain previously to the Berlin Decree
which are not strictly conformable to the rights of civilized war and to the approved usages and laws of nations. . . . I am commanded to inform you that his
Royal Highness cannot consent to blend the question
which has arisen upon the Orders in Council with any
discussion of the general principles of blockade."

In a note of two lines, Pinkney replied [1] that he
had no inducement to trouble his Lordship further
on the subject.   The same day he received a notice
that the Prince Regent would hold his first diplomatic levee February 19; but instead of accepting
the invitation, Pinkney wrote with the same brevity
to ask at what time the Prince Regent would do him
the honor to give his audience of leave.[2]

This abrupt course brought the Government partially to reason.   Within forty-eight hours Wellesley
wrote to Pinkney a private letter [3] of apology for the
delay in appointing a minister to Washington, and
of regret that this delay should have been misunder-

[1] Pinkney to Wellesley, Feb. 13, 1811; State Papers, iii. 412.
[2] Pinkney to Wellesley, Feb. 13, 1811; State Papers, iv. 413.
[3] Wellesley to Pinkney, Feb. 15, 1811; State Papers, iii. 413.

stood ; he announced that Augustus J. Foster, late British minister in Sweden, would be immediately gazetted as minister to the United States ; and his letter closed by a remark which came as near deprecation as Pinkney's temper would allow: " You will, of course, exercise your own judgment, under these circumstances, respecting the propriety of requiring an audience of leave on the grounds which you have stated." With this private letter, Lord Wellesley sent an official notice that the Prince Regent would receive Mr. Pinkney February 19, by his desire, for an audience of leave.

The responsibility thus thrown upon Pinkney was more serious than had ever before, or has ever since, fallen to the share of a minister of the United States in England. The policy of withdrawing the United States minister from London might be doubted, not so much because it was violent, as because it was likely to embarrass the President more than it embarrassed England. If the President was indeed bent on war, and wished to hasten its declaration, the recall of his minister in London might be proper ; but if he still expected to negotiate, London was the spot where he needed to keep his strongest diplomatist, and, if possible, more than one. Yet the worst possible mistake was to recede once more,— to repeat the comedy of American errors, and to let the British government assume that its policy was still safe.

Pinkney hesitated, and consulted his instructions.[1]

[1] Smith to Pinkney, Nov. 15, 1810; State Papers, iii. 375.

These were dated Nov. 15, 1810, and ordered Pinkney, in case no successor to F. J. Jackson should then have been appointed, to take leave of absence, entrusting the legation to a *chargé d'affaires ;* but this positive order was practically revoked in the concluding sentence: "Considering the season at which this instruction may have its effect, and the possibility of a satisfactory change in the posture of our relations with Great Britain, the time of your return to the United States is left to your discretion and convenience."

These instructions did not warrant Pinkney in demanding leave of absence on any other ground than that of failure to appoint a minister at Washington. They did not warrant him in returning to America at all if he saw the possibility of such an appointment. Pinkney was obliged to put a free construction on the President's language. Abandoning the ground that his departure was a necessary result of the absence of a British minister at Washington, he asked Lord Wellesley, in an official note, dated February 17, what Mr. Foster was to do when he arrived there ?[1] "I presume that for the restoration of harmony between the two countries, the Orders in Council will be relinquished without delay ; that the blockade of 1806 will be annulled ; that the case of the 'Chesapeake' will be arranged in the manner heretofore intended ; and in general that all such just and reasonable acts will be done as are necessary to

[1] Pinkney to Wellesley, Feb. 17, 1811; State Papers, iii. 414.

make us friends." So important a letter was probably never written by any other American diplomatist without instructions from his Government, — for it was in effect an ultimatum, preliminary to the rupture of relations and ultimate war ; yet even in this final list of American demands made by the American minister in withdrawing from London, impressment was not expressly mentioned.

Wellesley replied in a private letter [1] dated February 23, with the formal avowal that " it would be neither candid toward you, nor just toward this Government, to countenance any interpretation which might favor a supposition that it was intended by this Government to relinquish any of the principles which I have so often endeavored to explain to you." Nothing in Wellesley's letter showed a desire to irritate, and his refusals left less sting than was left by Canning's concessions ; but the issue was fairly joined, and America was at liberty to act upon it as she pleased.

In order to leave no doubt of his meaning, Pinkney instantly [2] claimed his audience of leave for February 28, declining, in the mean time, to attend the diplomatic levee which by postponement took place only February 26. His conduct was noticed and understood, as he meant it should be ; and as his audience

[1] Wellesley to Pinkney, Feb. 23, 1811 ; State Papers, iii. 415.

[2] Pinkney to Wellesley, Feb. 23, 1811 ; State Papers, iii. 415.

still remains the only occasion when an American
minister at London has broken relations in a hostile
manner, with resulting war, it has an interest peculiar
to itself. Several accounts were preserved of what
passed at the interview. Pinkney's official report
recorded the words used by him : [1] —

"I stated to the Prince Regent the grounds upon
which it had become my duty to take my leave and to
commit the business of the legation to a *chargé d'affaires;*
and I concluded by expressing my regret that my humble
efforts in the execution of the instructions of my Government to set to rights the embarrassed and disjointed
relations of the two countries had wholly failed ; and that
I saw no reason to expect that the great work of their
reconciliation was likely to be accomplished through any
other agency."

According to Pinkney, and according to the official
report of Lord Wellesley,[2] the Prince Regent replied
in terms of the utmost amity toward the United
States. Another account of the interview gave the
impression that the Prince Regent had not shown
himself so gracious toward the departing minister as
the official reports implied. Francis James Jackson,
who dogged Pinkney's footsteps with the personal
malevolence he had almost a right to feel, and who
haunted the Court and Foreign Office in the hope of
obtaining — what he never received — some public

[1] Pinkney to Robert Smith, March 1, 1811 ; State Papers,
iii. 415.

[2] Wellesley to Foster, April 29, 1811 ; Papers, etc., 1813,
p. 294.

mark of approval, wrote to Timothy Pickering a
long letter on Pinkney's departure:[1] —

" It has occasioned much surprise here that exactly at
the moment of Pinkney's demand being complied with
he should nevertheless take what he calls an inamicable
leave. . . . It was not expected that he would depart so
far from his usual urbanity as to decline the invitation
that was sent him in common with the rest of the foreign ministers to attend the Regent's levee.   It was
not probable after this that the audience of leave which
he claimed should answer his expectation.   It was very
short.   Mr. Pinkney was told that the Regent was desirous of cultivating a good understanding with the United
States ; that he had given a proof of it in the appointment of a minister as soon as his acceptance of the
Regency enabled him to appoint one ; that the Orders in
Council would have been repealed, but that his Royal
Highness never could or would surrender the maritime
rights of his country.   Mr. Pinkney then made some
profession of his personal sentiments, to which he was
answered : ' Sir, I cannot look into men's minds ; I can
only judge of men's motives by their conduct.'   And
then the audience ended."

So closed Pinkney's residence in London.   He
had passed there nearly five years of such violent
national hostility as no other American minister ever
faced during an equal length of time, or defied at last
with equal sternness ; but his extraordinary abilities
and character made him greatly respected and ad-

[1] F. J. Jackson to Pickering, April 24, 1811 ; New England
Federalism, p. 382.

mired while he stayed, and silenced remonstrance
when he left. For many years afterward, his suc-
cessors were mortified by comparisons between his
table-oratory and theirs. As a writer he was not'less
distinguished. Canning's impenetrable self-confidence
met in him powers that did not yield, even in self-
confidence, to his own; and Lord Wellesley's oriental
dignity was not a little ruffled by Pinkney's handling.
As occasion required, he was patient under irritation
that seemed intolerable, as aggressive as Canning
himself, or as stately and urbane as Wellesley; and
even when he lost his temper, he did so in cold
blood, because he saw no other way to break through
the obstacles put in his path. America never sent
an abler representative to the Court of London.

Pinkney sailed from England a few weeks afterward, leaving in charge of the legation John Spear
Smith, a son of Senator Samuel Smith, who had been
for a time attached to the Legation at St. Petersburg;
had thence travelled to Vienna and Paris, where he
received Pinkney's summons to London, — the most
difficult and important diplomatic post in the world.
Simultaneously, Lord Wellesley hurried Foster to the
United States. The new British minister was personally acceptable. By birth a son of the actual
Duchess of Devonshire by her first husband, he had
the advantage of social and political backing, while
he was already familiar with America, where he had
served as Secretary of Legation. Just dismissed
from Sweden by Bernadotte's election and the decla-

ration of war against England which followed it,
Foster would hardly have sought or taken the mission to Washington had not Europe been closed to
English diplomacy. Even F. J. Jackson, who spoke
kindly of few people, gave a pleasant account of his
successor.[1] "Foster is a very gentlemanlike young
man, quite equal to do nothing at his post, which is
now the best possible policy to follow;" but in the
same breath, "that most clumsy and ill-conditioned
minister," as Pinkney described Jackson,[2] added that
the police office was the proper place to train officials
for service at Washington. "One of the best magistrates as minister, and a good sharp thief-taker for
secretary, would put us in all respects much upon a
level with their Yankeeships." The phrase implied
that Jackson felt his own career at Washington to
have been mortifying, and that he had not been on
a level with his opponents. Possibly the sense of
mortification hurried the decline which ended in his
death, three years afterward, in the midst of the war
he did so much to cause.

Wellesley's instructions to Foster were dated April
10,[3] and marked another slight step toward concession. Once more he discussed the Orders in Council,
but on the ground taken by Pinkney could come to

[1] Bath Archives, Second Series, i. 219.

[2] Pinkney to Madison, Aug. 13, 1810 ; Wheaton's Pinkney,
p. 444.

[3] Papers relating to America, *C,* presented to Parliament,
February, 1813.

no other conclusion than that the President was mistaken in thinking the French Decrees repealed, and extravagant in requiring the blockade of 1806 to be repealed in consequence ; yet as long as any hope remained of prevailing with the President to correct his error, American ships, captured while acting in pursuance of it, should not be condemned. Even under the challenge expressly proclaimed by the non-importation, the British government anxiously desired to avoid a positive rupture. As for the "Chesapeake" affair, Foster was ordered to settle it to suit the American government, guarding only against the admission of insulting expressions. He was to remonstrate and protest against the seizure of the Floridas,[1] but was not to commit his Government further. Finally, a secret instruction [2] notified Foster that in case America should persist in her non-importation, England would retaliate, — probably by increasing her import duties, and excluding American commerce from the East Indies.

These instructions conformed with the general attitude of English society. Though sobered by the disasters that attended Tory government, England had not yet passed beyond the stage when annoyances created only the wish to ignore them. No one would admit serious danger from America. In Parliament, Pinkney's abrupt and hostile departure was barely mentioned, and ministers denied it importance. The

[1] Instruction No. 3; MSS. British Archives.
[2] Instruction No. 8; MSS. British Archives.

"London Times," of March 1, complained that no one could be induced to feel an interest in the American question. "There is certainly great apathy in the public mind generally upon the questions now at issue between us and our quondam colonies, which it is difficult to arouse, and perhaps useless to attempt." Here and there the old wish for a war with the United States was still felt;[1] but the public asked only to hear no more on American subjects. Even the "Times" refused, April 13, to continue discussion on matters "upon which the feelings of the great bulk of the nation are peculiarly blunt." Wellesley's course and Foster's instructions reflected only the lassitude and torpor of the day; but within eighteen months Wellesley, in open Parliament, criticised what he charged as the policy, not of himself, but of his colleagues, in language which implied that the public apathy was assumed rather than real. "The disposition of the American government was quite evident," he said, Nov. 30, 1812;[2] "and therefore common policy should have urged ministers to prepare fully for the event; and they should have made adequate exertion either to pacify, to intimidate, or to punish America." Knowing this, they sent out Foster, powerless either for defence or attack, to waste his time at Washington, where for ten years his predecessors had found the grave of their ambitions.

---

[1] Bath Archives, Second Series, i. 221.

[2] Cobbett's Debates, xxiv. 34.

CHAPTER II.

THE diplomatic insolvency inherited from Merry, Rose, Erskine, and Jackson became more complete with every year that passed; and even while Foster was on the ocean, a new incident occurred, which if it did not prove a catastrophe to be inevitable, showed at least how small was his chance of averting it.

On the renewal of trade between America and France, the British navy renewed its blockade of New York. If nothing more had happened, the recurrence of this vexation would alone have gone far to destroy the hopes of diplomacy; but this was not all.

The " Melampus " reappeared, having for a companion the " Guerriere," commanded by Captain Dacres, and supposed to be one of the best British frigates of her class. Early in May, when Foster sailed from England, these cruisers, lying off Sandy Hook, began to capture American vessels bound for France, and to impress American sailors at will. No sooner did these complaints reach Washington than Secretary Hamilton, May 6,[1] ordered Commodore John Rodgers, whose flag-ship, the 44-gun frigate " Presi-

[1] Secretary Hamilton to Commodore Rodgers, May 6, 1811; MSS. Navy Department Archives.

dent," was lying at Annapolis, to sail at once to
protect American commerce from unlawful interference by British and French cruisers. Rodgers sailed
from Annapolis May 10, and May 14 passed the capes.
The scene of the " Chesapeake's" unredressed outrage
lay some fifteen or twenty miles to the southward, and
the officers and crew of the " President" had reason
to think themselves expected to lose no fair opportunity of taking into their own hands the redress
which the British government denied. For the past
year Rodgers had carried orders " to vindicate the injured honor of our navy and revive the drooping
spirits of the nation ; . . . to maintain and support
at any risk and cost the honor " of his flag; and these
orders were founded chiefly on " the inhuman and
dastardly attack on our frigate ' Chesapeake,' — an
outrage which prostrated the flag of our country,
and has imposed on the American people cause of
ceaseless mourning." [1]

Rodgers was bound for New York, but on the
morning of May 16 was still about thirty miles from
Cape Charles and eighteen miles from the coast,
when toward noon he saw a ship to the eastward
standing toward him under a press of canvas. As
the vessel came near, he could make her out from
the shape of her upper sails to be a man-of-war; he
knew of no man-of-war except the " Guerriere " on
the coast; the new-comer appeared from the quarter

[1] Secretary Hamilton to Commodore Rodgers, June 9, 1810;
MSS. Navy Department Archives.

where that frigate would be looked for, and Rodgers reasoned that in all probability she was the "Guerriere." He decided to approach her, with the object of ascertaining whether a man named Diggio, said to have been impressed a few days before by Captain Dacres from an American brig, was on board. The spirit of this inquiry was new.

Until quarter before two o'clock in the afternoon the ships stood toward each other. The stranger showed no colors, but made signals, until finding them unanswered, she changed her course and stood to the southward. Rodgers then made sail in chase, his colors and pennant flying. At half-past three, the stranger's hull began to be visible from the "President's" deck, but as the wind failed the American frigate gained less rapidly. In latitude 37° the sun, May 16, sets at seven o'clock, and dusk comes quickly on. At quarter-past seven the unknown ship again changed her course, and lay to, presenting her broadside to the "President," and showing colors, which in the gathering twilight were not clearly seen. The ship had the look of a frigate.

At quarter before eight, Rodgers ordered his acting commandant to bring the "President" to windward of the supposed frigate within speaking distance, — a manoeuvre which naturally caused the stranger uneasiness, so that she wore three times to prevent the "President" from getting under her stern. At half-past eight, according to the American account, — at quarter-past eight, according to the British story, —

the "President" rounded to, within pistol-shot. On both ships every gun in the broadside was run out and trained on the opposite vessel, and out of every port a dozen eyes were strained to catch sight, through the dusk, of what passed in the stranger.

By the dim light Rodgers saw the supposed "Guerriere," her maintopsail to the mast, waiting with apparent confidence the next act of the audacious American frigate which had chased a British man-of-war all day, and had at last run up close to windward, — a manœuvre which British frigates were disposed to resent. To this point the reports showed no great disagreement; but in regard to what followed, one story was told by Rodgers and all his ship's company, while a wholly different story was told by the British captain and his officers.

Rodgers reported that while rounding to, he hailed the unknown vessel through his trumpet, calling out: "What ship is that?" The question, "What ship is that?" was immediately echoed back. Rodgers had time to tell his acting captain that the "President" was forging too fast ahead, before he hailed again: "What ship is that, I say?" Instantly a flash was seen from the dark where the stranger's hull lay, and a double report told that the ball had struck the "President," lodging in the mainmast. Taken by surprise, Rodgers turned to his commandant of marines and asked, "What the devil was that?" but before he gave an order his third lieutenant, Alexander James Dallas, who was watching at the first port forward of the gangway and saw the flash, leaped to one of the guns in his division and discharged it. The "Chesapeake's" disaster had done away with the old-fashioned logger-heads and matches; the "President's" guns were fitted with locks, and were discharged in an instant. Immediately afterward three guns were fired by the enemy, and the report of muskets was heard. Then Rodgers gave the order to fire, and the "President" opened with a whole broadside, followed by another. In about five minutes the enemy seemed to be silenced, and Rodgers gave the order to cease firing; but some three minutes afterward the stranger opened again, and the "President" resumed fire until she desisted. From the "President's" deck enough could be seen of the enemy's behavior to prove that whoever she might be, she was not the "Guerriere;" and Rodgers then made the remark that either she had received some unfortunate shot at the outset, or she was a vessel of force very inferior to what he had taken her for,— although she was still supposed to be nothing less than a 36-gun frigate. Disabled she certainly was, for she lay ungovernable, with her bow directly under the "President's" broadside.

Rodgers hailed once more, and understood the stranger to answer that she was a British ship-of-war in great distress. At nine o'clock at night the "President" began to repair damages, and beat about within reach, on different tacks, with lights displayed, until daybreak, when she ran down to the British vessel, and sent a boat on board. Then at last Rodgers learned, certainly to his great disappointment, that he had been fighting a single-decked vessel of less than half his force. His mistake was not so surprising as it seemed. The British cruiser might easily at a distance, or in the dark, be taken for a frigate. Her great length; her poop, top-gallants, forecastle; her deep bulwarks; the manner of stowing her hammocks; and room on each side to mount three more guns than she actually carried, — were decisive to any one who could not see that she carried but one tier of guns.[1]

Captain Bingham of the " Little Belt," a British corvette, rated at twenty guns, gave a very different account of the affair. He had been ordered from Bermuda to carry despatches to the " Guerriere; " had run north toward New York without finding her; and on his return southward, at eleven o'clock on the morning of May 16, had seen a strange sail, to which he gave chase. At two o'clock in the afternoon, concluding that she was an American frigate, he abandoned the chase, and resumed his course. The rest of his story is to be told in his own words : [2] —

" Hoisted the colors, and made all sail south, . . . the stranger edging away, but not making any more sail. At 3.30 he made sail in chase. . . . At 6.30, finding he

[1] Rodgers's Report of May 23, 1811; State Papers, Foreign Affairs, iii. 497.

[2] Niles's Register, i. 34.

gained so considerably on us as not to be able to elude him during the night, being within gunshot, and clearly discerning the stars in his broad pennant, I imagined the most prudent method was to bring to, and hoist the colors, that no mistake might arise, and that he might see what we were. The ship was therefore brought to, her colors hoisted, her guns double-shotted, and every preparation made in case of a surprise. By his manner of steering down, he evidently wished to lay his ship in a position for raking, which I frustrated by wearing three times. At about 8.15 he came within hail. I hailed and asked what ship it was. He again repeated my words and fired a broadside, which I instantly returned. The action then became general, and continued so for three quarters of an hour, when he ceased firing, and appeared to be on fire about the main hatchway. He then filled, . . . hailed, and asked what ship this was. He fired no more guns, but stood from us, giving no reason for his most extraordinary conduct."

Bingham's report was afterward supported by the evidence of his two lieutenants, his boatswain, purser, and surgeon, at the official inquiry made May 29, at Halifax.[1] Rodgers's report was sustained by the searching inquiry made by the American government to ascertain the truth of Bingham's assertions.[2] The American investigation was naturally much more thorough in consequence of Bingham's charges, so that not only every officer, but also every seaman of the " President's " company gave evidence under oath.

[1] American State Papers, Foreign Affairs, iii. 473.
[2] State Papers, iii, 477.

All agreed in swearing to the facts as they have been related in the American story.

About a month after the action, two sailors claiming to be deserters from the " President " arrived at Halifax and made affidavits,[1] which gave a third account quite different from the other two. One of these men, an Englishman, swore that he had been stationed in the second division, on the gun-deck of the " President ; " that a gun in that division went off, as he thought, by accident, four or five men leaning on it ; that he had turned to acquaint Lieutenant Belden, who commanded that division, of the fact, but before he could do this, though the lieutenant was only three guns from him, the whole broadside of the " President " was discharged. This story was the least probable of the three. The evidence of a deserter, under every motive to ingratiate himself with his future officers, would be suspicious, even if he were proved to have been in the " President's " crew, which was not the case ; but it became valueless when the rolls showed no Lieutenant Belden on board the " President," but that the second division on the gun-deck was commanded by Lieut. A. J. Dallas, — and Lieutenant Dallas swore that he himself fired the first gun from the " President," without orders, in answer to the " Little Belt's " discharge. The evidence of every other officer and man at the guns supported his assertion.

When the contradictory reports of Rodgers and

[1] London Times, Dec. 7, 1811 ; Palladium, Feb. 18, 1812.

Bingham were published, a controversy arose between the newspapers which sympathized with the different captains. Rodgers was vehemently attacked by the English and Federalist press ; Bingham was as hotly scouted by the American newspapers friendly to Madison. The dispute was never settled. Perhaps this was the only instance where the honor of the services was so deeply involved on both sides as to make the controversy important ; for if Rodgers, all his officers, and his whole crew behaved as Bingham alleged, and perjured themselves afterward to conceal it, they were not the men they were supposed to be ; and if Bingham swore falsely, he went far to establish the worst American charges against the character of the British navy.

For this reason some little effort to form an opinion on the subject deserves to be made, even at the risk of diffuseness. The elaborate investigation by the United States government settled the weight of testimony in favor of Rodgers. Other evidence raised doubts of the accuracy of Bingham's report.

This report was dated May 21, five days after the battle, in " lat. 36° 53' N.; long. 71° 49' W. Cape Charles bearing W. 48 miles," — which, according to the senior lieutenant's evidence, May 29, was about the spot of the action, from fifty to fifty-four miles east of Cape Charles. Yet a glance at the map showed that these bearings marked a point more than two hundred miles east of Cape Charles. This carelessness could not be set to the account of a misprint.

The date proved only inaccuracy; other parts of Bingham's report showed a willingness to confuse the facts. He claimed to have hoisted his colors at two o'clock in the afternoon, after making out the American commodore's pennant and resuming a southerly course. Rodgers averred that the " Little Belt" obstinately refused to show colors till darkness concealed them; and Bingham's report itself admitted that at 6.30 he decided to hoist his colors, " that no mistake might arise." During the five hours' chase his colors were not flying. His assertion, too, that at 6.30 the American frigate was within gunshot, and that the " Little Belt " was brought to because she could not escape, agreed ill with his next admission, that the " President " consumed nearly two hours in getting within hailing distance.

The most evident error was at the close of the British story. Bingham declared that the general action lasted three quarters of an hour, and that then the enemy ceased firing; appeared to be on fire about the main hatchway, and " stood from us," firing no more guns. The two lieutenants, boatswain, and purser of the " Little Belt " swore that the action lasted " about an hour; " the surgeon said " about forty-five minutes." Every American officer declared under oath that the entire action, including the cessation of firing for three minutes, did not exceed a quarter of an hour, or eighteen minutes at most. On this point the American story was certainly correct. Indeed, two years later, after the " Constitution" had silenced the "Guerriere" in thirty-five minutes, and the "United States" had, in a rough sea and at comparatively long range, left the "Macedonian" a wreck in less than two hours of action, no officer in the British service would have sacrificed his reputation for veracity by suggesting that a British corvette of eighteen guns could have lain nearly an hour within pistol-shot, in calm weather, under the hot fire of an American "line-of-battle ship in disguise." The idea of forcing her to "stand from us" would have seemed then mere gasconade. Some fifteen months afterward, the British sloop-of-war "Alert," of twenty guns, imitated the "Little Belt" by attacking Commodore Porter's 32-gun frigate "Essex," and in eight minutes struck her colors in a sinking condition. If the "President" had been no heavier than the "Essex," she should still have silenced the "Little Belt" in a quarter of an hour.

The "Little Belt" escaped destruction, but she suffered severely. Bingham reported: " I was obliged to desist from firing, as, the ship falling off, no gun would bear, and had no after-sail to help her to; all the rigging and sails cut to pieces; not a brace nor a bowline left. . . . I have to lament the loss of thirty-two men killed and wounded, among whom is the master. His Majesty's ship is much damaged in masts, rigging, and hull; . . . many shot through between wind and water, and many shots still remain inside, and upper works all shot away; starboard pump also." He did not know his good fortune.

Two years afterward he would have been well content to escape from the "President" on any terms, even though the "Little Belt" had been twice the size she was. The "President's" loss consisted of one boy wounded, and some slight damage to the rigging.

Bingham's report was accepted by the British government and navy with blind confidence, and caused no small part of the miscalculation which ended in disasters to British pride. "No one act of the little navy of the United States," said the British historian five years afterward, "had been at all calculated to gain the respect of the British. First was seen the 'Chesapeake' allowing herself to be beaten with impunity by a British ship only nominally superior to her. Then the huge frigate 'President' attacks and fights for nearly three quarters of an hour the British sloop 'Little Belt.'"[1] So self-confident was the British navy that Bingham was believed to have fought the "President" with credit and success; while, on the American side, Rodgers and his ship's company believed that the British captain deliberately delayed the meeting until dark, with the view of taking advantage of the night to punish what he thought the insolence of the chase.

Whatever opinion might be formed as to the conduct of the two captains, the vehemence of feeling on each side was only to be compared with the "Chesapeake" affair; but in this instance the grievance

[1] James. Naval Occurrences, p. 97.

belonged to the British navy, and Dacres and the " Guerriere" felt the full passion and duty of revenge. The news met Foster on his arrival at Norfolk, a few weeks afterward, and took away his only hope of a cordial reception. His instructions intended. him to conciliate good-will by settling the " Chesapeake" outrage, while they obliged him to take a tone of refusal or remonstrance on every other subject ; but he found, on arriving, that the Americans cared nothing for reparation of the " Chesapeake " outrage, since Commodore Rodgers had set off against it an outrage of his own, and had killed four men for every one killed by Captain Humphries. Instead of giving redress, Foster found himself obliged to claim it.

July 2 Foster was formally received by the President ; and the same day, as though he had no other hope but to take the offensive, he began his official correspondence by a letter on the seizure of West Florida, closing with a formal notice that if the United States persevered in their course, his orders required him to present the solemn protest of his Government " against an attempt so contrary to every principle of public justice, faith, and national honor."

The language was strong ; but unfortunately for Foster's influence, the world at the moment showed so little regard for justice, faith, or honor, that the United States had no reason to be singular in Quixotism ; and although in logic the *tu quoque* was an argument hardly deserving notice, in politics it was only less decisive than cannon. The policy of Foster's remonstrance was doubtful in another respect. In proportion as men exposed themselves to reprimands, they resented the reprimand itself. Madison and Monroe had each his sensitive point. Madison resented the suggestion that Napoleon's decrees were still in force, regarding the matter as involving his veracity. Monroe equally resented the assertion that West Florida belonged to Spain, for his character as a man of sense, if not of truth, was involved in the assertion that he had himself bought West Florida in his Louisiana purchase. Yet the mildness of his reply to Foster's severe protest proved his earnest wish to conciliate England. In a note [1] of July 8 he justified the seizure of West Florida by the arguments already used, and offered what he called a "frank and candid explanation" to satisfy the British government. In private he talked with more freedom, and — if Foster could be believed — showed himself in a character more lively if not more moral than any the American people would have recognized as his. July 5 Foster wrote to Wellesley : [2] —

"It was with real pain, my Lord, that I was forced to listen to arguments of the most profligate nature, such as that other nations were not so scrupulous ; that the United States showed sufficient forbearance in not assisting the insurgents of South America and looking to their own interests in the present situation of that country."

[1] Monroe to Foster, July 8, 1811; State Papers iii. 543.
[2] Foster to Wellesley, July 5, 1811 ; MSS. British Archives.

Foster was obliged to ignore the meaning of this
pointed retort ; while his inquiries how far the American government meant to carry its seizures of Spanish territory drew from Monroe no answer but a
laugh. The Secretary of State seemed a transformed
man. Not only did he show no dread of interference from England in Florida, but he took an equally
indifferent air on every other matter except one. He
said not a word about impressments ; he betrayed
no wish to trouble himself about the " Chesapeake "
affair ; he made no haste in apologizing for the attack
on the " Little Belt ; " but the Orders in Council —
these, and nothing else — formed the issue on which
a change of policy was to depend.

Precisely on the Orders in Council Foster could
offer no hope of concession or compromise. So far
from withdrawing the orders, he was instructed to
require that the United States should withdraw the
Non-intercourse Act, under threat of retaliation ; and
he carried out his instructions to the letter. After
protesting, July 2, against the seizure of West
Florida, he wrote, July 3, a long protest against the
non-importation.[1] His demand savored of Canning's
and Jackson's diplomacy ; but his arguments in its
support were better calculated for effect, and his cry
for justice claimed no little sympathy among men
who shared in the opinion of Europe that France
was the true object of attack, and that Napoleon's
overthrow, not the overthrow of England, was the

[1] Foster to Monroe, July 3, 1811; State Papers, iii. 435.

necessary condition of restoring public order. Foster's protest against including Fox's blockade among the admittedly illegal Orders in Council, brought the argument to a delicate issue of law and fact.

" In point of date," he said, " the blockade of May, 1806, preceded the Berlin Decree; but it was a just and legal blockade, according to the established law of nations, because it was intended to be maintained, and was actually maintained, by an adequate force appointed to guard the whole coast described in the notification, and consequently to enforce the blockade."

In effect this argument conceded Madison's principle; for the further difference between blockading a coast and blockading by name the several ports on a coast, was hardly worth a war; and the question whether an estuary, like the British Channel, the Baltic Sea, or Chesapeake Bay, could be best blockaded by a cruising or by a stationary squadron, or by both, called rather for naval than for legal opinion. Foster repudiated the principle of paper-blockades; and after showing that Fox's blockade was defended only as far as it was meant to be legal, he made the further concession of admitting that since it had been merged in the Orders in Council, it existed only as a part of the orders; so that if the orders were repealed, England must either make Fox's blockade effective, or abandon it. By this expedient, the issue was narrowed to the Orders in Council retaliatory on Bonaparte's decrees, and intended to last only as long as those decrees lasted.

Foster appealed to Napoleon's public and official language to prove that those decrees were still in force, and therefore that the United States government could not, without making itself a party to Napoleon's acts and principles, demand a withdrawal of the British Orders. If the orders were not to be withdrawn because they were illegal, they ought not to be withdrawn on the false excuse that Napoleon had withdrawn his decrees.   Against such a demand England might reasonably protest : —

" Great Britain has a right to complain that . . . not only has America suffered her trade to be moulded into the means of annoyance to Great Britain under the provisions of the French Decrees, but construing those decrees as extinct, upon a deceitful declaration of the French Cabinet, she has enforced her Non-importation Act against England. Under these circumstances I am instructed by my Government to urge to that of the United States the injustice of thus enforcing that Act against his Majesty's dominions ; and I cannot but hope that a spirit of justice will induce the United States government to reconsider the line of conduct they have pursued, and at least to re-establish their former state of strict neutrality."

President Madison had put himself, little by little, in a position where he had reason to fear the popular effect of such appeals ; but awkward as Madison's position was, that of Monroe was many degrees worse. He had accepted office in April as the representative of Republicans who believed that Napoleon's decrees were not repealed, and the objects of his ambition seemed to depend on reversing Madison's course. In July he found himself in painful straits. Obliged to maintain that Napoleon's decrees were repealed, he was reduced to sacrifice his own official agent in the effort. Foster reported, as a matter of surprise to himself, remarks of Monroe still more surprising to history.

" I have urged," reported Foster, July 7,[1] " with every argument I could think of, the injustice of the Non-importation Act which was passed in the last session of Congress, while there were doubts entertained even here as to the repeal of the Berlin and Milan Decrees ; but to my surprise I find it now maintained that there existed no doubt on the subject at the time of passing the Act, and Mr. Russell is censured by his Government for publicly averring that the ship ' New Orleans Packet ' was seized under their operation, — not that it is denied, however, that she was seized under them by our construction. Mr. Monroe, indeed, though he qualified his blame of Mr. Russell by praising his zeal, yet allowed to me that much of their present embarrassment was owing to his statement."

" It would be fatiguing to your Lordship," continued Foster, " were I to describe the various shadows of argument to which the American minister had recourse in order to prove his statement of the decrees having been repealed in as far as America had a right to expect."

These shadows of argument, however elaborately described, could be reduced to the compass of a few

[1] Foster to Wellesley, July 7, 1811 ; MSS. British Archives.

lines; for they all resulted in a doctrine which became thenceforward a dogma. Napoleon's decrees, so viewed, had two characters, — an international, and a municipal. The international character alone could give the right of international retaliation; and the Emperor, since November 1, had ceased to enforce his edicts in this character. The municipal character, whether enforced or not, in no way concerned England.

Such was, indeed, Napoleon's object in substituting customs regulations for the rules of his decrees in his own ports. After that change, he applied the decrees themselves to every other part of Europe, but made an apparent exception for American commerce with France, which was forced to conform to his objects by municipal licenses and prohibitory duties. Monroe took the ground that since November 2 the decrees stood repealed, and the "New Orleans Packet" had been seized under a "municipal operation" with which England had nothing to do. The argument, though perhaps casuistic, seemed to offer a sufficient excuse for England, in case she should wish to abandon her own system as she saw danger approaching; but it brought Monroe, who used it profusely, into daily mortification, and caused the President, who invented and believed it, a world of annoyance, — for Napoleon, as Monroe had personal reason to remember, never failed to sacrifice his allies, and was certain to fail in supporting a theory so infirm as this.

For the moment, Monroe made no written reply to
Foster's letter of July 3 ; he was tormented by the
crisis of his career, and Foster ceased to be important from the moment he could do nothing toward
a repeal of the orders. With the usual misfortune
of British diplomatists, Foster became aggressive as
he lost ground, and pushed the secretary vigorously
into Napoleon's arms. July 14 Foster wrote again,
in a threatening tone, that measures of retaliation
for the Act of March 2 were already before his
Government, and if America persisted in her injurious course of conduct, the most unfriendly situation
would result. While this threat was all that England offered for Monroe's friendship, news arrived
on the same day that Napoleon, May 4, had opened
his ports to American commerce. Not till then did
Monroe give way, and turn his back upon England
and his old political friends. The course taken by
Foster left no apparent choice ; and for that reason
chiefly Monroe, probably with many misgivings, abandoned the theory of foreign affairs which had for
five years led him into so many mortifications at
home and abroad.

July 23 Monroe sent his answer [1] to the British
minister's argument. In substance this note, though
long, contained nothing new ; but in effect it was
an ultimatum which left England to choose between
concession and war. As an ultimatum, it was weakened by the speciousness of its long argument to

[1] Monroe to Foster, July 23, 1811; State Papers, iii. 439.

prove that the French Decrees were repealed. The weakness of the ground required double boldness of assertion, and Monroe accepted the whole task. He showed further willingness to accept an issue on any point England might select. Foster's remonstrance in regard to the "Little Belt" called from Monroe a tart reference to the affair of the "Chesapeake," and a refusal to order an inquiry, as a matter of right, into the conduct of Commodore Rodgers. He showed equally little disposition to press for a settlement of the "Chesapeake" affair. Foster had been barely two weeks at Washington when he summed up the result of his efforts in a few words,[1] which told the situation, as Monroe then understood it, a year before war was declared : —

"On the whole, their view in this business [of the 'Little Belt'] is to settle this, with every other difference, in the most amicable manner, provided his Majesty's Orders in Council are revoked ; otherwise, to make use of it, together with all other topics of irritation, for the purpose of fomenting a spirit of hatred toward England, and thereby strengthening their party. Your Lordship cannot expect to hear of any change till Congress meet."

[1] Foster to Wellesley, July 18, 1811; MSS. British Archives.

CHAPTFR III.

BEFORE the familiar figure of Robert Smith quite fades from the story of his time, the mystery which he succeeded in throwing around his true sympathies needs explanation. When dismissed from the Cabinet in March, he was supposed to be a friend of France and of the President's French policy. In June he appeared before the public as an opponent of Madison and of French influence. Perhaps in reality he neither supported nor opposed either policy; but he deserves such credit as friendly hands gave him at the moment of his disgrace, and on no one had he made a happier impression than on Serurier, the new French minister. After six weeks' experience, Serurier, who looked upon Gallatin as little better than an enemy, regarded Robert Smith as a friend. March 5, while Gallatin was writing his resignation, Serurier wrote a despatch to Cadore giving his estimates of the two Cabinet officers:[1] —

"Mr. Gallatin, perhaps the most capable man in the Republic, under an exterior rigidly Republican hides his ambitious designs, his feelings of superiority, which

[1] Serurier to Champagny, No. 5, March 5, 1811. Archives des Aff. Étr. MSS.

torment him without his being able to satisfy them.
People maintain that all his system as a financier is
English, — a thing simple enough; and that, on another
side, he thinks himself obliged to expiate the sin of being
a stranger and born on our frontiers, by separating
himself from us in his political principles. I am told
also that he has seen with annoyance the occupation by
France of Geneva, his country, — whither he expected
to withdraw himself with his riches, if his ambition should
be crossed here by events. I have as yet no cause for
complaint in regard to him, but this is the way he is
talked about by the Frenchmen here, and by the party
most nearly in sympathy with us (*le parti qui se rap-
proche le plus de nous*)."

The fable of Gallatin's *richesses* revealed the source
of Serurier's information. The party most nearly
in sympathy with France was the "Aurora" faction, which spread stories of Gallatin's peculations
and treated him with vindictive enmity, but regarded
Robert Smith as a friend. Serurier's description of
Gallatin's character contrasted darkly with his por-
trait of Robert Smith: —

"Mr. Smith shows certainly a character equally decided, but more open. His system seems more Continental; at least he wishes me to think so. With perhaps
less breadth of mind, he has more elevation. I know
that he nourishes a secret admiration of the Emperor,
which he very wisely hides. I dined with him three days
ago; it was my first dinner. On leaving the table he
sent for a bust and an engraving of his Majesty, and on
this subject said to me things full of politeness. In the
conversation which followed, he became more expansive:

' The nation ' (it is he who is speaking) ' is bold and enterprising at sea ; and if war should break out with England, supposing this rupture to be accompanied by a full reconciliation with France, the commerce between Europe and America might become more active than ever. The Americans possess a sort of vessels called schooners, the swiftest sailers in the world, and for that reason beyond insult and capture ; while their sailors are full of confidence in the advantage given them by this sort of vessel in time of war.' He affirmed to me that the great majority of the nation, if satisfied on the side of France, will be much inclined to war with her rival ; but that the mild, prudent, and perhaps too timid administration of Mr. Jefferson heretofore, and now that of Mr. Madison, had thus far repressed the national enthusiasm ; but he was convinced that under the administration, for example, of the Vice-President General Clinton, or of any other statesman of his character, war would have already broken out."

This was not the only occasion when Robert Smith showed himself to the French minister as restive under restraint.

" I asked him," reported Serurier at another time,[1] " what the Government expected to do if the English resented its pretension to the independence of its flag? ' War,' he replied with perfect frankness, ' is the inevitable result of our position toward the English if they refuse to recognize our rights.' Mr. Smith then admitted to me that his Government certainly had the best founded hope that the establishment of the regency in England

[1] Serurier to Champagny, Feb. 17, 1811 ; Archives des Aff. Étr. MSS.

would bring about a change of ministry and probably of system, and that the Orders in Council would be repealed; that in this case, neutral rights being re-established, the motive for all this discussion would cease.   But he repeated to me that in the contrary case war would, in his eyes, be inevitable, and that the Americans, in deciding on this course, had perfectly foreseen where it would lead them, without being, on that account, deterred from a decision dictated by their honor or their interest."

These remarks were made February 17, the day when the President decided to accept Napoleon's conditions; and they helped to convince Serurier that Robert Smith was more " continental," or Napoleonic, than Gallatin.   For this reason, when he heard that Gallatin had prevailed, and Smith was to take the Russian Mission, he wrote to his Government with regret : [1] —

" The Secretary of State has taken his resolution like a man of courage.   Instead of sulking and going to intrigue in his province, he has preferred to remain attached to the government of his country, and to go for some time to enjoy the air of our Europe, whither his tastes lead him, and to reserve himself for more favorable circumstances.   His frank and open character makes him generally regretted.   I think he must have had a share at the time in the fit of energy which his Government has shown.   His language was measured; but very certainly his system drew him much nearer to France than to England."

[1] Serurier to Champagny, March 26, 1811; Archives des Aff. Étr. MSS.

Perhaps Serurier was misled by Robert Smith's habit of taking tone from the person nearest him; but as the French minister learned more of Monroe, his regrets for Smith became acute. " I regard as an evil," he wrote, April 5,[1] " the removal of a man whose elevated views, — noble in foreign policy at least, — and whose decided character, might have given to affairs a direction which must be at least counteracted by his absence, and especially by the way in which his place is filled."

Monroe took charge of the State Department April 1, and within a few days Serurier became unpleasantlv conscious of the change. He still met with civility, but he felt new hesitation. Joel Barlow had been appointed minister to France, and should have started instantly for his post. Yet Barlow lingered at Washington; and when Serurier asked the reason of the delay, Monroe merely said he was waiting for the arrival of the frigate " Essex " with despatches from France and England to the middle of April. The expected despatches did not arrive until July; and in the interval Serurier passed a season of discomfort. The new Secretary of State, unlike his predecessor, showed no admiration for Napoleon. Toward the end of June, the French consuls in the United States made known that they were still authorized and required by the Emperor to issue permits or certificates to American vessels destined for France.

[1] Serurier to Champagny, April 5, 1811 ; Archives des Aff. Étr. MSS.

Monroe sent at once for Serurier, and admonished him in language that seemed to the French minister altogether out of place : [1] —

" Mr. Monroe's countenance was absolutely distorted (*tout-à-fait décomposeé*). I could not conceive how an object, apparently so unimportant, could affect him so keenly. He continued thus : ' You are witness, sir, to the candor of our motives, to the loyalty of our principles, to our immovable fidelity to our engagements. In spite of party clamor and the extreme difficulty of the circumstances, we persevere in our system ; but your Government abandons us to the attacks of its enemies and ours, by not fulfilling on its side the conditions set forth in the President's proclamation. We are daily accused of a culpable partiality for France. These cries were at first feeble, and we flattered ourselves every day to be able to silence them by announcing the Emperor's arrangements in conformity with ours ; but they become louder by our silence. The Administration finds itself in the most extreme embarrassment (*dans le plus extrême embarras*) ; it knows neither what to expect from you, nor what to say to its constituents. Ah, sir ! ' cried Mr. Monroe, ' if your sovereign had deigned to imitate the promptness (*empressement*) which our President showed in publishing his proclamation ; if he had re-opened, with the necessary precautions, concerted with us, his ports and his vessels, — all the commerce of America was won for France. A thousand ships would have sailed at all risks to your ports, where they would have sought the products of your manufactures which are so much liked

[1] Serurier to Maret, June 30, 1811 ; Archives des Aff. Étr. MSS.

in this country. The English would have certainly opposed such a useful exchange between the two peoples ;
our honor and interest would have united to resist them ;
and the result, for which you are doubtless more desirous
than you admit, could not have failed to happen at
last.' "

Serurier tried in vain to soothe the secretary ;
Monroe was not to be appeased. Oratory so impassioned was not meant for mere show ; and as causes
of grievance multiplied, the secretary gathered one
after another, evidently to be used for a rupture with
France. Each stage toward his end he marked by
the regular shade of increasing displeasure that he
had himself, as a victim, so often watched. Enjoying the pleasure of doing to others what Cevallos
and Harrowby, Talleyrand and Canning had done
to him, Monroe, familiar with the accents of the
most famous school in European diplomacy, ran no
risk of throwing away a single tone.

When the secretary told Serurier that Joel Barlow's departure depended on the news to be brought
by the " Essex," he did not add that he was himself waiting for the arrival of Foster, the new British minister ; but as it happened, Foster reached
Washington July 1, at the same instant with the
despatches brought by the " Essex." The crisis of
Serurier's diplomatic fortune came with the arrival
of Foster, and during the next two weeks the French
minister passed through many uncomfortable scenes.
He knew too little of American affairs to foresee

that not himself, but Monroe, must in the end be
the victim. As soon as the " Essex " was announced,
bringing William Pinkney from London and Jonathan Russell's despatches from Paris, — including
his report of Napoleon's tirade to the Paris merchants, but no sign that his decrees were repealed,
— Serurier called at the Department to learn what
Monroe had to say. " I found him icy ; he told me
that, contrary to all the hopes of the Government,
the ' Essex ' had brought nothing decisive, and
asked if I was more fortunate." [1] Serurier had despatches, but as the story has shown [2] they were
emphatic in forbidding him to pledge himself in regard to the Emperor's course. Obliged to evade
Monroe's inquiry, he could only suggest hopes of
more decisive news by the next arrival, and then
turned the subject to Napoleon's zeal in revolutionizing Spanish America: —

" I was heard with politeness, but coldly. Then I
talked of the abrupt and improper tone of Mr. Russell's
correspondence. I said that it did not offend, because
Mr. Russell was not of enough consequence to give
offence ; but that it was considered altogether indeco-
rous. I made him aware, on this occasion, of the
necessity that the Republic should have a minister at
Paris. Mr. Monroe answered that the Government had
already made that remark ; he repeated to me that he
had intended, long before, to send away Mr. Barlow,

[1] Serurier to Maret, July 5, 1811 ; Archives des Aff Étr.
MSS.

[2] See vol. v. p. 393.

but that the daily expectation of despatches from France
had made him always delay. Here he stopped himself,
and returned for the tenth time upon the difficult position of the Government; upon the universal outcry
of commerce, which would become a kind of revolt in
the North if the Government could offer nothing to
counteract it. He recalled to me the effect produced
by the announcement of new licenses issued at Boston
and Baltimore, and the equally annoying effect of a pamphlet by the ex-Secretary of State, Mr. Smith, which
revealed to the public the declaration made by me on
my arrival, that the old confiscations made by way of
reprisals, could not be matter of discussion, — ' information,' said he, ' which had at the time profoundly
afflicted the Administration, and which it had counted
on publishing only at the moment when it could simultaneously announce a better outlook, and the absolute
restoration of commercial relations.' He ended, at last,
this conference by telling me that he had not yet finished
reading all his papers; that the Government was that
moment deliberating on its course, and that in a few
days we would have a new conference."

Serurier felt his danger, and expected to be sacrificed. Society turned against him. Even Duane
became abusive of France.

" Already, within a few days, I notice a change in the
manners of every one about me. The general attention
of which I was the object during the first five months
has been suddenly followed by a general reserve; people
are civil, but under a thousand pretexts they avoid being seen in conversation with me. The journals hitherto
most favorable to France begin to say that since we

will not keep our engagements, a rupture must take place."

Thinking that he had nothing to lose, the French minister took a high tone, and July 3, through a private channel, conveyed to the President a warning that the course threatened might lead too far.

"The person in question having answered that I might depend on the Government's fidelity to its engagements, I replied that I would believe it all if the new American minister should be despatched to Paris, and that I would believe nothing if this departure were again postponed."

Everything depended on Foster, who had been received by the President July 2, the day before Serurier's message was sent. Apparently, the first impression made by Foster's letters and conversation was decisive, for Monroe told the French minister at the public dinner of July 4, that Barlow was to start at once on his mission.

"This news," reported Serurier, "caused me great pleasure. This success, though doubtless inconsiderable, made all my ambition for the moment; it delays for several months the crisis that the English party was trying to force, in the hope of making it decisive against us; it neutralizes the effect of the arrival of the British minister, whose want of influence down to this point it reveals; it withdraws the initiative from the President and restores to his Majesty the decision of our great affairs."

No sooner had this decision been made, than Monroe seemed to repent it. The conduct of France had been of late more outrageous than that of England; and Monroe, who found his worst expectations fulfilled, could not easily resign himself to accepting a yoke against which he had for five years protested. The departure of Barlow, ordered July 4, was countermanded July 5; and this proof of Monroe's discontent led to a striking interview, July 9, in which the Secretary of State became more impassioned than ever.[1] Serurier began by asking what he was to think of the Government's conduct. Monroe replied by recalling what had happened since the appointment of Barlow as minister to France, a fortnight after Serurier's arrival. Then the Proclamation of November 2 had been supposed sufficient to satisfy the Emperor; the Non-intercourse Act followed, — yet the President was still waiting for the assurance that the French Decrees were repealed, without which knowledge Barlow's instructions could not be written.

" So we reached the day when the ' Essex ' arrived," continued Monroe. " Not an officer of the government, not a citizen in the Republic, but was convinced that this frigate brought the most satisfactory and the most decisive news. Yet to our great astonishment — even to our confusion — she has brought nothing. In spite of a deception so afflicting, the President had still decided to make a last attempt, and this was to send off Mr. Barlow. I had the honor to announce it to you; but on the news of our frigate's arrival without satis-

[1] Serurier to Maret, July 10, 1811; Archives des Aff. Étr. MSS.

factory information from France, a general cry of discontent rose all over the Republic, and public opinion
pronounced itself so strongly against Mr. Barlow's departure that the Government can to-day no longer give
the order without raising from all parts of the Union the
cry of treason. I am myself a daily witness of the general effervescence that this silence of your Government
excites. I cannot walk from my house to this office
without being accosted by twenty citizens, who say to
me : ' What, sir! shall you send off a minister to France,
when the Imperial government shows itself unwilling to
carry out its engagements ; when it treats our citizens
with so much injustice, and you yourself with so much
contempt?   No! the honor of the Republic will not
permit you to send your ambassador under such circumstances, and you will be responsible for it to the
country.' "

Monroe's objection seemed reasonable. The sending a new minister to France was in no way necessary for making an issue with England. Indeed, if
only a simple issue with England had been wanted,
the permanent presence of British frigates off Sandy
Hook, capturing American vessels and impressing
American seamen, was sufficient. No further protest against it needed to be made, seeing that it
had been the subject of innumerable protests.   If
President Madison wanted an issue that should oblige
Great Britain to declare war, or to take measures
equivalent to war, he could obtain it in a moment by
ordering Rodgers and Decatur to drive the British
frigates away and rescue their victims. For such a

purpose he needed no minister in France, and had no occasion to make himself a party to fraud. Monroe's language implied that he would have preferred some such issue.

" ' Believe me,' said Mr. Monroe in finishing, and as we were about to separate, ' the American government will not be inconsequent; but its patience is exhausted, and as regards foreign Powers it is determined to make itself respected. People in Europe suppose us to be merchants, occupied exclusively with pepper and ginger. They are much deceived, and I hope we shall prove it. The immense majority of citizens do not belong to this class, and are, as much as your Europeans, controlled by principles of honor and dignity. I never knew what trade was. The President is as much of a stranger to it as I; and we accord to commerce only the protection that we owe it, as every government owes it to an interesting class of its citizens.' "

Commerce would have listened with more amusement than conviction to Monroe's ideas on the " principles of honor and dignity " which led a government of Virginia and Pennsylvania farmers to accord protection in the form of embargoes and non-intercourses to commerce which it distrusted and despised; but Monroe meant only that France, as well as England, must reckon on a new national spirit in Virginia, — a spirit which they had themselves roused, and for whose bad qualities they had only themselves to blame.

Yet Monroe found himself in an attitude not flattering to his pride. All his life a representative of the Virginia school, — more conservative than Jefferson, and only to be compared with John Randolph, and John Taylor of Caroline, — he had come to the State Department to enforce his own principles and overrule the President; but he found himself helpless in the President's hands. That the contest was in reality between Monroe's will and Madison's became clear to Serurier; and that Monroe's pliable nature must succumb to Madison's pertinacity, backed as it was by authority, could not be doubtful. Six months seemed to Virginians a short time for Monroe's submission, but in truth Monroe had submitted long before; his rebellion itself had been due to William Pinkney and John Randolph rather than to impulses of his own; he regretted it almost as soon as it was made, and he suffered little in allowing Madison to control the course of events. Yet he would certainly have preferred another result, and his interview with Serurier, July 9, recorded the policy he had meant to impose, while preparing for its abandonment.

The secretary waited only for a pretext to accept Madison's dogma that the French Decrees were withdrawn, although his conversations with Serurier proved his conviction to the contrary. A few days later, a vessel arrived from England bringing unofficial news from France, to May 24, that the Emperor had released the American vessels kept in sequestration since November 1, and had admitted their cargoes for sale. Without the form of further struggle, Monroe followed the footsteps of his predecessor.

" The Secretary of State sent for me three days ago to his office," wrote Serurier, July 20.[1] " After having congratulated me on this decision [of the Emperor], he told me that he had no doubt of its producing on the public the same excellent impression it had made on the Government ; but he added that as it was not official, the President would like to have me write a letter as confirmative as possible, in the absence of instructions, both of these events and of his Majesty's good intentions ; and that if I could write him this letter, Mr. Barlow should immediately depart."

The only instructions possessed by Serurier on the subject of the decrees warned him against doing what Monroe asked ; but the temptation to win a success was strong, and he wrote a cautious letter,[2] dated July 19, saying that he had no official knowledge on the subject, but that " it is with reason, sir, that you reject the idea of a doubt on the fidelity of France in fulfilling her engagements ; for to justify such a doubt one must have some contradictory facts to cite, — one must show that judgments have been rendered in France on the principle of maintaining the Decrees of Berlin and Milan, or that a series of American ships coming from England to America, or from America to England, have been captured

[1] Serurier to Maret, July 20, 1811 ; Archives des Aff. Étr. MSS.

[2] Serurier to Monroe, July 19, 1811 ; MSS. State Department Archives.

by our privateers in virtue of the blockade of the British Isles. Nothing of the sort has become known to any of us, and, on the contrary," all advices showed that the decrees in France and on the ocean had ceased to affect American commerce.

Probably this letter disappointed the President, for it was never published, nor was any allusion made to it in the correspondence that followed. Without even such cover, Monroe ordered Barlow to depart, and made the decision public. Serurier, puzzled though delighted by his success, groped in the dark to discover how the Government had reached its decision. Foster's attitude failed to enlighten him; and he could see no explanation, except that the result was a personal victory of Madison over Monroe and the Cabinet.

"The joy is general among the authorities," he wrote July 20,[1] "except among some friends of Mr. Foster; but more than any one else, Mr. Madison seems enchanted to see himself confirmed (*raffermi*) in a system which is wholly his own, but which he began to see no means of maintaining. I do him the justice to say that if he had a movement of hesitation on the point of Mr. Barlow's departure, it was more the effect of public clamor than of his own sentiments, — a movement of spite (*dépit*) and discouragement, rather than of inclination toward England, which he frankly detests, as does his friend Mr. Jefferson, — and that he has not been for a moment unfaithful to his engagements with

[1] Serurier to Maret, July 20, 1811; Archives des Aff. Étr MSS.

us. I have never seen him more triumphant. The Secretaries of State, of the Treasury, and of War are doubtful, perhaps, and conduct themselves more according to events; but happily the President, superior to them in enlightenment as in position, governs entirely by himself, and there is no reason to fear his being crossed by them."

Serurier knew Madison and Jefferson only as a Frenchman might, and his ideas of their feelings toward England were such as a Frenchman could understand. In truth, Madison did not want a distinct issue of peace or war with England. Had he wished for such an issue, he would have made it. Disbelieving in war, as war approached, he clung to the last chances of peaceful coercion. The fiction that Napoleon's decrees were repealed enabled him to enforce his peaceful coercive measures to avoid war. Not because he wanted war, but because he wanted peace, Madison insisted that the decrees were withdrawn. As he carried each point, he stood more and more alone; he was misunderstood by his enemies and overborne by his friends; he failed in his policy of peace, and knew himself unfit to administer a policy of war. Yet he held to his principle, that commercial restrictions were the true safeguards of an American system.

A man of keen intelligence, Madison knew, quite as well as Monroe, Serurier, or Foster, that the French Decrees were not repealed. His alleged reason for despatching Barlow was unsatisfactory

to himself as to Monroe, and doubly worthless because unofficial.   Even while he insisted on his
measures, he made no secret of his discontent.
When official despatches arrived a few days later,
Serurier was puzzled at finding Madison well aware
that the Emperor had not withdrawn and did not
mean to withdraw his decrees.   July 23 Serurier
communicated [1] to Monroe the substance of the despatches from France.   The next day he called at
the Department and at the White House to watch
the effect of his letter, which announced the admission of American merchandise into French ports.

" Mr. Monroe showed himself less satisfied than I had
hoped, either because the President had so directed, in
order to reserve the right of raising new pretensions, or
because, already advised by Mr. Russell, he had been at
the same time informed that the prizes made since November by our privateers were not restored; and these
restrictions had been represented in an unfavorable light
by the *chargé d'affaires*.   He confined himself to telling
me that certainly there were things agreeable to the
American government in the Emperor's arrangements,
but that there were others wholly contrary to expectation, and that before his departure he would send me
a list of the complaints left unsatisfied. . . . As the
President is to start to-morrow for his estate in Virginia, I called this morning to bid him good-by.   I
had on this occasion with Mr. Madison an interview
which put the last stroke to my suspicions.   When I
told him that I was glad to see him a last time under

[1] Serurier to Monroe, July 23, 1811 ; State Papers, iii. 508.

auspices so happy as the news I had officially given him
the evening before, he answered me that he had learned
with pleasure, though without surprise, the release of
the sequestered ships and the Emperor's decision to
admit American products; but that one thing pained
him profoundly. This was that the American ships captured since last November, under pretext of the Berlin
and Milan Decrees, had not been released with those
which voluntarily entered French ports; and he pretended that this failure to execute the chief of our
engagements destroyed the effect of all the rest." [1]

The opinion scarcely admitted dispute. Reversing
Madison's theory, Napoleon had relieved American
vessels from the "municipal operation" of his decrees in France, while he enforced that international
operation on the high seas which alone Madison
declared himself bound by the law of nations to
resist. The blockade thus enforced by Napoleon
against England was more extravagant than any
blockade England had ever declared. Of his acts
in Denmark and on the Baltic Madison took no
notice at all, though these, more than the deten-
tion of American prizes in France, "destroyed the
effect of all the rest." If, then, the decrees were
still enforced on the ocean, — as Madison insisted
they were, — they could not have been repealed;
and Madison, by submitting to their enforcement
on the ocean, not only recognized their legality,
but also required England to make the same sub-

[1] Serurier to Maret, July 24, 1811; Archives des Aff. Étr.
MSS.

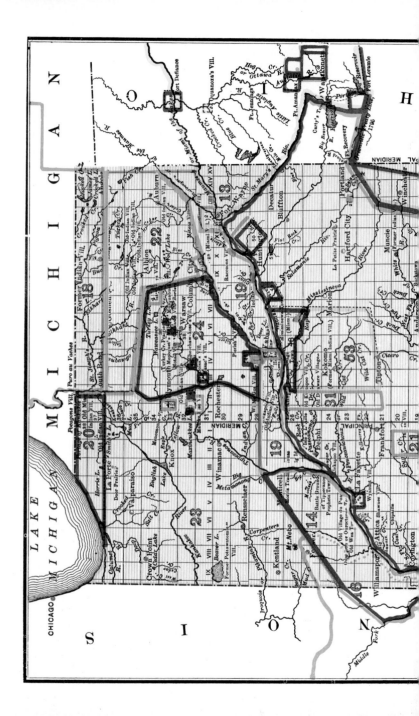

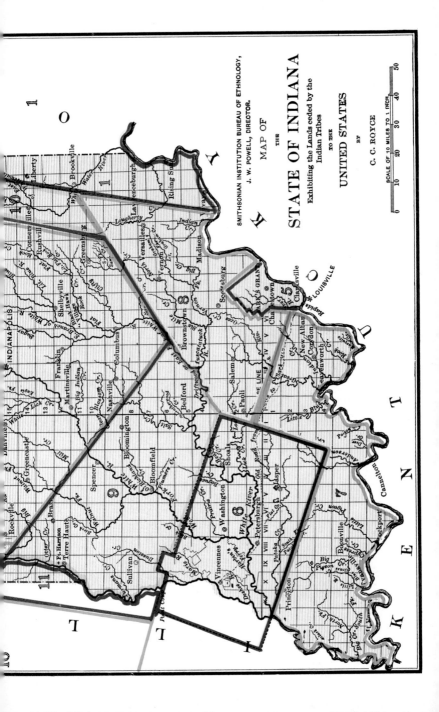

SMITHSONIAN INSTITUTION BUREAU OF ETHNOLOGY,
J. W. POWELL, DIRECTOR.

MAP OF

THE

STATE OF INDIANA

Exhibiting the Lands ceded by the
Indian Tribes

TO THE

UNITED STATES

BY

C. C. ROYCE

SCALE OF 10 MILES TO 1 INCH.

0   10   20   30   40   50

CESSIONS OF INDIAN TERRITORY IN INDIANA,
1795--1810.

———•———

1. *Tract ceded by Treaty of Greenville, August 3rd, 1795.*
2. *Tract about Fort Wayne, ceded by the same Treaty.*
3. *Two miles square on the Miami portage, ceded by the same Treaty.*
4. *Six miles square at Old Wea Town on the Wabash, ceded by the same Treaty.*
5. *Clark's Grant on the Ohio, reserved by the same Treaty.*
6. *Vincennes tract, reserved by the same Treaty.*
7. *Tract ceded by Treaties of August 18th and 27th, 1804.*
8. *Tract ceded by Treaty of August 21st, 1805.*
9, 10, 11. *Tracts ceded by Treaty of September 30th, 1809.*
12. *Tract ceded by Treaty of December 9th, 1809.*

mission, under penalty of a declaration of war from the United States. This dilemma threatened to overthrow Madison's Administration, or even to break up the Union. Serurier saw its dangers, and did his utmost to influence Napoleon toward concessions :

" The revocation of the Decrees of Milan and Berlin has become a personal affair with Mr. Madison. He announced it by proclamation, and has constantly maintained it since. The English party never stops worrying him on this point, and saying that he has been made a tool of France, — that the decrees have not been repealed. He fears the effect of this suspension, and foresees that it will cause great discussions in the next Congress, and that it alone may compromise the Administration, triumphant on all other points."

Under such circumstances, Monroe needed more than common powers in order to play his part. Talleyrand himself would have found his impassive countenance tried by assuring Foster in the morning that the decrees were repealed, and rating Serurier in the afternoon because they were in force. Such conversations, extended over a length of time, might in the end raise doubts of a statesman's veracity ; yet this was what Monroe undertook. On the day when Serurier communicated the news that disturbed the President, Monroe sent to the British minister the note maintaining broadly that France had revoked her decrees. Three days later, after the President had told Serurier that " the failure to execute the chief of our engagements destroyed the effect of all the rest," Monroe gave to Barlow his instructions founded on the revocation of the decrees. Doubtless this double-dealing exasperated all the actors concerned in it. Madison and Monroe at heart were more angry with France than with England, if indeed degrees in anger could be felt where the outrages of both parties were incessant and intolerable. Yet Barlow took his instructions and set sail for France; a proclamation appeared in the "National Intelligencer" calling Congress together for November 1; and the President and his Secretary of State left Washington for their summer vacation in Virginia, having accepted, once for all, the conditions imposed by Napoleon.

For some years afterward Monroe said no more about old Republican principles; but twelve months later he wrote to Colonel Taylor a letter [1] which began with a candid confession : —

" I have been afraid to write to you for some time past, because I knew that you expected better things from me than I have been able to perform. You thought that I might contribute to promote a compromise with Great Britain, and thereby prevent a war between that country and the United States ; that we might also get rid of our restrictive system. I own to you that I had some hope, though less than some of my friends entertained, that I might aid in promoting that desirable result. This hope has been disappointed."

[1] Monroe to Taylor, June 13, 1812; Monroe MSS.

CHAPTER IV.

ALTHOUGH no one doubted that the year 1812 was to witness a new convulsion of society, if signs of panic occurred they were less marked in crowded countries where vast interests were at stake, than in remote regions which might have been thought as safe from Napoleon's wars as from those of Genghis Khan. As in the year 1754 a petty fight between two French and English scouting parties on the banks of the Youghiogheny River, far in the American wilderness, began a war that changed the balance of the world, so in 1811 an encounter in the Indian country, on the banks of the Wabash, began a fresh convulsion which ended only with the fall of Napoleon. The battle of Tippecanoe was a premature outbreak of the great wars of 1812.

Governor William Henry Harrison, of the Indiana Territory, often said he could tell by the conduct of his Indians, as by a thermometer, the chances of war and peace for the United States as estimated in the Cabinet at London. The remark was curious, but not surprising. Uneasiness would naturally be greatest where least control and most irritation existed. Such a region was the Northwestern Terri-

tory.   Even the spot where violence would break
out might be predicted as somewhere on the water-
line of the Maumee and the Wabash, between Detroit
at one extremity and Vincennes at the other.   If a
guess had been ventured that the most probable
point would be found on that line, about half way
between Lake Erie and the Ohio River, the map
would have shown that Tippecanoe Creek, where it
flowed into the Wabash, corresponded with the rough
suggestion.

The Indiana Territory was created in 1800; and
the former delegate of the whole Northwestern Territory, William Henry Harrison, was then appointed
governor of the new division.   Until the year 1809,
Illinois formed part of the Indiana Territory; but
its single settlement at Kaskaskia was remote.   The
Indiana settlement consisted mainly of two tracts, —
one on the Ohio, opposite Louisville in Kentucky, at
the falls, consisting of about one hundred and fifty
thousand acres, called Clark's Grant; the other, at
Vincennes on the Wabash, where the French had
held a post, without a definite grant of lands, under an old Indian treaty, and where the Americans
took whatever rights the French enjoyed.   One hundred miles of wilderness separated these two tracts.
In 1800, their population numbered about twenty-
five hundred persons; in 1810, nearly twenty-five
thousand.

Northward and westward, from the bounds of
these districts the Indian country stretched to the

Lakes and the Mississippi, unbroken except by military posts at Fort Wayne and Fort Dearborn, or Chicago, and a considerable settlement of white people in the neighborhood of the fortress at Detroit. Some five thousand Indian warriors held this vast region, and were abundantly able to expel every white man from Indiana if their organization had been as strong as their numbers. The whites were equally eager to expel the Indians, and showed the wish openly.

Governor Harrison was the highest authority on matters connected with the northwestern Indians. During eight years of Harrison's government Jefferson guided the Indian policy; and as long as Jefferson insisted on the philanthropic principles which were his pride, Harrison, whose genius lay in ready adaptation, took his tone from the President, and wrote in a different spirit from that which he would have taken had he represented an aggressive chief. His account of Indian affairs offered an illustration of the law accepted by all historians in theory, but adopted by none in practice; which former ages called "fate," and metaphysicians called "necessity," but which modern science has refined into the "survival of the fittest." No acid ever worked more mechanically on a vegetable fibre than the white man acted on the Indian. As the line of American settlements approached, the nearest Indian tribes withered away.

Harrison reported conscientiously the incurable

evils which attended the contact of the two hostile forms of society. The first, but not the most serious, was that the white man, though not allowed to settle beyond the Indian border, could not be prevented from trespassing far and wide on Indian territory in search of game. The practice of hunting on Indian lands, in violation of law and existing treaties, had grown into a monstrous abuse. The Kentucky settlers crossed the Ohio River every autumn to kill deer, bear, and buffalo for their skins, which they had no more right to take than they had to cross the Alleghanies, and shoot or trap the cows and sheep in the farm-yards of Bucks County. Many parts of the Northwestern Territory which as late as 1795 abounded in game, ten years afterward contained not game enough to support the small Indian parties passing through them, and had become worthless for Indian purposes except as a barrier to further encroachment.[1]

The tribes that owned these lands were forced either to remove elsewhere, or to sell their old hunting-grounds to the government for supplies or for an annuity. The tribes that sold, remaining near the settlements to enjoy their annuity, were more to be pitied than those that removed, which were destined to destruction by war. Harrison reported that contact with white settlements never failed to ruin them. "I can tell at once," he wrote in 1801,[2]

---

[1] Dawson's Harrison, p. 8.
[2] Dawson's Harrison, p. 11.

"upon looking at an Indian whom I may chance to meet, whether he belongs to a neighboring or to a more distant tribe. The latter is generally well-clothed, healthy, and vigorous; the former half-naked, filthy, and enfeebled by intoxication, and many of them without arms excepting a knife, which they carry for the most villanous purposes." Harrison estimated the number of Indian warriors then in the whole valley of the Wabash as not exceeding six hundred; the sale of whiskey was unlawful, yet they were supposed to consume six thousand gallons of whiskey a year, and their drunkenness so often ended in murder that among three of the tribes scarcely a chief survived.

"I have had much difficulty," wrote Harrison in the same letter from Vincennes, "with the small tribes in this immediate neighborhood; namely the Piankeshaws, the Weas, and the Eel River Miamis. These three tribes form a body of the most depraved wretches on earth. They are daily in this town in considerable numbers, and are frequently intoxicated to the number of thirty or forty at once, when they commit the greatest disorders, drawing their knives and stabbing every one they meet with; breaking open the houses of the citizens, killing their cattle and hogs, and breaking down their fences. But in all their frolics they generally suffer the most themselves. They kill each other without mercy. Some years ago as many as four were found dead in a morning; and although those murders were actually committed in the streets of the town, yet no attempt to punish them has ever been made."

The Piankeshaws were reduced to twenty-five or thirty warriors; the Weas and Eel River Indians were mere remnants. The more powerful tribes at a distance saw with growing alarm the steady destruction of the border warriors; and the intelligent Indians everywhere forbade the introduction of whiskey, and tried to create a central authority to control the degraded tribes.

A third evil was much noticed by Harrison. By treaty, if an Indian killed a white man the tribe was bound to surrender the murderer for trial by American law; while if a white man killed an Indian, the murderer was also to be tried by a white jury. The Indians surrendered their murderers, and white juries at Vincennes hung them without scruple; but no jury in the territory ever convicted a white man of murdering an Indian. Harrison complained to the President of the wanton and atrocious murders committed by white men on Indians, and the impossibility of punishing them in a society where witnesses would not appear, criminals broke jail, and juries refused to convict. Throughout the territory the people avowed the opinion that a white man ought not in justice to suffer for killing an Indian; [1] and many of them, like the uncle of Abraham Lincoln,[2] thought it a virtuous act to shoot an Indian at sight. Harrison could combat this code of popular law only by proclamations offering rewards for the arrest of

[1] Dawson's Harrison, pp. 7, 31, 32.
[2] Life of Lincoln, by Hay and Nicolay, chap. i.

murderers, who were never punished when arrested. In 1801 the Delawares alone complained of six un-atoned murders committed on their tribe since the Treaty of Greenville, and every year increased the score.

" All these injuries," reported Harrison in 1801, " the Indians have hitherto borne with astonishing patience ; but though they discover no disposition to make war on the United States at present, I am confident that most of the tribes would eagerly seize any favorable opportunity for that purpose ; and should the United States be at war with any of the European nations who are known to the Indians, there would probably be a combination of more than nine tenths of the Northern tribes against us, unless some means are used to conciliate them."

So warmly were the French remembered by the Indians, that if Napoleon had carried out his Louisiana scheme of 1802 he could have counted on the active support of nearly every Indian tribe on the Mississippi and the Lakes ; from Pensacola to Detroit his orders would have been obeyed. Toward England the Indians felt no such sentimental attachment; but interest took the place of sentiment. Their natural line of trade was with the Lakes, and their relations with the British trading-post at Malden, opposite Detroit, became more and more close with every new quarrel between Washington and London.

President Jefferson earnestly urged the Indians to become industrious cultivators of the soil ; but even for that reform one condition was indispensable. The

Indians must be protected from contact with the whites; and during the change in their mode of life, they must not be drugged, murdered, or defrauded. Trespasses on Indian land and purchases of tribal territory must for a time cease, until the Indian tribes should all be induced to adopt a new system. Even then the reform would be difficult, for Indian warriors thought death less irksome than daily labor; and men who did not fear death were not easily driven to toil.

There President Jefferson's philanthropy stopped. His greed for land equalled that of any settler on the border, and his humanity to the Indian suffered the suspicion of having among its motives the purpose of gaining the Indian lands for the whites. Jefferson's policy in practice offered a reward for Indian extinction, since he not only claimed the territory of every extinct tribe on the doctrine of paramount sovereignty, but deliberately ordered [1] his Indian agents to tempt the tribal chiefs into debt in order to oblige them to sell the tribal lands, which did not belong to them, but to their tribes: —

" To promote this disposition to exchange lands which they have to spare and we want, for necessaries which we have to spare and they want, we shall push our trading-houses, and be glad to see the good and influential individuals among them in debt; because we observe that when these debts get beyond what the individuals can pay, they become willing to lop them off by a cession of lands."

[1] Jefferson to Harrison, Feb. 27, 1803; Works, iv. 471.

No one would have felt more astonishment than Jefferson had some friend told him that this policy, which he believed to be virtuous, was a conspiracy to induce trustees to betray their trusts; and that in morals it was as improper as though it were not virtuously intended. Shocked as he would have been at such a method of obtaining the neighboring estate of any Virginia family, he not only suggested but vigorously carried out the system toward the Indians.

In 1804 and 1805, Governor Harrison made treaties with the Miamis, Eel Rivers, Weas, Piankeshaws, and Delawares, — chiefly the tribes he called " a body of the most depraved wretches upon earth," — by which he obtained the strip of country, fifty miles wide, between the Ohio and the White rivers, thus carrying the boundary back toward the Wabash. The treaty excited deep feeling among the better Indians throughout the territory, who held long debates on their means of preventing its execution.

Among the settlers in Indiana, an internal dispute mingled with the dangers of Indian relations. For this misfortune Harrison himself was partially to blame. A Virginian by birth, naturally inclined toward Southern influences, he shared the feelings of the Kentucky and Virginia slave-owners who wanted the right of bringing their slaves with them into the Territory, contrary to the Ordinance of 1787. The men who stood nearest the governor were earnest and active in the effort to repeal or evade the prohibition of slavery, and they received from Harrison all the support he could give them. With his approval, successive appeals were made to Congress. Perhaps the weightiest act of John Randolph's career as leader of the Republican majority in the House was to report, March 2, 1803, that the extension of slavery into Indiana was "highly dangerous and inexpedient," and that the people of Indiana "would at no distant day find ample remuneration for a temporary privation of labor and immigration" in the beneficence of a free society. Cæsar Rodney, of Delaware, in March, 1804, made a report to a contrary effect, recommending a suspension for ten years of the anti-slavery clause in the Ordinance; but the House did not act upon it.

The advocates of a slave system, with Harrison's co-operation, then decided that the Territory should pass into the second grade, which under the Ordinance of 1787 could be done when the population should number five thousand male whites of full age. The change was effected in the winter of 1804–1805, by means open to grave objection.[1] Thenceforward Harrison shared his power with a Legislative Council and a House of Representatives; while the legislature chose a territorial delegate to Congress. The first territorial legislature, in 1805, which was wholly under Harrison's influence, passed an Act, subsequently revised and approved Sept. 17, 1807, permitting owners of slaves to bring them into the

[1] Dunn's Indiana (American Commonwealths), p. 324.

Territory and keep them there for a number of days, during which time the slave might be emancipated on condition of binding himself to service for a term of years to which the law set no limit.[1]

The overpowering influence and energy of the governor and his Southern friends gave them during these years undisputed control. Yet the anti-slavery sentiment was so strong as to make the governor uncomfortable, and almost to endanger his personal safety; until at last, in 1808, the issue was fairly brought before the people in the elections. Both in that and in the following year the opponents of slavery outvoted and defeated the governor's party. Feelings became exceedingly bitter, and the Territory was distracted by feuds which had no small influence on matters of administration, and on the Indian troubles most of all. Between the difficulties of introducing negroes and expelling Indians, Harrison found that his popularity had been lessened, if not lost.[2] He could not fail to see that a military exploit was perhaps his only hope of recovering it; and for such an exploit he had excuses enough.

The treaties of 1804–1805, which threatened the Indians with immediate loss of their hunting-grounds in the Wabash valley, caused a fermentation peculiarly alarming because altogether new. Early in 1806 Harrison learned that a Shawanee Indian,

[1] Dillon's History of Indiana, App. G. p. 617.

[2] Dunn's Indiana, p. 397.

claiming to be a prophet, had gathered a number of warriors about him at Greenville, in Ohio, and was preaching doctrines that threatened trouble. Harrison attributed the mischief to the Prophet; but he learned in time that the Prophet's brother Tecumseh — or more properly Tecumthe — gave the movement its chief strength.

Indians and whites soon recognized Tecumthe as a phenomenon. His father was a Shawanee warrior, in no way distinguished; his mother, a Creek or Cherokee Indian, captured and adopted by the Shawanee, — and of these parents three children at one birth were born about the year 1780, a few miles from Springfield, Ohio. The third brother lived and died obscure; Tecumthe and the Prophet became famous, although they were not chiefs of their tribe, and had no authority of office or birth. Such of the chiefs as were in the.pay or under the power of the United States government were jealous of their influence, and had every reason for wishing to suppress the leaders of a movement avowedly designed to overthrow the system of tribal independence. From the first, Tecumthe aimed at limiting the authority of the tribes and their chiefs in order to build up an Indian confederacy, embracing not the chiefs but the warriors of all the tribes, who should act as an Indian Congress and assume joint ownership of Indian lands.

This scheme was hostile to the plans though not to the professions of President Jefferson. Its ob-

ject was to prevent the piecemeal sale of Indian
lands by petty tribal chiefs, under pressure of government agents. No one could honestly deny that
the object was lawful and even regular; for in the
Treaty of Greenville in 1795, which was the only
decisive authority or precedent, the United States
had admitted and acted on the principle for which
Tecumthe contended, — of accepting its cessions of
land, not from single tribes, but from the whole
body of northwestern Indians, without entering on
the subject of local ownership.[1] Governor Harrison and President Jefferson were of course aware
of the precedent, and decided to disregard it[2] in
order to act on the rule better suited to their purposes; but their decision was in no way binding on
Tecumthe or the tribes who were parties to the treaty
of Greenville.

During the year 1807 Tecumthe's influence was
increased by the "Chesapeake" excitement, which
caused the Governor-general of Canada to intrigue
among the Indians for aid in case of war. Probably
their increase of influence led the Prophet and his
brother, in May or June, 1808, to establish themselves
on Tippecanoe Creek, the central point of Indian
strategy and politics. Vincennes lay one hundred
and fifty miles below, barely four-and-twenty hours
down the stream of the Wabash; Fort Dearborn, or

---

[1] Treaty of Greenville ; State Papers, Indian Affairs, p. 562.

[2] Harrison to the Secretary of War, March 22, 1814 ; Drake's
Tecumseh, p. 161.

Chicago, was a hundred miles to the northwest; Fort
Wayne the same distance to the northeast; and excepting a short portage, the Tippecanoe Indians could
paddle their canoes to Malden and Detroit in one
direction, or to any part of the waters of the Ohio and
Mississippi in the other. At the mouth of Tippecanoe
Creek the reformers laid out a village that realized
Jefferson's wish, for the Indians there drank no
whiskey, and avowed themselves to be tillers of the
soil. Their professions seemed honest. In August,
1808, the Prophet came to Vincennes and passed
two weeks with Governor Harrison, who was surprised to find that no temptation could overcome
the temperance of the Prophet's followers. The
speech then made in the public talk with the governor remains the only record of the Prophet's
words, and of the character he wished to pretend,
if not to adopt.

"I told all the redskins," he said to Harrison, "that
the way they were in was not good, and that they ought
to abandon it; that we ought to consider ourselves as one
man, but we ought to live agreeable to our several customs, — the red people after their mode, and the white
people after theirs; particularly that they should not
drink whiskey; that it was not made for them, but the
white people, who alone know how to use it; and that it
is the cause of all the mischiefs which the Indians suffer.
. . . Determine to listen to nothing that is bad; do not
take up the tomahawk, should it be offered by the British
or by the Long-knives; do not meddle with anything that

does not belong to you, but mind your own business, and cultivate the ground, that your women and your children may have enough to live on. I now inform you that it is our intention to live in peace with our father and his children forever."

Whatever want of confidence Harrison felt in these professions of peace, he recorded his great surprise at finding the temperance to be real; and every one who visited the settlement at Tippecanoe bore witness to the tillage, which seemed to guarantee a peaceful intent; for if war had been in Tecumthe's mind, he would not have placed town, crops, and stock within easy reach of destruction.

Nothing could be more embarrassing to Jefferson than to see the Indians follow his advice; for however well-disposed he might be, he could not want the Indians to become civilized, educated, or competent to protect themselves, — yet he was powerless to protect them. The Prophet asked that the sale of liquor should be stopped; but the President could no more prevent white settlers from selling liquor to the Indians than he could prevent the Wabash from flowing. The tribes asked that white men who murdered Indians should be punished; but the President could no more execute such malefactors than he could execute the smugglers who defied his embargo. The Indians had rights recognized by law, by treaty, and by custom, on which their existence depended; but these rights required force to maintain them, and on the Wabash President Jefferson had less police power than the Prophet himself controlled.

Wide separation could alone protect the Indians from the whites, and Tecumthe's scheme depended for its only chance of success on holding the white settlements at a distance. The Prophet said nothing to Harrison on that point, but his silence covered no secret. So notorious was the Indian hostility to land-cessions, that when Governor Hull of Michigan Territory, in November, 1807, negotiated another such cession at Detroit,[1] the Indian agent at Fort Wayne not only doubted its policy, but insinuated that it might have been dictated by the British in order to irritate the Indians; and he reported that the Northern Indians talked of punishing with death the chiefs who signed it.[2]

Aware of the danger, Harrison decided to challenge it. The people of his Territory wanted the lands of the Wabash, even at the risk of war. The settlement at Tippecanoe was supposed to contain no more than eighty or a hundred warriors, with four or five times that number within a radius of fifty miles. No immediate outbreak was to be feared; and Harrison, "conceiving that a favorable opportunity then offered"[3] for carrying the boundary from the White River to the Wabash, asked authority to make a new purchase. Secretary Eustis, July 15, 1809, wrote him

[1] Treaty of Nov. 7, 1807; State Papers, Indian Affairs, p. 747.

[2] Dawson's Harrison, p. 106.

[3] Dawson, p. 129.

a cautious letter,[1] giving the required permission, but insisting that, " to prevent any future dissatisfaction, the chiefs of all the nations who had or pretended right to these lands " were to be present as consenting parties to the treaty.   On this authority Harrison once more summoned together " the most depraved wretches upon earth," — Miamis, Eel Rivers, Delawares, Pottawatomies, and Kickapoos, — and obtained from them, Sept. 30, 1809, several enormous cessions of territory which cut into the heart of the Indian country for nearly a hundred miles up both banks of the Wabash valley.   These transfers included about three million acres.

Harrison knew that this transaction would carry despair to the heart of every Indian in his Territory. The Wabash valley alone still contained game.   Deprived of their last resource, these Indians must fall back to perish in the country of the Chippewas and Sioux, their enemies.[2]   Already impoverished by the decrees of Napoleon, the Orders in Council, and the embargo, which combined to render their peltry valueless, so that they could scarcely buy the powder and shot to kill their game,[3] the Indians had thenceforward no choice but to depend on British assistance. Harrison's treaty immediately strengthened the influence of Tecumthe and the Prophet.   The Wyandots,

[1] Eustis to Harrison, July 15, 1809.   Indian Affairs, p. 761.

[2] Harrison to the Secretary of War, March 22, 1814 ; Drake's Tecumseh, p. 162.

[3] Dawson, p. 142.

or Hurons, regarded by all the Indian tribes in the Territory as first in dignity and influence, joined Tecumthe's league, and united in a declaration that the late cessions were void, and would not be recognized by the tribes. The winter of 1809–1810 passed quietly; but toward May, 1810, alarming reports reached Vincennes of gatherings at the Prophet's town, and of violence to be expected. When the salt, which was part of the usual annuity, reached Tippecanoe, Tecumthe refused to accept it, and drove the boatmen away. He charged the American government with deceiving the Indians; and he insisted, as the foundation of future peace, that the cessions of 1809 should be annulled, and no future cession should be good unless made by all the tribes.

Harrison knew that his treaties of 1809 opened an aggressive policy, which must naturally end in an Indian war. Some of the best citizens in the Territory thought that the blame for the consequences ought not to rest on the Indians.[1] Since the election of Madison to the Presidency in November, 1808, war with England had been so imminent, and its effect on the Indians so marked, that Harrison could not help seeing the opportunity of a military career, and he had given much study to military matters.[2]

[1] Harrison to Eustis, July 4, 1810 ; Dawson, p. 149. Harrison to Governor Scott, Dec. 13, 1811 ; Dawson, p. 244. Badollet's Letters to Gallatin ; Gallatin MSS. Dillon's Indiana, p. 455.

[2] Harrison to Governor Scott of Kentucky, March 10, 1809 ; Dawson, p. 119.

His plans, if they accorded with his acts, included an Indian war, in which he should take the initiative. His treaties of 1809 left him no choice, for after making such a war inevitable, his only safety lay in crushing the Indians before the British could openly aid them.   Unfortunately, neither Madison nor Eustis understood his purpose, or would have liked it.   They approved his land-purchases, which no Administration and no citizen would have dared reject; but they were very unwilling to be drawn into an Indian war, however natural might be such a consequence of the purchases.

So it happened that as early as the summer of 1810 war was imminent in the Wabash and Maumee valleys, and perhaps only British influence delayed it. British interests imperatively required that Tecumthe's confederacy should be made strong, and should not be wrecked prematurely in an unequal war. From Malden, opposite Detroit, the British traders loaded the American Indians with gifts and weapons ; urged Tecumthe to widen his confederacy, to unite all the tribes, but not to begin war till he received the signal from Canada.   All this was duly reported at Washington.[1]   On the other hand, Harrison sent for Tecumthe; and August 12, 1810, the Indian chief came for a conference to Vincennes.   Indians and whites, in considerable numbers, armed and alert, fearing treachery on both sides, witnessed the interview.

[1] State Papers, Indian Affairs, p. 799.

Tecumthe took, as his right, the position he felt himself to occupy as the most powerful American then living, — who, a warrior himself, with five thousand warriors behind him, held in one hand an alliance with Great Britain, in the other an alliance with the Indians of the southwest. Representatives of the Wyandots, Kickapoos, Pottawatomies, Ottawas, and Winnebagoes announced the adhesion of their tribes to the Shawanee Confederacy and the election of Tecumthe as their chief. In this character he avowed to Harrison, in the broadest and boldest language, the scope of his policy : [1] —

" Brother, since the peace was made in 1795 you have killed some of the Shawanee, Winnebagoes, Delawares, and Miamis, and you have taken our land from us ; and I do not see how we can remain at peace with you if you continue to do so. . . . You try to force the red people to do some injury ; it is you that are pushing them on to do mischief. You endeavor to make distinctions ; you wish to prevent the Indians from doing as we wish them, — from uniting and considering their land as the common property of the whole. You take tribes aside and advise them not to come into this measure. . . . The reason, I tell you, is this : You want, by your distinctions of Indian tribes, in allotting to each a particular tract of land, to make them to war with each other. You never see an Indian come and endeavor to make the white people do so. You are continually driving the red people ; and at last you will drive them into the great lake, where they cannot either stand or work.

[1] War Department Archives, MSS.

" Since my residence at Tippecance we have endeavored to level all distinctions, to destroy village chiefs by
whom all mischief is done : it is they who sell our lands
to the Americans. Our object is to let all our affairs be
transacted by warriors. This land that was sold, and
the goods that were given for it, was only done by a
few. The treaty was afterward brought here, and the
Weas were induced to give their consent because of their
small numbers. . . . In future we are prepared to punish those chiefs who may come forward to propose to
sell their land. If you continue to purchase of them,
it will produce war among the different tribes, and at
last I do not know what will be the consequence to the
white people."

Earnestly denying the intention of making war,
Tecumthe still declared that any attempt on Harrison's part to enter into possession of the land lately
ceded would be resisted by force. In the vehemence
of discussion he used language in regard to the United
States which caused great excitement, and broke up
the meeting for that day ; but he lost no time in
correcting the mistake. After the conference closed,
he had a private interview with Harrison, and repeated his official ultimatum. He should only with
great reluctance make war on the United States,
against whom he had no other complaint than their
land-purchases ; he was extremely anxious to be their
friend, and if the governor would prevail upon the
President to give up the lands lately purchased, and
agree never to make another treaty without the con-

sent of all the tribes, Tecumthe pledged himself to be a faithful ally to the United States, and to assist them in all their wars with the English; otherwise he would be obliged to enter into an English alliance.

Harrison told him that no such condition had the least chance of finding favor with the Government. "Well," rejoined Tecumthe, as though he had expected the answer, "as the great chief is to decide the matter, I hope the Great Spirit will put sense enough into his head to induce him to direct you to give up this land. It is true, he is so far off he will not be injured by the war; he may sit still in his town and drink his wine, while you and I will have to fight it out."

Therewith Tecumthe and Harrison parted, each to carry on his preparations for the conflict. The Secretary of War wrote to Harrison in November instructing him to defer the military occupation of the new purchase on the Wabash, but giving no orders as to the policy intended to be taken by the Government. Wanting peace, he threw on Harrison the responsibility for war.[1]

"It has indeed occurred to me," wrote the secretary, "that the surest means of securing good behavior from this conspicuous personage [Tecumthe] and his brother, would be to make them prisoners; but at this time more particularly, it is desirable that peace with all the Indian

[1] Dawson, pp. 173, 174.

tribes should be preserved; and I am instructed by the President to express to your Excellency his expectation and confidence that in all your arrangements this may be considered (as I am confident it ever has been) a primary object with you."

CHAPTER V.

NOTWITHSTANDING the hostile spirit on both sides, the winter of 1810–1811 passed without serious disturbance on the Wabash, and the summer of 1811 arrived before Harrison thought proper to take the next step. Then, June 24, he sent to Tecumthe and the Prophet a letter, or speech, intended to force an issue.

" Brothers," he wrote,[1] " this is the third year that all the white people in this country have been alarmed at your proceedings. You threaten us with war; you invite all the tribes to the north and west of us to join against us. Brothers, your warriors who have lately been here deny this, but I have received the information from every direction. The tribes on the Mississippi have sent me word that you intended to murder me, and then to commence a war upon our people. I have also received the speech that you sent to the Pottawatomies and others to join you for that purpose; but if I had no other evidence of your hostility to us, your seizing the salt which I lately sent up the Wabash is sufficient."

Except the seizure of five barrels of salt intended for other Indians, in June, 1811, no overt act yet

[1] Dawson's Harrison, p. 179.

showed the intention to begin a war, and certainly no such immediate intention existed; but two white men were at that moment murdered in the Illinois Territory, a drunken Indian was murdered at Vincennes, and these acts of violence, together with the general sense of insecurity, caused the government officials to write from all quarters to the War Department that Tecumthe must be suppressed. Tecumthe himself seemed disposed to avoid cause for attack. July 4 he sent word that he would come to Vincennes; and to Harrison's alarm he appeared there, July 27, with two or three hundred warriors for an interview with the governor. The act proved courage, if not rashness. Harrison's instructions hinted advice to seize the two Indian leaders, if it could be done without producing a war, and Harrison had ample time to prepare his measures.

Tecumthe came and remained two days at Vincennes, explaining, with childlike candor, his plans and wishes. As soon as the council was over, he said, he should visit the Southern tribes to unite them with those of the North in a peaceful confederacy; and he hoped no attempt would be made to settle the disputed territory till his return in the spring. A great number of Indians were to come in the autumn to live at Tippecanoe; they must use the disputed region for hunting-ground. He wished everything to remain in its present situation till his return; he would then go and see the President and settle everything with him. The affairs of all the tribes in that quarter were in his own hands, and he would despatch messengers in every direction to prevent the Indians from doing further mischief.

Tecumthe seemed to think that his wish would prevent Harrison from further aggression for the time. A few days afterward he passed down the Wabash, with some twenty warriors, on his diplomatic errand to the Creeks ; but before he was fairly out of sight, July 31, a number of citizens met at Vincennes, and adopted resolutions demanding that the settlement at Tippecanoe should be broken up. Immediate action, before Tecumthe should return, was urged by Harrison's party, and by many frightened settlers. Harrison's personal wish could not be doubted.

The Secretary of War had already ordered the Fourth Regiment of U. S. Infantry, under Colonel Boyd, with a company of riflemen, — making in the whole a force of five hundred regular troops, — to descend the Ohio from Pittsburg as rapidly as possible, and place themselves under Harrison's orders ; but Eustis added instructions not easily followed or understood. July 17 he wrote to Harrison,[1] —

" In case circumstances shall occur which may render it necessary or expedient to attack the Prophet and his followers, the force should be such as to insure the most complete success. This force will consist of the militia and regular troops. . . . If the Prophet should com-

[1] Dawson, p. 190.

mence or seriously threaten hostilities, he ought to be attacked."

Under these instructions, Harrison was warranted in doing what he pleased. Not even Tecumthe denied the seriousness of his hostile threats, and Harrison had every reason to begin the war at once, if war must be; but although Eustis spoke his own mind clearly, he failed to reckon upon the President, and this neglect was the cause of another letter to Harrison, written three days later:[1] —

"Since my letter of the 17th instant, I have been particularly instructed by the President to communicate to your Excellency his earnest desire that peace may, if possible, be preserved with the Indians, and that to this end every proper means may be adopted. . . . Circumstances conspire at this particular juncture to render it peculiarly desirable that hostilities of any kind or to any degree, not indispensably required, should be avoided. The force under Colonel Boyd has been ordered to descend the Ohio, . . . and although the force is at the disposal of your Excellency, I am instructed to inform you that the President indulges the hope and expectation that your exertions and measures with the Indians will be such as may render their march to the Indian Territory unnecessary, and that they may remain liable to another disposition."

Without paying attention to the President's wishes emphatically expressed in these orders of July 20, Harrison passed the next month in raising forces for an expedition to satisfy the wishes of the Western

[1] Dawson, p. 191.

people. No doubt was felt on the Ohio that Harrison
meant to attack the Indians at Tippecanoe; and so
serious a campaign was expected that Kentucky became eager to share it. Among other Kentuckians,
Joseph H. Daveiss, Aaron Burr's persecutor, wrote,[1]
August 24, to Harrison, offering himself as a volunteer: "Under all the privacy of a letter," said he,
"I make free to tell you that I have imagined there
were two men in the West who had military talents;
and you, sir, were the first of the two. It is thus an
opportunity of service much valued by me." Daveiss
doubted only whether the army was to attack at
once, or to provoke attack.

Harrison accepted Daveiss's services, and gave him
command of the dragoons, a mounted force of about
one hundred and thirty men from Indiana and Kentucky. The Fourth U. S. Infantry, three hundred
strong according to Colonel Boyd who commanded
it,[2] arrived in the Territory at the beginning of September. As rapidly as possible Harrison collected
his forces, and sent them up the river to a point in
the new purchase about sixty-five miles above Vincennes. The exact force was afterward much disputed.[3] Harrison reported his effectives as a few
more than nine hundred men. Some sixty Kentucky
volunteers were of the number.

[1] Dawson, p. 200.

[2] Boyd to Eustis, Dec. 10, 1811; MSS. War Department
Records.

[3] Marshall's Kentucky, ii. 509.

The last instructions from the Department, dated August 29,[1] made no change in the tenor of the President's orders. When Harrison joined his army, October 6, at the camp above Vincennes, he wrote to Eustis,[2] —

" I sincerely wish that my instructions were such as to authorize me to march up immediately to the Prophet's town. The troops which I command are a fine body of men, and the proportion of regulars, irregulars, infantry, and dragoons such as I could wish it. I have no reason to doubt the issue of a contest with the savages, and I am much deceived if the greater part of both officers and men are not desirous of coming in contact with them."

In doubt what to do next, Harrison waited while his army built a small wooden fort, to which he gave his own name, and which was intended to establish formal possession of the new purchase. While the army was engaged in this work, one of the sentinels was fired at and wounded in the night of October 10 by some person or persons unseen and unknown. Harrison regarded this as a beginning of hostilities by the Prophet, and decided to act as though war was declared. October 12 he received from Secretary Eustis a letter dated September 18, never published though often referred to,[3] which is not found in the

[1] Dawson, p. 195. Cf. McAffee, p. 18.

[2] Harrison to Eustis, Oct. 6, 1811 ; MSS. War Department Archives.

[3] Dawson, p. 253.

records of the government.   Harrison replied the next day : [1] —

"Your letter of the 18th ult. I had the honor to receive yesterday. My views have hitherto been limited to the erection of the fort which we are now building, and to a march, by way of feint, in the direction of the Prophet's town, as high, perhaps, as the Vermilion River. But the powers given me in your last letter, and circumstances which have occurred here at the very moment on which it was received, call for measures of a more energetic kind."

With this despatch Harrison enclosed a return of the soldiers present under his command. "You will observe," he said, "that our effectives are but little over nine hundred." The rank-and-file consisted of seven hundred and forty-two men fit for duty. Harrison thought this force too small, and sent back to Vincennes for four companies of mounted riflemen. Two of the four companies joined him,[2] but their strength was not reported. These returns showed that the army, with the two additional companies, numbered at least one thousand effectives. One of the officers of the Fourth U. S. Infantry, writing November 21, said that the force was a little upward of eleven hundred men.[3]

[1] Harrison to Eustis, Oct. 13, 1811 ; MSS. War Department Archives.

[2] Harrison to Eustis, Nov. 2, 1811 ; MSS. War Department Archives.

[3] Letter in New England Palladium, Dec. 24, 1811.

While the Americans were determined not to return without a battle, the Indians had been strictly ordered by Tecumthe to keep the peace, and showed the intention to avoid Harrison's attack. As early as September 25, the Prophet sent a number of Indians to Vincennes to protest his peaceful intentions, and to promise that Harrison's demands should be complied with.[1] Harrison returned no answer and sent no demands. October 28 he broke up his camp at Fort Harrison, and the army began its march up the river. The governor remained one day longer at the fort, and from there, October 29, sent some friendly Indians to the Prophet with a message requiring that the Winnebagoes, Pottawatomies, and Kickapoos, at Tippecanoe, should return to their tribes; that all stolen horses should be given up, and that murderers should be surrendered. He intended at a later time to add a demand for hostages,[2] in case the Prophet should accede to these preliminary terms.

Harrison did not inform the friendly Indians where they would find him, or where they were to bring their answer.[3] Crossing to the west bank of the Wabash to avoid the woods, the troops marched over a level prairie to the mouth of the Vermilion River, where they erected a blockhouse to protect their boats. The Vermilion River was the extreme boundary of the recent land-cession; and to cross it, under such

[1] Dawson, p. 196.   [2] Dawson, p. 196.
[3] Speech of Captain Charley, July 10, 1814; State Papers, Indian Affairs, i. 830.

circumstances, was war. Harrison looked for resistance; but not an Indian was seen, and November 3 the army resumed its march, keeping in the open country, until on the evening of November 5 it arrived, still unmolested, within eleven miles of the Prophet's town. From the Vermilion River to Tippecanoe was fifty miles.

The next morning, November 6, the army advanced toward the town, and as the column approached, Indians were frequently seen in front and on the flanks. Interpreters tried to parley with them, but they returned no answer except insulting or threatening gestures. Two miles from the town the army unexpectedly entered a difficult country, thick with wood and cut by deep ravines, where Harrison was greatly alarmed, seeing himself at the mercy of an attack; but no attack was made. When clear of the woods, within a mile and a half of the town, he halted his troops and declared his intention to encamp. Daveiss and all the other officers urged him to attack the town at once; but he replied that his instructions would not justify his attacking the Indians unless they refused his demands, and he still hoped to hear something in the course of the evening from the friendly Indians sent from Fort Harrison. Daveiss remonstrated, and every officer in the army supported him. Harrison then pleaded the danger of further advance. "The experience of the last two days," he said,[1] "ought to convince every officer that no reliance

[1] Dawson, p. 206.

ought to be placed upon the guides as to the topography of the country; that, relying on their information, the troops had been led into a situation so unfavorable that but for the celerity with which they changed their position a few Indians might have destroyed them; he was therefore determined not to advance to the town until he had previously reconnoitred."

The candor of this admission did not prove the military advantages of the halt; and neither of Harrison's reasons was strengthened by a third, which he gave a month afterward in a letter to the Governor of Kentucky. " The success of an attack upon the town by day," he said,[1] " was very problematical. I expected that they would have met me the next day to hear my terms; but I did not believe that they would accede to them, and it was my determination to attack and burn the town the following night." Daveiss and the other officers, looking at the matter only as soldiers, became more urgent, until Harrison at last yielded, and resolving no longer to hesitate in treating the Indians as enemies,[2] ordered an advance, with the determination to attack. " I yielded to what appeared the general wish," he said in his official report,[3] " and directed the troops to advance." They advanced about four hundred yards, when three

[1] Harrison to Governor Scott, Dec. 13, 1811 ; Dawson, p. 244.

[2] McAffee, p. 25.   Dawson, p. 206.

[3] Harrison to Eustis, Nov. 18, 1811 ; State Papers, Indian Affairs, p. 776.

Indians sent by the Prophet came to meet them,
bringing a pacific message, and urging that hostilities
should if possible be avoided.   Harrison's conscience,
already heavy-ladened, again gave way at this entreaty.[1]
" I answered that I had no intention of attacking
them until I discovered that they would not comply
with the demands that I had made ; that I would go
on and encamp at the Wabash, and in the morning
would have an interview with the Prophet and his
chiefs, and explain to them the determination of the
President ; that in the mean time no hostilities should
be committed."

Had Harrison's vacillation been due to consciousness of strength, his officers would have had no just
reason for remonstrance ; but he estimated his force
at about eight hundred effective men, and the Indians at more than six hundred.[2]   He knew that no
victory over the Northern Indians had ever been
won where the numbers were anything like equal.[3]
Before him was an unknown wilderness ; behind him
was a line of retreat, one hundred and fifty miles
long, and he had supplies for very few days.   He
could not trust the Indians ; and certainly they could
not trust him, for he meant in any case to surprise
their town the next night.   Delay was dangerous only
to the whites, — advantageous only to the Indians.

[1] Harrison to Eustis, Nov. 18, 1811 ; State Papers, Indian
Affairs, p. 776.

[2] Dawson, p. 216.

[3] Dawson, pp. 216, 250.

Daveiss felt so strongly the governor's hesitation that he made no secret of his discontent, and said openly not only that the army ought to attack,[1] but also that it would be attacked before morning, or would march home with nothing accomplished.[2] Indeed, if Harrison had not come there to destroy the town, he had no sufficient military reason for being there at all.

Having decided to wait, Harrison had next to choose a camping-ground. The army marched on, looking for some spot on the river where wood as well as water could be obtained, until they came within one hundred and fifty yards of the town, when the Indians, becoming alarmed, called on them to stop. Harrison halted his men and asked the Indians to show him a place suitable for his purpose, which they did;[3] and the troops filed off in front of the town, at right angles to the Wabash, till they reached a creek less than a mile to the northwest. Next to the town was a marshy prairie; beyond the marsh the ground rose about ten feet to a level covered with oaks; and then about a hundred yards farther it suddenly dropped to the creek behind, where the banks were thick with willow and brushwood. No spot in the neighborhood was better suited for a camp than this saddle-back between the marsh and the brook, but Harrison saw that it offered seri-

---

[1] Dawson, p. 211.   [2] McAffee, p. 28.

[3] Harrison to Eustis, Nov. 18, 1811 ; State Papers, Indian Affairs, p. 776.

ous disadvantages. " I found the ground destined
for the encampment," he reported, " not altogether
such as I could wish it.   It was, indeed, admirably
calculated .for regular troops that were opposed to
regulars, but it afforded great facility to the approach
of the savages."

There Harrison camped.   The troops were stationed in a sort of triangle, following the shape of
the high land,[1] — the base toward the northeast, the
blunt apex toward the southwest ; but at no part of
the line was any attempt made to intrench, or pali-
sade, or in any way to cover the troops.   Harrison
afterward explained that he had barely axes enough
to procure firewood.   The want of axes had been
discovered at Fort Harrison, and hardly excused the
neglect to intrench at Tippecanoe, for it had not
prevented building the fort.   The army pitched its
tents and lighted its fires for the night, with no
other protection than a single line of sentries, although the creek in the rear gave cover to an
attack within a few yards of the camp.

The night was dark, with light rain at intervals ;
the troops slept on their arms, and their rest was disturbed by no sound.   Many accounts have been given
of what passed in the Prophet's town,[2] but none of
them deserve attention.   During the night neither
Harrison nor his sentinels heard or saw anything
that roused their suspicions.   Harrison, in a brief

[1] See Plan of Camp.   Lossing, p. 205.
[2] Lossing, p. 203.

report of the next day,[1] said that the first alarm was given at half-past four o'clock in the morning. His full report of November 18 corrected the time to a few minutes before four. Still another account, on the day after the battle, named five o'clock as the moment.[2] Harrison himself was about to leave his tent, before calling the men to parade, when a sentinel at the farthest angle of the camp above the creek fired a shot. In an instant the Indian yell was raised, and before the soldiers at that end of the camp could leave their tents, the Indians had pierced the line, and were shooting the men by the light of the camp-fires. Within a few moments, firing began along the whole line, until the camp, except for a space next the creek, was encircled by it. Fortunately for Harrison, the attacking party at the broken angle had not strength to follow up its advantage, and the American line was soon reformed in the rear. Harrison rode to the point, and at the northeast angle met Daveiss and his dismounted dragoons. Daveiss reported that the Indians, under cover of the trees, were annoying the troops severely, and asked leave to dislodge them. The order was given; and Daveiss, followed by only a few men, rushed forward among the trees, where he soon fell, mortally wounded. The troops,

[1] Harrison to Eustis, Nov. 8, 1811; National Intelligencer, Nov. 30, 1811. Niles, i. 255.

[2] William Taylor to ———, Nov. 8, 1811; National Intelligencer, Dec. 7, 1811.

after forming, held their position without further
disaster till daybreak, when they advanced and drove
the Indians into the swamp. With this success the
battle ended, having lasted two hours.

For the moment the army was saved, but only at
great cost. Daveiss, who held an anomalous position
almost as prominent as that of Harrison himself, died
in the afternoon. Captain Baen, acting major of the
Fourth Regiment, two lieutenants, and an ensign of
the same regiment, were killed or wounded; two
lieutenant-colonels, four captains, and several lieutenants of the Indiana militia were on the same list, and
the general's aid-de-camp was killed. One hundred
and fifty-four privates were returned among the
casualties, fifty-two of whom were killed or mortally
wounded. The total loss was one hundred and
eighty-eight, of whom sixty-one were killed or mortally wounded.[1] The bodies of thirty-eight Indians
were found on the field.

If the army had cause for anxiety before the battle,
it had double reason for alarm when it realized its
position on November 7. If Harrison's own account
was correct, he had with him only eight hundred men.
Sixty-one had been killed or mortally wounded, and
he had near a hundred and fifty wounded to carry
with him in his retreat. His effective force was diminished more than one fourth, according to his biog-
rapher;[2] his camp contained very little flour and no

[1] General Return; State Papers, Indian Affairs, i. 779.

[2] Dawson, p. 233.

meat, for the few beeves brought with the army were either driven away by the Indians or stampeded by the noise of the battle; and his only base of supplies was at Vincennes, one hundred and seventy miles away. The Indians could return in greater numbers, but his own force must steadily grow weaker. Harrison was naturally a cautious man; he felt strongly the dangers that surrounded him, and his army felt them not less.[1]

The number of Indian warriors engaged in the night attack was estimated by Harrison at six hundred.[2] The law of exaggeration, almost invariable in battle, warrants belief that not more than four hundred Indians were concerned in the attack. The Prophet's Indians were few. Tecumthe afterward spoke of the attack as an "unfortunate transaction that took place between the white people and a few of our young men at our village,"[3] — as though it was an affair in which the young warriors had engaged against the will of the older chiefs. Tecumthe commonly told the truth, even with indiscretion; and nothing in the American account contradicted his version of the affair at Tippecanoe. Harrison's ablest military manœuvre had been the availing himself of Tecumthe's over-confidence in quitting the country at so critical a moment.

Although Harrison did not venture to send out

[1] Dawson, p. 233. Lossing, p. 206, *note.*
[2] Report of Nov. 18, 1811; Niles, i. 304.
[3] Dawson, p. 267.

a scout for twenty-four hours, but remained in camp waiting attack, no further sign of hostilities was given. "Night," said one of the army,[1] "found every man mounting guard, without food, fire, or light, and in a drizzling rain. The Indian dogs, during the dark hours, produced frequent alarms by prowling in search of carrion about the sentinels." On the morning of November 8, the dragoons and mounted riflemen approached the town and found it deserted. Apparently the Indians had fled in haste, leaving everything, even a few new English guns and powder. The army took what supplies were needed, and set fire to the village. Meanwhile every preparation had been made for rapid retreat. The wagons could scarcely carry all the wounded, and Harrison abandoned the camp furniture and private baggage. "We managed, however, to bring off the public property," he reported. At noon of November 9 the train started, and by night-fall had passed the dangerous woods and broken country where a few enemies could have stopped it. No Indians appeared; the march was undisturbed; and after leaving a company of the U. S. Fourth Regiment at Fort Harrison, the rest of the force arrived, November 18, at Vincennes.

The battle of Tippecanoe at once became a point of pride throughout the Western country, and Harrison received the official applause and thanks of Kentucky, Indiana, and Illinois; but Harrison's account of his victory was not received without criticism, and the

[1] Lossing, p. 206, *note*.

battle was fought again in the press and in private. The Fourth Regiment more than hinted that had it not been for their steadiness the whole party would have been massacred. At Vincennes, Harrison was severely attacked. In Kentucky criticism was open, for the family and friends of Joseph Daveiss were old Federalists, who had no interest in the military triumphs of a Republican official. Humphrey Marshall, Daveiss's brother-in-law, published a sharp review of Harrison's report, and hinted plainly that Daveiss had fallen a victim to the General's blunders. With characteristic vigor of language, Marshall called Harrison " a little, selfish, intriguing busybody," and charged him with having made the war without just cause, for personal objects.[1] These attacks caused the Western Republicans to sustain with the more ardor their faith in Harrison's military genius, and their enthusiasm for the victory of Tippecanoe; but President Madison and Secretary Eustis guarded themselves with some care from expressing an opinion on the subject.

Whatever his critics might say, Harrison gained his object, and established himself in the West as the necessary leader of any future campaign. That result, as far as it was good, seemed to be the only advantage gained at Tippecanoe. Harrison believed that the battle had broken the Prophet's influence, and saved the frontier from further alarm; he thought that in the event of a British war, the Indians

[1] Marshall's Kentucky, ii. 507, 521.

would remain neutral having "witnessed the ineffi-
cacy of British assistance;"[1] he expected the tribes
to seek peace as a consequence of what he considered the severest defeat they had ever received
since their acquaintance with the white people;[2]
and the expectation was general that they would deliver the Prophet and Tecumthe into the hands of
the American government. For a time these impressions seemed reasonable. The Prophet lost influence,
and the peace was not further disturbed; but presently the Western people learned that the Prophet
had returned to Tippecanoe, and that all things had
resumed their old aspect, except that no one could
foresee when the Indians would choose to retaliate
for Harrison's invasion.

Toward January, Tecumthe returned from the
South, and sent word that he was ready to go to
Washington. March 1, 1812, a deputation of some
eighty Indians visited Vincennes, and told Harrison
that the whole winter had been passed in sending
messages to the different villages to consult on their
future course, and that all agreed to ask for peace.
They blamed the Prophet for the affair at Tippecanoe, and asked leave to visit Washington to obtain
peace from the President. Harrison gladly assented,
for a delegation of Indians sent to Washington was
a guaranty of peace during the time of their absence.

[1] Harrison to J. M. Scott, Dec. 2, 1811. Niles, i. 311.

[2] Harrison to Eustis, Dec. 4, 1811; State Papers, Indian
Affairs, p. 779.

He expected them to appear at Fort Wayne in April, ready for the journey.

The Indian hesitation was probably due to doubt whether war would take place between the United States and England. The whole influence of the British agents was exerted to unite the Indians and to arm them, but to prevent a premature outbreak. The British Indian agent at Amherstburg sent Tecumthe a message blaming the attack on Harrison. Tecumthe replied:[1] —

" You tell us to retreat or turn to one side should the Big Knives come against us. Had I been at home in the late unfortunate affair I should have done so; but those I left at home were (I cannot call them men) a poor set of people, and their scuffle with the Big Knives I compared to a struggle between little children who only scratch each other's faces. The Kickapoos, Winnebagoes have since been at Post Vincennes and settled the matter amicably."

The situation was well understood. " If we have a British war, we shall have an Indian war," wrote the commandant from Fort Wayne.[2] " From the best information I can get, I have every reason to believe we shall have an Indian war this spring, whether we have a British war or not." Harrison must himself have felt that the campaign to Tippecanoe could only add to his dangers unless it was

[1] MSS. Canadian Archives. C. 676, p. 147.
[2] J. Rhea to Eustis, March 14, 1812; State Papers, Indian Affairs, p. 806.

followed up.   After April 1, 1812, illusions vanished;
for Indian hostilities began all along the border.
April 6 two settlers were murdered within three
miles of Fort Dearborn, at Chicago; several murders
were committed near Fort Madison, above St. Louis,
on the Mississippi; but the warning which spread
wild alarm throughout Indiana was the murder of
a whole family early in April within five miles of
Vincennes, and April 14 that of a settler within a
few miles of the Ohio River.   Another murder a few
weeks afterward, on the White River, completed the
work of terror.

Then a general panic seized the people.   The militia dared not turn out; for while they collected at
one spot, the Indians might attack their isolated
cabins.   Even Vincennes was thought to be in danger, and the stream of fugitives passed through it
as rapidly as possible on their way southward, until
depopulation threatened the Territory.[1]   " Most of
the citizens in this country," reported Harrison, May
6,[2] " have abandoned their farms, and taken refuge
in such temporary forts as they have been able to
construct.   Nothing can exhibit more distress than
those wretched people crowded together in places
almost destitute of every necessary accommodation."
Misled by the previous peaceful reports, the Government had sent the Fourth Regiment to Detroit; not
even a company of militia could be procured nearer

---

[1] Dawson, p. 263.
[2] State Papers, Indian Affairs, p. 808.

than the falls of the Ohio ; and Harrison called for help in vain.

Fortunately, Tecumthe was not yet ready for war. Six weeks after the hostilities began he appeared at a grand council, May 16, at Massassinway on the Wabash, between Tippecanoe and Fort Wayne. His speech to the tribes assembled there was more temperate than ever.[1]

"Governor Harrison made war on my people in my absence," he said. "It was the will of God that he should do so. We hope it will please God that the white people may let us live in peace ; we will not disturb them, neither have we done it, except when they came to our village with the intention of destroying us. We are happy to state to our brothers present that the unfortunate transaction that took place between the white people and a few of our young men at our village has been settled between us and Governor Harrison ; and I will further state, had I been at home there would have been no bloodshed at that time."

He added that the recent murders had been committed by Pottawatomies not under his control, and he offered no excuse for them.

"Should the bad acts of our brothers the Pottawatomies draw on us the ill-will of our white brothers, and they should come again and make an unprovoked attack on us at our village, we will die like men ; but we will never strike the first blow. . . . We defy a living creature to say we ever advised any one, directly or indirectly, to make war on our white brothers. It has

[1] Dawson, p. 266.

constantly been our misfortune to have our views mis-
represented to our white brethren. This has been done
by pretended chiefs of the Pottawatomies and others
that have been in the habit of selling land to the white
people that did not belong to them."

This was the situation on the Wabash in May and
June, 1812. Not only was Tecumthe unwilling to
strike the first blow, but he would not even retaliate
Harrison's invasion and seizure of the disputed territory. He waited for Congress to act, but every one
knew that whenever Congress should declare war
against England, war must also be waged with the
Indians; and no one could doubt that after provok-
ing the Indian war, Americans ought to be prepared
to wage it with effect, and without complaint of its
horrors.

CHAPTER VI.

THE war fever of 1811 swept far and wide over the
country, but even at its height seemed somewhat in-
termittent and imaginary. A passion that needed to
be nursed for five years before it acquired strength to
break into act, could not seem genuine to men who
did not share it. A nation which had submitted to
robbery and violence in 1805, in 1807, in 1809, could
not readily lash itself into rage in 1811 when it had
no new grievance to allege; nor could the public feel
earnest in maintaining national honor, for every one
admitted that the nation had sacrificed its honor, and
must fight to regain it. Yet what honor was to be
hoped from a war which required continued submis-
sion to one robber as the price of resistance to another? President Madison submitted to Napoleon
in order to resist England; the New England Federalists preferred submitting to England in order to
resist Napoleon; but not one American expected the
United States to uphold their national rights against
the world.

Politicians of the old school looked coldly on the
war spirit. Nations like individuals, when driven to

choose between desperate courses, might at times be
compelled to take the chances of destruction, often
destroying themselves, or suffering irreparable harm.
Yet the opponents of war could argue that Americans
were not placed between desperate alternatives. They
had persevered hitherto, in spite of their leaders, in
the policy of peace; had suffered much injury and
acute mortification, but had won Louisiana and West
Florida, had given democracy all it asked, and had
remained in reasonable harmony with the liberal
movement of the world. They were reaping the fruit
of their patient and obstinate husbandry; for Russia
and Sweden were about to fight their battles without
reward. Napoleon offered them favors more or less
real, and even England could not long resist the pressure of her interests. Jefferson's policy had wrought
all the evil it could cause, — perhaps it had cost the
highest price the nation could pay; but after the
nation had suffered the evil and paid the price, it had
a right to the profit. With more force than in 1798,
the old Republicans pleaded that if they should throw
aside their principles and plunge into hostilities with
England, they would not only sacrifice the results of
six years' humiliation, but would throw the United
States athwart the liberal movement of Europe, destroy the hopes of pure government at home, and
with more eagerness than they had shown for the
past ten years in stripping government of its power,
must devote themselves to the task of rebuilding a
sovereignty as terrible in peace as in war.

The moment for fighting, conservatives argued, had come in 1807, had passed in 1809; and hencefor-ward good policy called only for perseverance in the course that had been so persistently preferred. Not merely old Republicans, but an actual majority of the people probably held these opinions; yet the youthful energy of the nation, which had at last come to its strength under the shelter of Jefferson's peaceful rule, cried out against the cowardice of further submis-sion, and insisted on fighting if only to restore its own self-respect.

The course of Massachusetts had much to do with changing the current of opinion. Hitherto this State had barred the way to a British war. Although the Republican party in Massachusetts several times elected their candidate for governor by majorities more or less decisive, they failed to gain full con-trol of the State legislature before 1811. In 1810 they elected Elbridge Gerry and a majority of the representatives, but they still lacked one vote to give them control of the Senate. In April, 1811, Gerry succeeded once more, defeating Christopher Gore, the Federalist candidate, by a majority of three thousand votes; while the House, which consisted of some six hundred and fifty members, chose a Republican speaker by a majority of thirty-one. For the first time the Republicans controlled also a majority, though only of one vote, in the State Senate. This success, gained in spite of the unpopular Non-importa-tion Act, gave extraordinary confidence to the Gov-

ernment, and left the Federalists powerless.   Timothy
Pickering lost his seat in the United States Senate,
and Speaker Varnum received it.   The Republicans
hastened to introduce, and to carry through the Massachusetts legislature, measures that threatened to
upturn the foundation of Federalist society.   Other
measures still more radical were expected.   Jefferson's hopes of reforming Massachusetts were almost
fulfilled ; but the success which gave reality to them
removed the last obstacle to war with England.

As the autumn advanced, the Republican newspapers broke into a general cry for war.   The British
minister's refusal to withdraw the Orders in Council,
the return of Pinkney from London, the affair of the
" Little Belt," the notorious relations between the
northwestern Indians and the British traders, — all
served to increase the ill-temper of a public trying to
lash itself into an act it feared.   Even the battle at
Tippecanoe, although evidently contrary to British
interest, was charged to British influence.   As though
England had not already given cause for a score of
wars, the press invented new grievances, and became
as eager to denounce imaginary crimes as to correct
flagrant and chronic wrongs.

The matter of impressments then began to receive
the attention which had never yet been given it.
Hitherto neither Government nor people had thought
necessary to make a *casus belli* of impressments.   Orders in Council and other measures of Great Britain
which affected American property had been treated

as matters of vital consequence ; but as late as the
close of 1811, neither the President, the Secretary of
State, nor Congress had yet insisted that the person of an American citizen was as sacred as his
property. Impressments occurred daily. No one
knew how many native-born Americans had been
taken by force from the protection of the American
flag ; but whether the number was small or great,
neither Republican nor Federalist had ventured to
say that the country must at all hazards protect
them, or that whatever rules of blockade or contraband the belligerents might adopt against property, they must at least keep their hands off the
persons of peaceable Americans whether afloat or
ashore.   President Madison had repeated, until the
world laughed in his face, that Napoleon no longer
enforced his decrees, and that therefore if England
did not withdraw her blockade, war would result ;
but he had never suggested that America would fight
for her sailors.   When he and his supporters in
earnest took up the grievances of the seamen, they
seemed to do so as an afterthought, to make out a
cause of war against England, after finding the public unwilling to accept the cause at first suggested.
However unjust the suspicion might be, so much
truth existed in this Federalist view of Madison's
course as warranted the belief that if England in
July, 1811, had yielded to the demand for commercial freedom, the Government would have become deaf
to the outcry of the imprisoned seamen.   Only by

slow degrees, and in the doubtful form of a political manœuvre, did this, the worst of all American grievances, take its proper place at the head of the causes for war.

Winter drew near, finding the public restless, irritable, more than half afraid of its own boldness, but outspoken at last. British frigates once more blockaded New York, seizing ships and impressing men without mercy, while the British prize-courts, after a moment's hesitation, declared that the French Decrees were not repealed, and that American vessels sailing to France were good prize. Under these irritations the temper of the American press became rapidly worse, until war was declared to be imminent, and the conquest of Canada became the favorite topic of newspaper discussion.

Yet the true intentions of the President and his Cabinet were as uncertain as those of the Twelfth Congress, which had not yet met. A very large part of the public could not believe war to be possible, and the Government itself shared so far in the doubt as to wait for Congress to give the impulse so often refused. When the President and his Cabinet met in Washington to prepare for the session of Congress called for November 4, a month earlier than usual, neither the Cabinet nor the congressmen felt a certainty of the future; and so little did the outside world believe in war, that Madison, Monroe, and Gallatin were supposed to be aiming at a diplomatic rather than at a military victory. In truth they had no well-defined plan. The process by which a scattered democracy decided its own will, in a matter so serious as a great and perhaps fatal war, was new to the world ; bystanders were surprised and amused at the simplicity with which the people disputed plans of war and peace, giving many months of warning and exact information to the enemy, while they showed no sign of leadership, discipline, or union, or even a consciousness that such qualities were needed. Men like Josiah Quincy, Rufus King, John Randolph, and even Madison and Gallatin, seeing that the people themselves, like the machine of government they had invented, were incompetent to the work of war, waited with varied emotions, but equally believing or fearing that at last a fatal crisis was at hand.

Monroe was far from easy ; but he had accepted, as was his wont, the nearest dominating will, and he drifted without an effort, although his old friends had already parted company with him. Though obliged to support the President in holding that Napoleon's decrees were withdrawn so that they had ceased to violate the neutral commerce of the United States, he showed that he did so, not so much because he thought it the truth, as because England gave him no choice. To Serurier, the French minister, Monroe made little concealment of his real wishes ; and when Serurier first called at the Department after Monroe's return from Virginia, he heard nothing that greatly pleased him.

" I found the Secretary of State," wrote Serurier, October 23,[1] " nearly in the same state of mind in which I left him at his departure for Virginia. He told me at the outset that although the information received by the President during the last two months had added to his hopes, it had not yet completed his conviction on the decrees ; that he could not believe them entirely repealed so long as there remained in our ports a single vessel captured by our privateers since November. . . . He pretended that very recent advices from Naples announced an order sent lately from Paris to sell the American prizes, and this news had been very disagreeble to the Executive, and had thrown it into new uncertainties. . . . He returned again to our customs-tariff, and the indispensability of its reduction."

Serurier exerted himself to infuse what he called proper spirit into the secretary's temper, complaining that England was actually engaged in making war on American commerce with France while enjoying all the advantages of American trade, —

" A very dangerous situation for an alliance, I added, where all the advantage is for your enemies, and all the loss is for your friends. Mr. Monroe agreed to all this ; but he pretended that this false position could be viewed only as a transition to a more decided state of things ; that the present situation was equally burdensome and intolerable to the citizens, and little suited to the dignity of the Government ; that it was necessary to wait for despatches from Mr. Barlow. Then he fell back once more on his theme, — that whenever they should be

[1] Serurier to Maret, Oct. 23, 1811; Archives des Aff. Étr. MSS

perfectly satisfied on the side of France, and also of the Emperor's friendship, they would certainly adopt very energetic measures toward England. . . . ' We shall not go backward,' said Mr. Monroe to me ; ' we shall be inflexible about the repeal of the Orders in Council. But in order to go further, to bring us to great resolutions, the Emperor must aid us ; private and public interest must make the same demand. The President does indeed hold the rudder of the Ship of State ; he guides, but it is public opinion which makes the vessel move. On France depends the winning of public opinion ; and we wish for it, as you can well conceive that in our position we should.' "

Serurier knew no more than this, which was no more than all the world could see. The British minister was not so well informed. After an exchange of notes with Monroe, which left matters where they were, Foster learned from Monroe, October 30, that the Government was waiting for Barlow's despatches, and if these should prove unsatisfactory, some restriction of French commerce would be imposed by way of retaliation on the restrictions imposed by Napoleon.[1] Foster hoped for a turn in affairs favorable to himself, and tried to bring it about, not only by suggesting to Lord Wellesley the wisdom of concessions from England, but also by offering a frank and fair reparation for the " Chesapeake " outrage. He wrote, November 1, to the Secretary of State renewing the formal disavowal of Berkeley's unauthorized act, and offering to restore the men to the

[1] Foster to Wellesley, Nov. 5, 1811 ; MSS. British Archives.

vessel from which they had been taken, with compensation to themselves and families. Somewhat coldly Monroe accepted the offer. The two surviving seamen were in due time brought from their prison at Halifax and restored to the deck of the "Chesapeake" in Boston harbor; the redress was made as complete as such tardy justice could ever be, but the time had passed when it could atone for the wrong.

Both Foster and Serurier felt that the people were further advanced than the Government in hostility to England, and that this was especially true in the matter of impressments; but no one, even at the White House, knew certainly what to expect from the new Congress assembling at Washington Nov. 4, 1811. That this body differed greatly from any previous Congress was clear, if only because it contained some seventy new members; but another difference, less easily measured, was more serious. The active leaders were young men. Henry Clay of Kentucky, William Lowndes, John Caldwell Calhoun, David R. Williams, Langdon Cheves of South Carolina, Felix Grundy of Tennessee, Peter Buell Porter of New York, Richard Mentor Johnson of Kentucky, had none of them reached his fortieth year; while Madison and his Cabinet belonged to a different generation. None of the new leaders could remember the colonial epoch, or had taken a share in public life except under the Constitution of 1789, or had been old enough to feel and understand the lessons taught by opposition to the Federalist rule. They knew the

Federalists only as a faction, more or less given to treasonable talk, controlling some thirty or forty votes in the House, and proclaiming with tedious iteration opinions no one cared to hear. The young war Republicans, as they were called, felt only contempt for such a party; while, as their acts showed, they were filled with no respect for the technicalities of their Executive head, and regarded Gallatin with distrust. Of statesmanship, in the old sense, they took little thought. Bent on war with England, they were willing to face debt and probable bankruptcy on the chance of creating a nation, of conquering Canada, and carrying the American flag to Mobile and Key West.

After ten years devoted to weakening national energies, such freshness of youth and recklessness of fear had wonderful popular charm. The reaction from Jefferson's system threatened to be more violent than its adoption. Experience seemed to show that a period of about twelve years measured the beat of the pendulum. After the Declaration of Independence, twelve years had been needed to create an efficient Constitution; another twelve years of energy brought a reaction against the government then created; a third period of twelve years was ending in a sweep toward still greater energy; and already a child could calculate the result of a few more such returns.

Had the majority of the House been in a gentler mood, its choice for Speaker should have fallen on Macon, once more a sound party man prepared to

support war; but Macon was set aside. Bibb of
Georgia, a candidate of the minority, received only
thirty-eight voices, while seventy-five were given for
Henry Clay. Clay was barely thirty-four years of age,
and was a new member of the House; but he was
the boldest and most active leader of the war Republicans. He immediately organized the committees for
war. That on Foreign Relations, the most immediately
important, was put into the hands of Porter, Calhoun,
and Grundy. Military affairs were placed in charge
of David R. Williams. Langdon Cheves became chairman of the Naval Committee. Ezekiel Bacon and
Cheves stood at the head of the Ways and Means.

November 5 the President's Message was read, and
its account of the situation seemed to offer hardly
the chance of peace. England, it said, had refused the
" reasonable step" of repealing its Orders in return
for the extinction of the French Decrees; while the
new British minister had made " an indispensable
condition of the repeal of the British Orders, that
commerce should be restored to a footing that would
admit the productions and manufactures of Great
Britain, when owned by neutrals, into markets shut
against them by her enemies, — the United States
being given to understand that in the mean time a
continuation of their Non-importation Act would lead
to measures of retaliation." Instead of repealing the
orders, the British government, " at a moment when
least to have been expected," put them into more
rigorous execution; " indemnity and redress for other

wrongs have continued to be withheld; and our coasts and the mouths of our harbors have again witnessed scenes not less derogatory to the dearest of our national rights than vexatious to the regular course of our trade." In some respects Madison's statement of grievances sounded almost needlessly quarrelsome; yet even in this list of causes which were to warrant a declaration of war, the President did not expressly mention impressments, in comparison with which his other grievances sank, in the afterthought, to insignificance.

Of France, also, the President spoke in language far from friendly. Although the decrees were revoked, " no proof is yet given," he said, " of an intention to repair the other wrongs done to the United States, and particularly to restore the great amount of American property seized and condemned under edicts . . . founded in such unjust principles that the reparation ought to have been prompt and ample." In addition to this, the United States had much reason to be dissatisfied with " the rigorous and unexpected restrictions " imposed on their trade with France, which if continued would lead to retaliation. Not a word did the Message contain of friendly or even civil regard for the French government.

Then followed the sentences which could be read only in the sense of an invitation to war : —

" I must now add that the period has arrived which claims from the legislative guardians of the national rights a system of more ample provisions for maintaining them.   Notwithstanding the scrupulous justice, the protracted moderation, and the multiplied efforts on the part of the United States to substitute for the accumulating dangers to the peace of the two countries all the mutual advantages of re-established friendship and confidence, we have seen that the British Cabinet perseveres not only in withholding a remedy for other wrongs so long and so loudly calling for it, but in the execution, brought home to the threshold of our territory, of measures which, under existing circumstances, have the character as well as the effect of war on our lawful commerce.   With this evidence of hostile inflexibility in trampling on rights which no independent nation can relinquish, Congress will feel the duty of putting the United States into an armor and an attitude demanded by the crisis, and corresponding with the national spirit and expectations."

The report of Secretary Gallatin, sent to the House November 22, bore also a warlike character.   For the past year Gallatin told a cheerful story.   In spite of the non-importation, the receipts from customs and other revenue exceeded $13,500,000, while the current expenses had not reached $8,000,000.   If war should be declared, the secretary asked only for an increase of fifty per cent in the duties, in order to make sure of a fixed revenue of nine million dollars; and should this increase of duty be insufficient for the purpose, the deficiency could be supplied without difficulty by a further increase of duties, by a restoration of the impost on salt, and by " a proper selection of moderate internal taxes."   With a revenue of nine

million dollars secured, the Treasury could rely on
loans to defray extraordinary expenses, and a few
years of peace would supply the means of discharging
the debt incurred.

If this was different finance from that which Gallatin had taught in other days, and by which he had
risen to popularity and power, it was at least as simple as all that Gallatin did; but the simplicity of his
methods, which was their chief professional merit,
caused also their chief reproach. History showed
the financial charlatan to be popular, not so much
because he was dishonest as because he gratified an
instinct for gambling as deep as the instinct of sel-
fishness; and a common notion of a financier was
that of a man whose merit lay in the discovery of
new sources of wealth, or in inventing means of
borrowing without repayment. Gallatin professed to
do neither. He did not recommend the issue of
paper money; he saw no secret hoards buried in
the unsold public lands; he would listen to no tricks
or devices for raising money. If money was needed
he would borrow it, and would pay whatever it was
worth; but he would not suggest that any device
could relieve the public from taxing itself to pay
whatever the public chose to spend.

" The ability and will of the United States faithfully
to perform their engagements are universally known;
and the terms of loans will in no shape whatever be
affected by want of confidence in either. They must,
however, depend not only upon the state of public credit,

and on the ability to lend, but also on the existing demand for capital required for other objects.   Whatever
this may be, the money wanted by the public must be
purchased at its market price. . . . The most simple and
direct is also the cheapest and safest mode."

Gallatin instanced, as an extreme case, the borrowing of forty millions at eight instead of the legal rate
of six per cent, which he declared an inconsiderable
difference if compared with the effects of other modes
of raising money.   No one whose judgment deserved
respect doubted the correctness of his opinion; but
Republican congressmen had for twelve years denounced the Federalist loan of 1798, when five millions had been borrowed at eight per cent, and they
hardly dared face their constituents when their own
Secretary of the Treasury talked of borrowing forty
millions at the same exorbitant rate.   Gently as
Gallatin hinted at "a proper selection of moderate
internal taxes," they remembered that these internal
taxes had broken the Federalist party to pieces.
They were angry with Gallatin for not providing
other means for the war than loans and taxes, and
they regarded him as not unwilling to check and
chill the military ardor of the nation.

The President's Message, as far as it regarded
foreign affairs, was referred in the House, November
11, to a select committee, the chairman of which was
Peter B. Porter, with Calhoun and Grundy to support
his well-known opinions.   Although the nature of
their report could hardly be doubted, no one seemed

confident that it would be taken seriously. Macon wrote privately, November 21, to his old friend Joseph Nicholson, that he was still ignorant of the leaders' intentions: [1] —

" At this place we are nearly all too wise or too mysterious to form hasty conclusions; it is, however, probable that there are not more than five or six opinions among us, varying from open war to repealing the present restrictive system. I have had but little communication with the knowing ones, and have in some degree guessed at the number of different opinions. I am almost certain that no plan is yet adopted by the leaders in the House."

Within a week Macon found that a plan was made, but it seemed to come wholly from the White House. The Secretary of War appeared before the Committee of Foreign Relations and explained what the President wanted; [2] at the same time Secretary Monroe communicated to the French minister the nature of the Executive plan.[3]

" Mr. Monroe added," wrote Serurier, November 28, " . . . that the situation of affairs should leave me no doubt as to his Excellency's [the President's] disposition; that the Government had lost every illusion as to the repeal of the Orders in Council, and was decided in adopting measures of rigor; that we might be assured it would not retreat; that ten thousand regulars were to

[1] Macon to Nicholson, Nov, 21, 1811; Nicholson MSS.

[2] Annals of Congress, 1811–1812, p. 715.

[3] Serurier to Maret, Nov. 28, 1811 ; Archives des Aff. Étr. MSS.

be raised and placed at the disposition of the Executive, with a great number of volunteers ; that the posts would be put in a state of defence, the navy increased, and merchants authorized to arm for the protection of their commerce ; that this measure, now that our decrees were withdrawn, could strike at England alone ; that the Administration in taking this resolution had perfectly seen where it led ; that evidently this situation would not last three months, and would inevitably lead to a decision for which the country was prepared ; that the Committee of Foreign Relations in the House of Representatives would report within a few days, and he had no doubt that these measures would pass by a great majority."

A few days later Serurier had conversations with Monroe and Madison on the subject of the Spanish American colonies, whose independence they agreed to assist not only by moral but also by material aid. The French minister closed his despatch by adding that Congress was at the moment listening to the report of the Committee of Foreign Relations. "Mr. Monroe repeated to me that he considered war as pretty nearly decided."

If the British minister knew less exactly what was happening behind the scenes, he still knew enough to alarm him. He reported that the Government was actively organizing its party in Congress ; that different sets of members met every evening in caucus, and were instilled with the ideas of the Administration ;[1] but that while the members of the Government were to all appearance still undecided themselves, it would

[1] Foster to Wellesley, Nov. 9, 1811 ; MSS. British Archives.

be rash for other persons to express a decided opinion. A few days after writing in this doubtful sense, Foster was electrified by an outburst of temper from Monroe, who told him that the Government would send no new minister to England, and that it "had reason to believe Great Britain really wished for war with the United States."[1] Monroe added that he felt some difficulty in talking openly about the views of the Government, as some of his disclosures might be regarded as menaces. The President, though less warm than the Secretary, talked not less decidedly:

"He owned to me that the situation of America was very embarrassing; that anything was better than remaining in such a state; and though he very strongly asserted the impossibility of America receding from the grounds she had taken, . . . said that he would ask no sacrifice of principle in Great Britain, and would have no objection to some conventional arrangement between the two countries if it should be judged necessary in the event of the Orders in Council being withdrawn. This was, however, an indispensable preliminary, for he must consider the French Decrees as revoked so far as Great Britain had a right to expect America should require their revocation."

Although Foster became more nervous from day to day, and showed strong symptoms of a wish that the Orders in Council might be modified or withdrawn, neither he nor the President informed the

[1] Foster to Wellesley, Nov. 21, 1811; Papers presented to Parliament in 1813, p. 417.

British government that any other cause of war existed, or that the United States meant to insist on further concessions. In secret, diplomacy flattered itself that war would still be avoided; but it reckoned without taking into account the temper of Congress.

CHAPTER VII.

THE leaders of the war party next performed in Congress a scene in some respects new in the drama of history.

November 29, Peter B. Porter of New York, from the Committee of Foreign Relations, presented to the House his report, in part.

"Your committee will not incumber your journals," it began, "and waste your patience with a detailed history of all the various matters growing out of our foreign relations. The cold recital of wrongs, of injuries, and aggressions known and felt by every member of this Union could have no other effect than to deaden the national sensibility, and render the public mind callous to injuries with which it is already too familiar."

Admission of weakness in the national sensibility gave the key-note of the report, and of the speeches that supported it. Even the allusion to the repeal of the French Decrees showed fear lest the truth might make the public mind callous to shame : —

"France at length . . . announced the repeal . . . of the Decrees of Berlin and Milan ; and it affords a subject of sincere congratulation to be informed, through the official organs of the Government, that those decrees are, so far at least as our rights are concerned, really and practically at an end."

Porter had not studied the correspondence of the Department of State so thoroughly as to learn that Russia and Sweden were in the act of making war to protect American rights from the operation of those decrees which, as he was informed, were "really and practically at an end." His report ignored these difficulties, but added that England affected to deny the practical extinction of the French Decrees. In truth, England not affectedly but positively denied the extinction of those decrees; the United States offered no sufficient evidence to satisfy even themselves; and a declaration of war founded on England's "affected" denial was in a high degree likely to deaden the national sensibility. With more reason and effect, the committee dwelt on the severity with which England enforced her blockades as far as the American coast; and last of all, added, almost in a tone of apology, an allusion to the practice of impressments : —

"Your committee are not, however, of that sect whose worship is at the shrine of a calculating avarice; and while we are laying before you the just complaints of our merchants against the plunder of their ships and cargoes, we cannot refrain from presenting to the justice and humanity of our country the unhappy case of our impressed seamen. Although the groans of these victims of barbarity for the loss of (what should be

dearer to Americans than life) their liberty; although
the cries of their wives and children, in the privation
of protectors and parents, have of late been drowned
in the louder clamors at the loss of property, — yet is
the practice of forcing our mariners into the British
navy, in violation of the rights of our flag, carried on
with unabated rigor and severity. If it be our duty to
encourage the fair and legitimate commerce of this country by protecting the property of the merchant, then indeed, by as much as life and liberty are more estimable
than ships and goods, so much more impressive is the
duty to shield the persons of our seamen, whose hard
and honest services are employed equally with those of
the merchants in advancing under the mantle of its laws
the interests of their country."

Truisms like these, matters of course in the oldest
despotisms of Europe, and the foundation of even
Roman society, sounded altogether new in the mouth
of a democratic Legislature, which uttered them as
though their force were not universally admitted.
The weakness of the report in its premises was
not strengthened by vigor in the self-excuses that
followed, more apologetic than convincing: —

" If we have not rushed to the field of battle, like the
nations who are led by the mad ambition of a single
chief or the avarice of a corrupted court, it has not
proceeded from a fear of war, but from our love of
justice and humanity."

As the sway of Jefferson's philosophy ceased, these
formulas, never altogether pleasing, became peculiarly

repulsive. Indeed, the only sentence in the committee's report that commanded respect was its concluding appeal to the people to abandon the policy which
had proceeded, as it claimed, from their love of justice and humanity : —

"The period has arrived when in the opinion of your
committee it is the sacred duty of Congress to call forth
the patriotism and resources of the country. By the aid
of these, and with the blessing of God, we confidently
trust we shall be enabled to procure that redress which
has been sought for by justice, by remonstrance, and
forbearance in vain."

The report closed with six Resolutions, recommending an increase of ten thousand men to the regular
army ; a levy of fifty thousand volunteers ; the out-
fit of all the vessels of war not in actual service ;
and the arming of merchant vessels.

In opening the debate on the report, Porter spoke
in language more candid than the report itself. "It
was the determination of the committee," he said,
"to recommend open and decided war, — a war as
vigorous and effective as the resources of the country
and the relative situation of ourselves and our enemy
would enable us to prosecute." He went so far as to
point out the intended military operations, — the destruction of British fisheries, and of British commerce
with America and the West Indies, and the conquest
of Canada. "By carrying on such a war at the public expense on land, and by individual enterprise at
sea, we should be able in a short time to remunerate

ourselves ten-fold for all the spoliations she had committed on our commerce."

Such ideas were not unbecoming to Porter, who began life as a Federalist, and had no philosophical theories or recorded principles to explain or defend; but what Porter might advise without a qualm, was much less simple for Republicans from the South; and while his speech had its value for the public as a straightforward declaration, it had little or none for individuals who were conscious that it advised what they had always condemned. The true spokesman of the committee was not Porter, but Felix Grundy of Tennessee.

Grundy, like Henry Clay a Virginian by birth and born the same year, 1777, like Clay began his career in Kentucky, where he rose to be chief-justice of the State before he was thirty years old. In 1807 he removed from Kentucky to Tennessee, and was next elected to the Twelfth Congress expressly to advocate war. As a new member, whose duty, like that of all new members, required him to exchange some controversial hostilities with John Randolph, he could not afford to miss his mark; and when Randolph called upon him by a sneering request to tell what were the constitutional resources of the committee and its talents, Grundy spoke. He apologized for his remarks as embarrassed, and indeed his speech showed less fluency than the subject and occasion seemed to warrant; but though it made no pretence of wit or rhetoric, it went to the heart of the sub-

ject, and dealt seriously with the difficulties which
Grundy and his party felt.

" What cost me more reflection than anything else,"
he admitted, " was the new test to which we are to put
this government. We are about to ascertain by actual
experiment how far our republican institutions are calculated to stand the shock of war ; and whether, after
foreign danger has disappeared, we can again assume our
peaceful attitude without endangering the liberties of the
people."

At the outset, Grundy stumbled upon the difficulty
which checked every movement of his party. Obliged
to reconcile his present action with the attitude taken
by his friends in opposition to the Federalist armaments of 1798, he could only charge that the armaments of 1798 were made not for war, but to provide
Executive patronage and affect domestic politics, — a
charge which, whether true or not, did not meet the
objection.

" If your minds are resolved on war," continued the
speaker, " you are consistent, you are right, you are still
Republican ; but if you are not resolved, pause and re-
flect, for should this Resolution pass and you then become faint-hearted, remember that you have abandoned
your old principles and trod in the paths of your
predecessors."

Thus, according to Grundy, from the moment a
party intended in earnest to make war against a
foreign enemy, armies, loans, patronage, taxes, and
every following corruption, with all the perils of

European practice, became Republican. Only when armies were to be raised for domestic purposes were they unrepublican. The Administration of 1798 would gladly have accepted this test, had the Republicans then been willing to permit armaments on any terms.

Grundy weakened the argument further by attempting to show that in the present case, unlike that of 1798, sufficient cause for war existed: "It is the right of exporting the productions of our own soil and industry to foreign markets." The statement, considering Grundy's reputation, was not skilfully made. The blockades maintained by England in 1811 were less hostile to American products and industry than were the decrees of Napoleon, or the French Decrees of 1798, which confiscated every American ship laden in whole or in part with goods of English origin, and closed France to every American ship that entered an English port. Grundy still maintained that the decrees of 1798 had not justified the Federalist armaments; he could hardly maintain that the British blockades of 1811 alone gave cause for armaments of the same kind, — yet this he did. " What are we now called on to decide ? " he asked. " It is whether we will resist by force the attempt . . . to subject our maritime rights to the arbitrary and capricious rule of her will."

Grundy spoke of impressments as an outrage which called loudly for the interposition of the government, but he did not allege them as in themselves a suffi-

cient cause for war. He laid more weight on the
influence of England in turning the minds of the
northwestern Indians toward hostilities. " War is
not to commence by land or sea; it is already begun,"
he said, alluding to the battle of Tippecanoe, fought
a month before; yet if ever a war was aggressive,
it was the war which Harrison had begun for no
other object than to win the valley of the Wabash,
and England had interfered neither directly nor indirectly to produce the outbreak of these hostilities.

Grundy's next argument was still less convincing.
The pledge given to France, he said, made necessary the Non-importation Law against England; but
this act was an intolerable burden to the United
States : —

" Ask the Northern man, and he will tell you that any
state of things is better than the present.   Inquire of the
Western people why their crops are not equal to what
they were in former years, they will answer that industry
has no stimulus left, since their surplus products have no
markets.   Notwithstanding these objections to the present restrictive system, we are bound to retain it; this,
and our plighted faith to the French government have
tied the Gordian knot.   We cannot untie it.   We can cut
it with the sword."

Reasoning like this was dear to John Randolph,
never so happy as when he had such a slip to expose.
In defiance of remonstrance, the President and Congress had insisted upon imposing the non-importation,
on the ground that they had entered into a contract

with France ; and no sooner had they done so, than, in order to free themselves from their contract with France, they insisted upon war with England. On the same reasoning their only means of rendering the contract void was by annexing themselves to the empire of Napoleon.

Finally Grundy appealed to an argument wholly new : —

" This war, if carried on successfully, will have its advantages. We shall drive the British from our continent. . . . I am willing to receive the Canadians as adopted brethren. It will have beneficial political effects ; it will preserve the equilibrium of the government. When Louisiana shall be fully peopled, the Northern States will lose their power ; they will be at the discretion of others ; they can be depressed at pleasure, and then this Union might be endangered. I therefore feel anxious not only to add the Floridas to the South, but the Canadas to the North of this empire."

Grundy was the first of Southern statesmen to express publicly the Southern belief that when Louisiana and Florida should be peopled, the Northern States would lose their power and be at the discretion of others, to be depressed at pleasure. Such was the theory of the time, and the political history of the United States seemed to support it ; but the Republican party in 1798 would have looked on any of its representatives as insane who had proposed to make war on England in order to give more power to the Northern States.

To this speech John Randolph replied in his usual keen and desultory style ; but Randolph's arguments had lost historical interest, for the question was not so much whether war should be made, as upon what new ground the United States should stand. The Federalists, conscious of the change, held their peace. The Republicans, laboring to convince not their opponents but themselves, argued day after day that cause for war existed, as though they doubted their own assertion ; but no sooner did they reach delicate ground than they became confused. Many of the speakers avoided argument, and resorted to declamation. The best representative of this class was R. M. Johnson of Kentucky, who, after five years of national submission to both European belligerents, declared that a sixth year would prove fatal : " We must now oppose the further encroachments of Great Britain by war, or formally annul the Declaration of Independence." On this doubtful foundation he imagined visionary conquests. " I should not wish to extend the boundary of the United States by war if Great Britain would leave us to the quiet enjoyment of independence ; but considering her deadly and implacable enmity, and her continued hostilities, I shall never die contented until I see her expulsion from North America, and her territories incorporated with the United States." Probably these appeals carried weight ·with the Western people ; but even earnest supporters of war might doubt whether men of sense could be conciliated or persuaded by such oratory, or by descriptions of Harrison's troops at Tippecanoe, " in the silent watches of the night, relieved from the fatigues of valor, and slumbering under the perfidious promises of the savages, who were infuriated and made drunk by British traders," and so massacred unawares.

Among the Republican speakers was J. C. Calhoun, who had lately taken his seat as a member for South Carolina. Of all the new men, Calhoun was the youngest. He had not yet reached his thirtieth birthday, and his experience in life was slight even for his years ; but his speech of December 12 much excelled that of Grundy in merit, showing more clearness of statement, and fairly meeting each successive point that had been made by Randolph. Little could be added to what Calhoun said, and no objection could be justly made against it, except that as an expression of principles it had no place in the past history of the Republican party.

" Sir," exclaimed Calhoun, " I know of but one principle to make a nation great, to produce in this country not the form but the real spirit of union ; and that is to protect every citizen in the lawful pursuit of his business. . . . Protection and patriotism are reciprocal. This is the road that all great nations have trod."

Of the tenets held by the Virginia school, none had been more often or more earnestly taught than that the United States ought not to be made a great nation by pursuing the road that all great nations had trod. Had Calhoun held such language in 1798, he would

have been branded as a monocrat by Jefferson, and
would not long have represented a Republican district; but so great was the revolution in 1811 that
Calhoun, thinking little of his party and much of the
nation, hardly condescended to treat with decent
respect the " calculating avarice " which, though he
alluded to its authors only in vague words, had been
the pride of his party.

" It is only fit for shops and counting-houses," he said,
" and ought not to disgrace the seat of sovereignty by
its squalid and vile appearance.   Whenever it touches
sovereign power, the nation is ruined.   It is too short-
sighted to defend itself.   It is an unpromising spirit,
always ready to yield a part to save the balance.   It is
too timid to have in itself the laws of self-preservation.
It is never safe but under the shield of honor."

Not without reason did Stanford of North Carolina
retort that he very well recollected to have heard
precisely the same doctrines in a strain of declamation at least equally handsome, upon the same subject, and from the same State ; but the time was in
1799, and the speaker was the Federalist leader of
the House, — Robert Goodloe Harper.

Troup of Georgia presently followed with a criticism that seemed more sensible than any yet made.
He was ready to vote, but he begged for some discretion in debate.   He threatened to call for the previous
question if idle verbiage and empty vociferations were
to take the place of energetic conduct.   " Of what
avail is argument, of what avail is eloquence, to con-

vince, to persuade — whom? Ourselves? The people? Sir, if the people are to be reasoned into a war now, it is too soon, much too soon, to begin it; if their representatives here are to be led into it by the flowers of rhetoric, it is too soon, much too soon, to begin it." The House, he said, had chosen to debate in public a subject which should have been discussed with closed doors, to announce that its measures were intended as measures of offensive hostilities, that its army was to attack Canada; and what was all this but a declaration of war, contrary to all warlike custom, — a magnanimous notice to the enemy when, where, and how the blow would fall? Troup protested against this novel strategy, and pointed out the folly of attacking Canada if England were given such liberal notice to reinforce it; but sensible as the warning was, the debate, which was meant to affect public opinion both in America and in England rather than to prepare for hostilities, went on as before. Even Macon insisted on the wisdom of talking, and pledged himself to support war in order to maintain "the right to export our native produce;" while old William Findley, who had sat in almost every Congress since 1790, voted for the Resolutions on the unrepublican principle that the best means to prevent war was to prepare for it. No concealment was affected of conquests to be made in the Canadas. " Ever since the report of the Committee on Foreign Relations came into the House," said Randolph on the last day of the debate, "we have heard but one

word, — like the whippoorwill, but one monotonous
tone, — Canada, Canada, Canada!"

Stanford of North Carolina made one of the peculiar speeches in which he delighted, but which had
ceased to irritate his party, even though he went so
far as to aver that the Federalists in 1798 had more
cause for war with France than existed in 1811 with
England, and though he declared the Sedition Law
of 1798 to be no more direct an attack on free discussion than was the "previous question" of 1810. He
showed little mercy to Grundy and Calhoun, and
he proved to the delight of the Federalists the inconsistency of his party; while Randolph, in another
speech, redoubled his bitter comments on the changes
of political faith which left no one but Stanford and
himself true to the principles for which they had
taken office. They talked to deaf ears. The Republican party no longer cared for principles. Under the
beneficent pressure of England, the theories of Virginia were, for the time, laid aside.

The Resolutions proposed by the Committee on
Foreign Relations were adopted, December 16, by
what was in effect a unanimous vote. Only twenty-
two members recorded their names against the increase of the regular army, and only fifteen voted
against fitting out the navy. A still stronger proof
of political revolution was the vote of ninety-seven to
twenty-two in favor of the Resolution which authorized merchant vessels to arm. This measure had the
effect of a declaration of war. In former years it had

been always rejected as improper, because it created a private war, taking from the Government and giving to private citizens the control over war and peace; but December 19 the House adopted this last and decisive measure, and while many Republicans would not vote at all, and even Lowndes and Macon voted against it, Josiah Quincy, Timothy Pitkin, and most of the extreme Federalists recorded their votes in its favor.

Meanwhile the Senate had acted. In the want of reports, no record remains of what passed in debate before December 17; but the Journal shows that William B. Giles was made chairman of the Committee on Foreign Relations, with Crawford and five other senators as his associates; and that Giles reported December 9 a bill for raising, not ten thousand regular troops, as the President recommended, but ten regiments of infantry, two of artillery, and one of cavalry, — in all twenty-five thousand men for five years, in addition to an existing army nominally ten thousand strong. Each regiment was to number two thousand men, and whether its ranks were filled or not, required a full complement of officers. Rumor reported, and Giles admitted, that his bill was not an Administration measure, but on the contrary annoyed the Administration, which had asked for all the regular force it could raise or organize within a year. The public, though unwilling to side with Giles against the President, could not but admit that the conquest of Canada by ten thousand men was uncer-

tain, even with the assistance of volunteers and
militia, while the entire scheme of war would become
a subject of ridicule if Congress avowed the intention
of vanquishing all the forces of Great Britain with
only ten thousand raw troops.

Perhaps a better economy would have covered the
ocean with cruisers, and have used the army only for
defence ; but although in any case the military result would probably have been what it was, the party
which undertook to wage a great war by a government not at all equipped for the purpose, without
experience and with narrow resources, proved wisdom in proportion as it showed caution. The President evidently held this opinion. Senator Anderson
of Tennessee, acting probably on Executive advice,
moved to amend the bill with a view of returning
to the original plan of ten or twelve thousand additional troops ; and on this motion, December 17,
Giles made a speech that could not have been more
mischievous had he aimed only to destroy public
trust in the Government. He avowed the difference
between himself and the Secretary of War in regard to the number of troops needed, and he showed
only too easily that the force he proposed was not
more than competent to the objects of the Government ; but not content with proving himself wiser
than the President and the Secretary of War, he
went out of his way to attack the Secretary of the
Treasury with virulence that surprised the Federalists themselves.

The decrepit state of the Treasury, said Giles, was the tenderest part of the discussion ; but instead of dealing tenderly with it, he denounced Gallatin, whose financial reputation, he declared, was made to his hand by others, and was founded less on facts than on anticipation. "If reliance can be placed on his splendid financial talents, only give them scope for action, apply them to the national ability and will, let them perform the simple task of pointing out the true *modus operandi*, and what reason have we to despair of the republic ? What reason have we to doubt of the abundance of the Treasury supplies ? Until now the honorable secretary has had no scope for the demonstration of his splendid financial talents." He went so far as to assert that during the last three years all the measures that had dishonored the nation were, in a great degree, attributable to the unwillingness of Jefferson and Madison to disturb Gallatin's popularity and repose ; that the repeal of the salt tax, the failure of the embarg the refusal to issue letters of marque, were all due to Gallatin's influence ; and that it would have been infinitely better to leave the national debt untouched, than to pay it by surrendering the smallest attribute of national sovereignty.

Giles had long been in open opposition to the President, he had intrigued with every other factious spirit to embarrass the Government, and had scandalized his own State by the bitterness of his personal hatreds ; but he had not before shown him-

self ready to sacrifice the nation to his animosities.
Every one knew that had he expected to give the
Administration the splendid success of a military
triumph, he would never have thrust upon it an
army competent to the purpose. Every one believed
that he hoped to ruin President Madison by the war
that was threatened, and wished to hasten the ruin
before the next autumn election. Those who had
watched Giles closely knew how successfully he had
exerted himself to cripple the Treasury. — how he
had guided the attacks on its resources ; had by his
single vote destroyed Gallatin's only efficient instrument, the Bank ; had again by his single vote repealed the salt tax against Gallatin's wishes ; and
how he had himself introduced and supported that
repeal of the embargo which broke the influence of
Gallatin and went far to ruin Madison's Administration before it was fairly in office. So notorious was
his conduct that Senator Anderson of Tennessee and
his colleague G. W. Campbell, in replying, went to the
verge of the rules in charging Giles with motives of
the blackest kind. Campbell pointed out that Giles's
army would frustrate its own objects ; would be unable to act against Canada as quickly as would be
necessary, and would cause needless financial difficulty. " I trust," continued Campbell, " it is not the
intention of any one by raising so large a regular
force, thereby incurring so great an expenditure beyond what it is believed is necessary, to drain your
treasury, embarrass your fiscal concerns, and paralyze

the best concerted measures of government. If, however, such are the objects intended, a more effectual mode to accomplish them could not be adopted." Giles's speech offered an example, unparalleled in American history, of what Campbell described as "the malignity of the human mind;" but although his object was evident, only twelve senators supported Madison, while twenty-one voted for Giles's army. As though to prove the true motive of the decision, every Federalist senator voted with Giles, and their votes gave him a majority.

Giles's bill passed the Senate December 19, and was referred at once to the House Committee on Foreign Relations, which amended it by cutting down the number of troops from twenty-five thousand to fifteen thousand men; but when this amendment was proposed to the House, it met, in the words of Peter B. Porter, with a gust of zeal and passion. Henry Clay and the ardent war democrats combined with the Federalists to force the larger army on the President, although more than one sound Democrat invoked past experience and ordinary common-sense to prove that twenty-five thousand men — or even half that number — could not be found in the United States willing to enlist in the regular army and submit for five years to the arbitrary will of officers whom they did not know and with whom they had nothing in common. The House voted to raise Giles's army, but still took the precaution of requiring that the officers of six regiments only should be commissioned, until three fourths of the privates for these six regiments should have been enlisted. Another amendment was proposed giving the President discretion to raise only these six regiments, if he thought circumstances rendered the larger force unnecessary ; but Grundy defeated this effort of caution by the argument that too much power had formerly been given to the Executive, and therefore Congress must insist on leaving him no discretion, but obliging him to take twice the army and double the patronage he had asked or could use.   More than twenty Federalists supported Grundy, and gave him a majority of sixty-six to fifty-seven.   Calhoun came to Grundy's assistance with a more reasonable argument.   Delay was becoming dangerous ; the New Year had arrived ; the public began to doubt whether Congress meant to act ; he would vote to prevent delay.

At length, January 6, the bill passed the House by a vote of ninety-four to thirty-four.   Six or eight Federalists, including Josiah Quincy, voted with the majority ; six or eight Republicans, including Macon, Randolph, and Stanford, voted with the minority. The bill returned to the Senate, where the amendments were immediately and almost unanimously struck out.   The House, in no kind temper, was obliged to discuss the subject once more.   Even the most zealous advocates of war were staggered at the thought that all the officers of thirteen new regiments in the regular army must be at once appointed, when no one felt confident that the ranks of these regiments could ever be filled. The support given by the Federalists to every extravagant measure increased the uneasiness of Republicans; and John Randolph's ridicule, founded as it was on truth, did not tend to calm it.

" After you have raised these twenty-five thousand men," said Randolph, " if I may reason on an impossibility, — for it has, I think, been demonstrated that these men cannot be raised, it will be an army on paper only, — shall we form a Committee of Public Safety, or shall we depute the power to the Speaker — I should not wish it in safer hands — to carry on the war? Shall we declare that the Executive, not being capable of discerning the public interest, or not having spirit to pursue it, we have appointed a committee to take the President and Cabinet into custody? . . . You have an agent to execute certain business; he asks from you a certain amount for effecting the business on hand; you give him double, — you force it upon him, you compel him to waste it! "

Again the Federalists decided the result. Half of the Federalist members voted with the extreme war Republicans. The House, by sixty-seven votes to sixty, abandoned its amendments; the bill passed, as Giles had framed it, and January 11 received the President's signature.

CHAPTER VIII.

THE Army Bill was understood to decide not so much the war as the change in domestic politics. That the party of Jefferson, Madison, Gallatin, and Monroe should establish a standing army of thirty-five thousand troops in time of peace, when no foreign nation threatened attack, and should do this avowedly for purposes of conquest, passed the bounds of inconsistency and proclaimed a revolution. This radical change was no longer disguised. Clay, Calhoun, Grundy, Lowndes, and Cheves made only a bare pretence of respecting the traditions of their party; while Giles, with a quality peculiar to himself, excused his assaults on Madison by doing public penance for his ancient errors in maligning Washington. "Further information and reflection," he said, "and practical experience of more than twenty years, have completely convinced me of the superiority of the talent of this great man as a statesman as well as a soldier, and have also admonished me of my former errors." If in America any politician could be found to whose public character such an admission was fatal, Giles might be regarded as the person; but conduct that ruined

Giles's character only raised the reputations of Clay, Lowndes, and Calhoun. These younger men were not responsible for what had been said and done ten or fifteen years before ; they had been concerned in no conspiracy to nullify the laws, or to offer armed resistance to the government ; they had never rested their characters as statesmen on the chance of success in governing without armaments, and in coercing Napoleon and Pitt by peaceable means ; they had no past to defend or excuse, and as yet no philosophical theories to preach, — but they were obliged to remove from their path the system their party had established, and they worked at this task with more energy and with much more success than they showed in conducting foreign war. Even a return to Washington's system would not answer their purpose, for they were obliged to restore the extreme practices of 1798, and to re-enact the laws which had then been denounced and discarded as the essence of monarchy.

Bitterly as all good Republicans regretted to create a standing army, that vote was easy compared with other votes it made necessary. Doubtless an army was an evil, but the effects of the evil were likely to appear chiefly in the form of taxes; and the stanchest war Republicans flinched at taxation. The British minister, who saw so much of these difficulties that he could not believe in the possibility of war, reported to his Government a story which showed how uneasily the Administration balanced itself between the two bodies of its supporters. In December, during the debate on the Army Bill, the Committee of Ways and Means was repeatedly urged to produce a scheme of war-finance, but failed to do so. Foster reported, on what he called good authority, that when the chairman of that committee went to Gallatin for information to meet questions in the House, the secretary declined giving estimates until the Army Bill should be disposed of; and he explained that if he submitted a plan of taxes, the Government would be charged with wanting to damp the ardor of Congress.[1] Every one knew that the ardor of Congress feared nothing so much as damping; but every one who knew Gallatin was persuaded that as long as he remained Secretary of the Treasury, taxes must proportionally increase with debt.

Foster's story was probably true; for although Ezekiel Bacon, chairman of the Ways and Means Committee, wrote as early as Dec. 9, 1811, to the secretary for advice, the secretary delayed his answer until January 10, the day when Congress agreed to pass the Army Bill. The letter was read to the House January 20, and proved, as had been foreseen, a serious discouragement to the war spirit. Yet Gallatin made an under-estimate of financial difficulties; for while he assumed the fixed charges at $9,600,000, and estimated the receipts from customs under the existing duties at only $2,500,000 during war, he assumed also the committee's estimate of $10,000,000

[1] Foster to Wellesley, Jan. 16, 1812; MSS. British Archives.

as the annual loan that would be required to meet the expense of war. In order to pay the fixed charges of government, the customs revenue must be raised to $6,000,000; and for this purpose he asked Congress not only to double the existing duties, but also to reimpose the old duty on salt. To meet the remaining charge of $3,600,000 and the accruing interest on new loans, he asked for internal taxes to the amount of $5,000,000.

Unfortunately Gallatin had carelessly said, in his annual report of November, that a revenue of nine millions would, with the aid of loans, answer the purposes of war; while his letter of January 10 required, as was proper, that the interest of each new loan should be added annually to the nine millions. The difference amounted to $600,000 for the first year alone, and in each successive year increased taxation by at least an equal sum. Gallatin himself was in a defiant mood, as he well might be, since he saw Congress in a position where it must either submit or take the responsibility of bankrupting the Treasury; and he did not content himself with demanding unpopular taxes, but read Congress a lecture on its own conduct that had made these taxes necessary. He recalled his promise of 1808 that " no internal taxes, either direct or indirect, were contemplated even in the case of hostilities carried on against the two great belligerent powers ; " and he showed that since 1808 Congress had thrown away his actual or expected balance of twenty millions, had refused to accept twenty

millions that might have been obtained from the
Bank, and had thus made internal taxes necessary,
while making loans more difficult to obtain even on
harder terms.

The sting of this reproof came at the end of the
secretary's letter, where he named the objects of internal taxation.   These were spirits, refined sugar,
licenses to retailers, auctions, stamps, and carriages
for conveyance of persons.   Here was the whole
armory of Federalism, that had once already roused
rebellion, and after causing the grievances which
brought the Republicans into power, appeared again
threatening to ruin them as it had ruined their
predecessors.   Standing army of thirty-five thousand
men, loans, protective duties, stamps, tax on distilla-
tion, — nothing but a Sedition Law was wanting;
and the previous question, as a means of suppressing discussion, was not an unfair equivalent for the
Sedition Law.

Gallatin's letter caused no little excitement in the
House. Congress recoiled, and for more than a month
left the subject untouched. The chance that England
might still give way, or that something might at the
last prevent actual war, made every member anxious
to avoid committing himself on matters of taxation.
The number of representatives who favored war was
supposed not to exceed forty or fifty in a House of
one hundred and forty-one, — as many more would
vote for war only in case they must; but the war
men and the peace men united in private to fall upon

Gallatin, — the first, because he had chilled the national spirit by saying that taxes must be laid; the last, because he had not said it earlier, and had not chilled the national spirit once for all.

Laying aside the question of taxes, Congress took up two other subjects of pressing importance. Every one doubted the possibility of raising a regular army, and those persons who knew best the character of the people were convinced that the war must be waged by militia on land, and by privateers on the ocean.

The House began with the militia. December 26 Porter brought in a bill authorizing the President "to accept of any company or companies of volunteers, either of artillery, cavalry, or infantry, who may associate and offer themselves for the service, not exceeding fifty thousand," officered according to the law of the State to which the companies belonged, and liable to service for one year, with the pay of regular troops. Evidently these volunteers were State militia, and were subject to be used only for purposes defined in the Constitution. In 1798 the attempt to raise such a corps had been denounced as unconstitutional, a device to separate a part of the State militia in order to put it under the President's power in a manner expressly forbidden by the Constitution and peculiarly dangerous to the public liberties; and although the device of 1798 was made more evident, as its efficiency was made more certain, by the provision that these corps should be officered by the

President, the device of 1812 was not less offensive
to men who held that Congress had no power to call
out the State militia except " to execute the laws of
the Union, suppress insurrections, and repel inva-
sions," of course only within the limits of the United
States. The chief service desired from these volunteer corps was the conquest of Canada and the occupation of Florida; but every principle of the Republican
party would be outraged by placing the militia at the
President's orders, to serve on foreign soil.

Porter, who wanted express legislation to overcome this difficulty, stated his dilemma to the House;
and the debate began quietly on the assumption that
these volunteers were not to serve in Canada or
Florida without their own consent, when, January 11,
Langdon Cheves, with much seriousness and even
solemnity of manner and language, informed the
House that the Republican party had hitherto taken
a wrong view of the subject. The distinguished South
Carolinian affirmed doctrines that had never before
been heard from Republican lips : —

" The power of declaring and making war is a great
sovereign power, whose limits and extent have long been
understood and well established. It has its attributes
and incidental powers, which are in the same degree less
equivocal than those of other powers as it excels those
powers in its importance. Do you ask then for the right
of Congress to employ the militia in war? It is found
among the attributes of the sovereign power which Congress has to make war. Do you ask for the limits to

which this employment may extend? They are coextensive with the objects of the war."

The President himself, added Cheves, was understood to hold this opinion, and ought to be left to act under the high responsibility attached to his office. Anxious as the party was to support the President, Cheves's speech met with protest after protest, until Henry Clay came to his support and adopted his argument. On the other hand, the Federalists, although consistency required them to take the same view, and even war Republicans, like Porter and Grundy, rejected the idea of an unlimited war power, and declared that the volunteers must be retained within the national boundaries. The point was left unsettled; January 17 the House passed the bill by a vote of eighty-seven to twenty-three, leaving the decision in the President's hands, or, what was worst of all, in the hands of the volunteers. In the Senate, Giles made an interesting speech against the bill, avoiding the constitutional question, but arguing that the volunteer force would prove inefficient, and that a regular army could alone serve the purposes of war. He had no difficulty in proving the correctness of his view and the fatal folly of short enlistments; but he could not explain how the ranks of the regular army were to be filled, and his objections took no practical form. The bill passed without a division, and February 6 was approved by the President.

In this matter Congress, without absolutely rejecting Cheves's doctrine, evaded a decision; but another subject remained which was not so gently treated. From the first, the Republican party had opposed a navy. The United States owned five or six frigates, but not one ship-of-the-line; New York or Philadelphia might be blockaded, perhaps ransomed, at any time by a single seventy-four with a frigate or two in company. To seafaring men, the idea of fighting England without ships seemed absurd, but the Republican party was pledged by every line of its history not to create a navy. The dilemma was singular. Either the Republican party must recant its deepest convictions, or the war must be fought without ships except privateers, and England must be left with no anxiety but the defence of Canada.

Once more Langdon Cheves took the lead. January 17, after the House voted on the Volunteer Bill, Cheves as chairman of the Naval Committee asked an appropriation to build twelve seventy-fours and twenty frigates at a cost of seven and a half million dollars.

"I know," he began, "how many and how strong are the prejudices, how numerous and how deeply laid are the errors which I have to encounter in the discussion of this question, — errors and prejudices the more formidable as they come recommended by the virtues and shielded by the estimable motives of those who indulge them. I have been told that this subject is unpopular, and it has been not indistinctly hinted that those who become the zealous advocates of the bill will not advance by their exertions the personal estimation in which they may be held by their political associates."

In few words Cheves avowed that while he preferred to act with the Republican party, he was in truth independent, and he warned his friends that on the subject of a navy they must in the end either conquer their prejudices or quit office.

After this preamble, Cheves struck once more at the foundations of his party. His argument, as a matter of expediency, was convincing ; for every American ship-of-war, even when blockaded in port, would oblige the British to employ three ships of equal or greater size to relieve each other in blockading and watching it. The blockading service of the American station was peculiarly severe. England had no port nearer than Halifax for equipments or repairs ; in general all her equipments must be made in Europe, and for only three months' service ; in winter she must for months at a time abandon the blockade, and leave the coast free. No method could be devised by which, with so small risk and so little waste of money and life, the resources of England could be so rapidly drained as by the construction of heavy war-vessels. Once at sea, an American seventy-four had nothing to fear except a squadron ; and even when dismantled in port, she required the attention of a hostile fleet.

The House had submitted with slowly rising ill-temper to each successive demand of the war it would have preferred to avoid ; but this last requirement threw it into open revolt. Cheves found himself for a time almost alone. Even Richard M.

Johnson, always ardent for war, became mournful
with prophecies of the evils that Cheves was about
to bring upon the country. " I will refer to Tyre and
Sidon, Crete and Rhodes, to Athens and to Carthage."
Plunder, piracy, perpetual war, followed the creation
of every navy known to history. Armies might be
temporary, but navies were permanent, and even
more dangerous to freedom. " Navies have been
and always will be engines of power, employed in
projects of ambition and war."

These were the old and respected Republican doctrines, still dear to a large majority of the party.
William Lowndes came to the support of his colleague, and ridiculed Johnson's lessons from ancient
history; Henry Clay protested against the unreasonable prejudice which refused naval assistance, and
which left New York and the commerce of the Mississippi at the mercy of single British ships; but
when the committee of the whole House came to
a vote, Cheves found a majority opposed to him on
every motion for the building additional ships of
any sort whatever. The House continued the debate for several days, but ended, January 27, by
refusing to build frigates. The division was close.
Fifty-nine members voted for the frigates; sixty-
two voted against them. While Cheves, Lowndes,
Calhoun, Troup, Porter, and the Federalists voted
for the ships, Ezekiel Bacon, Grundy, R. M. Johnson,
D. R. Williams, and the friends of the Administration
in general voted against them.

By the middle of February, Congress reached a
point of disorganization that threatened disaster.
The most ardent urged immediate war, while not a
practical step had yet been taken toward fighting.
Such was the chaos that Peter B. Porter, who had
himself reported the Army and Volunteer bills, asked
for a committee to raise another provisional army of
twenty thousand men, for the reason that the two
armies already provided were useless, — the regular
force, because it could not be put into the field within
the year; the volunteers, because they could not law-
fully be used for offensive war. "What force have
we given the President?" asked Porter. "We have
made a parade in passing laws to raise twenty-five
thousand regular troops, and fifty thousand volunteers; but in truth and in fact we have not given
him a single man." The House refused to follow
Porter's advice; but as usual the war Republicans
were obliged to coalesce with the Federalists in order
to maintain themselves against these Executive reproaches. What Porter said was mainly true. With
the exception of the peace establishment consisting of
nominally ten thousand men, and the vessels of war
actually afloat, the President had not yet been given
means of defending the coasts and frontiers from
hostile forces which, in the case of the northwestern
Indians, were already actually attacking them.

In the midst of this general discouragement, February 17, Ezekiel Bacon brought in fourteen Resolutions embodying a scheme for raising money.

Gallatin's measures were expected to be harsh, but
those proposed by Bacon seemed more severe than
had been expected. The customs duties were to
be doubled; twenty cents a bushel were laid on salt,
fifty cents a gallon on the capacity of stills; licenses
and stamps in proportion; and a direct tax of three
million dollars was to be apportioned among the
States. A loan bill for eleven millions at six per cent
was easily passed, but all the force of the war feeling
could not overcome the antipathy to taxation. The
Resolution for doubling the customs duties met little
resistance; but February 28 the House refused, by
sixty to fifty-seven, to impose a duty on imported salt,
and for the moment this vote threatened to ruin the
whole scheme. The House adjourned for reflection;
and on the following Monday a member from Virginia
moved to reconsider the vote. "It now seems," he
said, "that if the article of salt is excluded, the whole
system of taxation will be endangered. We are told
in conversation, since the vote on the salt tax, that
the system which has been presented by the Committee of Ways and Means is a system of compromise
and concession, and that it must be taken altogether,
the bad with the good; that if we pay the salt tax,
the eastern and the western country will suffer peculiarly by an increase of the impost, and by the land
tax." In short, he thought it better to take the whole
draught even if it were hemlock.

This view of the case did not find easy acceptance.
Nelson of Virginia exhorted the majority not under

any circumstances to accept the impost on salt; and
Wright of Maryland, a man best known for his extravagances, took the occasion to express against
Gallatin the anger which the friends of the Smiths,
Giles, and Duane had stored.   Gallatin, he said,
was trying to fix the odium of these taxes on Congress in order to disgust the people and chill the war
spirit; he was treading in the muddy footsteps of his
official predecessors, in attempting to strap around
the necks of the people this odious system of taxation, for which the Federalists had been condemned
and dismissed from power.   The salt tax would destroy the present as it had destroyed the old Administration; the true course was to lay taxes directly
on property.   Probably most of the Republican
members sympathized in private with the feelings
of Wright, but Gallatin had at last gained the advantage of position; the House voted to reconsider, and
by a majority of sixty-six to fifty-four accepted the
duty of twenty cents on imported salt.

The salt duty distressed the South, and in revenge
many Southerners wished to impose a tax of twenty-
five cents a gallon on whiskey, which would be felt
chiefly in the West; but this was no part of the
Treasury scheme.   Grundy and R. M. Johnson succeeded in defeating the motion; and after deciding
this contest, the House found no difficulty in adopting
all the other Resolutions.   March 4 the committee
was instructed to report by bill; Bacon sent the Resolutions to the Treasury, and the secretary waited for

events. Every one admitted that while war was still
uncertain, the financial policy undecided, and a Presidential election approaching, only the prospect of immediate bankruptcy would outweigh the dangers of
oppressive taxation.

Four months of continuous session had passed, and
spring was opening, when the Legislature reached this
point. The result of the winter's labor showed that
the young vigor of this remarkable Congress had succeeded only in a small part of the work required to
give Jefferson's peaceful system a military shape.
Although the nominal regular army had been raised
from ten thousand to thirty-five thousand men, the
Act of Congress which ordered these men to be enlisted could not show where they were to be found;
and meanwhile the sudden strain broke down the War
Department. Rumor pointed at Secretary Eustis as
incompetent, and the chances were great that any
secretary, though sufficiently good for peace, would
prove unequal to the task of creating an army without men or material to draw from. Whether the
secretary was competent or not, his situation exposed
him to ridicule. He had hitherto discharged the duties of Secretary of War, of Quartermaster-General,
Commissary-General, Indian Commissioner, Commissioner of Pensions, and Commissioner of Public
Lands; and although Congress promised to create a
quartermaster's department, and had the bill already
in hand, the task of organizing this department, as
well as all the other new machinery of war, fell on

the secretary and eight clerks, not one of whom had been twelve months in office. Any respectable counting-house would have allowed some distribution of authority and power of expansion ; but the secretary could neither admit a partner nor had he the right to employ assistance. Adapted by Jefferson, in 1801, to a peace establishment of three or four regiments, the Department required reorganization throughout, or Congress would be likely to find the operations of war brought to a quick end.

Had Congress undertaken to wage war on the ocean, the same difficulty would have been felt in the navy ; but this danger was evaded by the refusal to attempt naval operations. At all times the Republicans had avowed their willingness to part with the five frigates, and these were perhaps to be sent to sea with no great hope in the majority for their success ; but the Navy Department was required to make no other exertion. Secretary Hamilton, like Secretary Eustis, was supposed to be unequal to his post ; but his immediate burden amounted only to fitting out three frigates in addition to those in actual service, and the expenditure of two hundred thousand dollars annually for three years toward the purchase of ship-timber.

To meet the expenses thus incurred for military purposes, in the absence of taxes which, if imposed, could not be made immediately productive, Congress authorized a loan of eleven million dollars at six per cent, redeemable in twelve years.

An army of thirty-five thousand regulars which could not be raised within a year, if at all, and of fifty thousand volunteers who were at liberty to refuse service beyond the frontier, promised no rapid or extensive conquests. A navy of half-a-dozen frigates and a few smaller craft could not be expected to keep the ports open, much less to carry the war across the ocean. Privateers must be the chief means of annoyance, not so much to British pride or power as to British commerce, and this kind of warfare was popular because it cost the government nothing; but even the privateers were at a great disadvantage if the ports were to be closed to their prizes by hostile squadrons. Such means of offence were so evidently insufficient that many sensible persons could not believe in the threatened war; but these were only the most conspicuous weaknesses. Armies required equipment, and the United States depended on Europe, chiefly on England, for their most necessary supplies. The soldier in Canada was likely to need blankets; but no blankets were to be had, and the Non-importation Act prevented them from coming into the market, whatever price might be offered.

Not only was the machinery of government unsuited to energetic use, but the Government itself was not in earnest. Hardly one third of the members of Congress believed war to be their best policy. Almost another third were Federalists, who wished to overthrow the Administration; the rest were hon-

est and perhaps shrewd men, brought up in the
school of Virginia and Pennsylvania politics, who
saw more clearly the evils that war must bring than
the good it might cause, and who dreaded the reaction upon their constituents. They could not understand the need of carrying into every detail a
revolution in their favorite system of government.
Clay and Calhoun, Cheves and Lowndes asked them
to do in a single session what required half a century
or more of time and experience, — to create a new
government, and invest it with the attributes of old-
world sovereignty under pretext of the war power.
The older Republicans had no liking for such statesmanship, and would gladly have set the young Southerners in their right place.

By force of will and intellect the group of war
members held their own, and dragged Congress forward in spite of itself; but the movement was slow
and the waste of energy exhausting. Perhaps they
failed to carry their points more often than they
succeeded. Energetic as their efforts were, after
four months of struggle they had settled nothing,
and found themselves in March no further advanced
than in November. War should already have been
declared; but Congress was still trying to avoid it.

Federalists had much to do with causing the confusion of Republicans. Their conduct could seldom be
explained on rational grounds, but in January, 1812,
they seemed to lose reason. Their behavior, contra-
dicting their own principles, embarrassed their friends

still more than it confused their enemies.   The British minister wrote to his Government constant complaints of the dangerous course his Federalist allies
were pursuing.

"The Federal leaders," Foster wrote Dec. 11, 1811,[1]
"make no scruple of telling me that they mean to give
their votes for war, although they will remain silent in
the debates ; they add that it will be a short war of six
or nine months.   To my observations on the strange
and dangerous nature of such a policy, they shrug their
shoulders, telling me that they see no end to restrictions
and non-importation laws but in war ; that war will turn
out the Administration, and then they will have their
own way, and make a solid peace with Great Britain."

To this policy Federalist leaders adhered.   As the
weeks passed, Foster's situation grew more difficult.
Disgusted equally by the obstinacy of his Government
and by the vacillations of Congress, he found his worst
annoyances in the intrigues of his friends.   Toward
the close of the year he wrote : [2] —

"The situation that I find myself thus unexpectedly
placed in is, I must confess, exceedingly embarrassing.
I am aware that H. R. H. the Prince Regent wishes to
avoid a rupture with this country, and yet I see that the
efforts of a party, hitherto the most adverse to a war
with Great Britain, are united with those of another,
which till now has been supposed the most considerable
in point of numbers, for the purpose of bringing it on ;

[1] Foster to Wellesley, Dec. 11, 1811; MSS. British Archives.
[2] Foster to Wellesley, Dec. 11, 1811; MSS. British Archives.

while Government, although wishing for delay, are yet so weak and little to be depended on that it is to be feared if the two Houses were to decide on hostilities, they would not have resolution enough to oppose the measure."

January 16, 1812, he wrote again.[1] Somewhat encouraged by the evident difficulties of the war party in Congress, he was then disposed to look less severely at Federalist tactics : —

" The opposition know the embarrassment of the President, and endeavor to take advantage of it by pushing for measures so decisive as to leave him no retreat. It has been told me in confidence more than once by different leaders, that if the Orders in Council are not revoked he must eventually be ruined in the opinion of the nation. Some individuals have even gone so far as to reproach us for not concerting measures with them for that purpose, observing that the French have managed this country by concert with a party ; and that unless Great Britain do the same, the French party will always be predominant. I should mention to your Lordship that the Federalists are by no means united. From twelve to sixteen vote for peace measures, while eight only, though of the leaders, vote the contrary way."

February 1, a fortnight after this letter was written, two Federalist leaders, whose names Foster wisely suppressed, called on the British minister to give him their advice as to the best course his Government could take " in order to produce a thorough amalgamation of interests between America and

[1] Foster to Wellesley, Jan. 16, 1812 ; MSS. British Archives.

Great Britain." Their conversation, which seems to have been in no way invited by Foster, was reported by him to Lord Wellesley without comment of any kind.[1] Had the two Federalists foreseen the scandal to be caused, six weeks later, by the publication of John Henry's papers, they would hardly have dared approach the British minister at all; and they would at least have been reminded that such advice as they gave him was not only forbidden by law, but bordered closely upon treason.

" The sum of these suggestions was that we should neither revoke our Orders in Council nor modify them in any manner. They said this Government would, if we conceded, look upon our concessions as being the effect of their own measures, and plume themselves thereon; that they only wanted to get out of their present difficulties, and if we made a partial concession they would make use of it to escape fulfilling their pledge to go to war, still however continuing the restrictory system; whereas if we pushed them to the edge of the precipice by an unbending attitude, that then they must be lost, either by the disgrace of having nearly ruined the trade of the United States and yet failed to reduce Great Britain by their system of commercial restrictions, or else by their incapacity to conduct the government during war. These gentlemen declared they were for war rather than for the continuance of the restrictory system, even if the war should last four years. They thought no expense too great which would lead to the termination of the irritating, fretful feelings which had so long existed between

[1] Foster to Wellesley, Feb. 2, 1812 ; MSS. British Archives.

the two countries. They animadverted on the peevish nature of the answers given in the affairs of the ' Chesapeake' and to my note on the Indians, and whenever any spirit of conciliation was shown by Great Britain, and told me it would ever be so until the people felt the weight of taxes; that nothing would bring them to a right sense of their interests but touching their purses; and that if we did go to war for a time, we should be better friends afterward. In short, they seemed to think that Great Britain could by management bring the United States into any connection with her that she pleased."

The President, as his office required, stood midway between the masses of his followers, but never failed to approve the acts and meet the wishes of the war members. Early in March, at a moment when they were greatly embarrassed, he came to their aid by a manœuvre which excited much feeling on all sides, but especially among the Federalists engaged in abetting the war policy. He seemed to have fallen on the track of a conspiracy such as had overthrown the liberties and independence of classic republics, and which left no alternative but war or self-destruction; but the true story proved more modern, if not less amusing, than the conspiracies of Greece and Rome.

CHAPTER IX.

JOHN HENRY, whose reports from Boston to Sir James Craig at Quebec had been received with favor in 1808 and 1809 both in Canada and in London, not satisfied with such reward as he received from the governor-general, went to England and applied, as was said, for not less than thirty-two thousand pounds, or one hundred and sixty thousand dollars, as the price he thought suitable for his services and his silence.[1] Whatever was the sum he demanded, he failed to obtain it, and left England in ill humor on his return to Canada, carrying his papers with him and an official recommendation to the governor-general.

On the same ship was a Frenchman who bore the title of Count Edward de Crillon. His connections, he said, embraced the noblest and highest families of France ; among his ancestors was the "brave Crillon," who for centuries had been known to every French child as the Bayard of his time. The Count Edward's father was the Duc de Crillon ; by marriage he was closely connected with Bessières, the Maréchal Duc d'Istrie, Napoleon's favorite. Count Edward de

[1] Crillon's evidence; Annals of Congress, 1811–1812, p. 1222.

Crillon had fallen into disfavor with the Emperor, and for that reason had for a time quitted France, while waiting a restoration to the army. His manners were easy and noble; he wore the decoration of the Legion of Honor, received and showed letters from his family and from the Duc d'Istrie, and talked much of his personal affairs, especially of his estate called St. Martial, "in Lebeur near the Spanish border," and, he took pride in saying, near also to the Château de Crillon, the home of his ancestors. He had met John Henry in London society. When he appeared on the Boston packet, a friendship arose between these two men so hardly treated by fortune. Henry confided his troubles to the count, and Crillon gave himself much concern in the affair, urging Henry to have no more to do with an ungrateful government, but to obtain from the United States the money that England refused. The count offered to act as negotiator, and use his influence with Serurier, his minister, to approach the Secretary of State. The count even offered to provide for Henry's subsequent welfare by conveying to him the valuable estate at St. Martial in consideration of the money to be obtained for Henry's documents. At St. Martial, under the protection of the Crillons, John Henry would at last find, together with every charm of climate and scenery, the ease of life and the social refinement so dear to him.

Henry entered into a partnership with the Frenchman, and on their arrival at Boston Crillon wrote to

Serurier, introducing himself, and narrating the situation of Henry, whose papers, he said, were in his own control.[1] Serurier made no reply; but Crillon came alone to Washington, where he called on the minister, who after hearing his story sent him to Monroe, to whom he offered Henry's papers for a consideration of $125,000. Serurier liked Crillon, and after some months of acquaintance liked him still more : —

"His conduct and language during six weeks' residence here have been constantly sustained; the attention shown him by this Government, the repentance he displayed for having incurred the displeasure of his sovereign, the constant enthusiasm with which he spoke of the Emperor, the name he bore, the letters he showed from his sister and from the Maréchal Duc d'Istrie, the decoration of the Legion he carried, and finally the persecution he suffered from the British minister and the party hostile to France, — all this could not but win my regard for him." [2]

Yet Crillon did not owe to Serurier his introduction into society, or his success in winning the confidence of Madison and Monroe. Indeed, the French minister could not openly recommend a man who admitted himself to be banished from France by the Emperor's displeasure. On the contrary, the favor that Crillon rapidly won at the White House served rather to establish his credit with his legation. The President

[1] Les Etats Unis il y a quarante ans; Par Caraman. Revue Contemporaine, 31 Août, 1852, p. 26.

[2] Serurier to Maret, May 27, 1812 ; Archives des Aff. Étr. MSS.

and Cabinet ministers were civil to the count, who
became a frequent guest at the President's table;
and the services he promised to Serurier's great object were so considerable as to make the French
minister glad to assist him.   No French comedy was
suited with a happier situation or with more skilful
actors.   During several weeks in January and February, 1812, Count Edward de Crillon was the centre
of social interest or hostility at the White House, the
State Department, and the French and the British
Legations.

The negotiation through Serurier was successful.
Henry was secretly summoned to Washington, and
consented to desist from his demand for $125,000.
Secretary Monroe agreed to give him $50,000, and to
promise that the papers should not be made public
until Henry himself was actually at sea, while Crillon
received the money, delivering to Henry the title-deeds
to the estate of St. Martial.   The money was paid,
February 10, out of the contingent fund for foreign
intercourse.   Henry left Washington the next day to
sail from New York for France in a national ship-
of-war, but the Count Edward de Crillon remained.
March 2 Serurier reported,[1] —

" The Administration has decided to publish Henry's
documents.   The order has been sent to New York that
in case the ship which was to give him passage has not
arrived, he is to be embarked on a merchant-vessel; and

[1] Serurier to Maret, March 2, 1811; Archives des Aff. Étr.
MSS.

then all the papers are to be sent to Congress by special message. Much is expected from this exposition. The conduct of M. Crillon since his arrival here has never ceased to be consistent and thoroughly French. It has drawn on him the hatred of the British minister and of all the British party; but he bears up against it with the noblest firmness, and sometimes even with an intrepidity that I am obliged to restrain. He keeps me informed of everything that he thinks of service to the Emperor; and his loyalty of conduct attaches the members of the Administration to him. I have personally every motive to be satisfied with him, and I hope that the service he has just rendered, the sentiments he professes on all occasions, his so enthusiastic admiration for the Emperor, his devotion, his love of his country and his family, will create for him a title to the indulgence of his sovereign and the return of his favor. He will wait for them here, and I pray your Excellency to invoke them on my part."

The President waited only for the news that Henry had sailed, before sending to Congress the evidence of British intrigues and of Federalist treason; but as soon as this news arrived, Saturday, March 7, Monroe sent for Serurier : [1] —

"The Secretary of State asked me to come to his office to inform me of the determination. He asked me if I did not agree with him that it was better not to mention me in the Message, as such mention might injure its effect by giving it a French color. I told Mr. Monroe that I should leave the President entirely free to follow

[1] Serurier to Maret, March 2, 1811; Archives des Aff. Étr. MSS.

the course he thought best in the matter. He might say that the documents had come into my possession, and that I had at once sent them to him as interesting the Republic exclusively; or he might restrict himself to the communication of the papers without detail as to the route they had followed. That I had taken no credit, as he could remember, in regard to the service I had been so fortunate as to render the Administration; and that I had on my own account no need of newspaper notoriety or of public gratitude."

Monday, March 9, the President sent Henry's papers to Congress, with a message which said nothing as to the manner of acquiring them, but charged the British government with employing a secret agent " in fomenting disaffection to the constituted authorities of the nation, and in intrigues with the disaffected for the purpose of bringing about resistance to the laws, and eventually, in concert with a British force, of destroying the Union and forming the eastern part thereof into a political connection with Great Britain." Serurier reported that the Administration had great hopes through this discovery of deciding the result, inflaming the nation, and throwing it enthusiastically into the war : —

" The American people recalls to me the son of Ulysses on the rock of Calypso's isle ; uncertain, irresolute, he knows not to which of his passions to yield, when Minerva, flinging him into the sea, fixes his fate, leaving him no other choice than to overcome by his courage and strength the terrible elements she gives him for an enemy."

When John Henry's letters were read in Congress, March 9, 1812, the Federalists for a moment felt real alarm, for they knew not what Henry might have reported; but a few minutes of examination showed them that, as far as they were concerned, Henry had taken care to report nothing of consequence. That he came to Boston as a British agent was hitherto unknown to the Federalists themselves, and the papers showed that he never revealed his secret character to them. His letters were hardly more compromising than letters, essays, and leading articles, sermons, orations, and addresses that had been printed again and again in every Federalist paper in Boston and New York. Here and there they contained rows of mysterious asterisks, but no other sign of acquaintance with facts worth concealing. The Federalists naturally suspected, what is evident on comparison of the papers bought by Madison with the originals in the Record Office at London, that Henry intended to sell as little as possible at the highest price he could exact. His revelations told nothing of his first visit to Boston in 1808, nor was one of the letters published which had been written in that year, although his documents incidentally alluded to information then sent; but what was more singular and fatal to his credit, the letters which he sold as his own were not copies but paraphrases of the originals; the mysterious asterisks were introduced merely to excite curiosity; and except the original instructions of Sir James Craig and the recent letter from Lord Liverpool's secretary, showing that in view of an expected war Henry had been employed as a secret agent to obtain political information by the governor-general, and that his reports had been sent to the Colonial Office, nothing in these papers compromised any one except Henry himself. As for the British government, since war was to be waged with it in any case for other reasons, these papers distracted attention from the true issue.

After a night's reflection the Federalists returned to the Capitol convinced that the President had done a foolish act in throwing away fifty thousand dollars for papers that proved the Federalist party to be ignorant of British intrigues that never existed. Fifty thousand dollars was a large sum ; and having been spent without authority from Congress, it seemed to the Federalists chiefly their own money which had been unlawfully used by Madison for the purpose of publishing a spiteful libel on themselves. With every sign of passion they took up the President's personal challenge. A committee of investigation was ordered by the House, and found that Henry, with the Government's privity, had already sailed for Europe. Nothing remained but to examine Crillon, who gave evidence tending to prove only such facts as he thought it best that Congress should believe. In the Senate, March 10, Lloyd of Massachusetts moved a Resolution calling on the President for the names of any persons " who have in any way or manner whatever entered into, or most remotely countenanced," the projects of Sir James Craig. Monroe could only reply that, as John Henry had mentioned no names, the Department was not possessed of the information required. The reply made the Federalists only more angry; they were eager for revenge, and fortune did not wholly refuse it. They never learned that Henry's disclosure was the result of French intrigue, but they learned enough to make them suspect and exult over some mortification of the President.

Soon after Count Edward de Crillon gave his evidence to the investigating committee, news arrived that France was about to make war with Russia, and although Crillon had decided to wait in Washington for his recall to the Emperor's favor, he became suddenly earnest to depart. March 22, Serurier wrote:[1] —

"At the news of a possible rupture with Russia, the blood of M. de Crillon, always so boiling, has become hotter than ever, and he has decided to return to France without waiting an answer from your Excellency; he wants to throw himself at the Emperor's feet, tell him what he has done, invoke pardon for his errors, and go to expiate them in the advance guard of his armies."

April 1 Crillon left Washington bearing despatches from Monroe to Barlow, and from Serurier to Bassano. Neither he nor John Henry is known to have

[1] Serurier to Maret, March 22, 1811; Archives des Aff. Étr. MSS.

ever again visited the United States, and their names
would have been forgotten had not stories soon arrived that caused the Federalists great amusement,
and made President Madison very uncomfortable.
Barlow wrote to the President that Count Edward
de Crillon was an impostor ; that no such person
was known to the Crillon family or to the French
service. Private letters confirmed the report, and
added that the estate of St. Martial had no existence,
and that Crillon's draughts in Henry's favor were
drawn on a person who had been five years dead.

" The President, with whom he has often dined," continued Serurier,[1] " and all the secretaries, whose reception, joined with the political considerations known to
your Excellency, decided his admittance to my house, are
a little ashamed of the eagerness (*empressement*) they
showed him, and all the money they gave him. For my
own part, Monseigneur, I have little to regret. I have
constantly refused to connect myself with his affairs ; I
sent him to the Secretary of State for his documents ;
the papers have been published, and have produced an
effect injurious to England without my having bought
this good fortune by a single *denier* from the Imperial
treasury ; and I have escaped at the cost of some civilities, preceded by those of the President, the motive of
which I declared from the first to be the services which
the Administration told me had been rendered it by
this traveller."

Serurier continued to declare that he had honestly
believed Crillon to be " something like what he re-

[1] Serurier to Maret, May 27, 1812; Archives des Aff. Étr. MSS.

presented himself;" but he could not reasonably expect the world to accept these protestations. He had aided this person to obtain fifty thousand dollars from the United States Treasury for papers not his own, and instead of warning the President against an adventurer whose true character he admitted himself to have suspected, the French minister abetted the impostor. Although he afterwards asserted, and possibly believed, that Crillon was an agent of Napoleon's secret police, he was equally unwilling to admit that he had himself been either dupe or accomplice.[1]

That the President should be mortified was natural, but still more natural that he should be angry. He could not resent the introduction of a foreign impostor to his confidence, since he was himself chiefly responsible for the social success of the Count Edward de Crillon; but deception was a part of the French system, and Madison felt the Crillon affair sink into insignificance beside the other deceptions practised upon him by the government of France. He was as nearly furious as his temperament allowed, at the manner in which the Emperor treated him. Before Crillon appeared on the scene, Madison used language to Serurier that betrayed his extreme dissatisfaction at being paraded before the public as a dupe or tool of France. At Savannah a riot took place between French privateersmen and American

[1] Caraman. Revue Contemporaine, 31 août, 1852. Count Edward de Crillon, American Historical Review, October, 1895, pp. 51–69.

or English sailors; several men on both sides were killed; the privateers were burned; and Serurier complained in language such as Napoleon might be supposed to expect from his minister in regard to a violent outrage on the French flag. At the White House on New Year's day, 1812, the French minister renewed his complaints, and the President lost patience.

"The President," wrote Serurier,[1] "answered me with vivacity, that doubtless such indignities were subject for much regret; but it was not less distressing to learn what was passing every day in the Baltic and on the routes from America to England, where some American ships were burned, while others were captured and taken into European ports under French influence and condemned; that such proceedings were in his eyes hostilities as pronounced as were those of England, against whom the Republic was at that moment taking up arms. . . . Mr. Madison ended by telling me that he wished always to flatter himself that Mr. Barlow would send immediate explanation of these strange measures, and notice that they had ceased; but that for the moment, very certainly, matters could not be in a worse situation."

Disconcerted by this sharp rebuff from the President, Serurier went to Monroe, who was usually good-humored when Madison was irritable, and irritable when Madison became mild. This process of alternate coaxing and scolding seemed to affect Serurier more than it affected his master. Monroe

[1] Serurier to Maret, Jan. 2, 1812; Archives des Aff. Étr. MSS.

made no reproaches, but defended the President's position by an argument which the Republican party did not use in public : —

" He urged that the captures of these ships, though perhaps inconsiderable in themselves, had the unfortunate effect of giving arms to the English party, which obstinately maintains that the repeal of the Berlin and Milan Decrees has not taken place ; ' that repeal,' he added, ' on which nevertheless the whole actual system of the Administration is founded, and which, if it be not really absolute, would render the war we are undertaking with England very imprudent and without reasonable object.' "

This admission, although made in private, seemed humiliating enough ; but as weeks passed, Monroe's complaints became stronger.   March 2 Serurier reported him as avowing that he considered Barlow's mission fruitless ; [1] —

" After delays that have lasted three months beyond what we feared, we have as yet received only projects of arrangements, but nothing finished that we can publish. . . . You are witness to our embarrassment.   Our position is painful.   We will treat with England on no other ground than that of withdrawing the Orders in Council, and nothing promises this withdrawal.   We are then decided for war.   You see us every day making our preparations.   If these meet with obstacles, if they suffer some delay, if Congress seems to grow weak and to hesitate, this slackening is due to the fact that we come to no conclusion with France."

[1] Serurier to Maret, March 2, 1812; Archives des Aff. Étr. MSS.

Ships were still captured on their way to England.
"If your decrees are in fact repealed," asked Monroe,
"why this sequestration?" Serurier strove in vain
to satisfy Monroe that the decrees, though repealed in
principle, might be still enforced in fact. He failed
to calm the secretary or the President, whose temper became worse as he saw more clearly that he
had been overreached by Napoleon, and that his word
as President of the United States had been made a
means of deceiving Congress and the people.

Had the British government at that moment offered the single concession asked of it, no war
could have taken place, unless it were a war with
France; but the British government had not yet re-
covered its reason. Foster came to Washington with
instructions to yield nothing, yet to maintain peace;
to threaten, but still conciliate. This mixture of
policy, half Canning and half Fox, feeble and mischievous as it was, could not be altered by Foster;
his instructions were positive. "Nor can we ever
deem the repeal of the French hostile decrees to be
effectual," wrote Wellesley in April, 1811, "until neutral commerce shall be restored to the condition in
which it stood previously to the commencement of
the French system of commercial warfare." Wellesley hinted that the Decrees of Berlin and Milan were
no longer important; they were in effect superseded
by Napoleon's tariff of prohibitions and prohibitive
duties; and until this system of war was abandoned,
and neutral rights of trade were respected, Great

Britain could not withdraw her blockades. In obedience to these instructions, Foster was obliged to tell
Monroe in July, and again in October, 1811, that even
if the repeal of the decrees were genuine, it would not
satisfy the British government. Not the decrees, but
their principle, roused British retaliation.

When the President in his Annual Message represented Foster as requiring that the United States
should force British produce and manufactures into
France, Foster protested, explained, and remonstrated in vain; he found himself reduced to threats of
commercial retaliation which no one regarded, and
his position became mortifying beyond any in the
experience of his unfortunate predecessors. Compelled to witness constant insults to his country, he
was still ordered to maintain peace. As early as
Dec. 11, 1811, he notified his Government that unless
its system were changed, war was likely to follow.
The suggestions offered by the Federalist congressmen, February 1, could hardly fail to show the British government that at last it must choose between
war and concession. Feb. 26, 1812, Foster wrote
again that war might be declared within a fortnight.
March 9 the revelations of John Henry gave the
minister another anxiety, and called from him another lame disavowal. Yet throughout these trying
months Foster remained on friendly and almost
intimate terms with Monroe, whom he described
as " a very mild, moderate man." [1]

[1] Foster to Wellesley, March 12, 1812; MSS. British Archives.

Matters stood thus till March 21, 1812, when Washington was excited by news that Foster had received recent instructions from his Government, and the crisis of war and peace was at hand. " The anxiety and curiosity of both Houses of Congress," reported Foster, April 1,[1] " to know the real nature of the despatches was so great that some of the members on committees told me they could not get the common routine of business at all attended to. The Department of State was crowded with indi· viduals endeavoring to obtain information from Mr. Monroe, while I was questioned by all those with whom I happened to be acquainted." A report spread through Washington that the Orders in Council were repealed, and that an immediate accommodation of all differences between England and the United States might be expected.

Foster would have been glad to find his new instructions composed in such a sense; but he hardly expected to find them so positive as they were in an opposite spirit. Lord Wellesley's despatch of Jan. 28, 1812,[2] which may be said to have decided the declaration of war, was afterward published, and need not be quoted in detail. He remonstrated against the arming of merchant vessels, and ordered Foster to speak earnestly on the subject " for the purpose of preventing a state of affairs which might probably lead to acts of force." The pretended

[1] Foster to Wellesley, April 1, 1812; MSS. British Archives.
[2] Papers communicated to Parliament in 1813, p. 314.

revocation of the French Decrees, said Lord Wellesley, was in fact a fresh enactment of them, while
the measures of America tended to occasion such
acts of violence as might " produce the calamity
of war between the two countries." This usual for-
mula, by which diplomacy announced an expected
rupture, was reinforced by secret instructions warning Foster cautiously to " avoid employing any suggestions of compromise to the American government
which might induce them to doubt the sincerity or
firmness of his Majesty's government in their determination, already announced, of maintaining stead-
fastly the system of defence adopted by them until
the enemy shall relinquish his unwarrantable mode
of attack upon our interests through the violation
of neutral rights."

Foster regarded this order as a rebuke, for he had
talked freely, both to his own Government and in
Washington, of the possibility that the Orders in
Council might be withdrawn. The warning gave
him a manner more formal than usual when he
went, March 21, to assure Monroe that the Prince
Regent would never give way. Monroe listened with
great attention; " then merely said, with however
considerable mildness of tone, that he had hoped
his conversations with me at the early part of the
session would have produced a different result."
Foster left him without further discussion, and announced everywhere in public that, " far from being
awed and alarmed at the threatening attitude and

language " of Congress, his Government would maintain its system unimpaired.[1]

The President looked upon this declaration as final. Already every preparation had been made to meet it. Only a fortnight before, the papers of John Henry had been sent to Congress, and the halls of Congress, as well as the columns of every Republican newspaper in the country, were filled with denunciations of England's conduct, while the President prepared a message recommending an embargo for sixty days, — a measure preliminary to the declaration of war, — when March 23, two days after Foster's interview, news arrived that a French squadron, under open orders, had begun to burn and sink American commerce on the ocean. The American brig "Thames" reached New York March 9, and her captain, Samuel Chew, deposed before a magistrate that February 2, in the middle of the Atlantic, his brig on the return voyage from Portugal was seized by a French squadron which had sailed from Nantes early in January, and which had already seized and burned the American ship "Asia" and the brig "Gershom." The French commodore declared that he had orders to burn all American vessels sailing to or from an enemy's port. The American newspapers were soon deluged with affidavits to the same effect from the captains and seamen of vessels burned by these French frigates, and the news, arriving in Washington at a moment

[1] Foster to Wellesley, April 1, 1812; MSS. British Archives.

when the Federalists were most eager to retaliate the insult of the Henry letters, caused extreme sensation. In face of these piratical acts no one longer pretended that the French Decrees were repealed. Republicans were angrier than Federalists. Madison and Monroe were angriest of all. Serurier was in despair. "I am just from Mr. Monroe's office," he wrote March 23 ;[1] "I have never yet seen him more agitated, more discomposed. He addressed me abruptly : ' Well, sir, it is then decided that we are to receive nothing but outrages from France! And at what a moment too! At the very instant when we were going to war with her enemies.'" When the French minister tried to check his vehemence of reproach, Monroe broke out again : —

" Remember where we were two days ago. You know what warlike measures have been taken for three months past; adopted slowly, they have been progressively followed up. We have made use of Henry's documents as a last means of exciting (*pour achever d'exalter*) the nation and Congress ; you have seen by all the use we have made of them whither we were aiming ; within a week we were going to propose the embargo, and the declaration of war was the immediate consequence of it. A ship has arrived from London, bringing us despatches to February 5, which contain nothing offering a hope of repeal of the orders ; this was all that was needed to carry the declaration of war, which would have passed almost unanimously. It is at such a moment that your frigates

[1] Serurier to Maret, March 23, 1812; Archives des Aff. Étr. MSS.

come and burn our ships, destroy all our work, and put the Administration in the falsest and most terrible position in which a government can find itself placed."

For the hundredth time Monroe repeated the old story that the repeal of the French Decrees was the foundation of the whole American system; "that should the Executive now propose the embargo or the declaration of war, the whole Federal party — reinforced by the Clinton party, the Smith party, and the discontented Republicans — would rise in mass and demand why we persist in making war on England for maintaining her Orders in Council when we have proofs so recent and terrible that the French Decrees are not withdrawn." He added that if the question were put at such a moment, he did not doubt that the Government would lose its majority.

Foster also attempted to interfere in this complicated quarrel: —

" I took an occasion to wait on Mr. Monroe," wrote Foster April 1, " to hear what he would say relative to this outrage. He seemed much struck with the enormity of it, and . . . admitted that there were some circumstances in this particular instance of peculiar violence, and calling for the highest expressions of resentment on the part of this government. He told me that M. Serurier in an interview he had with him on the subject stated his disbelief in the fact."

Foster wrote an official note to Monroe, using the recent French outrages as new ground for demanding to see the instrument by which the decrees were said to be repealed.

Serurier himself was little pleased with the Emperor's conduct, and expressed his annoyance frankly to his Government ; but he consoled himself with the conviction that President Madison could no longer recede, even if serious in wishing to do so. Congress was equally helpless. Nothing could exceed the anger of congressmen with France. As Macon wrote to Nicholson, March 24,[1] after Captain Chew's deposition had been read in the House, " the Devil himself could not tell which government, England or France, is the most wicked." The cry for a double war with France as well as with England became strong enough to create uneasiness ; and although such a triangular war might be a military mistake, no one could explain the reasoning which led to a declaration of war with England, on the grounds selected by Madison, without a simultaneous declaration against France. The responsibility Madison had incurred would have broken the courage of any man less pertinacious. With difficulty could the best Republican conceive how the issue with England could have been worse managed.

At this moment, according to a Federalist legend, Madison was believed to hesitate, and Clay and Grundy coerced him into the recommendation of war by threats of opposing his renomination for the Presidency.[2] In reality, some of the moderate Republicans urged him to send a special mission to

---

[1] Macon to Nicholson, March 24, 1812; Nicholson MSS.

[2] Statesman's Manual, ii. 444, *note*.

England as a last chance of peace.[1] Perhaps Clay and Grundy opposed this suggestion with the warmth ascribed to them, but certainly no sign of hesitation could be detected in Madison's conduct between the meeting of Congress in November and the declaration of war in June.[2] Whatever were his private feelings, he acted in constant agreement with the majority of his party, and at most asked only time for some slight armaments. As to the unprepared state of the country, he said that he did not feel himself bound to take more than his share of the responsibility.[3] Even under the exasperation caused by the conduct of France, he waited only for his party to recover composure. March 31 Monroe held a conference with the House Committee of Foreign Relations, and told them that the President thought war should be declared before Congress adjourned, and that he would send an Embargo Message if he could be assured it would be agreeable to the House.[4] On the same day Foster called at the State Department for an answer to the note in which he had just asked for proof that the French Decrees were repealed. Monroe made him a reply of which Foster seemed hardly to appreciate the gravity.[5]

[1] Adams's Gallatin, pp. 457–459.

[2] Speech of John Smilie, April 1, 1812; Annals of Congress, p. 1592. Monroe to Colonel Taylor, June 13, 1812; Monroe MSS.

[3] Speech of John Randolph, April 1, 1812; Annals of Congress, p. 1593.

[4] Speech of John Randolph, April 1, 1812; Annals of Congress, p. 1593.

[5] Foster to Wellesley, April 1, 1812; MSS. British Archives.

" He told me, a good deal to my disappointment I confess, that the President did not think it would lead to any utility to order an answer to be written to either of my last notes ; that he could not now entertain the question as to whether the French Decrees were repealed, having already been convinced and declared that they were so. He said that the case of the two American ships which were burned could not be said to come under the Berlin and Milan Decrees, however objectionable the act was to this Government ; that the declaration of the French commodore of his having orders to burn all ships bound to or from an enemy's port was given only verbally, and might not have been well understood by the American captain, who did not very well understand French ; while the declaration in writing only alluded to ships bound to or from Lisbon and Cadiz."

Nothing could be more humiliating to Monroe than the resort to subterfuge like this ; but the President left no outlet of escape. The Committee of Foreign Relations decided in favor of an embargo ; and April 1, the day after this interview, Madison sent to Congress a secret Message, which was read with closed doors : —

" Considering it as expedient, under existing circumstances and prospects, that a general embargo be laid on all vessels now in port or hereafter arriving for the period of sixty days, I recommend the immediate passage of a law to that effect."

CHAPTER X.

WHEN news of this decisive step became public, the British minister hastened to Monroe for explanations.[1] Monroe " deprecated its being considered as a war measure. He even seemed to affect to consider it as an impartial measure toward the two belligerents, and as thereby complying with one of our demands ; namely, putting them on an equality. . . . He used an expression which I had some difficulty in comprehending, — that it was the wish of the Government to keep their policy in their own hands." In truth Monroe seemed, to the last, inclined to leave open a door by which the anger of America might, in case of reconciliation with England, be diverted against France. Madison had no such delusion. Foster went to the President, and repeated to him Monroe's remark that the embargo was not a war measure.[2] " Oh, no!" said Madison, " embargo is not war ;" but he added that in his opinion the United States would be amply justified in war, whatever might be its expediency, for Great Britain was actually waging

[1] Foster to Wellesley, April 2, 1812 ; Papers, 1813, p. 564.
[2] Foster to Wellesley, April 3, 1812 ; MSS. British Archives.

war on them, and within a month had captured eighteen ships of the estimated value of fifteen hundred thousand dollars. He said he should be glad still to receive any propositions England might have to make, and that Congress would be in session at the period fixed for terminating the embargo. Neither Madison nor Monroe could properly say more to the British minister, for they could not undertake to forestall the action of Congress ; but the rumor that France might be included in the declaration of war as in the embargo, made the French minister uneasy, and he too asked explanation. To him the secretary talked more plainly.[1]

" Mr. Monroe answered me," wrote Serurier April 9, " that the embargo had been adopted in view of stopping the losses of commerce, and of preparing for the imminent war with England; he protested to me his perfect conviction that war was inevitable if the news expected from France answered to the hopes they had formed. He gave me his word of honor that in the secret deliberations of Congress no measure had been taken against France. He admitted that in fact the affair of the frigates had produced a very deep impression on that body; that it had, even in Republican eyes, seemed manifest proof that the Imperial Decrees were not repealed, and that this unfortunate accident had shaken (*ébranlé*) the whole base of the Administration system ; that the Executive, by inclination as much as by system, had always wished to believe in

[1] Serurier to Maret, April 9, 1812 ; Archives des Aff. Étr. MSS.

this repeal, without which it was impossible to make issue (*engager la querelle*) with England; that its interest in this respect was perfectly in accord with that of France, but that he had found it wholly impossible to justify the inconceivable conduct of the commander of the frigates. . . . Mr. Monroe insisted here on his former declarations, that if the Administration was abandoned by France it would infallibly succumb, or would be obliged to propose war against both Powers, which would be against its interests as much as against its inclination."

The Embargo Message surprised no one. The Committee of Foreign Relations made no secret of its decision. Calhoun warned Josiah Quincy and other representatives of commercial cities; and on the afternoon of March 31 these members sent an express, giving notice to their constituents that the embargo would be proposed on the following day. Every ship-owner on the seaboard and every merchant in the great cities hurried ships and merchandise to sea, showing that they feared war less than they feared embargo, at the moment when Congress, April 1, went into secret session to discuss the measure intended to protect ship-owners and merchants by keeping their property at home. Porter introduced the bill laying an embargo for sixty days;[1] Grundy declared it to be intended as a measure leading directly to war; Henry Clay made a vehement speech approving the measure on that ground. On the other side

[1] Supplemental Journal, April 1, 1812; Annals of Congress, 1811–1812, p. 1588.

Randolph declared war to be impossible; the President dared not be guilty of treason so gross and unparalleled as that of plunging an unprepared nation into such a conflict. Randolph even read memoranda of Monroe's remarks to the Committee of Foreign Relations : " The embargo would leave the policy as respected France, and indeed of both countries, in our hands ; " and from this he tried to convince the House that the embargo was not honestly intended as a war measure. The debate ran till evening, when by a vote of sixty-six to forty the previous question was ordered. Without listening to the minority the House then hurried the bill through all its stages, and at nine o'clock passed it by a vote of seventy to forty-one.

The majority numbered less than half the members. In 1807 the House imposed the embargo by a vote of eighty-two to forty-four, yet the country failed to support it. The experience of 1807 boded ill for that of 1812. In the Senate the outlook was worse. The motion to extend the embargo from sixty to ninety days was adopted without opposition, changing the character of the bill at a single stroke from a strong war measure into a weak measure of negotiation ; but even in this weaker form it received only twenty votes against thirteen in opposition. The President could not depend on a bare majority in the Senate. The New England Democrats shrank from the embargo even more than from war. Giles and Samuel Smith stood in open opposition. The

Clintons had become candidates of every discontented faction in the country. Had the vote in the Senate been counted by States, only six would have been thrown for the embargo, and of these only Pennsylvania from the North. In face of such distraction, war with England seemed worse than a gambler's risk.

Madison, watching with that apparent neutrality which irritated both his friends and his enemies, reported to Jefferson the progress of events.[1] He was not pleased with the Senate's treatment of his recommendations, or with " that invariable opposition, open with some and covert with others, which has perplexed and impeded the whole course of our public measures." He explained the motives of senators in extending the embargo from sixty to ninety days. Some wished to make it a peace measure, some to postpone war, some to allow time for the return of their constituents' ships; some intended it as a ruse against the enemy. For his own part he had regarded a short embargo as a rational and provident measure, which would be relished by the greater part of the nation; but he looked upon it as a step to immediate war, and he waited only for the Senate to make the declaration.

The President asked too much. Congress seemed exhausted by the efforts it had made, and the country showed signs of greater exhaustion before having made any efforts at all. The complaints against

[1] Madison to Jefferson, April 24, 1812; Writings, ii. 532.

France, against the non-importation, against the embargo, and against the proposed war were bitter and
general.   April 6 Massachusetts held the usual State
election.   Gerry was again the Republican candidate
for governor, and the Federalists had little hope of
defeating him; but the Republican Administration
had proved so unpopular, the famous Gerrymander
by which the State had been divided into districts
in party interests had so irritated the conservative
feeling, that the new embargo and the expected war
were hardly needed to throw the State again into
opposition.   Not even the revelations of John Henry
restored the balance.   More than one hundred and
four thousand votes were cast, and a majority of
about twelve hundred appeared on the Federalist side.
Caleb Strong became governor once more at a moment when the change paralyzed national authority
in New England ; and meanwhile throughout the
country the enlistments for the new army produced
barely one thousand men.

The month of April passed without legislation that
could strengthen Government, except an Act, approved April 10, authorizing the President to call out
one hundred thousand militia for six months' service.
Congress showed so strong a wish to adjourn that the
Administration was obliged to exert its whole influence to prevent the House from imitating the
Senate, which by a vote of sixteen to fifteen adopted
a Resolution for a recess until June 8.   Secretary
Gallatin ventured to bring no tax bills before Con-

gress; Lowndes and Cheves made a vigorous effort
to suspend the Non-importation Act; and a general
belief prevailed that the Government wished to admit
English goods in order to evade, by increase of
customs-revenue, the necessity of taxation.

Serurier, much discomposed by these signs of vacillation, busied himself in the matter, declaring to his
friends in Congress that he should look on any suspension of the Non-importation Act as a formal in-
fraction of the compact with France. When he
pressed Monroe with remonstrances,[1] Monroe told
him, April 22, that the President and Cabinet had
positively and unanimously declared to the Committee
of Foreign Relations against the suspension, because
it would seem to indicate indecision and inconse-
quence in their foreign policy; that this remonstrance
had caused the plan to be given up, but that the
Administration might still be obliged to consent to
a short adjournment, so great was the wish of members to look after their private affairs. In fact,
Congress showed no other wish than to escape, and
leave the President to struggle with his difficulties
alone.

If the war party hesitated in its allegiance to
Madison, its doubts regarded his abilities rather than
his zeal. Whatever might be Madison's genius, no
one supposed it to be that of administration. His
health was delicate; he looked worn and feeble; for

[1] Serurier to Maret, April 24, 1812; Archives des Aff. Étr.
MSS.

many years he had shown none of the energy of
youth ; he was likely to succumb under the burden
of war ; and, worst of all, he showed no consciousness of needing support.   The party was unanimous
in believing Secretary Eustis unequal to his post, but
Madison made no sign of removing him.   So general
was the impression of Eustis's incapacity that when,
April 24, the President sent to Congress a message
asking for two Assistant Secretaries of War to aid
in conducting the Department, the request was commonly regarded as an evasion of the public demand
for a new Secretary of War, and as such was unfavor-
ably received.   In the House, where the subject was
openly discussed, Randolph defended Eustis in the
style of which he was master : " I will say this much
of the Secretary of War, — that I do verily believe,
and I have grounds to believe it to be the opinion
of a majority of this House, that he is at least as
competent to the exercise of his duties as his colleague who presides over the Marine."   The Senate,
wishing perhaps· to force the President into recon-
structing his Cabinet, laid aside the bill creating
two Assistant Secretaries of War ; and with this action, May 6, ended the last chance of efficiency in
that Department.

While Eustis ransacked the country for generals,
colonels, and the whole staff of officers, as well as the
clothing, arms, and blankets for an army of twenty-
five thousand men who could not be found, Gallatin
labored to provide means for meeting the first year's

expenses. Having no longer the Bank to help him, he dealt separately with the State Banks through whose agency private subscriptions were to be received. The subscriptions were to be opened on the first and second days of May. The Republican newspapers, led by the "National Intelligencer,"[1] expressed the hope and the expectation that twice the amount of the loan would be instantly subscribed. Their disappointment was very great. Federalist New England refused to subscribe at all; and as the Federalists controlled most of the capital in the country, the effect of their abstention was alarming. In all New England not one million dollars were obtained. New York and Philadelphia took each about one and a half million. Baltimore and Washington took about as much more. The whole Southern country, from the Potomac to Charleston, subscribed seven hundred thousand dollars. Of the entire loan, amounting to eleven million dollars, a little more than six millions were taken; and considering the terms, the result was not surprising. At a time when the old six-per-cent loans, with ten or twelve years to run, stood barely at par, any new six-per-cent loan to a large amount, with a vast war in prospect, could hardly be taken at the same rate.

The Federalists, delighted with this failure, said, with some show of reason, that if the Southern States wanted the war they ought to supply the means, and had no right to expect that men who thought the

[1] National Intelligencer, April 23, 1812.

war unjust and unnecessary should speculate to make money from it. Gallatin put a good face on his failure, and proposed soon to reopen subscriptions; but the disappointment was real.

"Whatever the result may be," wrote Serurier to his Government,[1] "they had counted on more national energy on the opening of a first loan for a war so just. This cooling of the national pulse, the resistance which the Northern States seem once more willing to offer the Administration, the defection it meets every day in Congress, — all this, joined to its irritation at our measures which make its own system unpopular, adds to its embarrassment and hesitation."

Gallatin made no complaints, but he knew only too well what lay before him. No resource remained except treasury notes bearing interest. Neither Gallatin, nor any other party leader, cared to suggest legal-tender notes, which were supposed to be not only an admission of national bankruptcy at the start, but also forbidden by the spirit of the Constitution; yet the government could hardly fail to experience the same form of bankruptcy in a less convenient shape. After the destruction of the United States Bank, a banking mania seized the public. Everywhere new banks were organized or planned, until the legislature of New York, no longer contented with small corporations controlling capital of one or two hundred thousand dollars, prepared to incorporate the old Bank of the United States under a new form,

[1] Serurier to Maret, May 4, 1812; Archives des Aff. Étr. MSS.

with a capital of six millions. Governor Tompkins stopped the project by proroguing the legislature ; but his message gave the astonishing reason that the legislature was in danger of yielding to bribery.[1] The majority protested against the charge, and denounced it as a breach of privilege; but whether it was well or ill founded, the influence of the banking mania on State legislatures could not fail to be corrupting. The evil, inherent in the origin of the new banks, was aggravated by their management. Competition and want of experience or of supervision, inevitably led to over-issue, inflation of credit, suspension of specie payments, and paper-money of the worst character. Between a debased currency of private corporations and a debased currency of government paper, the former was the most expensive and the least convenient; yet it was the only support on which the Treasury could depend.

Early in May a double election took place, which gave more cause of alarm. New York chose a Federalist Assembly, and Massachusetts chose a General Court more strongly Federalist than any one had ventured to expect. In the face of such a revolution in two of the greatest and richest States in the Union, President, Cabinet, and legislators had reason to hesitate; they had even reason to fear that the existence of the Union might hang on their decision. They knew the Executive Department to be incompetent for war; they had before their eyes the spectacle

[1] Message of March 27, 1812 ; Niles, ii. 39.

of an incompetent Congress; and they saw the people
declaring, as emphatically as their democratic forms
of government permitted, their unwillingness to undertake the burden. Even bold men might pause
before a situation so desperate.

Thus the month of May passed, full of discouragement. Congress did not adjourn, but the members
went home on leave, with the understanding that
no further action should be taken until June. At
home they found chaos. Under the coercion of embargo, commerce ceased. Men would do little but
talk politics, and very few professed themselves satisfied with the condition into which their affairs had
been brought. The press cried for war or for peace,
according to its fancy; but although each of the old
parties could readily prove the other's course to be
absurd, unpatriotic, and ruinous, the war men, who
were in truth a new party, powerless to restore order
by legitimate methods, shut their ears to the outcry, and waited until actual war should enforce a
discipline never to be imposed in peace.

The experiment of thrusting the country into war
to inflame it, as crude ore might be thrown into a
furnace, was avowed by the party leaders, from President Madison downward, and was in truth the only
excuse for a course otherwise resembling an attempt
at suicide. Many nations have gone to war in pure
gayety of heart; but perhaps the United States were
first to force themselves into a war they dreaded, in
the hope that the war itself might create the spirit

they lacked. One of the liveliest and most instructive discussions of the session, May 6, threw light upon the scheme by which the youthful nation was to reverse the process of Medea, and pass through the caldron of war in confidence of gaining the vigor of age. Mr. Bleecker of New York, in offering petitions for the repeal of the embargo, argued that the embargo could not be honestly intended. "Where are your armies; your navy? Have you money? No, sir! Rely upon it, there will be, there can be, no war — active, offensive war — within sixty days." War would be little short of treason; would bring shame, disgrace, defeat; and meanwhile the embargo alienated the people of States which must necessarily bear much of the burden. These arguments were supported by John Randolph.

"I am myself," he said, "in a situation similar to what would have been that of one of the unfortunate people of Caracas, if preadvised of the danger which overhung his country. I know that we are on the brink of some dreadful scourge, some great desolation, some awful visitation from that Power whom, I am afraid, we have as yet in our national capacity taken no pains to conciliate. . . . Go to war without money, without men, without a navy! Go to war when we have not the courage, while your lips utter war, to lay war taxes! when your whole courage is exhibited in passing Resolutions! The people will not believe it!"

Richard M. Johnson undertook first to meet these criticisms. Johnson possessed courage and abilities, but he had not, more than other Kentuckians of his day, the caution convenient in the face of opponents. He met by threats the opposition he would not answer. "It was a Tory opposition, in the cities and seaports; and an opposition which would not be quite so bold and powerful in a time of war; and he trusted in that Heaven to which the gentleman from Virginia had appealed, that sixty days would not elapse before all the traitorous combinations and opposition to the laws and the acts of the general government would in a great measure cease, or change, and moderate their tone." Calhoun, who followed Johnson, expressed the same idea in less offensive form, and added opinions of his own which showed the mental condition in which the young war leaders exulted: "So far from being unprepared, sir, I believe that in four weeks from the time that a declaration of war is heard on our frontiers the whole of Upper and a part of Lower Canada will be in our possession."

Grundy, following in the debate, used neither threats like Johnson, nor prophecies like Calhoun; but his argument was not more convincing. "It is only while the public mind is held in suspense," he said; "it is only while there is doubt as to what will be the result of our deliberations, — it is only while we linger in this Hall that any manifestations of uneasiness will show themselves. Whenever war is declared, the people will put forth their strength to support their rights." He went so far as to add that when war should be once begun, the distinction between Federalists and Republicans would cease. Finally, Wright of Maryland, whose words fortunately carried little weight, concluded the debate by saying that if signs of treason and civil war should discover themselves in any part of the American empire, he had no doubt the evil would soon be radically cured by hemp and confiscation ; and his own exertions should not be spared to employ the remedy.

The President himself had no other plan than to " throw forward the flag of the country, sure that the people would press onward and defend it." [1] The example he had himself given to the people in 1798 tended to cast doubt on the correctness of his judgment,[2] but his candidacy for the Presidency also shook confidence in his good faith. So deep was the conviction of his dislike for the policy he supported as to lead the British minister, May 3, to inform his Government that the jealousies between the younger and older members of Congress threatened an open schism, in which the President was supposed likely to be involved.[3]

" The reason why there has been no nomination made in caucus yet, by the Democratic members, of Mr. Madison as candidate for the Presidency is, as I am assured in confidence, because the war party have suspected him not to have been serious in his late hostile

[1] Adams's Gallatin, p. 460, *note.*
[2] Ante, vol. i. pp. 139, 142.
[3] Foster to Castlereagh, May 3, 1812; MSS. British Archives.

measures, and wish previously to ascertain his real sentiments. I have been endeavoring to put the Federalists
upon insinuating that they will support him, if he will
agree to give up the advocates for war."

This intrigue was stopped by the positive refusal
of the eastern Federalists to support Madison on
any terms, — they preferred coalition with DeWitt
Clinton and the Republican malcontents ; but the
time had come when some nomination must be made,
and when it arrived, all serious thought of an open
Republican schism at Washington vanished. The
usual Congressional caucus was called May 18, and
was attended by eighty-three members and senators,
who unanimously renominated Madison. Seventeen
senators, just one half the Senate, and sixty-six
members, almost one half the House, joined in the
nomination ; but only three New York members took
part, and neither Giles nor Samuel Smith was present, — they had ceased to act with the Republican
party. Only a few weeks before, Vice-President Clinton had died in office, and whatever respect the Administration may have felt for his great name and
Revolutionary services, the party was relieved at the
prospect of placing in the chair of the Senate some
man upon whom it could better depend. The caucus
named John Langdon of New Hampshire ; and when
he declined, Elbridge Gerry, the defeated Governor
of Massachusetts, was selected as candidate for the
Vice-presidency.

So little cordiality was felt for President Madison

by his party that only the want of a strong rival reconciled a majority to the choice; but although Clay, Crawford, and Calhoun accepted the necessity, the State of New York flatly rebelled. At Albany, when the news arrived that the Washington caucus had named Madison for the Presidency, the Republican members of the State legislature called for May 29 a caucus of their own. Their whole number was ninety-five; of these, all but four attended, and eighty-seven voted that it was expedient to name a candidate for the Presidency. Ninety members then voted to support DeWitt Clinton against Madison, and Clinton formally accepted the nomination. This unusual unanimity among the New York Republicans raised the movement somewhat above the level of ordinary New York politics, and pointed to a growing jealousy of Virginia, which threatened to end in revival of the old alliance between New York and New England. Even in quiet times this prospect would have been alarming; in face of war, it threatened to be fatal.

During the entire month of May Congress passed, with only one exception, no Act for war purposes. While the absent members attended to their private affairs, Government waited for the last despatches from abroad. The sloop-of-war "Hornet," after long delay, arrived at New York, May 19, and three days afterward the despatches reached Washington. Once more, but for the last time, the town roused itself to learn what hope of peace they contained.

As far as concerned Great Britain, the news would at any previous time have checked hostile action, for it showed that the British government had taken alarm, and that for the first time a real change of policy was possible; but this news came from un-official sources, and could not be laid before Con-gress. Officially, the British government still stoutly maintained that it could not yield. Lord Wellesley had given place to Lord Castlereagh. In a very long despatch,[1] dated April 10, the new Foreign Minister pleaded earnestly that England could not submit herself to the mercy of France. The argu-ment of Lord Castlereagh rested on an official report made by the Duc de Bassano to the Emperor, March 10, in which Napoleon reasserted his rules regarding neutrals in language quite as strong as that of his decrees, and reasserted the validity of those decrees, without exception, in regard to every neutral that did not recognize their provisions. Certainly, no proof could be imagined competent to show the con-tinued existence of the decrees if Bassano's report failed to do so; and Castlereagh, with some reason, relied on this evidence to convince not so much the American government as the American people that a deception had been practised, and that England could not act as America required without submit-ting to Napoleon's principles as well as to his arms.

Embarrassing as this despatch was to President Madison, it was not all, or the worst; but Serurier

[1] Papers presented to Parliament, 1813, p. 475.

himself described the other annoyance in terms as lively as his feelings : [1] —

" The ' Hornet' has at last arrived. On the rumor of this news, the avenues of the State Department were thronged by a crowd of members of both Houses of Congress, as well as by strangers and citizens, impatient to know what this long-expected vessel had brought. Soon it was learned that the ' Hornet' had brought nothing favorable, and that Mr. Barlow had as yet concluded nothing with your Excellency. On this news, the furious declamations of the Federalists, of the commercial interests, and of the numerous friends of England were redoubled ; the Republicans, deceived in their hopes, joined in the outcry, and for three days nothing was heard but a general cry for war against France and England at once. . . . I met Mr. Monroe at the Speaker's house ; he came to me with an air of affliction and discouragement ; addressed me with his old reproach that decidedly we abandoned the Administration, and that he did not know henceforward how they could extricate themselves from the difficult position into which their confidence in our friendship had drawn them."

Serurier had no reason for uneasiness on his own account. The President and his party could not go backward in their path ; yet no enemy could have devised a worse issue than that on which the President had placed the intended war with England. Every Act of Congress and every official

[1] Serurier to Maret, May 27, 1812; Archives des Aff. Étr. MSS.

expression of Madison's policy had been founded on the withdrawal of the French Decrees as they affected American commerce. This withdrawal could no longer be maintained, and Madison merely shook confidence in his own good faith by asserting it; yet he could do nothing else. "It is understood," he wrote to Jefferson at this crisis,[1] "that the Berlin and Milan Decrees are not in force against the United States, and no contravention of them can be established against her. On the contrary, positive cases rebut the allegation." Yet he said that "the business has become more than ever puzzling;" he was withheld only by political and military expediency from favoring war with France. He wrote to Joel Barlow,[2] after full knowledge of Napoleon's conduct, that "in the event of a pacification with Great Britain the full tide of indignation with which the public mind here is boiling will be directed against France, if not obviated by a due reparation of her wrongs; war will be called for by the nation almost *unâ voce*."

A position so inconsistent with itself could not be understood by the people. Every one knew that if the decrees were not avowedly enforced in France against the United States, they were relaxed only because Madison had submitted to their previous enforcement, and had, in Napoleon's opinion, recognized their legality. The Republican press, which

[1] Madison to Jefferson, May 25, 1812 ; Works ii. 535.
[2] Madison to Barlow, Aug. 11, 1812; Works ii. 540.

supported Madison most energetically, made no concealment of its active sympathies with Napoleon, even in Spain. What wonder if large numbers of good citizens who believed Napoleon to be anti-Christ should be disposed to resist, even to the verge of treason, the attempt to use their lives and fortunes in a service they regarded with horror!

CHAPTER XI.

CASTLEREAGH'S long note of April 10, communicated by Foster to the American government, contained a paragraph defining the British doctrine of retaliation : —

"What Great Britain always avowed was her readiness to rescind her orders as soon as France rescinded, absolutely and unconditionally, her decrees. She never engaged to repeal those orders as affecting America alone, leaving them in force against other States, upon condition that France would except, singly and especially, America from the operation of her decrees. She could not do so without the grossest injustice to her allies, as well as all other neutral nations ; much less could she do so upon the supposition that the special exception in favor of America was to be expressly granted by France, as it has been hitherto tacitly accepted by America, upon conditions utterly subversive of the most important and indisputable maritime rights of the British empire."

Long afterward Madison objected [1] to the common accounts of the war, that they brought too little into view "the more immediate impulse to it" given

[1] Madison to Henry Wheaton, Feb. 26, 1827 ; Works iii. 553.

by this formal notice communicated to him officially by Foster, which left .no choice between war and degradation. He regarded this notice as making further discussion impossible. His idea was perhaps too strongly asserted, for Foster offered, under other instructions, a new and important concession, — that England should give up altogether her system of licensing trade with the Continent, and in its place should enforce a rigorous blockade; [1] but Madison and Monroe declined listening to any offer that did not admit in principle the right of the United States to trade with every European country. [2] Thus at the last moment the dispute seemed to narrow itself to the single point of belligerent right to blockade a coast.

Acting at once on the theory that Castlereagh's instructions of April 10 gave the last formal notice intended by the British government, President Madison prepared a Message recommending an immediate declaration of war. This Message was sent to Congress June 1; the two Houses instantly went into secret session, and the Message was read. No one could dispute the force of Madison's long recital of British outrages. For five years, the task of finding excuses for peace had been more difficult than that of proving a *casus belli;* but some interest

[1] Castlereagh to Foster, April 10, 1812 ; Papers, etc., 1813, p. 511.

[2] Foster to Castlereagh, June 6, 1812 ; Papers, etc., 1813, p. 577.

still attached to the arrangement and relative weight
of the many American complaints.

Madison, inverting the order of complaints previously alleged, began by charging that British
cruisers had been " in the continued practice of
violating the American flag on the great highway
of nations, and of seizing and carrying off persons
sailing under it." The charge was amply proved,
was not denied, and warranted war; but this was
the first time that the Government had alleged impressment as its chief grievance, or had announced,
either to England or to America, the intention to
fight for redress, — and England might fairly complain that she had received no notice of intended war
on such ground. The second complaint alleged that
British cruisers also violated the peace of the coasts,
and harassed entering and departing commerce.
This charge was equally true and equally warranted
war, but it was open to the same comment as that
made upon the first. The third grievance on which
the President had hitherto founded his coercive
measures consisted in " pretended blockades, without the presence of an adequate force and sometimes
without the practicability of applying one," by means
of which American commerce had been plundered
on every sea, — a practice which had come to its
highest possible development in the fourth grievance, the sweeping system of blockades known as
the Orders in Council. These four main heads of
complaint covered numbers of irritating consequen-

ces, but no other separate charge was alleged, beyond
an insinuation that the hostile spirit of the Indians
was connected with their neighborhood to Canada.

On the four great grievances thus defined every
American could in theory agree; but these admitted
wrongs had hitherto been endured as a matter of
expediency, rather than resort to war; and the opposition still stood on the ground that had been so
obstinately held by Jefferson, — that war, however
just, was inexpedient. If union in the war policy
was to be hoped, the President must rather prove
its expediency than its justice. Even from his own
point of view, two doubts of expediency required
fresh attention. For the first time, England showed
distinct signs of giving way; while on the other hand
France showed only the monomania of insisting on
her decrees, even to the point of conquering Russia.
In the face of two such movements, the expediency
of war with England became more than ever doubtful; and if the President wished for harmony, he
must remove these doubts. This he did not attempt,
further than by alluding to the sense of Castlereagh's
late despatch, as yet not in his possession. What
was still more remarkable, he said nothing in regard
to the contract with France, which since November,
1809, he had made the ground for every measure of
compulsion against England. Indeed, not only was
the contract ignored, but if any meaning could be
placed on his allusions to France, the theory of contract seemed at last to be formally abandoned.

" Having presented this view of the relations of the
United States with Great Britain, and of the solemn
alternative growing out of them, I proceed to remark
that the communications last made to Congress on the
subject of our relations with France will have shown
that since the revocation of her decrees, as they violated the neutral rights of the United States, her government has authorized illegal captures by its privateers
and public ships; and that other outrages have been
practised on our vessels and our citizens. It will have
been seen, also, that no indemnity had been provided,
or satisfactorily pledged, for the extensive spoliations
committed under the violent and retrospective orders
of the French government against the property of our
citizens, seized within the jurisdiction of France.   I
abstain at this time from recommending to the consideration of Congress definite measures with respect to
that nation."

The war of 1812 was chiefly remarkable for the
vehemence with which, from beginning to end, it
was resisted and thwarted by a very large number
of citizens who were commonly considered, and who
considered themselves, by no means the least respectable, intelligent, or patriotic part of the nation.
That the war was as just and necessary as any war
ever waged, seemed so evident to Americans of
another generation that only with an effort could
modern readers grasp the reasons for the bitter
opposition of large and respectable communities
which left the government bankrupt, and nearly
severed the Union; but if students of national his-

tory can bear with patience the labor of retaining in mind the threads of negotiation which President Madison so thoroughly tangled before breaking, they can partially enter into the feelings of citizens who held themselves aloof from Madison's war. In June, 1812, the reasons for declaring war on Great Britain, though strong enough, were weaker than they had been in June, 1808, or in January, 1809. In the interval the British government had laid aside the arrogant and defiant tones of Canning's diplomacy; had greatly modified the Orders in Council; had offered further modifications; and had atoned for the "Chesapeake" outrage. In 1807 England would have welcomed a war with the United States; in 1812 she wanted peace, and yielded much to secure it. In 1808 America was almost unanimous, her government still efficient, well supplied with money, and little likely to suffer from war; in 1812 the people were greatly divided, the government had been weakened, and the Treasury was empty. Even Gallatin, who in 1809 had been most decided for war, was believed in 1812 to wish and to think that it might be avoided. Probably four fifths of the American people held the same opinion. Not merely had the situation in every other respect changed for the worse, but the moral convictions of the country were outraged by the assertion of a contract with Napoleon — in which no one believed — as the reason for forcing religious and peaceful citizens into what they regarded as the service of France.

The war Message of June 1 rather strengthened than removed grounds of opposition. The President alleged but one reason for thinking war expedient at that moment rather than at another; but when in after years he insisted that Castlereagh's instructions were the immediate cause which precluded further negotiation, he admitted his own mistake, and presumed that had Congress known what was then passing in England the declaration of war would have been suspended and negotiations renewed.[1] Such a succession of mistakes, admitted one after another almost as soon as they were made, might well give to Madison's conduct the air so often attributed to it, of systematic favor to Napoleon and equally systematic hostility to England.

The House went at once into secret session; the Message was referred to the Committee of Foreign Relations; and two days afterward, June 3, Calhoun brought in a report recommending an immediate appeal to arms. As a history of the causes which led to this result, Calhoun's report was admirable, and its clearness of style and statement forced comparisons not flattering to the President's Message; but as an argument for the immediate necessity of war, the report like the Message contented itself with bare assertions. " The United States must support their character and station among the nations of the earth, or submit to the most shameful degradation."

[1] Madison to Wheaton, Feb. 26, 1827; Madison's Works, iii. 553.

Calhoun's arguments were commonly close in logic, and avoided declamation; but in the actual instance neither he nor his followers seemed confident in the strength of their reasoning.

After the House had listened in secret session, June 3, to the reading of this report, Josiah Quincy moved that the debate should be public. The demand seemed reasonable. That preliminary debates should be secret might be proper, but that war with any Power, and most of all with England, should be declared in secret could not be sound policy, while apart from any question of policy the secrecy contradicted the professions of the party in power. Perhaps no single act, in a hundred years of American history, showed less regard for personal and party consistency than the refusal by the Republicans of 1812 to allow society either rights or privileges in regard to the declaration of war upon England. Quite apart from military advantages to be hoped from secrecy, Henry Clay and his friends were weary of debate and afraid of defeat. Only a few days before, May 29, Clay forced Randolph from the floor by tactics which showed that no more discussion was to be allowed. The secret session gave the Speaker absolute power, and annihilated opposition. By seventy-six votes to forty-six, the House rejected Quincy's motion; and a similar motion by Randolph shared the same fate.

This demand being refused, the minority declined further discussion. They said that any act of theirs

which admitted the validity of what they held to be
a flagrant abuse of power could do no good, and
might create a dangerous precedent. Henceforward
they contented themselves with voting. On the same
day Calhoun presented the bill declaring war against
England, and on the second reading the opposition
swelled to forty-five votes ; while of the Republican
majority, numbering about one hundred and five
members, only seventy-six could be brought to the
test. June 4 the third reading was carried by a vote
of seventy-eight to forty-five, and the same day the bill
passed by a vote of seventy-nine to forty-nine.

Proverbially wars are popular at their beginning ;
commonly, in representative governments, they are
declared by aid of some part of the opposition. In the
case of the War of 1812 the party in power, instead
of gaining strength by the declaration, lost about
one fourth of its votes, and the opposition actually
gained nearly one fifth of the Administration's
strength. In the Senate the loss was still greater.
There too the President's Message was debated in
secret, but the proceedings were very deliberate. A
select committee, with Senator Anderson of Tennessee at its head, took charge of the Message, and
consumed a week in studying it. June 8 the committee reported the House bill with amendments.
June 11 the Senate, by a vote of seventeen to thirteen, returned the bill to the committee for further
amendment. June 12 the committee reported the
amendments as instructed. The Senate discussed

them, was equally divided, and accordingly threw out its own amendments. June 15 the Senate voted the third reading of the House bill by a vote of nineteen to thirteen. June 16, after a strong speech for delay from Senator James A. Bayard, the Senate again adjourned without action; and only June 18, after two weeks of secret discussion, did the bill pass. Nineteen senators voted in its favor; thirteen in opposition. Samuel Smith, Giles, and Leib, the three Republican senators most openly hostile to Madison, voted with the majority. Except Pennsylvania, the entire representation of no Northern State declared itself for the war; except Kentucky, every State south of the Potomac and the Ohio voted for the declaration. Not only was the war to be a party measure, but it was also sectional; while the Republican majority, formerly so large, was reduced to dependence on the factious support of Smith, Giles, and Leib.

The bill with its amendments was at once returned to the House and passed. Without a moment's delay the President signed it, and the same day, June 18, 1812, the war began.

" The President's proclamation was issued yesterday," wrote Richard Rush, the comptroller, to his father, June 20; [1] . . . " he visited in person — a thing never known before — all the offices of the departments of war and the navy, stimulating everything in a manner worthy of a little commander-in-chief, with his little round hat and huge cockade."

[1] Richard Rush to Benjamin Rush, June 20, 1812; Rush MSS.

In resorting to old-fashioned methods of violence, Congress had also to decide whether to retain or to throw away its weapons of peaceful coercion. The Non-importation Act stopped importations from England. If war should be considered as taking the place of non-importation, it would have the curious result of restoring trade with England. Opinions were almost as hotly divided on the question of war with, or war without, non-importation as on the question of war and peace itself; while even this detail of policy was distorted by the too familiar interference of Napoleon, — for the non-importation was a part of his system, and its retention implied alliance with him, while the admission of English merchandise would be considered by him almost an act of war. The non-importation was known to press severely on the industries of England, but it threatened to paralyze America. In the absence of taxation, nothing but the admission of British goods into the United States could so increase the receipts of the Treasury as to supply the government with its necessary resources. Thus, two paths lay open. Congress might admit British goods, and by doing so dispense with internal taxes, relieve the commercial States, and offend France ; or might shut out British goods, disgust the commercial States, double the burden of the war to America, but distress England and please Napoleon.

War having been declared June 18, on June 19 Langdon Cheves introduced, from the Committee of

Ways and Means, a bill partially suspending the Non-importation Act. He supported his motion by a letter from Gallatin, accepting this bill as an alternative to the tax bills. On the same day news arrived of more American vessels burned by French frigates. Chaos seemed beyond control. War with England was about to restore commerce with her; alliance with France was a state of war with her. The war party proposed to depend on peace taxes at the cost of France their ally, in the interests of England their enemy; the peace party called for war taxes to discredit the war; both parties wanted trade with England with whom they were at war; while every one was displeased with the necessity of assisting France, the only ally that America possessed in the world. Serurier went to the Secretary of State to discuss this extraordinary situation, but found Monroe in no happy temper.[1]

" He began by complaining to me of what, for that matter, I knew already, — that a considerable number of new American ships, going to Spain and Portugal and returning, had been very recently burned by our frigates, and that others had been destroyed on the voyage even to England. The Secretary of State on this occasion, and with bitterness, renewed to me his complaints and those of the Government and of Congress, whose discontent he represented as having reached its height. I am, Monseigneur, as weary of hearing these eternal grumblings as of having to trouble you with them; but I

[1] Serurier to Maret, June 13, 1812 ; Archives des Aff. Étr. MSS.

think myself obliged to transmit to you whatever is said
of an official character. Mr. Monroe averred that for
his part, as Secretary of State, since he had never ceased
down to this moment to maintain the repeal of our decrees, he found himself suddenly compromised in the
face of his friends and of the public, and he must admit
he had almost lost the hope of an arrangement with us.
Such were, Monseigneur, his expressions ; after which
he retraced to me the system that the Administration
had never ceased pursuing with constancy and firmness
for eighteen months, and the last act of which had at
length been what I had seen, a formal declaration of war
against England by the republic, — ' at a moment,' he
added, ' when it feels ill-assured of France, and is so ill-
treated by her.' He finished at last by saying to me,
with a sort of political coquetry, that he was among his
friends obliged to admit that they had been too weak
toward France, and that perhaps they had been too quick
in regard to England."

Serurier wrote that the bitterness against France
was really such as would have caused a declaration
of war against her as well as against England, if the
Administration had not stopped the movement in
Congress ; nothing prevented the double war except
the military difficulties in its way. At the moment
when, June 23, the French minister was writing in
these terms to the Duc de Bassano, the House of
Representatives was considering the action he feared.
Cheves had proposed to modify the non-importation,
— the Federalists moved to repeal it altogether ; and
although they were defeated that day in committee,

when Cheves's bill came before the House no less a
champion than Calhoun rose to advocate the reopen-
ing of trade.

Whatever Calhoun in those days did, was boldly
and well done ; but his speech of June 24, 1812,
against commercial restrictions, was perhaps the boldest and the best of his early efforts. Neither great
courage nor much intelligence was needed to support
war, from the moment war became a party measure ;
but an attack on the system of commercial restriction
was a blow at Madison, which belittled Jefferson, and
threw something like contempt on the Republican
party from its beginning twenty years before, down
to the actual moment. How gently Calhoun did this,
and yet how firmly he laid his hands on the rein that
was to guide his party into an opposite path, could be
seen in his short speech.

"The restrictive system, as a mode of resistance," he
said, "and a means of obtaining a redress of our wrongs,
has never been a favorite one with me. I wish not to
censure the motives which dictated it, or to attribute
weakness to those who first resorted to it for a restoration of our rights. . . . I object to the restrictive system, and for the following reasons, — because it does not
suit the genius of our people, or that of our government,
or the geographical character of our country."

With a single gesture, this young statesman of the
new school swept away the statesmanship of Jefferson and Madison, and waved aside the strongest
convictions of his party ; but he did it with such

temperate statement, and with so serious a manner, that although he said in effect little less than had been said for years by Federalists and enemies, he seemed rather to lead than to oppose. " We have had a peace like a war : in the name of heaven let us not have the only thing that is worse, — a war like a peace." That his voice should be at once obeyed was not to be expected ; but so many Republican members followed Calhoun, Cheves, and Lowndes, that the Federalists came within three votes of carrying their point ; and so equally divided was the House that, June 25, when the Federalists returned to the attack and asked for a committee to report a bill repealing the non-importation, the House divided sixty against sixty, and the Speaker's vote alone defeated the motion.

Greatly to the French minister's relief the storm passed over ; but the heroic decision of Congress not only to punish England, but to punish itself by deprivation of everything English, — not only to fight Napoleon's battles, but also to fight them under every disadvantage that Napoleon chose to exact, — could not but increase the vehemence of Northern hatred against the war, as it was certain to increase Southern hatred against taxes. Gallatin knew not what to expect. June 26 he wrote to a friend,[1] —

" We have not money enough to last till January 1 next, and General Smith is using every endeavor to run us aground by opposing everything, — treasury notes,

[1] Adams's Gallatin, p. 466.

double duties, etc. The Senate is so nearly divided, and the division so increased by that on the war question, that we can hardly rely on carrying anything."

Although Gallatin caused the necessary bills for the war taxes to be reported to the House June 26, he had no idea of passing them, and was not surprised when by a vote of seventy-two to forty-six the House postponed them to the next session, Calhoun and Cheves voting with the Federalists against postponement. This chronic helplessness could not last in face of war without stopping government itself; and Congress, with a bad grace, yielded at last to necessity. Even while Gallatin was complaining, the Senate passed the bill for issuing five millions in treasury notes. June 30 it passed the bill doubling the duties on imports. In rapid succession, such other bills as were most needed by Government were put upon their passage; and July 6 the exhausted Congress adjourned, glad to escape its struggle with the novel problems of war.

In American history few sessions of Congress left a deeper mark than that of 1811–12; but in the midst of the war excitement several Acts of high importance almost escaped public notice. As far-reaching as the declaration of war itself was the Act, approved April 8, 1812, declaring the State of Louisiana to be admitted into the Union. Representatives of the Eastern States once more protested against the admission of new territory without consulting the States themselves; but Congress followed up the act by one more open to question. West Florida had remained hitherto in the condition of its military occupation a year before. Congress had then found the problem too hard to solve on any theory of treaty or popular rights; but in the excitement of the war fever Government acted on the new principle that West Florida, which had been seized because it was a part of Louisiana, should be treated as though it were a conquered territory. An Act of Congress, approved April 14, divided the district in halves at the Pearl River, and annexed the western half — against the expressed wishes of its citizens [1] — to the new State of Louisiana; the eastern portion was incorporated in the Mississippi Territory by an Act approved May 14, 1812.

To the territory of West Florida the United States had no right. Their ownership of the country between the Iberville and the Perdido was a usurpation which no other country was bound to regard; indeed, at the moment when Congress subjected the shores of Mobile Bay to the Mississippi Territorial government, Mobile was still garrisoned by a Spanish force and ruled by the Spanish people. The case of West Florida was the more curious, because in after years the United States government, in order to obtain a title good beyond its own borders, accepted the territory as a formal grant from the King of Spain. Ferdinand VII., the grantor and only rightful inter-

[1] Petition of inhabitants; Annals of Congress, 1811–1812, p. 2157.

preter of his own grant,[1] inserted an article into the treaty of 1819 which was intended by him to discredit, and did in fact ignore, the usurpations of the United States: " His Catholic Majesty cedes to the United States, in full property and sovereignty, all the territories which belong to him situated to the eastward of the Mississippi, known by the names of East and West Florida." [2] According to the Acts of Congress, no territory known as West Florida belonged to the King of Spain ; it had been ceded to the United States as a part of Louisiana. The admission by treaty in 1819 that Ferdinand VII. was still sovereign over any territory known by the name of West Florida, threw discredit on the previous acts of President and Congress, and following the confusion due to the contradictory systems they had pursued, created a chaos which neither proclamations, Acts of Congress, treaties, nor decisions of the courts, numerous and positive as they might be, could reduce to order. History cannot tell by what single title the United States hold West Florida.

East Florida threatened to become a worse annoyance. In January, 1811, as the story has told, the President, under authority of a secret Act of Congress, sent George Matthews and John McKee to take possession, under certain circumstances, of Mobile and Fernandina. Their written instructions

[1] United States *vs*. Arredondo, 6 Peters, p. 741.
[2] State Papers, Foreign Relations, iv. 617, 623; Diary of J. Q. Adams, Feb. 15, 1819, iv. 254, 255.

were singularly loose.[1]   In general they were to take
possession of East Florida only in case the Spanish
authorities or " the existing local authority " should
wish it, or in case of actual British interference ; but
their conduct was to be " regulated by the dictates of
their own judgments, on a close view and accurate
knowledge of the precise state of things there, and
of the real disposition of the Spanish government."
Besides these written instructions, Matthews professed to be guided by verbal explanations of a
stronger character.   With the precedent of Baton
Rouge before his eyes, Matthews could not but assume that he was sent to St. Mary's for a practical
object ; and he found there a condition of affairs that
seemed to warrant him in acting with energy.   St.
Mary's River was filled with British vessels engaged
in smuggling British merchandise into the United
States in defiance of the Non-importation Act ; while
Amelia Island, on which the town of Fernandina
stood, was a smuggling depot, and the Spanish authority an empty form, useful only for the protection
of illicit trade.

Matthews's official reports assumed as a matter of
course an intention in his Government to possess
itself of East Florida.   His letters made no disguise
of his own acts or intentions.   After six months
of inquiry, he wrote to Secretary Monroe, Aug. 3,

[1] Secretary of State to Gen. George Matthews and John
McKee, Jan. 26, 1811 ; State Papers, Foreign Affairs, iii.
571.

1811, a plain account of the measures necessary to be taken : [1] —

" I ascertained that the quiet possession of East Florida could not be obtained by an amicable negotiation with the powers that exist there ; . . . that the inhabitants of the province are ripe for revolt. They are, however, incompetent to effect a thorough revolution without external aid. If two hundred stand of arms and fifty horsemen's swords were in their possession, I am confident they would commence the business, and with a fair prospect of success. These could be put into their hands by consigning them to the commanding officer at this post, subject to my order. I shall use the most discreet management to prevent the United States being committed ; and although I cannot vouch for the event, I think there would be but little danger."

In October, Matthews communicated freely his plans and wishes to Senator Crawford, and commissioned him to explain them to the Government.[2] The President was fully acquainted with them, and during six months offered no objection, but waited in silence for Matthews to effect the revolution thus prepared.

Matthews carried out his mission by following the West Florida precedent as he understood it. March 16, 1812, some two hundred self-styled insurgents

[1] Matthews to Monroe, Aug. 3, 1811; Secret Acts, Resolutions, and Instructions under which East Florida was invaded in 1812 and 1813. Washington.

[2] Matthews to Monroe, Oct. 14, 1811; Secret Acts, Resolutions, and Instructions under which East Florida was invaded in 1812 and 1813. Washington.

crossed the river, landed on Amelia Island, and summoned the garrison of Fernandina to surrender. At the same time the American gunboats, stationed on the river, took a position to watch the movement. The Spanish commandant sent to inquire whether the American gunboats meant to assist the insurgents, and receiving an answer in the affirmative, he capitulated to the so-called patriots.[1] Independence was declared; an independent flag was raised; and when this formality ended, the patriots summoned General Matthews, who crossed the river with a company of the regular army, and March 19 took possession of Amelia Island, subject to the President's approval.

Matthews supposed his measures to be warranted by his instructions, and thought the Government bound to sustain him; but the Government took an opposite course. April 4 Monroe wrote to Matthews [2] disavowing the seizure of Amelia Island, and referring to the precedent of Baton Rouge as the proper course to have followed. "The United States did not take possession until after the Spanish authority had been subverted by a revolutionary proceeding, and the contingency of the country being thrown into foreign hands had forced itself into view." Matthews failed to see why one "revolutionary proceeding" was not as good as another, or why the fiction of foreign interference might not serve as well at Fernandina as at Baton Rouge. He was excessively indignant, and

[1] Niles, ii. 93.
[2] State Papers, Foreign Affairs, iii. 572.

believed his disavowal to be due to the publication
of John Henry's letters, which had made the President suddenly sensitive to the awkwardness of doing
openly acts which he imputed as a crime in the
governor-general of Canada to imagine. Senator
Crawford afterward wrote to Monroe [1] that this impression was by no means confined to Matthews; indeed, Crawford himself seemed to share it. Yet
governments were not bound to make explanations to
their instruments; and Matthews was told only that
he had mistaken the President's wishes, and that his
instructions were meant in good faith to require that
the Spaniards should of their own accord ask to surrender their territory to the United States.

April 24 Madison wrote to Jefferson: [2] " In East
Florida Matthews has been playing a strange comedy
in the face of common-sense as well as of his instructions. His extravagances place us in the most distressing dilemma." The dilemma consisted in the
President's wish to maintain possession of Amelia
Island, and the difficulty of doing it. In explaining
the matter to the French minister, Monroe made no
secret of the President's wishes: [3] —

" Mr. Monroe, in communicating the facts to me at
one of our last conversations, told me that General Mat-

[1] Crawford to Monroe, Aug. 6, 1812; Monroe MSS. State
Dep. Archives.

[2] Works, ii. 532.

[3] Serurier to Maret, May 4, 1812; Archives des. Aff.
Etr. MSS.

thews had gone beyond his orders ; that he was told to observe only ; and in case a third Power, which could be only England, should present itself to occupy the island, he was to prevent it if possible, and in case of necessity repulse the disembarking troops. He added that nevertheless, now that things had reached their present condition, there would be more danger in retreating than in advancing ; and so, while disavowing the General's too precipitate conduct, they would maintain the occupation."

This decision required some double dealing. April 10 Monroe wrote [1] to the governor of Georgia, requesting him to take Matthews's place and to restore Amelia Island to the Spanish authorities ; but this order was for public use only, and not meant to be carried into effect. May 27 Monroe wrote again,[2] saying : —

" In consequence of the compromitment of the United States to the inhabitants, you have been already instructed not to withdraw the troops unless you find that it may be done consistently with their safety, and to report to the Government the result of your conferences with the Spanish authorities, with your opinion of their views, holding in the mean time the ground occupied."

Governor Mitchell would have been a poor governor and still poorer politician, had he not read such instructions as an order to hold Amelia Island as long as possible. Instead of re-establishing the Spanish authority at Fernandina, he maintained the

[1] State Papers, iii. 572.   [2] State Papers, iii. 573.

occupation effected by Matthews.[1] June 19, the day
after declaring war against England, the House took
up the subject on the motion of Troup of Georgia,
and in secret session debated a bill authorizing the
President not to withdraw the troops, but to extend
his possession over the whole country of East and
West Florida, and to establish a government there.[2]
June 25, by a vote of seventy to forty-eight, the
House passed this bill, which in due time went successfully through all its stages in the Senate until
July 3, when the vote was taken on its passage.
Only then three Northern Republicans, — Bradley
of Vermont, Howell of Rhode Island, and Leib of
Pennsylvania, — joining Giles, Samuel Smith, and
the Federalists, defeated, by a vote of sixteen to fourteen, this bill which all the President's friends in
both Houses supported as an Administration measure,
and upon which the President promised to act with
decision ; but even after its failure the President
maintained possession of Fernandina, with no other
authority than the secret Act of Congress which had
been improperly made by Matthews the ground of
usurping possession.

From the pacific theories of 1801 to the military
methods of 1812 was a vast stride. When Congress
rose, July 6, 1812, the whole national frontier and

[1] Governor Garzia to Governor Mitchell, Dec. 12, 1812 ;
Niles, iii. 311.

[2] An Act, etc., Annals of Congress ; 12th Congress, 1811–
1812, Part I. p. 324.

coast from Prairie du Chien to Eastport, from Eastport to St. Mary's, from St. Mary's to New Orleans,
— three thousand miles, incapable of defence, — was
open to the attacks of powerful enemies ; while the
Government at Washington had taken measures for
the military occupation of the vast foreign territories
northward of the Lakes and southward to the Gulf
of Mexico.

CHAPTER XII.

W<small>HILE</small> the Twelfth Congress at Washington from November, 1811, until July, 1812, struggled with the declaration which was to spread war westward to the Mississippi River, Napoleon at Paris prepared the numberless details of the coming campaign that was to ravage Europe eastward as far as Moscow ; and in this fury for destruction, no part remained for argument or diplomacy. Yet Joel Barlow, full of hope that he should succeed in solving the problem which had thus far baffled his Government, reached Paris, Sept. 19, 1811, and began a new experience, ended a year later at Zarnovitch in Poland by a tragedy in keeping with the military campaign to which Barlow was in a fashion attached.

Joel Barlow felt himself at home in Paris. In 1788, at the age of thirty-four, he had first come abroad, and during seventeen exciting years had been rather French than American. In 1792 the National Convention conferred on him the privileges of French citizenship, — an honor then shared only by Washington and Hamilton among Americans. He felt himself to be best understood and appreciated by Frenchmen. His return to France in 1812 was, he

said, attended by a reception much more cordial and
friendly than that which he had received in America,
in 1805, on his return to his native country after
seventeen years of absence. He settled with delight
into his old society, even into his old house in the
Rue Vaugirard, and relished the pleasure of recovering, with the highest dignity of office, the atmosphere
of refinement which he always keenly enjoyed. Yet
when these associations lost their freshness, and he
turned to his diplomatic task, he found that few lots
in life were harder than that of the man who bound
himself to the destinies of Napoleon.

On the success of Barlow's mission the fate of
President Madison might depend. As long as France
maintained her attitude of hostility to the United
States, war against England would be regarded by a
majority of the Northern people with distrust and
dislike. On that point Madison was justly timid.
The opposition of New England and New York must
be quieted, and in order to quiet it Madison must
prove France to be honest in respecting American
rights ; he must show that the decrees had been
really repealed as he had so often and still so obstinately asserted, and that the vast confiscations of
American property under the authority of those decrees would receive indemnity. The public had
commonly supposed France to be comparatively a
slight aggressor; but to the general surprise, when
Congress, before the declaration of war against England, called for a return of captures under the bellig-

erent edicts, Monroe's report showed that the seizures
by France and by the countries under her influence
in pursuance of the decrees were not less numerous
than those made by England under the Orders in
Council. The precise values were never known. The
confiscations ordered by Napoleon in Spain, Naples,
Holland, Denmark, Hamburg, and on the Baltic outnumbered those made in his empire; but all these
taken together probably exceeded the actual condem-
nations in British prize-courts. This result, hardly
expected by the American government, added to its
embarrassment, but was only a part of its grievances
against Napoleon. Not only had France since 1807
surpassed England in her outrages on American
property, but while England encouraged American
commerce with her own possessions, Napoleon sys-
tematically prohibited American commerce with his
empire. He forbade American vessels to import
sugar or other colonial produce except by special
license; he imposed a duty of sixty cents a pound on
Georgia cotton worth twenty or twenty-five cents; he
refused to take tobacco except in small quantities as
a part of the government monopoly; and he obliged
every American ship to carry for its return cargo two
thirds in silks and the other third in wines, liquors,
and such other articles of French produce as he might
direct. The official returns made to Congress showed
that in 1811 the United States exported domestic produce to the amount of $45,294,000, of which France
and Italy took only $1,164,275.

Barlow's instructions required him to reform these evils, but they especially insisted upon indemnity for seizures under the decrees. Haste was required; for Congress could not be expected to adopt extreme measures against England until France should have made such concessions as would warrant the American government in drawing a distinction between the two belligerents. Barlow arrived in Paris September 19, only to learn that on the same day the Emperor set out for Antwerp and Amsterdam. The Duc de Bassano received him kindly, assured him of the Emperor's order to begin upon business at once, and listened courteously to the American complaints and demands. Then he too departed for Holland, whence he returned only November 9, when at Washington Congress had been already a week in session.

Nothing showed this delay to be intentional; but Napoleon never allowed delay when he meant to act, and in the present instance he was not inclined to act. Although the Duc de Bassano made no reply to Barlow, he found time at Amsterdam to write instructions to Serurier.[1] In these he declared that all American vessels captured since November, 1810, had been released, except those coming by way of England, which were not yet condemned, but only sequestered.

"The French government would like to know, before making a decision, how England would act toward Amer-

[1] Maret to Serurier, October, 1811 ; Archives des Aff. Étr. MSS.

ican ships bound for France. If I return once more on the motives for this delay, it is only for your personal instruction and without making it a subject of an official declaration on your part. On this question you should speak as for yourself ; appear ignorant what are the true motives for still detaining some American ships which have had communication with England ; restrict yourself to receiving the representations sent you, and to declaring that you will render an account of them ; in short, give no explanation that would imply that the Decrees of Berlin and Milan are not entirely revoked."

While the Emperor was thus secretly determined to enforce his decrees, he was equally determined to pay no indemnities. Against sacrifices of money Napoleon always made unconquerable resistance.

In due time Barlow had his audience of reception, and made to the Emperor a speech, not without flattery. He ventured to mention his commercial objects, in the hope of calling out an answer that would suit his purpose. Napoleon's reply proved for the hundredth time the danger of risking such experiments : —

" As to the commerce between the two Powers, I desire to favor it. I am great enough to be just. But on your part you must defend your dignity against my enemies and those of the Continent. Have a flag, and I will do for you all that you can desire."

In reporting the interview to Monroe, Barlow added that the ambiguity of the Emperor's reply made it unfit for publication.[1] Ambiguity was not the quality

[1] Barlow to Monroe, Nov. 17, 1812 ; MSS. State Department Archives.

that a more sensitive man would have ascribed to a
rebuff so sharp; but whatever the President may
have thought, he took Barlow's advice. The interview was never made known to Congress.

During the month of November Napoleon busied
himself in commercial questions only in order to show
liberality to England at the expense of America. He
extended his system of licenses to the exchange of
French wines for sugar in large quantities, and even
to the importation of coffee, indigo, tea, wool, dye-
woods, and other articles, all to be obtained from
England by license.[1] He discovered that his ex-
changes would benefit France more than England in
the proportion of three to one. " It is therefore the
perfected system that has produced this result, which
had not been expected for several years. Evidently
the system thus established is a permanent system,
which can be made perpetual." [2] The motive for this
discovery might be traced throughout all his economi-
cal experiments. He needed money.

Never had Napoleon's ministers a harder task to
give his acts a color of consistency. During the
months of November and December Barlow held
many interviews with Bassano, and made earnest
efforts to obtain some written pledge in favor of
American interests, but without success. December

[1] Notes dictées en conseil, 25 nov. 1811 ; Correspondance,
xxiii. 36.

[2] Note sur le Blocus continental, 13 janvier, 1812 ; Correspondance, xxiii. 167.

19 he wrote that he was almost discouraged by the
unexpected and unreasonable delay.[1] Napoleon made
no more seizures, and released such American vessels
as were held for violation of the decrees ; but he conceded nothing in principle, and was far from abandoning his fiscal system against the United States.
In order to meet Barlow's complaints, Bassano gathered together every token of evidence that the decrees were not in force ; but while he was asking the
American minister how these facts could be doubted,
a French squadron, Jan. 8, 1812, sailed from Nantes
with orders to destroy all neutral ships bound to or
from an enemy's port. For several months American commerce was ravaged by these ships under the
Emperor's order, in pursuance of his decrees. January 19 Napoleon issued another order of the gravest
character. His quarrel with Bernadotte the new king
of Sweden had reached a rupture, and he carried out
his threat of seizing the Swedish provinces south of
the Baltic ; but his orders to Marshal Davout were
almost as hostile to the United States as to Sweden : [2]
" As soon as you shall be sure of seizing a great
quantity of colonial merchandise in Swedish Pomerania, you will take possession of that province ; and
you will cause to be seized both at Stralsund and
Anklam, in short at all points in Pomerania, what-

[1] Barlow to Monroe, Dec. 19, 1811 ; State Papers, Foreign
Affairs, iii. 515.

[2] Napoleon to Davout, Jan. 19, 1812 ; Correspondance,
xxiii. 182.

ever colonial merchandise may be found." January 28 he wrote again : [1] " I wait with impatience your report on the colonial merchandise you shall have found in Pomerania." He made no exceptions in favor of American property, for his need of money was greater than ever.

While Bassano amused Joel Barlow with conversations that resulted in nothing, he drew up a report to the Emperor, to be laid before the conservative Senate, dealing wholly with the question of neutrals. Circumstances made the appearance of this report peculiarly mortifying to Barlow. Jonathan Russell, who had been sent to act as American *chargé* at London, wrote to Barlow asking for additional proofs to satisfy Lord Castlereagh that the decrees were repealed. Barlow replied, March 2, by a letter to Russell, recounting seven cases of ships which had been admitted to French ports contrary to the decrees, while in no case had the decrees been enforced.[2] " It is difficult to conceive," he added, " probably impossible to procure, and certainly insulting to require, a mass of evidence more positive than this or more conclusive to every unprejudiced mind." Hardly had he written this letter when news arrived that French frigates were burning American vessels on the ocean for infringing the decrees. March 12 he wrote to

[1] Napoleon to Davout, Jan. 19, 1812; Correspondance, p. 194.

[2] Barlow to Russell, March 2, 1812; State Papers, Foreign Affairs, iii. 518.

Bassano a letter of strong protest against these depredations, and a demand for redress. His letter received no answer. Had this been all, gross as the outrage was, nothing need have become public; but on the heels of this scandal came another more flagrant. March 16 the "Moniteur" published Bassano's official report to the Emperor, which had the character of an Imperial message to the conservative Senate. This document began by defining neutral rights as claimed by France; and while one of these claims required that the flag should cover all goods except arms and other munitions of war, another declared that no blockade was real except of a port "invested, besieged, in the presumption of being taken;" and until these principles should be restored to force by England, "the Decrees of Berlin and Milan must be enforced toward Powers that let their flags be denationalized; the ports of the Continent are not to be opened to denationalized flags or to English merchandise." Barlow could imagine no way of reconciling this language with Bassano's assertions that the decrees were withdrawn, and he enclosed the report to Monroe in a letter speculating upon the reason of this contradiction:[1] —

"You will notice that the minister in his report says nothing particular of the United States, and nothing more precise than heretofore on the revocation of the decrees. . . . I am afraid he is forbidden to designate the United

[1] Barlow to Monroe, March 16, 1812; MSS. State Department Archives.

States as out of the gripe of those decrees, because the Emperor did not like the bill we have seen before Congress for admitting English goods contracted for before the Non-importation Law went into operation."

Barlow could not but maintain that the decrees were repealed; yet the British government could hardly be required to hold the same opinion. Taking Bassano's report as proof that the United States would no longer maintain the repeal, the Prince Regent issued, April 21, 1812, a formal declaration, that in case those decrees should at any future time by an authentic act publicly promulgated be expressly and unconditionally repealed, then the Orders in Council should be wholly and absolutely revoked. This step brought matters to a crisis. As soon as the Prince Regent's declaration reached Paris, May 1, 1812, Barlow wrote to the French government a letter declaring that, between Bassano's report and the Prince Regent's declaration, proof that the decrees were repealed had become absolutely necessary for the United States, and he followed up his notes by a conversation in which he pressed on the French minister the danger of further trifling.[1]

Then came the climax of Imperial diplomacy. Neither Talleyrand nor Champagny had shown repugnance to falsehood; whatever end they wished, they used naturally and without hesitation the most convenient means. Yet free as they were from scruples, one might doubt whether Talleyrand or Cham-

[1] Barlow to Bassano, May 1, 1812; State Papers, iii. 602.

pagny would have done what Bassano did; for when
the American minister impatiently demanded some
authentic evidence that the decrees were repealed,
Bassano complained that such a demand should be
made when the American government possessed the
repealing decree itself. Barlow was struck dumb
with astonishment when the French minister then
passed to him a decree signed by Napoleon at St.
Cloud, April 28, 1811, declaring his previous decrees non-existent for American vessels after Nov.
1, 1810.[1]

That the American minister should have lost self-
possession in the face of an act so surprising and so
unexpected was natural, for Talleyrand himself could
hardly have controlled his features on seeing this
document, which for an entire year had been sought
by the whole world in vain, and which suddenly appeared as a paper so well known as to need only an
allusion. In his embarrassment Barlow asked the
vacant question whether this decree had been published, as though his surprise could be no greater had
the document been printed in the " Moniteur " and
the " National Intelligencer," or been sent to Congress with the President's Annual Message. Bassano
replied that it had not been published, but had been
communicated at the time to Jonathan Russell and
sent to Serurier with orders to communicate it to the
Secretary of State. These assertions increased the
American minister's embarrassment, for they implied

[1] Barlow to Monroe, May 12, 1812; State Papers, iii. 603.

a reflection on the American government which he
could not resent without in his turn implying that
Napoleon had invented the story so gravely told.
Barlow said no more, but asked for a copy of the
repealing decree, which was sent to him May 10.

If evidence were necessary to show that no such
decree was issued April 28, 1811, Napoleon's correspondence proves that the Emperor did not consider
the subject until April 29, and his note to the Council
dated that day is proof that no such decree had then
been adopted.[1]   Yet such a decree might naturally
have been afterward ante-dated without objection.
Had the Emperor signed it within the year 1811 he
might have set what date upon it he liked, and
need have made no mystery of the delay.   The interest of Bassano's conduct lay not so much in his
producing an ante-dated paper as in his averring
that the paper was not ante-dated, but had been
communicated to the American government at the
time.   The flagrancy of the falsehood relieved it
from the usual reproach of an attempt to deceive ;
but if it did not embarrass Bassano in the telling,
it embarrassed President Madison beyond calculation
in admitting.

Still more characteristic than the calmness with
which Bassano made these announcements to the
American minister at Paris, was the circumstantial
gravity with which he repeated them to his own minister at Washington.   Writing the same day, May 10,

[1] See *ante*, Vol. v. p. 402.

1812, he enclosed a copy of the decree, explaining his reasons for doing so : [1] —

" I have learned from Mr. Barlow that he is not acquainted with the Decree of April 28, 1811, . . . and I have addressed a copy to him. You yourself, sir, have never acknowledged its reception ; you have never mentioned it in any of your despatches ; you have never dwelt upon it in any of your interviews with the American Secretary of State. This silence makes me fear that the communication made of it to you under date of May 2, 1811, did not reach you, and I think it proper to enclose herewith a new copy."

He explained at some length why he had ignored this decree in his report to the conservative Senate :

" It had become useless to recall in this report a measure in respect to which no one could longer raise a doubt ; it would have been even improper to specify the Americans by name ; it would have entailed other citations ; it would have required too much prominence to be given to the true motives of the Senatus Consultum which was to be proposed. The Emperor had reason to complain of the numerous infractions made by Russia in the Continental system, in spite of her engagement to co-operate with and maintain it. Therefore against Russia were directed the provisions of that report ; but although various circumstances rendered war inevitable, it was still necessary to avoid naming her while preparing forces against her."

Bold and often rash a diplomatist as Napoleon was, he still felt that at the moment of going to war with

[1] Maret to Serurier, May 10, 1812 ; Archives des Aff. Étr. MSS.

Russia he could not entirely disregard the wishes of
the United States. In appearance he gave way, and
sacrificed the system so long and so tenaciously defended; but in yielding, he chose means that involved
the United States government in common responsibility for his previous acts.

Even had the Emperor's deception stopped there, it
would have offered the most interesting example in
American experience of one peculiarity of his genius;
but this was not all. He seemed to grudge the success which Barlow had wrung from him. One is
tempted to think that this victory cost Barlow his
life. The decree he had gained was flung at him
like a missile. Bassano's letter was dated May 10;
the Emperor already, the day before, had left Paris
to take command of his Grand Army on the Russian
frontier, and as yet the negotiation had not advanced
a step. Meanwhile Barlow took a course of his own.
Monroe and Madison cared little for a commercial
treaty, but insisted upon indemnities. Barlow, finding that indemnity was for the present out of the
question, showed great earnestness to make a commercial treaty, and admitted suggestions altogether
displeasing to his Government. Thus June arrived,
producing no change in the attitude of France other
than the new decree, which was as grave an offence
to the President's dignity as though it had been
couched in terms of the lie direct.

Deceived and deserted, Madison was driven without an ally into a war that required the strongest

alliances. Mortified at the figure he had been made to present, he wrote to Barlow that the shameful conduct of the French government would be an everlasting reproach to it, and that if peace were made with England, "the full tide of indignation with which the public mind here is boiling" would be directed against France. His anger was the more bitter because of his personal outrage. The repealing Decree of April, 1811, spared no kind of humiliation, for it proved, even to himself, his error in asserting that Napoleon imposed no condition precedent on the original promise to withdraw his decrees.[1] On that point the Federalists were shown to be right, and Madison could offer no defence against their charge that he had made himself a tool of Napoleon.

When Bassano left Paris to follow Napoleon into Russia he intrusted the negotiation with Barlow to the Duc Dalberg, by birth a German, who was in the Imperial service. While Dalberg listened to Barlow and wrote long reports to Bassano, Napoleon, entering Russia June 23, five days after Congress declared war against Great Britain, advanced to Wilna in Poland, where he remained until July 17, and then with five hundred thousand men plunged into the heart of Russia, leaving Bassano at Wilna with general charge of matters of state. These events made Barlow conscious that his negotiation was hopeless. His communications with Dalberg must be sent from Paris to Wilna, and thence to Napoleon on the

[1] Madison to Barlow, Aug. 11, 1812; Works, ii. 540.

road to Moscow, with the certainty of receiving no
attention during the active campaign; while even if
Napoleon had been able to give them ample attention, he would soon have taken offence at the increasing ill-temper of their tone, and would have
been more likely to show anger than to grant favors.
Under new instructions from Monroe, which were
almost a reprimand, Barlow said less and less about
a commercial treaty, and pressed harder for indemnities. Under instructions from Bassano, dated August
10,[1] Dalberg was obliged to avoid the discussion of
indemnities and to talk only about commerce. Barlow insisted upon explanations in regard to seventeen
American vessels recently burned at sea under the
Decrees of Berlin and Milan; but no explanation
could be obtained from Bassano. When the news
arrived that Congress had declared war against England, Bassano, August 10, renewed his instructions to
Dalberg without essential change: [2] —

"As for the commercial advantages that his Majesty
may be disposed to grant the Americans, particularly
since the last measures their Government has taken,
communicate to the Minister of Commerce the different
demands of Mr. Barlow; consult with him to what
points and in what proportion these advantages might
be granted, and communicate the result of these interviews to me before concluding anything in that respect

[1] Bassano to Dalberg, 10 August, 1812; Archives des Aff.
Étr. MSS.

[2] Bassano to Dalberg, 10 August, 1812; Archives des Aff.
Étr. MSS.

with Mr. Barlow. You are to encourage his hopes and his confidence in the benevolent views of his Majesty toward the United States; explain, on the score of his Majesty's distance and the importance of his actual occupations, the kind of languor of the negotiation which has been begun, and the failure to decide some of the questions proposed by that minister; and you can point him to the American declaration of war against England as a motive the more for removing from their proposed arrangements with France whatever would tend to complicate them and too long delay their adoption."

These instructions showed no change in the Imperial policy even in consequence of the war declared by the United States against England. The Decrees of Berlin and Milan were no more repealed by the Decree of 1811, so unexpectedly produced by Bassano, than they had been by Champagny's famous letter of August 5, 1810; no order was ever given to any official of the empire that carried the revocation into effect. While Bassano protested to Barlow against implications of the Emperor's good faith, Bassano's colleagues equally protested to Barlow that they had no authority to exempt American ships from the operation of the decrees. Decrès, the Minister of Marine, gave orders to his cruisers to destroy all vessels infringing the decrees, and not even an apology could be wrung from him for the act. If Barlow lost patience at this conduct, the Duc Dalberg, with German simple-mindedness, felt even more acutely the odium of his part, and sent to Bassano remonstrances as strong as those he received from Barlow. August

11, only one day after Bassano wrote from Wilna the instruction just quoted, Dalberg wrote from Paris in language such as had been of late seldom used in the Emperor's service : [1] —

" If we wish to inspire any confidence in the American government, of what use is an isolated proof of revocation if a little while afterward another proof overthrows it, and if Mr. Barlow, by his means of information at the Department of Commerce, at that of the Marine, at the Council of Prizes, learns that they are ignorant of it ; that nothing is changed in that legislation, and that it may at any instant be again enforced? Under such circumstances, I pray you, Monsieur le Duc, to consider what is the good of all the fine phrases and fair words that I may use to Mr. Barlow when he is every moment receiving news that our privateers in the Baltic and on the coast permit themselves the most reckless (*les plus fortes*) violations against the property of Americans. In such circumstances the art of diplomacy becomes insufficient, a sorry game (*triste métier*) of which no one is long the dupe."

Dalberg seemed to suspect that Bassano himself knew little of the true situation : —

" Your Excellency is perhaps not informed of the complaints made by Americans to Mr. Barlow. If you believe that, while nothing is settled in regard to American navigation, the Americans enjoy the favor of navigating freely, of being well treated in our ports, and of being exposed to no annoyance, you deceive yourself. What with the Decrees of Berlin and Milan, whose revo-

[1] Dalberg to Bassano, Aug. 11, 1812 ; Archives des Aff. Étr. MSS.

cation is not yet known to the authorities; what with
our forms of custom-house examinations; what with the
multiplied obstacles to all commercial movement, — this
is impossible."

Plain as such language was, it could have no
effect; for Bassano could do nothing without Napoleon's approval, and Napoleon was already beyond
reach. September 7 he fought the battle of Borodino;
September 15 he entered Moscow.

During all these months Barlow received by every
packet despatches more and more decided from Monroe, letters more and more threatening from Madison.
He told Dalberg in substance that these orders left
no choice except between indemnities and war. Dalberg reported his language faithfully to Bassano; and
Bassano, struggling with the increasing difficulties of
his position, invented a new expedient for gaining
time. While Napoleon remained at Moscow, unable
to advance and unwilling to retreat, Bassano wrote,
October 11, from Wilna a letter to Barlow saying that
the Emperor, regretting the delay which attended negotiation conducted at so great a distance, had put
an end to the Duc Dalberg's authority and requested
Barlow to come in person to Wilna. The request
itself was an outrage, for its motive could not be
mistaken. For an entire year Barlow had seen the
French government elude every demand he made, and
he could not fail to understand that the journey to
Wilna caused indefinite further delay, when a letter
of ten lines to Dalberg might remove every obstacle;

but however futile the invitation might be, refusal
would have excused the French government's inac-
tion.   Throughout life Barlow exulted in activity; a
famous traveller, no fatigue or exposure checked his
restlessness, and although approaching his sixtieth
year he feared no journey.   He accepted Bassano's
invitation, and October 25 wrote that he should set
out the following day for Wilna.   A week earlier,
Napoleon quitted Moscow, and began his retreat to
Poland.

Ten days brought Barlow to Berlin, and already
Napoleon's army was in full flight and in danger of
destruction, although the winter had hardly begun.
November 11 Barlow reached Königsberg and plunged
into the wastes of Poland.   Everywhere on the road
he saw the devastation of war, and when he reached
Wilna, November 18, he found only confusion.   Every
one knew that Napoleon was defeated, but no one yet
knew the tragedy that had reduced his army of half
a million men to a desperate remnant numbering some
fifty thousand.   While Barlow waited for Napoleon's
arrival, Napoleon struggled through one obstacle after
another until the fatal passage of the Beresina, November 27, which dissolved his army and caused him
to abandon it.   December 5, at midnight, he started
for Paris, having sent a courier in advance to warn
the Duc de Bassano, who lost no time in dismissing
his guests from Wilna, where they were no longer
safe.   Barlow quitted Wilna for Paris the day before
Napoleon left his army; but Napoleon soon passed

him on the road. The weather was very cold, the thermometer thirteen degrees below zero of Fahrenheit; but Barlow travelled night and day, and after passing through Warsaw, reached a small village called Zarnovitch near Cracow. There he was obliged to stop. Fatigue and exposure caused an acute inflammation of the lungs, which ended his life Dec. 24, 1812. A week earlier Napoleon had reached Paris.

Barlow's death passed almost unnoticed in the general catastrophe of which it was so small a part. Not until March, 1813, was it known in America; and the news had the less effect because circumstances were greatly changed. Madison's earnestness in demanding satisfaction from France expressed not so much his own feelings as fear of his domestic opponents. The triumph of Russia and England strengthened the domestic opposition beyond hope of harmony, and left the President in a desperate strait. No treaty, either with or without indemnities, could longer benefit greatly the Administration, while Napoleon's overthrow threatened to carry down Madison himself in the general ruin. In his own words,[1] —

" Had the French emperor not been broken down, as he was to a degree at variance with all probability and which no human sagacity could anticipate, can it be doubted that Great Britain would have been constrained by her own situation and the demands of her allies to

[1] Madison to Wheaton, Feb. 26, 1827 ; Works, iii. 553.

listen to our reasonable terms of reconciliation? The moment chosen for war would therefore have been well chosen, if chosen with a reference to the French expedition against Russia; and although not so chosen, the coincidence between the war and the expedition promised at the time to be as favorable as it was fortuitous."

Thus the year 1812 closed American relations with France in disappointment and mortification. Whatever hopes Madison might still cherish, he could not repeat the happy diplomacy of 1778 or of 1803. From France he could gain nothing. He had challenged a danger more serious than he ever imagined; for he stood alone in the world in the face of victorious England.

CHAPTER XIII.

WHILE Napoleon thus tried the temper of America, the Government of England slowly and with infinite reluctance yielded to American demands. Not for the first time experience showed that any English minister whose policy rested on jealousy of America must sooner or later come to ruin and disgrace.

After the departure of Pinkney and Foster in May, 1811, diplomatic action was for a time transferred to Washington. The young American *chargé* in London, John Spear Smith, could only transmit news that came officially to his hands. The Marquess Wellesley, still struggling to reorganize the Ministry, found the Prince Regent less and less inclined to assist him, until at last he despaired. American affairs resumed their old position. In June, 1811, Sir William Scott, after some months of hesitation, rendered final decision that the French Decrees were still in force, and that in consequence all American vessels falling within the range of the British Orders in Council were liable to condemnation.[1] In the Cabinet, Wellesley urged his colleagues either to ne-

[1] State Papers, iii. 421

gotiate with America or to show themselves prepared for war; but his colleagues would do neither.[1] Convinced that the United States would not and could not fight, Perceval and Eldon, Bathurst and Liverpool, were indifferent to Wellesley's discomfort. In the autumn of 1811 nothing in the attitude of the British government, except its previous hesitation, held out a hope of change.

Yet many reasons combined to show that concessions were inevitable. The sweeping ruin that overwhelmed British commerce and industry in 1810 sank deep among the laboring classes in 1811. The seasons doubled the distress. The winter had been intense, the summer was unfavorable; wheat rose in the autumn to one hundred and forty-five shillings, or about thirty-six dollars the quarter, and as the winter of 1811 began, disorders broke out in the manufacturing districts. The inland counties reached a state of actual insurrection which no exercise of force seemed to repress. The American non-importation aggravated the trouble, and worked unceasingly to shake the authority of Spencer Perceval, already one of the most unpopular ministers England had ever seen.

Popular distress alone could hardly have effected a change in Perceval's system; so great a result was not to be produced by means hitherto so little regarded. The moment marked an era in English history, for the new class of laborers, the mill-opera-

[1] The Courier, Sept. 22, 1812; Letter signed "Vetus."

tives and other manufacturing workmen, took for the first time an active share in shaping legislation. In their hostility to Perceval's policy they were backed by their employers; but the united efforts of employers and workmen were not yet equal to controlling the Government, even though they were aided by the American non-importation. They worried Perceval, but did not break him down. At the close of 1811 he showed still no signs of yielding; but news then arrived that the American Congress had met, and that the President's Message, the debates in the House, the tone of the press, and the feelings of the American people announced war. This was a new force with which Perceval could not deal.

No man of common-sense could charge England with want of courage, for if ever a nation had fought its way, England had a right to claim whatever credit such a career bestowed; but England lived in war, she knew its exact cost, and at that moment she could not afford it. The most bigoted Tory could see that if Napoleon succeeded in his coming attack on Russia, as he had hitherto succeeded in every war he had undertaken in Europe even when circumstances were less favorable, he would need only the aid of America to ruin beyond redemption the trade and finances of Great Britain. Little as Englishmen believed in the military capacity of the United States, they needed too much the markets and products of America to challenge war.

The gradual decline of the domineering tone which Canning had made fashionable offered a curious study in politics. In 1807 the affair of the "Little Belt" would have caused violent anger; in 1812 it created hardly a flurry. The Tory "Courier" talked wildly, but the "Times" took the matter with calmness; the Ministry showed no offence, and within a few weeks the affair was forgotten. Even after this irritation, the British public seemed pleased rather than angered to learn that Lord Wellesley had yielded complete apology and redress to America for the "Chesapeake" outrage. The commercial class for many months expected energetic retaliation by their government against the American Non-importation Act; but in September this idea was laid aside, and no one complained. Little by little the press took a defensive tone. In the place of threats the newspapers were filled with complaints. America was unfair, unreasonable, unjust; she called on England to admit that the French Decrees were repealed when in fact they were still in force; she threatened war; she hectored and bullied, — but the more dignified course required England to be temperate though firm.

Parliament met Jan. 7, 1812, and the Prince Regent's speech was studiously moderate in its reference to the United States. In the Commons, January 8, Whitbread attacked ministers for their failure to conciliate America; and Spencer Perceval replied in a manner that could hardly have satisfied himself.

" He would allow," he said,[1] " that a war with America would be an evil to Great Britain, but he also knew that such a war would be a greater evil to America. As an evil to America he was anxious to avert it; he looked upon America as accessory to the prosperity and welfare of Great Britain, and would be sorry to see her impoverished, crushed, or destroyed. . . . Sure he was that no one could construe those truly conciliatory dispositions of England into fear; but he was of the opinion that England, conscious of her own dignity, could bear more from America for peace's sake than from any other Power on earth."

This sentiment was the more significant because the latest news showed that England in the immediate future would be obliged to bear a great deal from America. The news became every day more and more alarming, and was reinforced by steadily increasing outcry from Birmingham, Liverpool, Nottingham, Hull, ending in a general agitation organized by active radicals, with Brougham at their head. So rapidly was one attack followed by another, that Perceval and his lieutenants — George Rose and James Stephen — could no longer carry their points by mere weight of office. The Marquess Wellesley, refusing to serve longer under Perceval, resigned from the Cabinet January 16, and no one felt confident that Perceval could supply his place. During more than a month negotiations continued without result, until, February 22, Lord Castlereagh received the appointment of Foreign Secretary.

[1] Cobbett's Debates, xxi. 61.

During this interval the movement against the Orders in Council gained strength. In the Commons, February 13, another debate occurred when Whitbread, in a strong American speech, moved for the diplomatic correspondence with the United States, and was answered with some temper by Stephen and Perceval. Stephen went so far as to declare, — and whatever he declared he certainly believed, — that " nothing but the utmost aversion to a quarrel with America would have enabled this country to have borne so much. So far from having done anything to provoke a rupture with America, the strongest, most persevering, and almost even humiliating means had been employed to avoid it; " [1] but he would not surrender to her the carrying and coasting trade of Europe even to prevent a war. Perceval spoke more evasively than usual, defending his commercial system as one that had been begun by his Whig predecessors, and throwing the blame for its irregularities on Napoleon's decrees; but although that day he was supposed to be in extreme peril of losing his majority, he closed his speech by declaring that sooner than yield to the repeal of the Orders in Council he would refuse share in any Administration. Alexander Baring answered that in this case war could hardly be avoided, and made an earnest appeal, founded on the distress of the manufacturing towns, in favor of the direct interference of Parliament to overrule

[1] Cobbett's Debates, xxi. 773.

the minister. Even William Wilberforce, whose speeches sometimes recalled those of Polonius, and whose hesitations generally marked the decline rather than the rise of a Ministry in power, felt himself constrained to say that "there was not at all times a sufficient attention in this country to the spirit of conciliation toward other countries, and particularly toward America. It would be well if persons in high situations in government had been more abundant in their civilities to that nation."

Again, five days afterward, Baring attacked Perceval by an embarrassing motion on the subject of licenses. No such scandal as the license system had been known in England since the monopolies of the Tudors and Stuarts. Most of the trade between Great Britain and the Continent was conducted by the Board of Trade on one side and Napoleon on the other, under special licenses issued for the carriage of specified articles. In 1807 the number of such licenses amounted to sixteen hundred; in 1810 they reached eighteen thousand. Owing to practical difficulties and to Napoleon's dislike, American vessels took few licenses. A nondescript class of so-called neutrals under the flags of Pappenberg, Kniphausen, and Varel, carrying double licenses and double sets of papers, served as the agents for this curious commerce which reeked with fraud and perjury. In the case of the "Æolus," Aug. 8, 1810, the Court said: "It is a matter perfectly notorious that we are carrying on the trade of the whole world

under simulated and disguised papers.   The commerce of the world unavoidably assumes a disguise ;
these disguises we ourselves are under the necessity
of employing, with simulation and dissimulation."
Dr. Joseph Phillimore, perhaps the highest authority
on civil law in England, in two strong pamphlets [1]
declared that ancient rules and practices had been
rendered obsolete, so that the Admiralty Courts were
no longer occupied with the law of nations, but only
with the interpretation of licenses ; and while the
property of enemies was as invariably restored as
formerly it had been condemned, the condemnation
of true neutral property had become as much a
matter of course as had been its restitution a few
years before.   No one, even among the sternest
supporters of the Orders in Council, ventured to defend the licenses on any other ground than that of
their necessity.

Baring's motion called up Perceval again.   " The
only principle on which Government acted," said he,[2]
" was to secure to the natives of England that trade
by means of licenses, the profits of which without
them would devolve to the hands of aliens."   This
admission, or avowal, seemed to yield the whole
ground of complaint which America had taken ;
neither Perceval nor Rose ventured to defend the
licenses as in themselves deserving support ; they

[1] Reflections, etc. ; Letter, etc., February, 1812.   By Joseph
Phillimore.

[2] Cobbett's Debates, **xxi. 847**.

stood only by the system.   Their attitude led to
another and more famous debate, which added an
interesting chapter to the history of England.

In the Lords, February 28, the Marquess of Lansdowne moved for a committee to consider the subject
of the Orders in Council.   Like all that Lord Lansdowne did, his speech was temperate and able; but
his arguments were the same that have been so often
repeated.   Lord Bathurst, President of the Board of
Trade, replied.   Bathurst's argument was singularly
free from the faults of Perceval and Rose; and he
went to the verge of destroying his own case by
avowing that in the clamor raised about the Orders
in Council no one could say what those orders were,
or what would be the consequences of yielding to
American demands.   He was sure that France had
suffered from the effect of the system, but he was
not so certain that England had been also a sufferer, while he maintained that the licenses tended
to diminish the spirit of perjury, and that the abandonment of licenses would only place an additional
obstacle in the way of trade.   " Were they to put
restraints on the freedom of British commerce for
the simple purpose of giving the trade of Europe to
the Americans?"   This avowal, like those made by
Perceval and Stephen, seemed to concede the justice
of American complaints; but perhaps it admitted
only the reply made by Lord Holland, who said in
plain words that the choice lay between the orders
and war, and that he could not suppose the orders to

be their Lordships' preference. Lansdowne's motion was rejected by a vote of one hundred and thirty-five to seventy-one.

In the Commons the great debate took place March 3, when Henry Brougham repeated Lansdowne's motion for a committee, after a speech showing as much self-restraint as clearness and force. In reply, George Rose offered a general denial of the facts which Brougham alleged. He denied that the orders injured the British export trade; that the license system injured British shipping or increased perjury; or that the orders caused manufacturing distress. On all these points he arrayed statistics in his support; but toward the close of his speech he made a remark — such as had been made many times by every defender of the system — surrendering in effect the point in diplomatic dispute between England and the United States. "The honorable gentleman," he said,[1] "had not been correct in calling these orders a system of retaliation; they were rather a system of self-defence, a plan to prevent the whole trade of the world from being snatched away from her." He was followed by Alexander Baring, who condemned the policy which built up the shipping of France at the cost of American shipping, and manufactures in Massachusetts at the cost of British manufactures; and after Baring came James Stephen, who repeated his old arguments

[1] Times report, March 4 ; National Intelligencer, April 25, 1812. Cf. London Morning Chronicle, March 4, 1812.

without essential change. Then toward midnight, after these four long, serious, statistical speeches, such as usually emptied the House, George Canning rose; and so keen was the interest and anxiety of the moment that more than four hundred members crowded in, curious to learn by what ingenuity Canning would defend a threatened vote against those Orders in Council of which he had been so long the champion.[1]

"For these Orders in Council," he said, "so far as he had been connected with their adoption, he was ready to take his full share of responsibility. What orders were truly meant? Why, they were the Orders in Council which, until he had heard the speech of the right honorable gentleman (Mr. Rose), he had always looked upon as retaliatory upon the enemy; which had been so understood in every instance, until the Vice-President of the Board of Trade, in contradiction to every statement which had hitherto been given to the public on the subject, — in contradiction to every document in office respecting these Orders, — in contradiction to every communication which he (Mr. Canning) had made, and every despatch written in his official character explanatory of their nature and spirit, — in contradiction to every speech which had been made in Parliament in defence of them, — had thought proper to represent them not as measures retaliatory upon the enemy, but as measures of self-defence. Self-defence, but not retaliatory! . . . If they were to be in no larger a sense retaliatory than as self-defensive, — if they were not to retaliate directly against the enemy,

[1] Memoirs of R. Plumer Ward, i. 446.

but to be defensive against a rival in trade, — if they were not to be belligerent measures, but purely defensive, — then all the arguments by which they had hitherto been supported would fail to apply."

Again and again Canning returned to this slip of the tongue by which Rose had given him pretext for turning against the Administration.

" If at any time it should appear that these orders did not retort his aggression upon the enemy, but operated solely to the injury of the neutrals; if even the British government should appear to have interfered to relieve their pressure upon the enemy, — they would stand upon far different principles than those upon which he had supported them, and would in his opinion be very proper objects for examination and revision. . . . Were he called upon to state his opinion of what he conceived the Orders in Council should be, he could not do it more fully than by saying that they were most perfect as they approached toward a belligerent measure and receded from a commercial one. Let them have for their object the pressure and distress of the enemy, for the purpose of compelling him to listen to terms of accommodation, and not for the narrow policy of wringing temporary concessions from him with which they might go to his own market."

To the amazement of friend and foe Canning next attacked the license system as one of which he had little knowledge, but whose details required investigation. As for America, as he was the last man who would lay the honor of the country at her feet, so would he be among the first to go far in the work of honorable conciliation, and he would not oppose the motion before the House because it might have incidentally the effect of conciliating her. Finally, if the account of Plumer Ward be true, "he concluded the first dull and flat speech I ever heard him make, without the smallest support from the House, and sat down without a cheer and almost without its being known that he had finished."

Plumer Ward was a passionate admirer of Spencer Perceval, and his anger with Canning showed the soreness caused by Canning's sudden change of front. Perceval was obliged to rescue Rose, but in doing so made the case worse rather than better as far as regarded America. Having declared that the orders were strictly retaliatory, he added, in the same breath, that "the object of Government was to protect and to force the trade of this country. . . . The object of the Orders in Council was not to destroy the trade of the Continent, but to force the Continent to trade with us." Had this assertion been made by Madison or Brougham it would have been instantly contradicted; but Perceval's silence was still less creditable than his avowals. No one knew so well as Perceval where to strike with effect at Canning; for not only could he show that from the first Canning was privy to the system of forcing commerce upon France, but he had preserved the letter in which Canning at the outset advised him to keep out of sight the exceptions which gave the measure the air of a commercial rather than a political transaction. Never had a distinguished man exposed himself with less caution than Canning, by declaring that in his opinion the orders required revision from the moment the British government should appear to intervene to relax their pressure upon the enemy ; for during two years of his official life he had given steady though silent support to the Board of Trade in its persistent efforts to supply France, by means of licenses in thousands and smuggling without limit, with every product known to commerce.   Such conduct challenged the severest retort, but Perceval made none.   He would have been superior to the statesmen of his time had he felt the true nature of that sleight-of-hand which he and Canning practised, and which, like the trick of blacklegs on the race-course, consisted in shuffling together the two words, " Retaliation — Self-defence ! Self-defence — Retaliation ! " but he could at least understand the impossibility of exposing Canning without also exposing himself.

The debate ended in a division.   One hundred and forty-four members, including Canning and Wilberforce, went into the lobby with Brougham.   Only a majority of seventy-two remained to be overcome ; and to Brougham's energetic nature such a majority offered an incentive to exertion.   Perceval's friends, on the other hand, exulted because this majority of seventy-two stood by him against the combined forces of Wellesley, Canning, the Radicals, and the Whigs.[1]   Except for one danger, Perceval and his system were

[1] Memoirs of R. Plumer Ward, i. 450.

still secure ; but the fear that the Americans meant at last to fight gave him no rest, — it dogged his steps, and galled him at every motion. Neither Rose nor James Stephen could prove, by any statistics under the control of the Board of Trade, that their system would benefit British commerce if it produced an American war. Already the north and west of England, the inland counties, the seaports, had risen in insurrection against the orders. Stephen and Rose exhausted themselves and the House to prove that the balance of profit was still in England's favor ; but what would become of their balance-sheet if they were obliged to add the cost of an American war to the debtor side of their account ?

In the effort to strengthen his Ministry Perceval persuaded Lord Sidmouth to enter the Cabinet, but only on condition that the orders should be left an open question. Sidmouth plainly said that he would rather give up the orders than face an American war.[1] He also asked that the license system should be renounced. Perceval replied that this would be a greater sacrifice than if the licenses had never been granted.[2] Lord Sidmouth was not a great man, — Canning despised his abilities, and the Prince of Wales called him a blockhead ;[3] but he was, except Lord Castlereagh, the only ally to be found, and Perceval accepted him on his own terms. The new Cabi-

[1] Memoirs of R. Plumer Ward, i. 441.
[2] Life of Sidmouth, iii. 74.
[3] Memoirs of R. Plumer Ward, i. 478.

net at once took the American question in hand, and
Castlereagh then wrote his instructions of April 10
to Foster, making use of Bassano's report to justify
England's persistence in the orders ; but besides this
despatch Castlereagh wrote another of the same date,
in which Sidmouth's idea took shape. If the United
States would restore intercourse with Great Britain,
the British government would issue no more licenses
and would resort to rigorous blockades.[1] This great
concession showed how rapidly Perceval lost ground ;
but this was not yet all. April 21 the Prince Regent
issued his formal declaration that whenever the
French government should publish an authentic Act
expressly and unconditionally repealing the Berlin
and Milan Decrees, the Orders in Council, including
that of Jan. 7, 1807, should be wholly and absolutely
revoked.

Had the United States at that moment been so
fortunate as to enjoy the services of Pinkney in
London, or of any man whose position and abilities
raised him above the confusion of party politics, he
might have convinced them that war was unnecessary. The mere threat was sufficient. Sidmouth's
entrance into the Cabinet showed the change of current, and once Perceval began to give way, he could
not stop. Unfortunately the United States had no
longer a minister in England. In July, 1811, the
President ordered Jonathan Russell to London to act

[1] Castlereagh to Foster, April 10, 1812 ; Papers of 1813, No.
4, p. 505.

as *chargé* until a minister should be appointed, which
he added would be done as soon as Congress met;[1]
but he changed his mind and appointed no minister,
while Jonathan Russell, seeing that Perceval commanded a majority and was determined to maintain
his system, reported the situation as hopeless.[2]

Brougham, without taking the precaution of giving
Russell the daily information he so much needed,
devoted all his energies to pressing the popular
movement against the Orders in Council. Petition
after petition was hurried to Parliament, and almost
every petition caused a new debate. George Rose,
who possessed an unhappy bluntness, in conversation
with a Birmingham committee said that the two
countries were like two men with their heads in
buckets of water, whose struggle was which of the
two could hold out longest before suffocation. The
phrase was seized as a catchword, and helped agitation. April 28 Lord Stanley, in the House, renewed
the motion for a committee on the petitions against
the orders. Perceval had been asked whether he
would consent to the committee, and had refused;
but on consulting his followers he found such symptoms of disaffection as obliged him to yield rather
than face a defeat. George Rose then announced,
greatly against his will, that as a matter of respect
to the petitioners he would no longer oppose their
request; Castlereagh and Perceval, cautioning the

[1] Monroe to Russell, July 27, 1811 ; State Papers, iii. 422.
[2] Russell to Monroe, March, 1812 ; State Papers, iii. 426, 427.

House that nothing need be expected from the investigation, followed Rose; while Stephen, after denouncing as a foul libel the charge that the orders had been invented to extend the commerce of Great Britain, also yielded to the committee "as a negative good, and to prevent misconstruction."

Stimulated by the threatening news from America, Brougham pressed with his utmost energy the victory he had won. The committee immediately began its examination of witnesses, who appeared from every quarter to prove that the Orders in Council and the subsequent non-importation had ruined large branches of British trade, and had lopped away a market that consumed British products to the value of more than ten million pounds sterling a year. Perceval and Stephen did their best to stem the tide, but were slowly overborne, and seemed soon to struggle only for delay.

Then followed a melodramatic change. May 11, as the prime minister entered the House to attend the investigation, persons about the door heard the report of a pistol, and saw Spencer Perceval fall forward shot through the heart. By the hand of a lunatic moved only by imaginary personal motives, this minister, who seemed in no way a tragical figure, became the victim of a tragedy without example in modern English history; but although England had never been in a situation more desperate, the true importance of Spencer Perceval was far from great, and when he vanished in the flash of a pistol from the stage where he seemed to fill the most considerable part, he stood already on the verge of overthrow. His death relieved England of a burden. Brougham would not allow his inquiry to be suspended, and the premier's assassination rather concealed than revealed the defeat his system must have suffered.

During the negotiations which followed, in the midst of difficulties in forming a new Ministry, Castlereagh received from Jonathan Russell Napoleon's clandestine Decree of Repeal. Brougham asked, May 22, what construction was to be put by ministers on this paper. Castlereagh replied that the decree was a trick disgraceful to any civilized government, and contained nothing to satisfy the conditions required by England. Apart from the subordinate detail that his view of the decree was correct, his remarks meant nothing. The alarm caused by news that Congress had imposed an embargo as the last step before war, the annoyance created by John Henry's revelations and Castlereagh's lame defence, the weight of evidence pressing on Parliament against the Orders in Council, the absence of a strong or permanent Ministry, — these influences, gaining from day to day, forced the conviction that a change of system must take place. June 8 Lord Liverpool announced that he had formed an Administration, and would deal in due course with the Orders in Council. June 16 Brougham made his motion for a repeal of the orders. When he began his speech he did not know what part the new Ministry would take, but while he unfolded his long and luminous argument he noticed that James Stephen failed to appear in the House. This absence could mean only that Stephen had been deserted by ministers ; and doubt ceased when Brougham and Baring ended, for then Lord Castlereagh — after Perceval's death the leader of the House — rose and awkwardly announced that the Government, though till within three or four days unable to deliberate on the subject, had decided to suspend immediately the Orders in Council.

Thus ended the long struggle waged for five years by the United States against the most illiberal Government known in England within modern times. Never since the Definitive Treaty of Peace had America won so complete a triumph, for the surrender lacked on England's part no element of defeat. Canning never ceased taunting the new Ministry with their want of courage in yielding without a struggle. The press submitted with bad grace to the necessity of holding its tongue. Every one knew that the danger, already almost a certainty, of an American war chiefly caused the sudden and silent surrender, and that the Ministry like the people shrank from facing the consequences of their own folly. Every one cried that England should not suffer herself to be provoked by the irritating conduct of America ; and at a moment when every word and act of the American government announced war in the rudest terms, not a voice was heard in England for accepting the challenge, nor was a musket made ready for defence.

The new Ministry thought the war likely to drive them from office, for they were even weaker than when Spencer Perceval led them. The "Times" of June 17 declared that whatever might be the necessity of defending British rights by an American war, yet it would be the most unpopular war ever known, because every one would say that with happier talents it might have been avoided. "Indeed," it added, "every one is so declaring at the present moment; so that we who have ever been the most strenuous advocates of the British cause in this dispute are really overwhelmed by the general clamor." Bitter as the mortification was, the headlong abandonment of the Orders in Council called out reproaches only against the ministers who originally adopted them. "We are most surprised," said the "Times" of June 18, "that such acts could ever have received the sanction of the Ministry when so little was urged in their defence."

Such concessions were commonly the result rather than the prelude of war; they were not unlike those by which Talleyrand succeeded, in 1799, in restoring friendly relations between France and America. Three months earlier they would have answered their purpose; but the English were a slow and stubborn race. Perhaps that they should have repealed the orders at all was more surprising than that they should have waited five years; but although they acted more quickly and decidedly than was their custom, Spencer Perceval lived three months too long. The Orders in Council were abandoned at Westminster June 17; within twenty-four hours at Washington war was declared; and forty-eight hours later Napoleon, about to enter Russia, issued the first bulletin of his Grand Army.

CHAPTER XIV.

For civil affairs Americans were more or less trained; but they had ignored war, and had shown no capacity in their treatment of military matters. Their little army was not well organized or equipped; its civil administration was more imperfect than its military, and its military condition could hardly have been worse. The ten old regiments, with half-filled ranks, were scattered over an enormous country on garrison service, from which they could not be safely withdrawn; they had no experience, and no organization for a campaign, while thirteen new regiments not yet raised were expected to conquer Canada.

If the army in rank and file was insufficient, its commanding officers supplied none of its wants. The senior major-general appointed by President Madison in February, 1812, was Henry Dearborn, who had retired in 1809 from President Jefferson's Cabinet into the Custom-House of Boston. Born in 1751, Dearborn at the time of his nomination as major-general was in his sixty-second year, and had never held a higher grade in the army than that of deputy quartermaster-general in 1781, and colonel

of a New Hampshire regiment after active service in
the Revolutionary War had ended.

The other major-general appointed at the same
time was Thomas Pinckney, of South Carolina,
who received command of the Southern Department.
Pinckney was a year older than Dearborn; his
military service was chiefly confined to the guerilla
campaigns of Marion and Sumter, and to staff duty
as aide to General Gates in the Southern campaign
of 1780; he had been minister in England and
Envoy Extraordinary to Spain, where he negotiated
the excellent treaty known by his name; he had
been also a Federalist member of Congress in the
stormy sessions from 1797 to 1801, — but none of
these services, distinguished as they were, seemed to
explain his appointment as major-general. Macon,
whose opinions commonly reflected those of the
Southern people, was astonished at the choice.

"The nomination of Thomas Pinckney for major-
general," he wrote,[1] "is cause of grief to all men who
wish proper men appointed; not that he is a Federal
or that he is not a gentleman, but because he is thought
not to possess the talents necessary to his station. I
imagine his nomination must have been produced through
the means of P. Hamilton, who is about as fit for his
place as the Indian Prophet would be for Emperor of
Europe. I never was more at a loss to account for any
proceeding than the nomination of Pinckney to be major-
general."

[1] Macon to Nicholson, March 25, 1812; Nicholson MSS.

Even the private report that Pinckney had become a Republican did not reconcile Macon, whose belief that the "fighting secretaries" would not do for real war became stronger than ever, although he admitted that some of the military appointments were supposed to be tolerably good.

Of the brigadier-generals the senior was James Wilkinson, born in 1757, and fifty-five years old in 1812. Wilkinson had recently been tried by court-martial on a variety of charges, beginning with that of having been a pensioner of Spain and engaged in treasonable conspiracy; then of being an accomplice of Aaron Burr; and finally, insubordination, neglect of duty, wastefulness, and corruption. The court acquitted him, and February 14 President Madison approved the decision, but added an irritating reprimand. Yet in spite of acquittal Wilkinson stood in the worst possible odor, and returned what he considered his wrongs by bitter and contemptuous hatred for the President and the Secretary of War.

The next brigadier was Wade Hampton, of South Carolina, who entered the service in 1808, and was commissioned as brigadier in 1809. Born in 1754, he was fifty-seven years old, and though understood to be a good officer, he had as yet enjoyed no opportunity of distinguishing himself. Next in order came Joseph Bloomfield of New Jersey, nominated as brigadier-general of the regular army March 27, 1812; on the same day James Winchester, of Tennessee, was named fourth brigadier; and April 8

William Hull, of Massachusetts, was appointed fifth
in rank. Bloomfield, a major in the Revolutionary
War, had been for the last ten years Governor of
New Jersey. Winchester, another old Revolutionary
officer, originally from Maryland, though mild, gen-
erous, and rich, was not the best choice that might
have been made from Tennessee. William Hull,
civil Governor of Michigan since 1805, was a third
of the same class. All were sixty years of age or
thereabout, and none belonged to the regular service. Excepting Hull, none seems ever before to have
commanded a regiment in face of an enemy.

Of the inferior appointments, almost as numerous
as the enlistments, little could be said. Among the
officers of the regiment of Light Artillery raised in
1808, after the " Chesapeake " alarm, was a young
captain named Winfield Scott, born near Petersburg,
Virginia, in 1786, and in the prime of his energies
when at the age of twenty-six he saw the chance of
distinction before him. In after life Scott described
the condition of the service as he found it in 1808.

" The army of that day," he said,[1] " including its
general staff, the three old and the nine new regiments,
presented no pleasing aspect. The old officers had very
generally sunk into either sloth, ignorance, or habits of
intemperate drinking. . . . Many of the appointments
were positively bad, and a majority of the remainder
indifferent. Party spirit of that day knew no bounds,
and of course was blind to policy. Federalists were

[1] Autobiography, p. 31.

almost entirely excluded from selection, though great numbers were eager for the field, and in New England and some other States there were but very few educated Republicans; hence the selections from those communities consisted mostly of coarse and ignorant men. In the other States, where there was no lack of educated men in the dominant party, the appointments consisted generally of swaggerers, dependants, decayed gentlemen, and others, ' fit for nothing else,' which always turned out utterly unfit for any military purpose whatever."

This account of the army of 1808 applied equally, said Scott, to the appointments of 1812. Perhaps the country would have fared as well without a regular army, by depending wholly on volunteers, and allowing the States to choose general officers. In such a case Andrew Jackson would have taken the place of James Winchester, and William Hull would never have received an appointment from Massachusetts.

No one in the government gave much thought to the military dangers created by the war, yet these dangers seemed evident enough to warrant keen anxiety. The sea-shore was nowhere capable of defence; the Lakes were unguarded; the Indians of the Northwestern Territory were already in arms, and known to be waiting only a word from the Canadian governor-general; while the whole country beyond the Wabash and Maumee rivers stood nearly defenceless. At Detroit one hundred and twenty soldiers garrisoned the old British fort; eighty-five

men on the Maumee held Fort Wayne; some fifty
men guarded the new stockade called Fort Harrison, lately built on the Wabash; and fifty-three men,
beyond possibility of rescue, were stationed at Fort
Dearborn, or Chicago; finally, eighty-eight men occupied the Island of Michillimackinaw in the straits
between Lake Huron and Lake Michigan.   These
were all the military defences of a vast territory,
which once lost would need another war to regain;
and these petty garrisons, with the settlers about
them, were certain, in the event of an ordinary mis-
chance, to be scalped as well as captured.   The
situation was little better in the South and Southwest, where the Indians needed only the support of
a British army at New Orleans or Mobile to expel
every American garrison from the territory.

No serious preparations for war had yet been made
when the war began.   In January, Congress voted
ten new regiments of infantry, two of artillery, and
one of light dragoons; the recruiting began in March,
and in June the Secretary of War reported to Congress that although no returns had been received
from any of the recruiting offices, yet considering
the circumstances " the success which has attended
this service will be found to have equalled any reasonable expectations." [1]   Eustis was in no way responsible for the failure of the service, and had no
need to volunteer an opinion as to the reasonable

[1] Eustis to Anderson, June 6, 1812; State Papers, Military
Affairs, i. 319.

expectations that Congress might entertain. Every one knew that the enlistments fell far below expectation; but not the enlistments alone showed torpor. In February, Congress authorized the President to accept fifty thousand volunteers for one year's service. In June, the number of volunteers who had offered themselves was even smaller than that of regular recruits. In April, Congress authorized the President to call out one hundred thousand State militia. In June, no one knew whether all the States would regard the call, and still less whether the militia would serve beyond the frontier. One week after declaring war, Congress fixed the war establishment at twenty-five regiments of infantry, four of artillery, two of dragoons, and one of riflemen, — making, with the engineers and artificers, an army of thirty-six thousand seven hundred men; yet the actual force under arms did not exceed ten thousand, of whom four thousand were new recruits. Toward no part of the service did the people show a sympathetic spirit before the war was declared; and even where the war was most popular, as in Kentucky and Tennessee, men showed themselves determined to fight in their own way or not at all.

However inexperienced the Government might be, it could not overlook the necessity of providing for one vital point. Detroit claimed early attention, and received it. The dangers surrounding Detroit were evident to any one who searched the map for that remote settlement, within gunshot of British terri-

tory and surrounded by hostile Indian tribes. The
Governor of Michigan, William Hull, a native of
Connecticut, had done good service in the Revolutionary War, but had reached the age of sixty years
without a wish to resume his military career. He
preferred to remain in his civil post, leaving to some
officer of the army the charge of military operations;
but he came to Washington in February, 1812, and
urged the Government to take timely measures for
holding the Indians in check. He advised the President and Cabinet to increase the naval force on Lake
Erie, although he already had at Detroit an armed
brig ready to launch, which he thought sufficient to
control the upper lakes. The subject was discussed;
but the delay necessary to create a fleet must have
risked, if it did not insure, the loss of the whole
Northwestern Territory, and the President necessarily decided to march first a force to Detroit strong
enough to secure the frontier, and, if possible, to
occupy the whole or part of the neighboring and
friendly British territory in Upper Canada. This
decision Hull seems to have suggested, for he wrote,[1]
March 6, to Secretary Eustis, —

"A part of your army now recruiting may be as well
supported and disciplined at Detroit as at any other
place. A force adequate to the defence of that vulner-
able point would prevent a war with the savages, and
probably induce the enemy to abandon the province of
Upper Canada without opposition. The naval force on

[1] Hull to Eustis, March 6, 1812; Hull's Defence, pp. 29–32.

the Lakes would in that event fall into our possession, and we should obtain the command of the waters
without the expense of building such a force."

This hazardous plan required energy in the American armies, timely co-operation from Niagara if not
from Lake Champlain, and, most of all, assumed both
incompetence and treason in the enemy. Assuming
that Hull would capture the British vessels on the
Lakes, the President made no further provision for
a fleet; but, apparently to provide for simultaneous
measures against Lower Canada, the Secretary of
War sent to Boston for General Dearborn, who was
to command operations on Lake Ontario and the
St. Lawrence River. Dearborn hastened to Washington in February, where he remained until the last
of April. He submitted to the Secretary of War
what was called a plan of campaign,[1] recommending
that a main army should advance by way of Lake
Champlain upon Montreal, while three corps, composed chiefly of militia, should enter Canada from
Detroit, Niagara, and Sackett's Harbor. Neither
Dearborn, Hull, Eustis, nor Madison settled the details of the plan or fixed the time of the combined
movement. They could not readily decide details
before Congress acted, and before the ranks of the
army were filled.

While these matters were under discussion in
March, the President, unable to find an army officer

[1] Defence of Dearborn, by H. A. S. Dearborn, p. 1.   Boston,
1824.

fitted to command the force ordered to Detroit,
pressed Governor Hull to reconsider his refusal;
and Hull, yielding to the President's wish, was
appointed, April 8, 1812, brigadier-general of the
United States army, and soon afterward set out for
Ohio. No further understanding had then been
reached between him and Dearborn, or Secretary
Eustis, in regard to the military movements of the
coming campaign.

The force destined for Detroit consisted of three
regiments of Ohio militia under Colonels McArthur,
Findlay, and Cass, a troop of Ohio dragoons, and
the Fourth Regiment of United States Infantry which
fought at Tippecanoe, — in all about sixteen hundred
effective men, besides a few volunteers. April 1 the
militia were ordered to rendezvous at Dayton, and
there, May 25, Hull took command. June 1 they
marched, and June 10 were joined at Urbana by the
Fourth Regiment. Detroit was nearly two hundred
miles away, and the army as it advanced was obliged
to cut a road through the forest, to bridge streams
and construct causeways; but for such work the
militia were well fitted, and they made good progress. The energy with which the march was conducted excited the surprise of the British authorities
in Canada,[1] and contrasted well with other military
movements of the year; but vigorous as it was it
still lagged behind events. Hull had moved only

[1] Prevost to Brock, July 31, 1812. Tupper's Life of Brock,
p. 209.

some seventy-five miles, when, June 26,[1] he received from Secretary Eustis a despatch, forwarded by special messenger from the Department, to warn him that war was close at hand. " Circumstances have recently occurred," wrote Secretary Eustis, " which render it necessary you should pursue your march to Detroit with all possible expedition. The highest confidence is reposed in your discretion, zeal, and perseverance."

The despatch, dated June 18, was sent by the secretary on the morning of that day in anticipation of the vote taken in Congress a few hours later.[2] Hull had every reason to understand its meaning, for he expected to lead his army against the enemy. " In the event of hostilities," he had written June 24,[3] " I feel a confidence that the force under my command will be superior to any which can be opposed to it. It now exceeds two thousand rank and file." On receiving the secretary's pressing orders Hull left his heavy camp-equipage behind, and hurried his troops to the Miami, or Maumee, River thirty-five miles away. There he arrived June 30, and there, to save transportation, loading a schooner with his personal baggage, his hospital stores, entrenching tools, and even a trunk containing his instructions and the muster-rolls of his army, he despatched it, July 1, up the Lake toward Detroit.

[1] Hull's Trial ; Defence, pp. 21, 22.
[2] Hull's Trial ; Evidence of Eustis, Appendix, p. 4.
[3] Defence of Dearborn, p. 9.

He took for granted that he should receive from his own government the first notice of war; yet he knew that the steamboat from New York to Albany and the road from Albany to Buffalo, which carried news to the British forces at Malden, was also the regular mode of conveyance for Detroit; and he had every reason to suspect that as his distance in time from Washington was greater, he might learn of war first from actual hostilities. Hull considered "there was no hazard" in sending his most valuable papers past Malden;[1] but within four-and-twenty hours he received a despatch from Secretary Eustis announcing the declaration of war, and the same day his schooner was seized by the British in passing Malden to Detroit.

This first disaster told the story of the campaign. The declaration made at Washington June 18 was published by General Bloomfield at New York June 20, and reached Montreal by express June 24; the same day it reached the British Fort George on the Niagara River and was sent forward to Malden, where it arrived June 30. The despatch to Hull reached Buffalo two days later than the British express, for it went by ordinary mail; from Cleveland it was forwarded by express, June 28, by way of Sandusky, to Hull, whom it reached at last, July 2, at Frenchtown on the river Raisin, forty miles below Detroit.

The slowness of transportation was made con-

[1] Memoirs, p. 36.

spicuous by another incident. John Jacob Astor,
being engaged in extensive trade with the Northwestern Indians, for political reasons had been encouraged by government. Anxious to save the large
amount of property exposed to capture, he not only
obtained the earliest intelligence of war, and warned
his agents by expresses, but he also asked and received from the Treasury orders [1] addressed to the
Collectors on the Lakes, directing them to accept and
hold such goods as might be brought from Astor's
trading-posts. The business of the Treasury as well
as that of Astor was better conducted than that of
the War Department. Gallatin's letters reached
Detroit before Eustis's despatch reached Hull; and
this incident gave rise to a charge of misconduct
and even of treason against Gallatin himself.[2]

Hull reached Detroit July 5. At that time the
town contained about eight hundred inhabitants
within gunshot of the British shore. The fort was
a square enclosure of about two acres, surrounded
by an embankment, a dry ditch, and a double row
of pickets. Although capable of standing a siege,
it did not command the river; its supplies were insufficient for many weeks; it was two hundred miles
distant from support, and its only road of communication ran for sixty miles along the edge of Lake
Erie, where a British fleet on one side and a horde
of savages on the other could always make it impass-

[1] Gallatin's Writings, ii. 503–511.
[2] Armstrong's Notices, i. 48.

able.   The widely scattered people of the territory, numbering four or five thousand, promised to become a serious burden in case of siege or investment.   Hull knew in advance that in a military sense Detroit was a trap.

July 9, four days after his arrival, Hull received orders from Washington authorizing him to invade Canada : —

" Should the force under your command be equal to the enterprise, consistent with the safety of your own post, you will take possession of Malden, and extend your conquests as circumstances may justify."

He replied immediately the same day : [1] —

" I am preparing boats, and shall pass the river in a few days.   The British have established a post directly opposite this place.   I have confidence in dislodging them, and of being in possession of the opposite bank. . . . The British command the water and the savages. I do not think the force here equal to the reduction of Amherstburg (Malden) ; you therefore must not be too sanguine."

Three days later, July 12, his army crossed the river.   Not a gun was fired.   The British militia force retired behind the Canard River, twelve miles below, while Hull and his army occupied Sandwich, and were well received by the inhabitants.

Hull had many reasons for wishing to avoid a battle.   From the first he looked on the conquest of

[1] Hull's Trial; Hull to Eustis, July 9, 1812, Appendix, p. 9; Clarke's Life of Hull, p. 335.

Canada as a result of his mere appearance. He began by issuing a proclamation [1] intended to win a peaceful conquest.

" You will be emancipated," said the proclamation to the Canadians, " from tyranny and oppression, and restored to the dignified station of freemen. . . . I have a force which will break down all opposition, and that force is but the vanguard of a much greater. . . . The United States offer you peace, liberty, and security, — your choice lies between these and war, slavery, or destruction. Choose then; but choose wisely." . . .

This proclamation, dated July 12, was spread throughout the province with no small effect, although it contained an apparently unauthorized threat, that " no white man found fighting by the side of an Indian will be taken prisoner; instant death will be his lot." The people of the western province were strongly American, and soon to the number of three hundred and sixty-seven, including deserters from the Malden garrison, sought protection in the American lines.[2] July 19 Hull described the situation in very hopeful terms: [3] —

" The army is encamped directly opposite to Detroit. The camp is entrenched. I am mounting the 24-pounders and making every preparation for the siege of Malden. The British force, which in numbers was superior to the American, including militia and Indians, is daily dimin-

[1] Hull's Memoirs, pp. 45, 46. Trial, App. (18).
[2] Hull's Trial; Evidence of Col. Joseph Watson, p. 151.
[3] Hull to Eustis, July 19, 1812; War Department MSS.

ishing. Fifty or sixty (of the militia) have deserted daily since the American standard was displayed, and taken protection. They are now reduced to less than one hundred. In a day or two I expect the whole will desert. The Indian force is diminishing in the same proportion. I have now a large council of ten or twelve nations sitting at Brownstown, and I have no doubt but the result will be that they will remain neutral. The brig 'Adams' was launched on the 4th of July. I have removed her to Detroit under cover of the cannon, and shall have her finished and armed as soon as possible. We shall then have the command of the upper lakes."

To these statements Hull added a warning, which carried at least equal weight : —

"If you have not a force at Niagara, the whole force of the province will be directed against this army. . . . It is all important that Niagara should be invested. All our success will depend upon it."

While Hull reached this position, July 19, he had a right to presume that the Secretary of War and Major-General Dearborn were straining every nerve to support him ; but in order to understand Hull's situation, readers must know what Dearborn and Eustis were doing. Dearborn's movements, compared day by day with those of Hull, show that after both officers left Washington in April to take command of their forces, Hull reached Cincinnati May 10, while Dearborn reached Albany May 3, and wrote, May 8, to Eustis that he had fixed on a site to be purchased for a military station. "I shall remain here

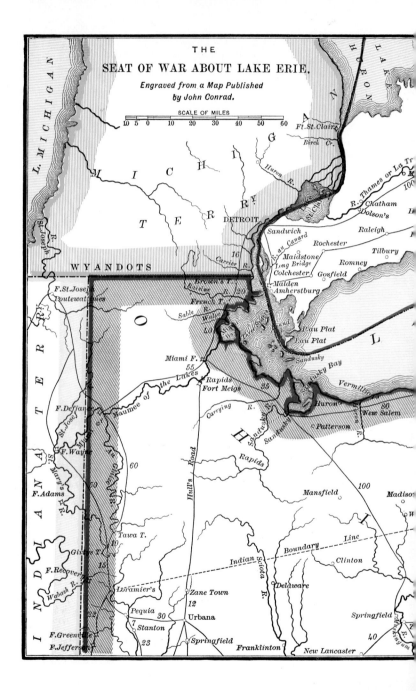

THE
SEAT OF WAR ABOUT LAKE ERIE.

Engraved from a Map Published
by John Conrad.

SCALE OF MILES
10 5 0 · 10 · 20 · 30 · 40 · 50 · 60

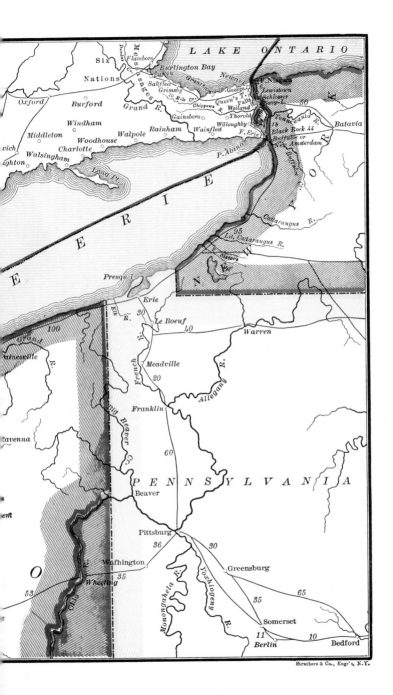

until the erection of buildings is commenced. . . . The recruiting seems going on very well where it has been commenced. There are nearly three hundred recruits in this State." [1] If Dearborn was satisfied with three hundred men as the result of six weeks' recruiting in New York State in immediate prospect of a desperate war, he was likely to take his own duties easily; and in fact, after establishing his headquarters at Albany for a campaign against Montreal, he wrote, May 21, to the Secretary announcing his departure for Boston: "As the quartermaster-general arrived here this day I hope to be relieved from my duties in that line, and shall set out for Pittsfield, Springfield, and Boston; and shall return here as soon as possible after making the necessary arrangements at those places."

Dearborn reached Boston May 26, the day after Hull took command at Dayton. May 29 he wrote again to Eustis: "I have been here three days. . . . There are about three hundred recruits in and near this town. . . . Shall return to Albany within a few days." Dearborn found business accumulate on his hands. The task of arranging the coast defences absorbed his mind. He forgot the passage of time, and while still struggling with questions of gunboats, garrisons, field-pieces, and enlistments he was surprised, June 22, by receiving the declaration of war. Actual war threw still more labor and anxiety upon him. The State of Massachusetts behaved as ill as

[1] Dearborn to Eustis, May 8, 1812; War Department MSS.

possible. " Nothing but their fears," he wrote,[1] " will prevent their going all lengths." More used to politics than to war, Dearborn for the time took no thought of military movements.

Madison and Eustis seemed at first satisfied with this mode of conducting the campaign. June 24 Eustis ordered Hull to invade West Canada, and extend his conquests as far as practicable. Not until June 26 did he write to Dearborn,[2] —

" Having made the necessary arrangements for the defence of the sea-coast, it is the wish of the President that you should repair to Albany and prepare the force to be collected at that place for actual service. It is understood that being possessed of a full view of the intentions of Government, and being also acquainted with the disposition of the force under your command, you will take your own time and give the necessary orders to the officers on the sea-coast. It is altogether uncertain at what time General Hull may deem it expedient to commence offensive operations. The preparations it is presumed will be made to move in a direction for Niagara, Kingston, and Montreal. On your arrival at Albany you will be able to form an opinion of the time required to prepare the troops for action."

Such orders as those of June 24 to Hull, and of June 26 to Dearborn, passed beyond bounds of ordinary incapacity, and approached the line of culpable neglect. Hull was to move when he liked, and Dearborn was to take his own time at Boston before be-

[1] Dearborn to Eustis, June 26, 1812 ; War Department MSS.

[2] Clarke's Life of Hull, p. 417. Hull's Memoirs, p. 173.

ginning to organize his army. Yet the letter to Dearborn was less surprising than Dearborn's reply. The major-general in charge of operations against Montreal, Kingston, and Niagara should have been able to warn his civil superior of the risks incurred in allowing Hull to make an unsupported movement from an isolated base such as he knew Detroit to be; but no thought of Hull found place in Dearborn's mind. July 1 he wrote:[1] —

"There has been nothing yet done in New England that indicates an actual state of war, but every means that can be devised by the Tories is in operation to depress the spirits of the country. Hence the necessity of every exertion on the part of the Government for carrying into effect the necessary measures for defence or offence. We ought to have gunboats in every harbor on the coast. Many places will have no other protection, and all require their aid. I shall have doubts as to the propriety of my leaving this place until I receive your particular directions after you shall have received my letter."

Dearborn complained with reason of the difficulties that surrounded him. Had Congress acted promptly, a large body of volunteers would have been already engaged, general officers would have been appointed and ready for service, whereas no general officer except himself was yet at any post north of New York city. Every day he received from every quarter complaints of want of men, clothing, and sup-

[1] Dearborn to Eustis, July 1, 1812; War Department MSS.

plies ; but his remaining at Boston to watch the conduct of the State government was so little likely to overcome these difficulties that at last it made an unfavorable impression on the Secretary, who wrote, July 9, a more decided order from Washington : [1] —

"The period has arrived when your services are required at Albany, and I am instructed by the President to direct, that, having made arrangements for placing the works on the sea-coast in the best state of defence your means will permit, . . . you will then order all the recruits not otherwise disposed of to march immediately to Albany, or some station on Lake Champlain, to be organized for the invasion of Canada."

With this official letter Eustis sent a private letter [2] of the same date, explaining the reason for his order : —

"If . . . we divide, distribute, and render inefficient the force authorized by law, we play the game of the enemy within and without. District among the field-officers the sea-board ! . . . Go to Albany or the Lake ! The troops shall come to you as fast as the season will admit, and the blow must be struck. Congress must not meet without a victory to announce to them."

Dearborn at Boston replied to these orders, July 13,[3] a few hours after Hull's army, six hundred miles away, crossed the Detroit River into Canada and challenged the whole British force on the lakes.

[1] Eustis to Dearborn, July 9, 1812; War Department MSS.
[2] Eustis to Dearborn, July 9, 1812; Dearborn MSS.
[3] Dearborn to Eustis, July 13, 1812; War Department MSS.

" For some time past I have been in a very unpleasant situation, being at a loss to determine whether or not I ought to leave the sea-coast. As soon as war was declared [June 18] I was desirous of repairing to Albany, but was prevented by your letters of May 20 and June 12, and since that time by the extraordinary management of some of the governors in this quarter. On the receipt of your letter of June 26 I concluded to set out in three or four days for Albany, but the remarks in your letter of the 1st inst. prevented me. But having waited for more explicit directions until I begin to fear that I may be censured for not moving, and having taken such measures as circumstances would permit for the defence of the sea-coast, I have concluded to leave this place for Albany before the end of the present week unless I receive orders to remain."

A general-in-chief unable to decide at the begin ning of a campaign in what part of his department his services were most needed was sure to be taught the required lesson by the enemy. Even after these warnings Dearborn made no haste. Another week passed before he announced, July 21, his intended departure for Albany the next day, but without an army. " Such is the opposition in this State as to render it doubtful whether much will be done to effect in raising any kind of troops." The two months he passed in Boston were thrown away ; the enlistments were so few as to promise nothing, and the governor of Massachusetts barely condescended to acknowledge without obeying his request for militia to defend the coast.

July 26, one week after Hull had written that all his success depended on the movements at Niagara, Dearborn reached Albany and found there some twelve hundred men not yet organized or equipped. He found also a letter, dated July 20, from. the Secretary of War, showing that the Government had begun to feel the danger of its position.[1] "I have been in daily expectation of hearing from General Hull, who probably arrived in Detroit on the 8th inst." In fact Hull arrived in Detroit July 5, and crossed into Canada July 12; but when the secretary wrote, July 20, he had not yet heard of either event. "You will make such arrangements with Governor Tompkins," continued Eustis, "as will place the militia detached by him for Niagara and other posts on the lakes under your control; and there should be a communication, and if practicable a co-operation, throughout the whole frontier."

The secretary as early as June 24 authorized Hull to invade Canada West, and his delay in waiting till July 20 before sending similar orders to the general commanding the force at Niagara was surprising; but if Eustis's letter seemed singular, Dearborn's answer passed belief. For the first time General Dearborn then asked a question in regard to his own campaign, — a question so extraordinary that every critic found it an enigma: "Who is to have command of the operations in Upper Canada? I take

[1] Eustis to Dearborn, July 20, 1812; MSS. War Department Records.

it for granted that my command does not extend to that distant quarter." [1]

July 26, when Hull had been already a fortnight on British soil, a week after he wrote that his success depended on co-operation from Niagara, the only force at Niagara consisted of a few New York militia, not co-operating with Hull or under the control of any United States officer, while the major-general of the Department took it for granted that Niagara was not included in his command. The Government therefore expected General Hull, with a force which it knew did not at the outset exceed two thousand effectives, to march two hundred miles, constructing a road as he went; to garrison Detroit; to guard at least sixty miles of road under the enemy's guns; to face a force in the field equal to his own, and another savage force of unknown numbers in his rear; to sweep the Canadian peninsula of British troops; to capture the fortress at Malden and the British fleet on Lake Erie, — and to do all this without the aid of a man or a boat between Sandusky and Quebec.

[1] Dearborn to Eustis, July 28, 1812. Defence of Dearborn, p. 4.

CHAPTER XV.

GENERAL HULL, two days after entering Canada, called a council of war, which decided against storming Malden and advised delay. Their reasons were sufficiently strong. After allowing for the sick-list and garrison-duty, the four regiments could hardly supply more than three hundred men each for active service, besides the Michigan militia, on whom no one felt willing to depend. Hull afterward affirmed that he had not a thousand effectives; the highest number given in evidence two years later by Major Jesup was the vague estimate of sixteen or eighteen hundred men. Probably the utmost exertion could not have brought fifteen hundred effectives to the Canadian shore. The British force opposed to them was not to be despised. Colonel St. George commanding at Malden had with him two hundred men of the Forty-first British line, fifty men of the Royal Newfoundland regiment, and thirty men of the Royal Artillery.[1] Besides these two hundred and eighty veteran troops with their officers, he had July 12 about six hun-

[1] Richardson, p. 5; Christie, ii. 34; Prevost to Bathurst, Aug. 26, 1812; Brock to Prevost, Aug. 7, 1812; Niles, iii. 265, 266.

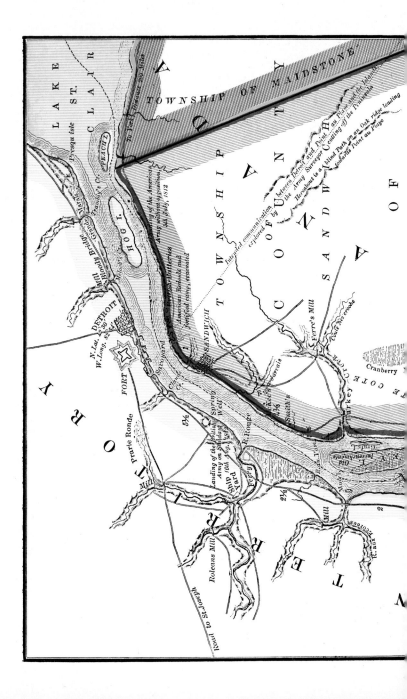

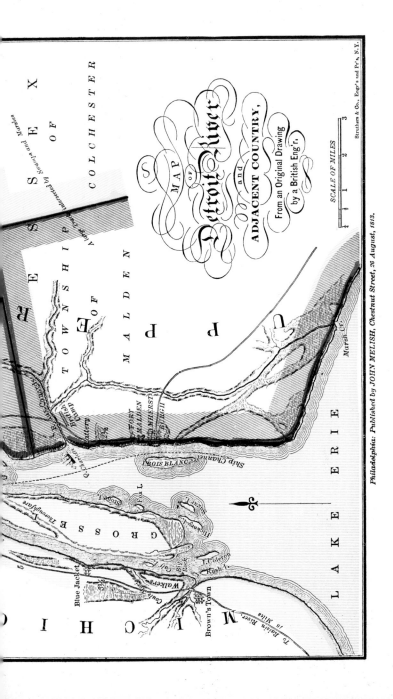

MAP
OF
Detroit River,
and
ADJACENT COUNTRY,
From an Original Drawing
by a British Eng'r.

SCALE OF MILES

Struthers & Co., Eng'r's and Pr's, N.Y.

Philadelphia: Published by JOHN MELISH, Chestnut Street, 26 August, 1813.

dred Canadian militia and two hundred and thirty Indians.[1] The militia deserted rapidly ; but after allowing for the desertions, the garrison at Malden, including Indians, numbered nearly nine hundred men. The British had also the advantage of position, and of a fleet whose guns covered and supported their left. They were alarmed and cautious, but though they exaggerated Hull's force they meant to meet him in front of their fortress.[2] Hull's troops would have shown superiority to other American forces engaged in the campaign of 1812 had they won a victory.

The Ohio militia, although their officers acquiesced in the opinion of the council of war, were very unwilling to lose their advantage. If nothing was to be gained by attack, everything was likely to be lost by delay. Detachments scoured the country, meeting at first little resistance, one detachment even crossing the Canard River, flanking and driving away the guard at the bridge ; but the army was not ready to support the unforeseen success, and the bridge was abandoned. Probably this moment was the last when an assault could have been made with a chance of success. July 19 and 24 strong detachments were driven back with loss, and the outlook became suddenly threatening.

Hull tried to persuade himself that he could take

[1] Lieutenant-Colonel Raby to Captain Gleg, July 27, 1812. Proctor to Brock, July 26, 1812. MSS. Canadian Archives.

[2] Richardson, p. 9.

Malden by siege. July 22 he wrote to Eustis that he was pressing the preparation of siege guns : [1] —

"I find that entirely new carriages must be built for the 24-pounders and mortars. It will require at least two weeks to make the necessary preparations. It is in the power of this army to take Malden by storm, but it would be attended in my opinion with too great a sacrifice under the present circumstances. . . . If Malden was in our possession, I could march this army to Niagara or York (Toronto) in a very short time."

This was Hull's last expression of confidence or hope. Thenceforward every day brought him fatal news. His army lost respect for him in consequence of his failure to attack Malden ; the British strengthened the defences of Malden, and August 8 received sixty fresh men of the Forty-first under Colonel Proctor from Niagara ; [2] but worse than mutiny or British reinforcement, news from the Northwest of the most disastrous character reached Hull at a moment when his hopes of taking Malden had already faded. August 3 the garrison of Michillimackinaw arrived at Detroit as prisoners-of-war on parole, announcing that Mackinaw had capitulated July 17 to a force of British and savages, and that Hull must prepare to receive the attack of a horde of Indians coming from the Northwest to fall upon Detroit in the rear.

[1] Hull to Eustis, July 22, 1812. Hull's Defence, App. No. 2 (10).

[2] Richardson, p. 18.

Hull called another council of war August 5, which, notwithstanding this news, decided to attack Malden August 8, when the heavy artillery should be ready; but while they were debating this decision, a party of Indians under Tecumthe crossing the river routed a detachment of Findlay's Ohio regiment on their way to protect a train of supplies coming from Ohio. The army mail-bags fell into British hands. Hull then realized that his line of communication between Detroit and the Maumee River was in danger, if not closed. On the heels of this disaster he received, August 7, letters from Niagara announcing the passage of British reinforcements up Lake Ontario to Lake Erie and Malden. Thus he was called to meet in his front an intrenched force nearly equal to his own, while at least a thousand Indian warriors were descending on his flank from Lake Huron, and in the rear his line of communication and supply could be restored only by detaching half his army for the purpose.

Hull decided at once to recross the river, and succeeded in effecting this movement on the night of August 8 without interference from the enemy; but his position at Detroit was only one degree better than it had been at Sandwich. He wished to abandon Detroit and retreat behind the Maumee, and August 9 proposed the measure to some of his principal officers. Colonel Cass replied that if this were done every man of the Ohio militia would refuse to obey, and would desert their general;[1] that the army

[1] Hull's Trial, Cass's testimony. Hull's Memoirs, p. 64.

would fall to pieces if ordered to retreat. Hull considered that this report obliged him to remain where he was.

This was the situation at Detroit August 9,—a date prominent in the story; but Hull's true position could be understood only after learning what had been done in Canada since the declaration of war.

The difficulties of Canada were even greater than those of the United States. Upper Canada, extending from Detroit River to the Ottawa within forty miles of Montreal, contained not more than eighty thousand persons. The political capital was York, afterward Toronto, on Lake Ontario. The civil and military command of this vast territory was in the hands of Brigadier-General Isaac Brock, a native of Guernsey, forty-two years old, who had been colonel of the Forty-ninth regiment of the British line, and had served since 1802 in Canada. The appointment of Brock in October, 1811, to the chief command at the point of greatest danger was for the British a piece of good fortune, or good judgment, more rare than could have been appreciated at the time, even though Dearborn, Hull, Winchester, Wilkinson, Sir George Prevost himself, and Colonel Proctor were examples of the common standard. Brock was not only a man of unusual powers, but his powers were also in their prime. Neither physical nor mental fatigue such as followed his rivals' exertions paralyzed his plans. No scruples about bloodshed stopped him midway to victory. He stood alone in his superiority as a soldier. Yet his civil difficulties were as great as his military, for he had to deal with a people better disposed toward his enemies than toward himself; and he succeeded in both careers.

Under Brock's direction, during the preceding winter vessels had been armed on Lake Erie, and Malden had been strengthened by every means in his power. These precautions gave him from the outset the command of the lake, which in itself was almost equivalent to the command of Detroit. Of regular troops he had but few. The entire regular force in both Canadas at the outbreak of the war numbered six thousand three hundred and sixty rank and file, or about seven thousand men including officers. More than five thousand of these were stationed in Lower Canada. To protect the St. Lawrence, the Niagara, and the Detroit, Brock had only fourteen hundred and seventy-three rank and file, or including his own regiment, — the Forty-ninth, then at Montreal, — two thousand one hundred and thirty-seven men at the utmost.[1]

When the news of war reached him, not knowing where to expect the first blow, Brock waited, moving between Niagara and Toronto, until Hull's passage of the Detroit River, July 12, marked the point of danger and startled the province almost out of its dependence on England. "Sir George Prevost, the

[1] Abstracts of General Returns of Troops in Upper and Lower Canada, July 30, 1812. Freer Papers, 1812–1813. MSS. Canadian Archives.

governor-general, reported with much mortification the effect of Hull's movement on Upper Canada :

"Immediately upon the invasion of the province," wrote Sir George, August 17,[1] "and upon the issuing of the proclamation by General Hull, which I have the honor of herewith transmitting, it was plainly perceived by General Brock that little reliance could be placed upon the militia, and as little dependence upon the active exertions of any considerable proportion of the population of the country, unless he was vested with full power to repress the disaffected spirit which was daily beginning to show itself, and to restrain and punish the disorders which threatened to dissolve the whole militia force which he had assembled.   He therefore called together the provincial legislature on July 27 in the hope that they would adopt prompt and efficient measures for strengthening the hands of the Government at a period of such danger and difficulty. . . . In these reasonable expectations I am sorry to say General Brock has been miserably disappointed ; and a lukewarm and temporizing spirit, evidently dictated either by the apprehension or the wish that the enemy might soon be in complete possession of the country, having prevented the Assembly from adopting any of the measures proposed to them, they were prorogued on the 5th instant."

Brock himself wrote to Lord Liverpool a similar account of his trials : —

"The invasion of the western district by General Hull," he wrote August 29,[2] "was productive of very

[1] Prevost to Bathurst, Aug. 17, 1812; MSS. British Archives.
[2] Brock to Liverpool, Aug. 29, 1812; MSS. British Archives.

unfavorable sensations among a large portion of the population, and so completely were their minds subdued that the Norfolk militia when ordered to march peremptorily refused. The state of the country required prompt and vigorous measures. The majority of the House of Assembly was likewise seized with the same apprehensions, and may be justly accused of studying more to avoid by their proceedings incurring the indignation of the enemy than the honest fulfilment of their duty. . . . I cannot hide from your Lordship that I considered my situation at that time extremely perilous. Not only among the militia was evinced a disposition to submit tamely, five hundred in the western district having deserted their ranks, but likewise the Indians of the Six Nations, who are placed in the heart of the country on the Grand River, positively refused, with the exception of a few individuals, taking up arms. They audaciously announced their intention after the return of some of their chiefs from General Hull to remain neutral, as if they wished to impose upon the Government the belief that it was possible they could sit quietly in the midst of war. This unexpected conduct of the Indians deterred many good men from leaving their families and joining the militia ; they became more apprehensive of the internal than of the external enemy, and would willingly have compromised with the one to secure themselves from the other."

Brock's energy counterbalanced every American advantage. Although he had but about fifteen hundred regular troops in his province, and was expected to remain on the defensive, the moment war was declared, June 26, he sent to Amherstburg all the

force he could control, and ordered the commandant
of the British post at the island of St. Joseph on
Lake Huron to seize the American fort at Michillimackinaw.   When Hull issued his proclamation of
July 12, Brock replied by a proclamation of July 22.
To Hull's threat that no quarter should be given to
soldiers fighting by the side of Indians, Brock responded by " the certain assurance of retaliation ; "
and he justified the employment of his Indian allies
by arguments which would have been more conclusive had he ventured to reveal his desperate situation.   In truth the American complaint that the
British employed Indians in war meant nothing to
Brock, whose loss of his province by neglect of any
resource at his command might properly have been
punished by the utmost penalty his Government could
inflict.

Brock's proclamation partly restored confidence.
When his legislature showed backwardness in supporting him he peremptorily dismissed them, August
5, after they had been only a week in session, and the
same day he left York for Burlington Bay and Lake
Erie.   Before quitting Lake Ontario he could not fail
to inquire what was the American force at Niagara
and what it was doing.   Every one in the neighborhood must have told him that on the American side
five or six hundred militiamen, commanded by no
general officer, were engaged in patrolling thirty-six
miles of river front ; that they were undisciplined,
ill-clothed, without tents, shoes, pay, or ammunition,

and ready to retreat at any sign of attack.[1]   Secure
at that point, Brock hurried toward Malden.   He had
ordered reinforcements to collect at Long Point on
Lake Erie; and August 8, while Hull was withdrawing his army from Sandwich to Detroit, Brock passed
Long Point, taking up three hundred men whom he
found there, and coasted night and day to the Detroit
River.

Meanwhile, at Washington, Eustis sent letter after
letter to Dearborn, pressing for a movement from
Niagara.   July 26 he repeated the order of July 20.[2]
August 1 he wrote, enclosing Hull's despatch of July
19 : " You will make a diversion in his favor at
Niagara and at Kingston as soon as may be practicable, and by such operations as may be within your
control."

Dearborn awoke August 3 to the consciousness
of not having done all that man could do.   He began arrangements for sending a thousand militia to
Niagara, and requested Major-General Stephen Van
Rensselaer of the New York State militia to take
command there in person.   In a letter of August 7 to
the Secretary of War, he showed sense both of his
mistakes and of their results : [3] —

" It is said that a detachment [of British troops] has
been sent from Niagara by land to Detroit; if so, I
should presume before they can march two hundred and

[1] Van Rensselaer's Narrative, pp. 9, 10.

[2] Dearborn's Defence of Dearborn, p. 4.

[3] Dearborn's Defence of Dearborn, p. 4.

fifty miles General Hull will receive notice of their approach, and in season to cut them off before they reach
Fort Malden. It is reported that no ordnance or ammunition have reached Niagara this season, and that there
is great deficiency of these articles. Not having considered any part of the borders of Upper Canada as within
the command intended for me, I have received no reports
or returns from that quarter, and did not until since my
last arrival at this place give any orders to the commanding officers of the respective posts on that frontier."

The consequences of such incapacity showed themselves without an instant's delay. While Dearborn
was writing from Albany, August 7, General Brock,
as has been told, passed from Lake Ontario to Lake
Erie; and the next morning, when Brock reached his
detachment at Long Point, Hull evacuated Sandwich
and retired to Detroit. Had he fallen back on the
Maumee or even to Urbana or Dayton, he would have
done only what Wellington had done more than once
in circumstances hardly more serious, and what Napoleon was about to do three months afterward in
leaving Moscow.

Desperate as Hull's position was, Dearborn succeeded within four-and-twenty hours by an extraordinary chance in almost extricating him, without being
conscious that his action more than his neglect affected Hull's prospects. This chance was due to
the reluctance of the British government to accept
the war. Immediately after the repeal of the Orders
in Council the new Ministry of Lord Liverpool or-

dered their minister, Foster, to conclude an armistice
in case hostilities had begun, and requested their
governor-general to avoid all extraordinary preparations. These orders given in good faith by the British government were exceeded by Sir George Prevost,
who had every reason to wish for peace. Although
he could not make an armistice without leaving General Hull in possession of his conquests in Upper
Canada, which might be extensive, Prevost sent his
adjutant-general, Colonel Baynes, to Albany to ask a
cessation of hostilities, and the same day, August 2,
wrote to General Brock warning him of the proposed
step.[1] Colonel Baynes reached headquarters at Albany August 9, and obtained from Dearborn an agreement that his troops, including those at Niagara,
should act only on the defensive until further orders
from Washington : —

" I consider the agreement as favorable at this period,"
wrote Dearborn to Eustis, " for we could not act offensively except at Detroit for some time, and there it will
not probably have any effect on General Hull or his
movements." [2]

What effect the armistice would have on Hull
might be a matter for prolonged and serious doubt,
but that it should have no effect at all would have
occurred to no ordinary commander. Dearborn had
been urgently ordered, August 1, to support Hull by
a vigorous offensive at Niagara, yet August 9 he

[1] Life of Prevost, p. 39; Life of Brock, p. 214.
[2] Dearborn to Eustis, Aug. 9, 1812; Dearborn's Defence, p. 6.

agreed with the British general to act only on the defensive at Niagara. Detroit was not under Dearborn's command, and therefore was not included in the armistice ; but Dearborn stipulated that the arrangement should include Hull if he wished it. Orders were sent to Niagara August 9, directing the commanding officers " to confine their respective operations to defensive measures," and with these orders Dearborn wrote to Hull proposing a concurrence in the armistice. Had Brock moved less quickly, or had the British government sent its instructions a week earlier, the armistice might have saved Detroit. The chance was narrow, for even an armistice unless greatly prolonged would only have weakened Hull, especially as it could not include Indians other than those actually in British service ; but even the slight chance was lost by the delay until August 9 in sending advices to Niagara and Detroit, for Brock left Long Point August 8, and was already within four days of Detroit when Dearborn wrote from Albany. The last possibility of saving Hull was lost by the inefficiency of American mail-service. The distance from Albany to Buffalo was about three hundred miles. A letter written at Albany August 9 should have reached Niagara by express August 13; Dearborn's letter to Hull arrived there only on the evening of August 17, and was forwarded by General Van Rensselaer the next morning.[1] Even through

[1] Van Rensselaer to Dearborn, Aug. 18, 1812 ; Van Rensselaer's Narrative, App. p. 25.

the British lines it could hardly reach Detroit before August 24.

Slowness such as this in the face of an enemy like Brock, who knew the value of time, left Hull small chance of escape. Brock with his little army of three hundred men leaving Long Point August 8 coasted the shore of the lake, and sailing at night reached Malden late in the evening of August 13, fully eight days in advance of the armistice.

Meanwhile Hull was besieged at Detroit. Immediately after returning there, August 8, he sent nearly half his force — a picked body of six hundred men, including the Fourth U. S. Regiment — to restore his communications with Ohio. Toward afternoon of the next day, when this detachment reached the Indian village of Maguaga fourteen miles south of Detroit, it came upon the British force consisting of about one hundred and fifty regulars of the Forty-first Regiment, with forty or fifty militia and Tecumthe's little band of twenty-five Indians, — about two hundred and fifty men, all told.[1] After a sharp engagement the British force was routed and took to its boats, with a loss of thirteen men or more, while the Indians disappeared in the woods. For some unsatisfactory reason the detachment did not then march to the river Raisin to act as convoy for the supplies, and nothing but honor was acquired by the victory. " It is a painful consideration," reported Hull,[2] " that

[1] Richardson, pp. 16, 24; James's Military Occurrences, i. 65.
[2] Hull to Eustis, Aug. 26, 1812; Niles, iii. 46.

the blood of seventy-five gallant men could only open
the communication as far as the points of their bayonets extended." On receiving a report of the battle
Hull at first inclined to order the detachment to the
Raisin, but the condition of the weather and the
roads changed his mind, and August 10 he recalled
the detachment to Detroit.

The next four days were thrown away by the
Americans. August 13 the British began to establish
a battery on the Canadian side of the river to bom-
bard Detroit. Within the American lines the army
was in secret mutiny. Hull's vacillations and evident alarm disorganized his force. The Ohio colonels
were ready to remove him from his command, which
they offered to Lieutenant-Colonel Miller of the U. S.
Fourth Regiment; but Colonel Miller declined this
manner of promotion, and Hull retained control. August 12 the three colonels united in a letter to the
governor of Ohio, warning him that the existence of
the army depended on the immediate despatch of at
least two thousand men to keep open the line of
communication. "Our supplies must come from our
State; this country does not furnish them." A post-
script added that even a capitulation was talked of
by the commander-in-chief.[1] In truth Hull, who like
most commanders-in-chief saw more of the situation
than was seen by his subordinates, made no concealment of his feelings. Moody, abstracted, wavering
in his decisions, and conscious of the low respect in

[1] McAffee, pp. 83, 84.

which he was held by his troops, he shut himself up and brooded over his desperate situation.

Desperate the situation seemed to be; yet a good general would still have saved Detroit for some weeks, if not altogether. Hull knew that he must soon be starved into surrender;[1] but though already short of supplies he might by vigorous preparations and by rigid economy have maintained himself a month, and he had always the chance of a successful battle. His effective force, by his own showing, still exceeded a thousand men to defend the fort; his supplies of ammunition were sufficient;[2] and even if surrender were inevitable, after the mortifications he had suffered and those he foresaw, he would naturally have welcomed a chance of dying in battle. Perhaps he might have chosen this end, for he had once been a brave soldier; but the thought of his daughter and the women and children of the settlement left to the mercy of Indians overcame him. He shrank from it with evident horror, exaggerating the numbers and brooding over the "greedy violence" of the bands, "numerous beyond any former example," who were descending from the Northwest.[3] Doubtless his fears were well-founded, but a general-in-chief whose mind was paralyzed by such thoughts could not measure himself with Isaac Brock.

[1] Hull to Eustis, Aug. 26, 1812; Niles, iii. 55.

[2] Hull's Trial; Evidence of James Dalliby, pp. 80, 81. Life of Brock, p. 289.

[3] Hull to Eustis, Aug. 26, 1812; Niles, iii. 55.

On the evening of August 14 Hull made one more effort. He ordered two of the Ohio colonels, McArthur and Cass, to select the best men from their regiments, and to open if possible a circuitous route of fifty miles through the woods to the river Raisin. The operation was difficult, fatiguing, and dangerous; but the supplies so long detained at the Raisin, thirty-five miles away by the direct road, must be had at any cost, and the two Ohio colonels aware of the necessity promptly undertook the service. Their regiments in May contained nominally about five hundred men each, all told. Two months of severe labor with occasional fighting and much sickness had probably reduced the number of effectives about one half. The report of Colonel Miller of the U. S. Fourth Regiment in regard to the condition of his command showed this proportion of effectives,[1] and the Fourth Regiment was probably in better health than the militia. The two Ohio regiments of McArthur and Cass numbered perhaps six or seven hundred effective men, and from these the two colonels selected three hundred and fifty, probably the best. By night-time they were already beyond the river Rouge, and the next evening, August 15, were stopped by a swamp less than half way to the river Raisin.

After their departure on the night of August 14 Hull learned that Brock had reached Malden the night before with heavy reinforcements. According to Hull's later story, he immediately sent orders to

[1] Hull's Trial; Evidence of Colonel Miller, p. 111.

McArthur and Cass to return to Detroit, giving the reasons for doing so ;[1] in fact he did not send till the afternoon of the next day,[2] and the orders reached the detachment four-and-twenty miles distant only at sunset August 15. So it happened that on the early morning of August 16 Hull was guarding the fort and town of Detroit with about two hundred and fifty effective men of the Fourth Regiment, about seven hundred men of the Ohio militia, and such of the Michigan militia and Ohio volunteers as may have been present, — all told, about a thousand effectives. Hull estimated his force as not exceeding eight hundred men ;[3] Major Jesup, the acting adjutant-general, reported it as one thousand and sixty, including the Michigan militia.[4] If the sickness and loss of strength at Detroit were in proportion to the waste that soon afterward astonished the generals at Niagara, Hull's estimate was perhaps near the truth.

Meanwhile Brock acted with rapidity and decision. After reaching Malden late at night August 13, he held a council the next day, said to have been attended by a thousand Indian warriors.[5]

" Among the Indians whom I found at Amherstburg," he reported to Lord Liverpool,[6] " and who had arrived from distant parts of the country, I found some extraor-

[1] Memoir, p. 110.
[2] Hull to Eustis, Aug. 26, 1812; Niles, iii. 55.
[3] Hull to Eustis, Aug. 26, 1812; Niles, iii. 55.
[4] Hull's Trial; Evidence of Major Jesup, p. 96.
[5] Life of Brock, p. 228.
[6] Despatch of Aug. 29, 1812; MSS. British Archives.

dinary characters. He who attracted most my attention
was a Shawnee chief, Tecumset, brother to the Prophet,
who for the last two years has carried on contrary to
our remonstrances an active warfare against the United
States. A more sagacious or more gallant warrior does
not, I believe, exist. He was the admiration of every
one who conversed with him."

Brock consumed one day in making his arrangements with them, and decided to move his army
immediately across the Detroit River and throw it
against the fort.

" Some say that nothing could be more desperate than
the measure," [1] he wrote soon afterward ; " but I answer
that the state of the province admits only of desperate
remedies. I got possession of the letters my antagonist
addressed to the Secretary of War, and also the sentiments which hundreds of his army uttered to their
friends. Confidence in their general was gone, and evident despondency prevailed throughout. I crossed the
river contrary to the opinion of Colonel Proctor, etc. It
is therefore no wonder that envy should attribute to good
fortune what, in justice to my own discernment, I must
say proceeded from a cool calculation of the *pours* and
contres."

Probably Brock received then Sir George Prevost's
letter of August 2 warning him of the intended armistice, for Hull repeatedly and earnestly asserted
that Brock spoke to him of the armistice August 16 ;
and although twelve days was a short time for an
express to pass between Montreal and Malden, yet it

---

[1] Letter of Sept. 3, 1812; Life, p. 267.

might have been accomplished at the speed of about fifty miles a day. If Brock had reason to expect an armistice, the wish to secure for his province the certainty of future safety must have added a motive for hot haste.

At noon August 15 Brock sent a summons of surrender across the river to Hull. "The force at my disposal," he wrote, "authorizes me to require of you the surrender of Detroit. It is far from my inclination to join in a war of extermination, but you must be aware that the numerous body of Indians who have attached themselves to my troops will be beyond my control the moment the contest commences." The threat of massacre or Indian captivity struck Hull's most sensitive chord. After some delay he replied, refusing to surrender, and then sent orders recalling McArthur's detachment; but the more he thought of his situation the more certain he became that the last chance of escape had vanished. In a few days or weeks want of provisions would oblige him to capitulate, and the bloodshed that would intervene could serve no possible purpose. Brock's movements increased the general's weakness. As soon as Hull's reply reached the British lines, two British armed vessels — the "Queen Charlotte" of seventeen guns and the "Hunter" of ten guns — moved up the river near Sandwich, while a battery of guns and mortars opened fire from the Canadian shore and continued firing irregularly all night on the town and fort. The fire was returned, but no energetic measures were taken to prepare either for an assault or a siege.

During the night Tecumthe and six hundred Indians crossed the river some two miles below and filled the woods, cutting communication between McArthur's detachment and the fort. A little before daylight of August 16 Brock himself, with three hundred and thirty regulars and four hundred militia, crossed the river carrying with them three 6-pound and two 3-pound guns. He had intended to take up a strong position and force Hull to attack it; but learning from his Indians that McArthur's detachment, reported as five hundred strong, was only a few miles in his rear he resolved on an assault, and moved in close column within three quarters of a mile of the American 24-pound guns. Had Hull prayed that the British might deliver themselves into his hands, his prayers could not have been better answered. Even under trial for his life, he never ventured to express a distinct belief that Brock's assault could have succeeded ; and in case of failure the small British force must have retreated at least a mile and a half under the fire of the fort's heavy guns, followed by a force equal to their own, and attacked in flank and rear by McArthur's detachment, which was within hearing of the battle and marching directly toward it.

" Nothing but the boldness of the enterprise could have insured its success," said Richardson, one of Brock's volunteers.[1] " When within a mile and a half of the

[1] Richardson, p. 30.

rising ground commanding the approach to the town we distinctly saw two long, heavy guns, afterward proved to be 24-pounders, planted in the road, and around them the gunners with their fuses burning. At each moment we expected that they would be fired, . . . and fearful in such case must have been the havoc; for moving as we were by the main road, with the river close upon our right flank and a chain of alternate houses and close fences on our left, there was not the slightest possibility of deploying. In this manner and with our eyes riveted on the guns, which became at each moment more visible, we silently advanced until within about three quarters of a mile of the formidable battery, when General Brock, having found at this point a position favorable for the formation of the columns of assault, caused the whole to be wheeled to the left through an open field and orchard leading to a house about three hundred yards off the road, which he selected as his headquarters. In this position we were covered."

All this time Hull was in extreme distress. The cannon-shot from the enemy's batteries across the river were falling in the fort. Uncertain what to do, the General sat on an old tent on the ground with his back against the rampart. "He apparently unconsciously filled his mouth with tobacco, putting in quid after quid more than he generally did; the spittle colored with tobacco-juice ran from his mouth on his neckcloth, beard, cravat, and vest." [1] He seemed preoccupied, his voice trembled, he was greatly agitated, anxious, and fatigued. Knowing that sooner

[1] Hull's Trial; Evidence of Major Snelling, p. 40.

or later the fort must fall, and dreading massacre for
the women and children; anxious for the safety of
McArthur and Cass, and treated with undisguised
contempt by the militia officers, — he hesitated, took
no measure to impede the enemy's advance, and at
last sent a flag across the river to negotiate. A
cannon-ball from the enemy's batteries killed four
men in the fort; two companies of the Michigan
militia deserted, — their behavior threatening to leave
the town exposed to the Indians, — and from that
moment Hull determined to surrender on the best
terms he could get.

As Brock, after placing his troops under cover,
ascended the brow of the rising ground to reconnoitre
the fort, a white flag advanced from the battery before
him, and within an hour the British troops, to their
own undisguised astonishment, found themselves in
possession of the fortress. The capitulation included
McArthur's detachment and the small force covering
the supplies at the river Raisin. The army, already
mutinous, submitted with what philosophy it could
command to the necessity it could not escape.

On the same day at the same hour Fort Dearborn
at Chicago was in flames. The Government provided
neither for the defence nor for the safe withdrawal
of the little garrison, but Hull had sent an order to
evacuate the fort if practicable. In the process of
evacuation, August 15, the garrison was attacked and
massacred by an overwhelming body of Indians. The
next morning the fort was burned, and with it the

last vestige of American authority on the western lakes disappeared. Thenceforward the line of the Wabash and the Maumee became the military boundary of the United States in the Northwest, and the country felt painful doubt whether even that line could be defended.

CHAPTER XVI.

ALTHOUGH the loss of Detroit caused the greatest loss of territory that ever before or since befell the United States, the public at large understood little of the causes that made it inevitable, and saw in it only an accidental consequence of Hull's cowardice. Against this victim, who had no friend in the world, every voice was raised. He was a coward, an imbecile, but above all unquestionably a traitor, who had, probably for British gold, delivered an army and a province, without military excuse, into the enemy's hands. If any man in the United States was more responsible than Hull for the result of the campaign it was Ex-President Jefferson, whose system had shut military efficiency from the scope of American government; but to Jefferson, Hull and his surrender were not the natural products of a system, but objects of hatred and examples of perfidy that had only one parallel. "The treachery of Hull, like that of Arnold, cannot be a matter of blame to our government," he wrote [1] on learning the story of Lewis Cass and the Ohio militia officers, who told with the usual bitter-

[1] Jefferson to Duane, Oct. 1, 1812; Works, vi. 79.

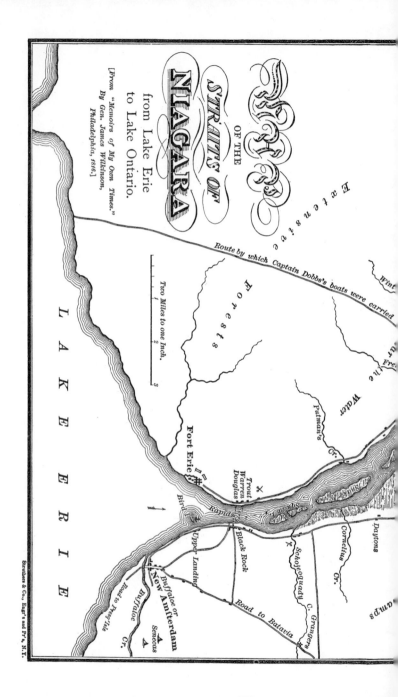

Maps
OF THE
STRAITS OF
NIAGARA
from Lake Erie
to Lake Ontario.

[From "Memoirs of My Own Times,"
By Gen. James Wilkinson,
Philadelphia, 1816.]

LAKE ERIE

Two Miles to one Inch.

Route by which Captain Dobbs's boats were carried

Extensive Forests

Fort Erie

Trout
Warren
Douglas

Putnam's Cr.

Rapids

Bird

Black Rock

Upper Landing

Buffaloe or
New Amsterdam

Road to Batavia

Schojequady

Cornelius Cr.

Daytons

C. Grangers

Road to Pres'q'isle

Buffaloe
Cr.

Senecas

Struthers & Co., Engr's and Pr's, N.Y.

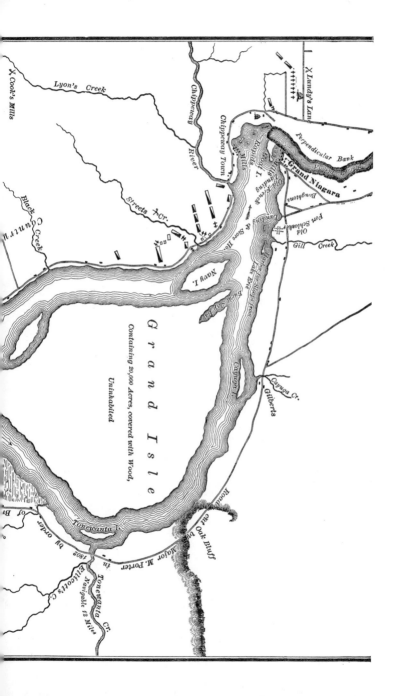

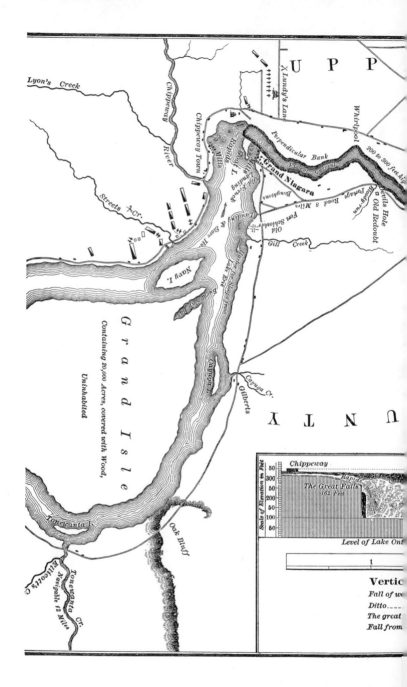

Lyon's Creek

Chippeway River

Chippeway Town

U P P

Whirlpool

200 to 300 feet high

Lundy's Lane

Perpendicular Bank

Mills

Rapids I.

Grand Niagara

Out of the Landing

Boughams

Devils Hole

Portage

Bloody run

Old Redoubt

Streets Cr.

Old Fort Schlosser

Portage Road 8 Mils

Gill Creek

Navy I.

Grand Island from Black Rock

Long Sault & Slow Horse

Lower Lake End

Rapids

G r a n d   I s l e

Cayuga Cr.

Gilberts

Containing 20,000 Acres, covered with Wood,

Uninhabited

U N T Y

Tonewanta I.

Oak Bluff

Tonewanta Cr.

Navigable 12 Miles

Ellicott's Cr.

Chippeway

Scale of Elevation in Feet

50
300
50
200
50
100
50

Rapids

The Great Falls
162 Feet

Level of Lake Ont

1

Vertic

Fall of we

Ditto____

The great

Fall from

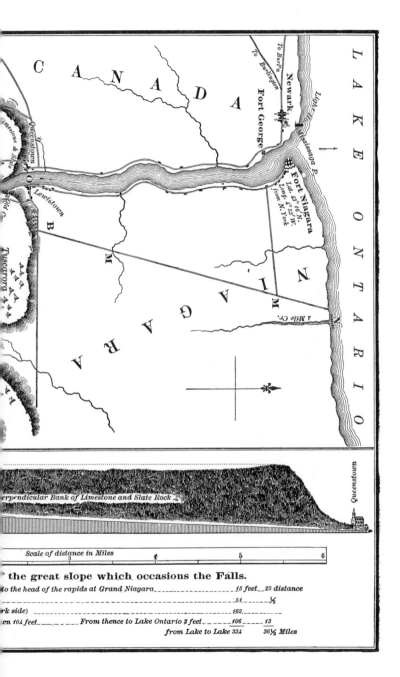

ness of betrayed men what they knew of the causes
that had brought their betrayal to pass. " The de-
testable treason of Hull," as Jefferson persisted in
calling it, was the more exasperating to him because,
even as late as August 4, he had written with entire
confidence to the same correspondent that " the ac-
quisition of Canada this year, as far as the neighborhood of Quebec, will be a mere matter of marching,
and will give us experience for the attack of Halifax
the next, and the final expulsion of England from the
American continent." Perhaps the same expectation explained the conduct of Hull, Madison, Eustis,
and Dearborn ; yet at the moment when Jefferson
wrote thus, Madison was beginning to doubt. August
8, the often-mentioned day when Brock reached Long
Point and Hull decided to retreat from Canada, Madison wrote to Gallatin : [1] —

" Should he [Hull] be able to descend upon Niagara
and an adequate co-operation be there afforded, our prospect as to Upper Canada may be good enough. But
what is to be done with respect to the expedition against
Montreal? The enlistments for the regular army fall
short of the most moderate calculation ; the Volunteer
Act is extremely unproductive ; and even the militia detachments are either obstructed by the disaffected governors or chilled by the Federal spirit diffused throughout the region most convenient to the theatre. I see
nothing better than to draw on this resource as far as

[1] Madison to Gallatin, Aug. 8, 1812 ; Gallatin's Writings,
i. 524.

the detachments consist of volunteers, who, it may be
presumed, will cross the line without raising Constitutional or legal questions."

In contrast with these admissions and their satiri-
cal "it may be presumed," the tone of the governor-
general, Sir George Prevost, at the same crisis was
masterful.[1]

"The Eighth or King's Regiment," he wrote August
17 from Montreal, "has arrived this morning from Quebec to relieve the Forty-ninth Regiment. This fine and
effective regiment of the Eighth, together with a chain
of troops established in the vicinity of this place consisting of a regular and militia force, the whole amounting
to near four thousand five hundred men, effectually serve
to keep in check the enemy in this quarter, where alone
they are in any strength."

The Canadian outnumbered the American forces at
every point of danger on the frontier. A week later
Sir George claimed another just credit : [2] —

"The decided superiority I have obtained on the Lakes
in consequence of the precautionary measures adopted
during the last winter has permitted me to move without interruption, independently of the arrangement [ar-
mistice], both troops and supplies of every description
toward Amherstburg, while those for General Hull, having several hundred miles of wilderness to pass before
they can reach Detroit, are exposed to be harassed and
destroyed by the Indians."

[1] Prevost to Bathurst, Aug. 17, 1812 ; MSS. British Archives.
[2] Prevost to Bathurst, Aug. 24, 1812 ; MSS. British Archives.

Not only were the British forces equal or superior to the American at Detroit, Niagara, and Montreal, but they could be more readily concentrated and more quickly supplied.

The storm of public wrath which annihilated Hull and shook Eustis passed harmless over the head of Dearborn. No one knew that Dearborn was at fault, for he had done nothing; and a general who did nothing had that advantage over his rivals whose activity or situation caused them to act. Dearborn threw the whole responsibility on the War Department. August 15 he wrote to President Madison: [1]

" The particular circumstances which have created the most unfortunate embarrassments were my having no orders or directions in relation to Upper Canada (which I had considered as not attached to my command) until my last arrival at this place, and my being detained so long at Boston *by direction*. If I had been directed to take measures for acting offensively on Niagara and Kingston, with authority such as I now possess, for calling out the militia, we might have been prepared to act on those points as early as General Hull commenced his operations at Detroit; but unfortunately no explicit orders had been received by me in relation to Upper Canada until it was too late even to make an effectual diversion in favor of General Hull. All that I could do was done without any delay."

For the moment, such pleas might serve; but after the capture of Detroit, Dearborn's turn came, and

[1] Dearborn to Madison, Aug. 15, 1812; Madison MSS. State Department Archives.

nothing could save him from a fate as decided if not as fatal as that of Hull. His armistice indeed would have answered the purpose of protection had the Government understood its true bearing; but Dearborn's letter announcing the armistice reached Washington August 13, and the Secretary of War seeing the dangers and not the advantages of a respite replied, August 15, in language more decided than he had yet used: [1] —

"I am commanded by the President to inform you that there does not appear to him any justifiable cause to vary or desist from the arrangements which are in operation; and I am further commanded to instruct you that from and after the receipt of this letter and allowing a reasonable time in which you will inform Sir George Prevost thereof, you will proceed with the utmost vigor in your operations. How far the plan originally suggested by you of attacking Niagara, Kingston, and Montreal at the same time can be rendered practicable, you can best judge. Presuming that not more than a feint, if that should be deemed expedient, with the troops on Lake Champlain aided by volunteers and militia can be immediately effected against Montreal, and considering the urgency of a diversion in favor of General Hull under the circumstances attending his situation, the President thinks it proper that not a moment should be lost in gaining possession of the British posts at Niagara and Kingston, or at least the former, and proceeding in co-operation with General Hull in securing Upper Canada."

[1] Eustis to Dearborn, Aug. 15, 1812; Hull's Memoirs, p. 87.

The same day, August 15, the eve of Hull's surrender, Dearborn wrote to the Secretary of War,[1] —

"If the troops are immediately pushed on from the southward, I think we may calculate on being able to possess ourselves of Montreal and Upper Canada before the winter sets in. . . . I am pursuing measures with the view of being able to operate with effect against Niagara and Kingston, at the same time that I move toward Lower Canada. If the Governor of Pennsylvania turns out two thousand good militia from the northwesterly frontier of his State, as I have requested him to do, and the quartermaster-general furnishes the means of transportation and camp-equipage in season, I am persuaded we may act with effect on the several points in the month of October at farthest."

As yet nothing had been done. August 19 General Van Rensselaer reported[2] from Lewiston that between Buffalo and Niagara he commanded less than a thousand militia, without ordnance heavier than 6-pounders and but few of these, without artillerists to serve the few pieces he had, and the troops in a very indifferent state of discipline. In pursuance of his orders he collected the force within his reach, but August 18 received notice of Dearborn's armistice and immediately afterward of Hull's surrender. August 23 Brock, moving with his usual rapidity, reappeared at Fort George with Hull's army as captives.

[1] Dearborn to Eustis, Aug. 15, 1812 ; War Department MSS.

[2] Van Rensselaer to Tompkins, Aug. 19, 1812; Narrative, Appendix, p. 27.

Fortunately, not only were the Americans protected by the armistice, but both Prevost and Brock were under orders, and held it good policy, to avoid irritating the Americans by useless incursions. Prevost, about the equal of Madison as a military leader, showed no wish to secure the positions necessary for his safety. Had he at once seized Sackett's Harbor, as Brock seized Detroit, he would have been secure, for Sackett's Harbor was the only spot from which the Americans could contest the control of Lake Ontario. Brock saw the opportunity, and wanted to occupy the harbor, but Prevost did not encourage the idea ; [1] and Brock, prevented from making a correct movement, saw no advantage in making an incorrect one. Nothing was to be gained by an offensive movement at Niagara, and Brock at that point labored only to strengthen his defence.

Van Rensselaer, knowing the whole American line to be at Brock's mercy, felt just anxiety. August 31 he wrote to Governor Tompkins,[2] —

" Alarm pervades the country, and distrust among the troops. They are incessantly pressing for furloughs under every possible pretence. Many are without shoes ; all clamorous for pay ; many are sick. . . . While we are thus growing weaker our enemy is growing stronger. They hold a very commanding position on the high ground above Queenstown, and they are daily strengthening themselves in it with men and ordnance. Indeed,

[1] Life of Brock, pp. 293, 294.
[2] Van Rensselaer's Narrative, Appendix, p. 35.

they are fortifying almost every prominent point from Fort Erie to Fort George. At present we rest upon the armistice, but should hostilities be recommenced I must immediately change my position. I receive no reinforcements of men, no ordnance or munitions of war."

Dearborn replied to this letter September 2, and his alarm was certainly not less than that of Van Rensselaer: [1] —

"From the number of troops which have left Montreal for Upper Canada, I am not without fear that attempts will be speedily made to reduce you and your forces to the mortifying situation of General Hull and his army. If such an attempt of the enemy should be made previous to the arrival of the principal part of the troops destined to Niagara, it will be necessary for you to be prepared for all events, and to be prepared to make good a secure retreat as the last resort."

To the Secretary of War, Dearborn wrote that he hoped there would be nothing worse than retreat.[2] Under such circumstances the armistice became an advantage, for the offensive had already passed into the enemy's hands. Detroit and Lake Erie were lost beyond salvation, but on Lake Ontario supplies and cannon were brought to Niagara by water from Oswego; the vessels at Ogdensburg were moved to Sackett's Harbor and became the nucleus of a fleet; while all the troops, regular and militia, that could be gathered from New England, New York, and Penn-

[1] Van Rensselaer's Narrative, Appendix, p. 42.
[2] Dearborn to Eustis, Sept. 14, 1812; War Department MSS.

sylvania were hurried to the front.   September 1
Dearborn wrote to Eustis [1] that he had at Plattsburg,
on Lake Champlain, or under marching orders there,
five thousand troops, more than half of them regulars,
while six thousand, including three regular regiments
from the southward, were destined for Niagara.

" When the regular troops you have ordered for
Niagara arrive at that post,' he wrote to Eustis, September 1, " with the militia and other troops there or
on their march, they will be able I presume to cross
over into Canada, carry all the works in Niagara, and
proceed to the other posts in that province in triumph."

Yet the movement of troops was slow.   September
15 Van Rensselaer had only sixteen hundred militia.[2]
Not till then did the reaction from Hull's disaster
make itself felt.   Commodore Chauncey came to
Lake Ontario with unbounded authority to create a
fleet, and Lieutenant Elliott of the navy was detached
to Lake Erie for the same purpose; ordnance and
supplies were hurried to Buffalo, and Dearborn sent
two regiments from Albany with two companies of
artillery.

" When they arrive," he wrote September 17 to Van
Rensselaer,[3] " with the regular troops and militia from
the southward and such additional numbers of militia as

[1] Dearborn to Eustis, Sept. 1, 1812; War Department MSS.
[2] Van Rensselaer to Tompkins, Sept. 15, 1812 ; Narrative,
Appendix, p. 50.
[3] Dearborn to Van Rensselaer, Sept. 17, 1812 ; Narrative,
Appendix, p. 56.

I reckon on from this State, the aggregate force will I presume amount to upward of six thousand. It is intended to have a force sufficient to enable you to act with effect, though late."

The alarm still continued; and even a week afterward Dearborn wrote as though he expected disaster : [1]

" A strange fatality seems to have pervaded the whole arrangements. Ample reinforcements of troops and supplies of stores are on their way, but I fear their arrival will be too late to enable you to måintain your position. . . . By putting on the best face that your situation admits, the enemy may be induced to delay an attack until you will be able to meet him and carry the war into Canada. At all events we must calculate on possessing Upper Canada before winter sets in."

In Dearborn's letters nothing was said of the precise movement intended, but through them all ran the understanding that as soon as the force at Niagara should amount to six thousand men a forward movement should be made. The conditions supposed to be needed for the advance were more than fulfilled in the early days of October, when some twenty-five hundred militia, with a regiment of Light Artillery without guns, and the Thirteenth U. S. Infantry were in the neighborhood of Lewiston ; while a brigade of United States troops, sixteen hundred and fifty strong, commanded by Brigadier-General Alexander Smyth, were on the march to Buffalo. October 13 Dearborn

[1] Dearborn to Van Rensselaer, Sept. 26, 1812; Narrative, Appendix, p. 59.

wrote to Van Rensselaer:[1] "I am confidently sure
that you will embrace the first practicable opportunity
for effecting a forward movement." This opportunity
had then already arrived. Smyth reached Buffalo,
September 29, and reported by letter to General Van
Rensselaer; but before seeing each other the two
generals quarrelled. Smyth held the opinion that
the army should cross into Canada above the Falls,
and therefore camped his brigade at Buffalo. Van
Rensselaer had made his arrangements to cross below the Falls. October 5 Van Rensselaer requested
Smyth to fix a day for a council of war, but Smyth
paid no attention to the request; and as he was
independent of Van Rensselaer, and could not be
compelled to obey the orders of a major-general of
New York militia, Van Rensselaer decided to act
without regard to Smyth's brigade or to his opinions.
He knew that the force under his immediate orders
below the Falls was sufficient for his purpose.[2]

Van Rensselaer's decision was supported by many
different motives, — the lateness of the season, the
weather, the sickness and the discontent of the militia
threatening actual disbandment, the jealousy of a
militia officer toward the regular service, and the additional jealousy of a Federalist toward the Government; for Van Rensselaer was not only a Federalist,
but was also a rival candidate against Tompkins for

[1] Dearborn to Van Rensselaer, Oct. 13, 1812; War Department
MSS.

[2] Narrative, p. 19.

the governorship of New York, and the Republicans were eager to charge him with intentional delay. A brilliant stroke by Lieutenant Elliott at the same moment added to the restlessness of the army. On the night of October 8 Elliott and Captain Towson of the Second Artillery, with fifty sailors and fifty soldiers of Smyth's brigade, cut out two British vessels under the guns of Fort Erie.[1]   One of these vessels was the " Adams," captured by Brock at Detroit, the other had belonged to the Northwestern Fur Company, and both were of great value to the British as a reinforcement to their fleet on Lake Erie. The larger was destroyed ; the smaller, named the " Caledonia," was saved, and served to increase the little American fleet.   Brock felt keenly the loss of these two vessels, which " may reduce us to incalculable distress," he wrote to Prevost, October 11. He watched the progress of Elliott's and Chauncey's naval preparations with more anxiety than he showed in regard to Dearborn's military movements, although he spared no labor in fortifying himself against these.

General Van Rensselaer conceived a plan for a double attack by throwing one body of troops across the river to carry Queenston, while a strong force of regulars should be conveyed in boats by way of the Lake and landed on the Lake shore in the rear of Fort George to take the fort by storm, — a movement

[1] Report of Lieutenant Elliott, Oct. 9, 1812.   Official Letters, p. 66.

afterward successfully made; but owing to Smyth's conduct the double attack was abandoned, and Van Rensselaer decided to try only the simpler movement against Queenston. Brock with less than two thousand men guarded nearly forty miles of front along the Niagara River, holding at Queenston only two companies of the Forty-ninth Regiment with a small body of militia, — in all about three hundred men. Brock was himself at Fort George, some five miles below Queenston, with the greater part of the Forty-first Regiment, which he had brought back from Detroit, and a number of Indians. The rest of his force was at Chippawa and Fort Erie, opposite Buffalo, where the real attack was expected.

Van Rensselaer fixed the night of October 10 for his movement, and marched the troops to the river at the appointed time; but the crossing was prevented by some blunder in regard to boats, and the troops after passing the night exposed to a furious storm returned to camp. After this miscarriage Van Rensselaer would have waited for a council of war, but the tone of his officers and men satisfied him that any sign of hesitation would involve him in suspicion and injure the service.[1] He postponed the movement until the night of October 12, giving the command of the attack to Colonel Solomon Van Rensselaer of the State militia, whose force was to consist of three hundred volunteers and three hun-

[1] Van Rensselaer to Secretary Eustis, Oct. 14, 1812; Narrative, Appendix, p. 62.

dred regular troops under Lieutenant-Colonel Christie of the Thirteenth Regiment.

At three o'clock on the morning of October 13 the first body of troops embarked. Thirteen boats had been provided. Three of these lost their way, or were forced by the current down stream until obliged to return. Colonel Christie was in one of the boats that failed to land. The command of his men fell to young Captain Wool of the Thirteenth Regiment. The British were on the alert, and although after a volley of musketry they withdrew toward Queenston they quickly returned with reinforcements and began a sharp action, in which Colonel Van Rensselaer was severely wounded and the advance on Queenston was effectually stopped. Daylight appeared, and at a quarter before seven Brock himself galloped up and mounted the hill above the river to watch the contest from an 18-pounder battery on the hill-top.[1] At the same moment Captain Wool with a few men of his regiment climbed up the same heights from the river-side by a path which had been reported to Brock as impassable, and was left unguarded. Reaching the summit, Wool found himself about thirty yards in the rear of the battery from which Brock was watching the contest below. By a rapid flight on foot Brock escaped capture, and set himself immediately to the task of recovering the heights. He had early sent for the Forty-first Regiment under General Sheaffe from Fort George, but without waiting rein-

[1] Life of Brock, p. 330.

forcements he collected a few men — about ninety, it
is said — of the Forty-ninth Regiment who could be
spared below, and sent them to dislodge Wool. The
first British attack was beaten back. The second,
in stronger force with the York Volunteers, was
led by Brock in person; but while he was still at
the foot of the hill, an American bullet struck him
in the breast and killed him on the spot.

At ten o'clock in the morning, Captain Wool,
though painfully wounded, held the heights with two
hundred and fifty men; but the heights had no value
except to cover or assist the movement below, where
the main column of troops with artillery and intrenching tools should have occupied Queenston, and advanced or fortified itself. When Lieutenant-Colonel
Christie, at about seven o'clock, having succeeded in
crossing the river, took command of the force on the
river bank, he could do nothing for want of men,
artillery, and intrenching tools.[1] He could not even
dislodge the enemy from a stone house whence two
light pieces of artillery were greatly annoying the
boats. Unable to move without support he recrossed the river, found General Van Rensselaer half
a mile beyond, and described to him the situation.
Van Rensselaer sent orders to General Smyth to
march his brigade to Lewiston " with every possible
despatch," and ordered Captain Totten of the Engineers across the river, with intrenching tools, to lay
out a fortified camp.

[1] Christie's Report, Feb. 22, 1813 ; Armstrong's Notices, i. 207.

Toward noon General Van Rensselaer himself crossed with Christie to Queenston and climbed the hill, where Lieutenant-Colonel Winfield Scott had appeared as a volunteer and taken the command of Captain Wool's force. Toward three o'clock Lieutenant-Colonel Christie joined the party on the hill. Brigadier-General William Wadsworth of the New York militia was also on the ground, and some few men arrived, until three hundred and fifty regulars and two hundred and fifty militia are said to have been collected on the heights. From their position, at two o'clock, Van Rensselaer and Scott made out the scarlet line of the Forty-first Regiment advancing from Fort George. From Chippawa every British soldier who could be spared hurried to join the Forty-first, while a swarm of Indians swept close on the American line, covering the junction of the British forces and the turning movement of General Sheaffe round the foot of the hill. About one thousand men, chiefly regulars, were concentrating against the six hundred Americans on the heights.[1] General Van Rensselaer, alarmed at the sight, hastened to recross the river to Lewiston for reinforcements.

"By this time," concluded Van Rensselaer in his report of the next day,[2] "I perceived my troops were embarking very slowly. I passed immediately over to accelerate their movements; but to my utter astonishment I found that at the very moment when complete

[1] Life of Brock, p. 324.
[2] Van Rensselaer to Dearborn, Oct. 14, 1812 ; Niles, iii. 138.

victory was in our hands the ardor of the unengaged troops had entirely subsided. I rode in all directions, urged the men by every consideration to pass over; but in vain. Lieutenant-Colonel Bloom who had been wounded in the action returned, mounted his horse, and rode through the camp, as did also Judge Peck who happened to be here, exhorting the companies to proceed; but all in vain."

More unfortunate than Hull, Van Rensselaer stood on the American heights and saw his six hundred gallant soldiers opposite slowly enveloped, shot down, and at last crushed by about a thousand men who could not have kept the field a moment against the whole American force. Scott and his six hundred were pushed over the cliff down to the bank of the river. The boatmen had all fled with the boats. Nothing remained but to surrender; and under the Indian fire even surrender was difficult. Scott succeeded only by going himself to the British line through the Indians, who nearly killed him as he went.

In this day's work ninety Americans were reported as killed. The number of wounded can only be estimated. Not less than nine hundred men surrendered, including skulkers and militia-men who never reached the heights. Brigadier-General William Wadsworth of the New York militia, Lieutenant-Colonel Fenwick of the U. S. Light Artillery, Lieutenant-Colonel Winfield Scott of the Second Artillery, and, among officers of less rank, Captain Totten of the Engineers were among the prisoners. Van Rensselaer's campaign did not, like that of Hull, cost a province, but it sacrificed nearly as many effective troops as were surrendered by Hull.

General Van Rensselaer the next day sent his report of the affair to General Dearborn, and added a request to be relieved of his command. Dearborn, who knew little of the circumstances, ordered him to transfer the command to General Smyth, and wrote to Washington a bitter complaint of Van Rensselaer's conduct, which he attributed to jealousy of the regular service.[1]

Hitherto the military movements against Canada had been directed by Eastern men. Alexander Smyth belonged to a different class. Born in Ireland in 1765, his fortunes led him to Virginia, where he became a respectable member of the Southwestern bar and served in the State legislature. Appointed in 1808 by President Jefferson colonel of the new rifle regiment, in 1812 he became inspector-general, with the rank of brigadier. By his own request he received command of the brigade ordered to Niagara, and his succession to Van Rensselaer followed of course. Dearborn, knowing little of Smyth, was glad to intrust the army to a regular officer in whom he felt confidence; yet an Irish temperament with a Virginian education promised the possibility

[1] Dearborn to Eustis, Oct. 21, 1812; War Department MSS. Dearborn to Madison, Oct. 24, 1812; Madison MSS., State Department Archives.

of a campaign which if not more disastrous than that led by William Hull of Massachusetts, or by Stephen Van Rensselaer of New York, might be equally eccentric.

October 24 Smyth took command at Buffalo, and three weeks later the public read in the newspapers an address issued by him to the " Men of New York," written in a style hitherto unusual in American warfare.

" For many years," Smyth announced to the Men of New York,[1] " you have seen your country oppressed with numerous wrongs. Your government, although above all others devoted to peace, has been forced to draw the sword, and rely for redress of injuries on the valor of the American people. That valor has been conspicuous. But the nation has been unfortunate in the selection of some of those who have directed it. One army has been disgracefully surrendered and lost. Another has been sacrificed by a precipitate attempt to pass it over at the strongest point of the enemy's lines with most incompetent means. The cause of these miscarriages is apparent. The commanders were popular men, ' destitute alike of theory and experience ' in the art of war."

Unmilitary as such remarks were, the address continued in a tone more and more surprising, until at last it became burlesque.

" In a few days the troops under my command will plant the American standard in Canada. They are men accustomed to obedience, silence, and steadiness. They will conquer, or they will die.

[1] Niles, iii. 203.

" Will you stand with your arms folded and look on this interesting struggle? Are you not related to the men who fought at Bennington and Saratoga? Has the race degenerated? Or have you, under the baneful influence of contending factions, forgot your country? Must I turn from you and ask the men of the Six Nations to support the government of the United States? Shall I imitate the officers of the British king, and suffer our ungathered laurels to be tarnished by ruthless deeds? Shame, where is thy blush! No!"

The respectable people of the neighborhood were not wholly discouraged by this call or by a second proclamation, November 17, as little military as the first; or even by an address of Peter B. Porter offering to lead his neighbors into Canada under the command of the " able and experienced officer " who within a few days could and would " occupy all the British fortresses on the Niagara River." A certain number of volunteers offered themselves for the service, although not only the attack but also its details were announced in advance. The British responded by bombarding Black Rock and Fort Niagara; and although their cannon did little harm, they were more effective than the proclamations of the American generals.

November 25 General Smyth issued orders for the invasion, which were also unusual in their character, and prescribed even the gestures and attitudes of the attacking force:[1] "At twenty yards distance the

[1] Lossing, p. 427 *note*.

soldiers will be ordered to trail arms, advance with shouts, fire at five paces distance, and charge bayonets. The soldiers will be *silent* above all things." In obedience to these orders, everything was prepared, November 27, for the crossing, and once more orders were issued in an inspiring tone:[1]

"Friends of your country! ye who have 'the will to do, the heart to dare!' the moment ye have wished for has arrived! Think on your country's honors torn! her rights trampled on! her sons enslaved! her infants perishing by the hatchet! Be strong! be brave! and let the ruffian power of the British king cease on this continent!"

Two detachments were to cross the river from Black Rock before dawn, November 28, to surprise and disable the enemy's batteries and to destroy a bridge five miles below; after this should be done the army was to cross. The British were supposed to have not more than a thousand men within twenty miles to resist the attack of three thousand men from Buffalo. Apparently Smyth's calculations were correct. His two detachments crossed the river at three o'clock on the morning of November 28 and gallantly, though with severe loss, captured and disabled the guns and tore up a part of the bridge without destroying it. At sunrise the army began to embark at the navy yard, but the embarkation continued so slowly that toward afternoon, when all the boats were occupied, only twelve hundred men, with artil-

[1] State Papers, Military Affairs, i. 501.

lery, were on board. "The troops thus embarked," reported Smyth,[1] "moved up the stream to Black Rock without sustaining loss from the enemy's fire. It was now afternoon, and they were ordered to disembark and dine."

This was all. No more volunteers appeared, and no other regulars fit for service remained. Smyth would not cross without three thousand men, and doubtless was right in his caution; but he showed want of courage not so much in this failure to redeem his pledges, as in his subsequent attempt to throw responsibility on subordinates, and on Dearborn who had requested him to consult some of his officers occasionally, and be prepared if possible to cross into Canada with three thousand men at once.[2] Smyth consulted his officers at the moment when consultation was fatal.

"Recollecting your instructions to cross with three thousand men *at once*, and to consult some of my principal officers in ' all important movements,' I called for the field officers of the regulars and twelve-months volunteers embarked."

The council of war decided not to risk the crossing. Winder, who was considered the best of Smyth's colonels, had opposed the scheme from the first, and reported the other officers as strongly against it. Smyth was aware of their opinions, and his

[1] Smyth to Dearborn, Dec. 4, 1812 ; Niles, iii. 282.

[2] Dearborn to Smyth, Oct. 21, 1812; State Papers, Military Affairs, i. 493.

appeal to them could have no object but to shift responsibility. After receiving their decision, Smyth sent a demand for the surrender of Fort Erie, "to spare the effusion of blood," and then ordered his troops to their quarters. The army obeyed with great discontent, but fifteen hundred men still mustered in the boats, when two days afterward Smyth issued another order to embark. Once more Smyth called a council of war, and once more decided to abandon the invasion. With less than three thousand men in the boats at once, the General would not stir.

Upon this, General Smyth's army dissolved. "A scene of confusion ensued which it is difficult to describe," wrote Peter B. Porter soon afterward,[1] — "about four thousand men without order or restraint discharging their muskets in every direction." They showed a preference for General Smyth's tent as their target, which caused the General to shift his quarters repeatedly. A few days afterward Peter B. Porter published a letter to a Buffalo newspaper, attributing the late disgrace "to the cowardice of General Smyth."[2] The General sent a challenge to his subordinate officer, and exchanged shots with him. Smyth next requested permission to visit his family, which Dearborn hastened to grant; and three months afterward, as General Smyth did not request an inquiry into the causes of his failure, the President without express authority of law dropped his name from the army roll.

[1] Niles, iii. 284.   [2] Niles, iii. 264.

When Dearborn received the official report of Smyth's grotesque campaign, he was not so much annoyed by its absurdities as he was shocked to learn that nearly four thousand regular troops sent to Niagara in the course of the campaign could not supply a thousand for crossing the river.[1] Further inquiry explained that sickness had swept away more than half the army. The brigade of regulars at Buffalo, which with the exception of Winder's regiment had never fired a musket, was reduced to less than half its original number, and both officers and men were unfit for active duty.[2] Only rest and care could restore the army to efficiency.

The failures of Hull, Van Rensselaer, and Smyth created a scandal so noisy that little was thought of General Dearborn; yet Dearborn still commanded on Lake Champlain the largest force then under arms, including seven regiments of the regular army, with artillery and dragoons. He clung to the idea of an attack on Montreal simultaneous with Smyth's movement at Niagara.[3] November 8, he wrote from Albany to Eustis that he was about to join the army under General Bloomfield at Plattsburg.[4]

[1] Dearborn to Eustis, December 11, 1812; War Department MSS.

[2] Major Campbell to General Smyth, Nov. 27, 1812 ; Military Affairs, i. 500. General Winder to General Smyth, Dec. 2, 1812 ; Military Affairs, i. 507.

[3] Dearborn to Smyth, Oct. 28 and Nov. 8, 1812; Military Affairs, i. 495, 497.

[4] Dearborn to Eustis, Nov. 8, 1812; War Department MSS.

" I have been detained several days by a severe rheumatic attack, but I shall, by the aid of Dr. Mann, be able to set off this day toward Lake Champlain, where I trust General Bloomfield will be able to move toward Montreal, and with the addition of three thousand regular troops that place might be carried and held this winter; but I cannot consent to crossing the St. Lawrence with an uncertainty of being able to remain there."

Whatever were Dearborn's motives for undertaking the movement, his official report [1] explained that on arriving at Plattsburg he found General Bloomfield ill, and was himself obliged to take command, November 19, when he marched the army about twenty miles to the Canadian line. At that point the militia declined to go further, and Dearborn as quietly as possible, November 23, marched back to Plattsburg. His campaign lasted four days, and he did not enter Canada.

Whether Dearborn, Smyth, or William Hull would have improved the situation by winning a victory or by losing a battle was a question to be answered by professional soldiers; but the situation at best was bad, and when the report of Smyth's crowning failure reached Dearborn it seemed for a moment to overcome his sorely tried temper. "I had anticipated disappointment and misfortune in the commencement of the war," he wrote to Eustis, [2] " but I did by no means apprehend such a deficiency of regular troops

---

[1] Dearborn to Eustis, Nov. 24, 1812; War Department MSS.
[2] Dearborn to Eustis, Dec. 11, 1812; War Department MSS.

and such a series of disasters as we have witnessed."
He intimated his readiness to accept the responsibility
which properly belonged to him, and to surrender his
command. "I shall be happy to be released by any
gentleman whose talents and popularity will command the confidence of the Government and the
country." To the President he wrote at the same
time:[1] "It will be equally agreeable to me to employ such moderate talents as I possess in the service of my country, or to be permitted to retire to
the shades of private life, and remain a mere but
interested spectator of passing events."

[1] Dearborn to Madison, Dec. 13, 1812 ; Madison MSS., State
Department Archives.

CHAPTER XVII.

CULPABLE as was the helplessness of the War Department in 1812, the public neither understood nor knew how to enforce responsibility for disasters which would have gone far to cost a European war minister his life, as they might have cost his nation its existence. By fortune still kinder, the Navy Department escaped penalty of any sort for faults nearly as serious as those committed by its rival. The navy consisted, besides gunboats, of three heavy frigates rated as carrying forty-four guns; three lighter frigates rated at thirty-eight guns; one of thirty-two, and one of twenty-eight; besides two ships of eighteen guns, two brigs of sixteen, and four brigs of fourteen and twelve, — in all sixteen sea-going vessels, twelve of which were probably equal to any vessels afloat of the same class. The eight frigates were all built by Federalist Congresses before President Jefferson's time; the smaller craft, except one, were built under the influence of the war with Tripoli. The Administration which declared war against England did nothing to increase the force. Few of the ships were in first-rate condition. The officers complained that the practice of laying up the frigates in port hastened their decay, and declared that hardly a frigate in the service was as sound as she should be. For this negligence Congress was alone responsible; but the Department perhaps shared the blame for want of readiness when war was declared.

The only ships actually ready for sea, June 18, were the "President," 44, commanded by Commodore Rodgers, at New York, and the "United States," 44, which had cruised to the southward with the "Congress," 38, and "Argus," 16, under the command of Commodore Decatur. Secretary Hamilton, May 21, sent orders to Decatur to prepare for war, and June 5 wrote more urgently:[1] "Have the ships under your command immediately ready for extensive active service, and proceed with them to New York, where you will join Commodore Rodgers and wait further orders. Prepare for battle, which I hope will add to your fame." To Rodgers he wrote on the same day in much the same words:[2] "Be prepared in all respects for extensive service." He asked both officers for their advice how to make the navy most useful. Rodgers's reply, if he made one, was not preserved; but Decatur answered from Norfolk, June 8,[3] —

[1] Hamilton to Decatur, June 5, 1812; MSS. Navy Department Records.

[2] Hamilton to Rodgers, June 5, 1812; MSS. Navy Department Records.

[3] Decatur to Hamilton, June 8, 1812; MSS. Navy Department Records.

" The plan which appears to me to be the best calculated for our little navy . . . would be to send them
out with as large a supply of provisions as they can
carry, distant from our coast and singly, or not more
than two frigates in company, without giving them any
specific instructions as to place of cruising, but to rely
on the enterprise of the officers."

The Department hesitated to adopt Decatur's advice, and began by an effort to concentrate all its
ships at New York, — an attempt in which Secretary
Hamilton could not wholly succeed, for the " Constellation " and the " Chesapeake," 38-gun frigates,
and the " Adams," 28, were not in condition for
sea ; the " Essex," 32, was not quite ready, and
the " Wasp," 18, was bringing despatches from
Europe, while the " Constitution," 44, detained at
Annapolis by the difficulty of shipping a new crew,
could not sail within three weeks. The secretary
ordered Captain Hull, who commanded the " Constitution," to make his way to New York with the
utmost speed, and if his crew were in proper condition, to look for the British frigate " Belvidera "
on the way. The only ships that could be brought
to New York without delay were those of Decatur
at Norfolk. To him the secretary, on the declaration of war, sent orders to proceed with all despatch
northwards, and " to notice the British flag if it
presents itself " on the way. " The ' Belvidera ' is
said to be on our coast," added the secretary.[1] Be-

[1] Hamilton to Decatur, June 18, 1812 ; MSS. Navy Department Records.

fore this letter reached Norfolk, Decatur and his squadron sailed from the Chesapeake and were already within sight of Sandy Hook; so that the only orders from the Navy Department which immediately affected the movement of the frigates were those sent to New York for Commodore Rodgers and the frigate "President," but which included Decatur's squadron when it should arrive.

"For the present," wrote the secretary to Rodgers,[1] "it is desirable that with the force under your command you remain in such position as to enable you most conveniently to receive further more extensive and more particular orders, which will be conveyed to you through New York. But as it is understood that there are one or more British cruisers on the coast in the vicinity of Sandy Hook, you are at your discretion free to strike them, returning immediately after into port. You are free to capture or destroy them."

These orders reached New York June 21. Rodgers in his fine frigate the "President," with the "Hornet," 18, was eager to sail. The hope of capturing the "Belvidera," which had long been an intolerable annoyance to New York commerce, was strong both in the Navy Department and in the navy; but the chance of obtaining prize money from the British West India convoy, just then passing eastward only a few days' sail from the coast, added greatly to the commodore's impatience.[2]

[1] Hamilton to Rodgers, June 18, 1812; MSS. Navy Department Records.

[2] Rodgers to Hamilton. Sept. 1, 1812 ; Official Letters, p. 52.

Decatur's squadron arrived off Sandy Hook June 19.   June 21, within an hour after receiving the secretary's orders of June 18, the whole fleet, including two forty-four and one thirty-eight-gun frigates, with the "Hornet" and the "Argus," stood out to sea.

The secretary might have spared himself the trouble of giving further orders, for many a week passed before Rodgers and Decatur bethought themselves of his injunction to return immediately into port after striking the "Belvidera." They struck the "Belvidera" within forty-eight hours, and lost her; partly on account of the bursting of one of the "President's" main-deck guns, which blew up the forecastle deck, killing or wounding sixteen men, including Commodore Rodgers himself, whose leg was broken; partly, and according to the British account chiefly, on account of stopping to fire at all, when Rodgers should have run alongside, and in that case could not have failed to capture his enemy. Whatever was the reason, the "Belvidera" escaped; and Rodgers and Decatur, instead of returning immediately into port as they had been ordered, turned in pursuit of the British West India convoy, and hung doggedly to the chase without catching sight of their game, until after three weeks' pursuit they found themselves within a day's sail of the British Channel and the convoy safe in British waters.

This beginning of the naval war was discouraging.

The American ships should not have sailed in a squadron, and only their good luck saved them from disaster. Rodgers and Decatur showed no regard to the wishes of the Government, although had they met with misfortune, the navy would have lost its last hope. Yet if the two commodores had obeyed the secretary's commands their cruise would probably have been in the highest degree disastrous. The Government's true intentions have been a matter of much dispute ; but beyond a doubt the President and a majority of his advisers inclined to keep the navy within reach at first, — to use them for the protection of commerce, to drive away the British blockaders ; and aware that the British naval force would soon be greatly increased, and that the American navy must be blockaded in port, the Government expected in the end to use the frigates as harbor defences rather than send them to certain destruction.

With these ideas in his mind Secretary Hamilton, in his orders of June 18, told Rodgers and Decatur that "more extensive" orders should be sent to them on their return to New York. A day or two afterward Secretary Gallatin complained to the President that these orders had not been sent.

"I believe the weekly arrivals from foreign ports," said Gallatin,[1] "will for the coming four weeks average from one to one-and-a-half million dollars a week. To protect these and our coasting vessels, while the British

[1] Adams's Gallatin, p. 465.

have still an inferior force on our coasts, appears to me of primary importance. I think that orders to that effect, ordering them to cruise accordingly, ought to have been sent yesterday, and that at all events not one day longer ought to be lost."

June 22 the orders were sent according to Gallatin's wish. They directed Rodgers with his part of the squadron to cruise from the Chesapeake eastwardly, and Decatur with his ships to cruise from New York southwardly, so as to cross and support each other and protect with their united force the merchantmen and coasters entering New York harbor, the Delaware, and the Chesapeake. Rodgers and Decatur were then beginning their private cruise across the ocean, and never received these orders until the commerce they were to protect either reached port in safety or fell into British hands.

Probably this miscarriage was fortunate, for not long after Rodgers and Decatur passed the Banks the British Vice-Admiral Sawyer sent from Halifax a squadron to prevent the American navy from doing what Secretary Hamilton had just ordered to be done. July 5 Captain Broke, with his own frigate the "Shannon," 38, the "Belvidera," 36, the "Africa," 64, and "Æolus," 32, put to sea from Halifax and was joined, July 9, off Nantucket by the "Guerriere," 38. Against such a force Rodgers and Decatur, even if together, would have risked total destruction, while a success would have cost more than it was worth. The Americans had nothing to gain and everything to lose by fighting in line-of-battle.

As Broke's squadron swept along the coast it seized whatever it met, and July 16 caught one of President Jefferson's 16-gun brigs, the "Nautilus." The next day it came on a richer prize. The American navy seemed ready to outstrip the army in the race for disaster. The "Constitution," the best frigate in the United States service, sailed into the midst of Broke's five ships. Captain Isaac Hull, in command of the "Constitution," had been detained at Annapolis shipping a new crew, until July 5,[1] — the day when Broke's squadron left Halifax; — then the ship got under way and stood down Chesapeake Bay on her voyage to New York. The wind was ahead and very light. Not till July 10 did the ship anchor off Cape Henry lighthouse,[2] and not till sunrise of July 12 did she stand to the eastward and northward. Light head-winds and a strong current delayed her progress till July 17, when at two o'clock in the afternoon, off Barnegat on the New Jersey coast, the lookout at the masthead discovered four sails to the northward, and two hours later a fifth sail to the northeast. Hull took them for Rodgers's squadron. The wind was light, and Hull being to windward determined to speak the

[1] Hull to Secretary Hamilton, July 7, 1812; MSS. Navy Department.

[2] Hull to Secretary Hamilton, July 10, 1812; MSS. Navy Department.

nearest vessel, the last to come in sight. The afternoon passed without bringing the ships together,
and at ten in the evening, finding that the nearest
ship could not answer the night signal, Hull decided
to lose no time in escaping.

Then followed one of the most exciting and sustained chases recorded in naval history. At daybreak the next morning one British frigate was
astern within five or six miles, two more were to
leeward, and the rest of the fleet some ten miles
astern, all making chase. Hull put out his boats
to tow the "Constitution;" Broke summoned the
boats of his squadron to tow the "Shannon." Hull
then bent all his spare rope to the cables, dropped
a small anchor half a mile ahead, in twenty-six
fathom water, and warped his ship along. Broke
quickly imitated the device, and slowly gained on
the chase. The "Guerriere" crept so near Hull's
lee-beam as to open fire, but her shot fell short.
Fortunately the wind, though slight, favored Hull.
All night the British and American crews toiled
on, and when morning came the "Belvidera," proving to be the best sailer, got in advance of her
consorts, working two kedge-anchors, until at two
o'clock in the afternoon she tried in her turn to
reach the "Constitution" with her bow guns, but in
vain. Hull expected capture, but the "Belvidera"
could not approach nearer without bringing her
boats under the "Constitution's" stern guns ; and
the wearied crews toiled on, towing and kedging, the

ships barely out of gunshot, till another morning came. The breeze, though still light, then allowed Hull to take in his boats, the " Belvidera" being two and a half miles in his wake, the " Shannon" three and a half miles on his lee, and the three other frigates well to leeward. The wind freshened, and the " Constitution" drew ahead, until toward seven o'clock in the evening of July 19 a heavy rain-squall struck the ship, and by taking skilful advantage of it Hull left the " Belvidera" and " Shannon" far astern; yet until eight o'clock the next morning they were still in sight keeping up the chase.

Perhaps nothing during the war tested American seamanship more thoroughly than these three days of combined skill and endurance in the face of an irresistible enemy. The result showed that Hull and the " Constitution" had nothing to fear in these respects. There remained the question whether the superiority extended to his guns; and such was the contempt of British naval officers for American ships, that with this experience before their eyes they still believed one of their 38-gun frigates to be more than a match for an American forty-four, although the American, besides the heavier armament, had proved his capacity to out-sail and out-manœuvre the Englishman. Both parties became more eager than ever for the test. For once, even the Federalists of New England felt their blood stir; for their own President and their own votes had called these frigates into existence, and a victory won by the " Constitution," which had been built by their hands, was in their eyes a greater victory over their political opponents than over the British.   With no half-hearted spirit, the sea-going Bostonians showered well-weighed praises on Hull when his ship entered Boston harbor, July 26, after its narrow escape ; and when he sailed again, New England waited with keen interest to learn his fate.

Hull could not expect to keep command of the " Constitution."   Bainbridge was much his senior, and had the right to a preference in active service. Bainbridge then held and was ordered to retain command of the " Constellation," fitting out at the Washington Navy Yard ; but Secretary Hamilton, July 28, ordered him to take command also of the " Constitution " on her arrival in port.   Doubtless Hull expected this change, and probably the expectation induced him to risk a dangerous experiment ; for without bringing his ship to the Charlestown Navy Yard, but remaining in the outer harbor, after obtaining such supplies as he needed, August 2, he set sail without orders, and stood to the eastward. Having reached Cape Race without meeting an enemy he turned southward, until on the night of August 18 he spoke a privateer, which told him of a British frigate near at hand.   Following the privateersman's directions the " Constitution " the next day, August 19, at two o'clock in the afternoon, latitude 41° 42', longitude 55° 48', sighted the " Guerriere."

The meeting was welcome on both sides. Only three days before, Captain Dacres had entered on the log of a merchantman a challenge to any American frigate to meet him off Sandy Hook. Not only had the " Guerriere " for a long time been extremely offensive to every sea-faring American, but the mistake which caused the " Little Belt " to suffer so seriously for the misfortune of being taken for the " Guerriere " had caused a corresponding feeling of anger in the officers of the British frigate. The meeting of August 19 had the character of a preconcerted duel.

The wind was blowing fresh from the northwest, with the sea running high. Dacres backed his main-top-sail and waited. Hull shortened sail and ran down before the wind. For about an hour the two ships wore and wore again, trying to get advantage of position; until at last, a few minutes before six o'clock, they came together side by side, within pistol-shot, the wind almost astern, and running before it they pounded each other with all their strength. As rapidly as the guns could be worked, the " Constitution " poured in broadside after broadside, double- shotted with round and grape, — and, without exaggeration, the echo of these guns startled the world. " In less than thirty minutes from the time we got alongside of the enemy," reported Hull,[1] " she was left without a spar standing, and the hull

[1] Hull to Secretary Hamilton, Aug. 28, 1812; MSS. Navy Department.

cut to pieces in such a manner as to make it difficult to keep her above water."

That Dacres should have been defeated was not surprising ; that he should have expected to win was an example of British arrogance that explained and excused the war. The length of the "Constitution" was 173 feet; that of the "Guerriere" was 156 feet; the extreme breadth of the "Constitution" was 44 feet; that of the "Guerriere" was 40 feet, or within a few inches in both cases. The "Constitution" carried thirty-two long 24-pounders, the "Guerriere" thirty long 18-pounders and two long 12-pounders; the "Constitution" carried twenty 32-pound carronades, the "Guerriere" sixteen. In every respect, and in proportion of ten to seven, the "Constitution" was the better ship; her crew was more numerous in proportion of ten to six. Dacres knew this very nearly as well as it was known to Hull, yet he sought a duel. What he did not know was that in a still greater proportion the American officers and crew were better and more intelligent seamen than the British, and that their passionate wish to repay old scores gave them extraordinary energy. So much greater was the moral superiority than the physical, that while the "Guerriere's" force counted as seven against ten, her losses counted as though her force were only two against ten.

Dacres' error cost him dear, for among the "Guerriere's" crew of two hundred and seventy-two, seventy-nine were killed or wounded; and the ship was injured beyond saving before Dacres realized his mistake, although he needed only thirty minutes of close fighting for the purpose. He never fully understood the causes of his defeat, and never excused it by pleading, as he might have done, the great superiority of his enemy.[1]

Hull took his prisoners on board the " Constitutution," and after blowing up the " Guerriere " sailed for Boston, where he arrived on the morning of August 30. The Sunday silence of the Puritan city broke into excitement as the news passed through the quiet streets that the " Constitution " was below, in the outer harbor, with Dacres and his crew prisoners on board. No experience of history ever went to the heart of New England more directly than this victory, so peculiarly its own; but the delight was not confined to New England, and extreme though it seemed it was still not extravagant, for however small the affair might appear on the general scale of the world's battles, it raised the United States in one half hour to the rank of a first-class Power in the world.

Hull's victory was not only dramatic in itself, but was also supremely fortunate in the moment it occurred. The " Boston Patriot " of September 2, which announced the capture of the " Guerriere," announced in the next column that Rodgers and Decatur, with their squadron, entered Boston harbor within four-and-twenty hours after Hull's arrival,

[1] Niles, ii. 333.

returning empty-handed after more than two months
of futile cruising; while in still another column the
same newspaper announced " the melancholy intelli.
gence of the surrender of General Hull and his whole
army to the British General Brock."   Isaac Hull was
nephew to the unhappy General, and perhaps the
shattered hulk of the " Guerriere," which the nephew
left at the bottom of the Atlantic Ocean, eight hundred miles east of Boston, was worth for the moment
the whole province which the uncle had lost, eight
hundred miles to the westward ; it was at least the
only equivalent the people could find, and they made
the most of it.   With the shock of new life, they
awoke to the consciousness that after all the peace
teachings of Pennsylvania and Virginia, the sneers
of Federalists and foreigners; after the disgrace of
the " Chesapeake " and the surrender of Detroit, —
Americans could still fight.   The public had been
taught, and had actually learned, to doubt its own
physical courage; and the reaction of delight in satisfying itself that it still possessed the commones.
and most brutal of human qualities was the natural result of a system that ignored the possibility
of war.

  Hull's famous victory taught the pleasures of war
to a new generation, which had hitherto been sedu-
lously educated to think only of its cost.   The first
taste of blood maddens; and hardly had the " Constitution " reached port and told her story than the
public became eager for more.   The old Jeffersonian

jealousy of the navy vanished in the flash of Hull's first broadside.   Nothing would satisfy the craving of the popular appetite but more battles, more British frigates, and more daring victories.   Even the cautious Madison was dragged by public excitement upon the element he most heartily disliked.

The whole navy, was once more, September 1, safe in port, except only the " Essex," a frigate rated at thirty-two but carrying forty-four guns, commanded by Captain David Porter. She left New York, July 3, with orders,[1] dated June 24, to join Rodgers, or failing this to cruise southwardly as far as St. Augustine.   June 11 she met a convoy of seven transports conveying a battalion of the First Regiment, or Royal Scots, from the West Indies to reinforce Prevost and Brock in Canada.   Porter cut out one transport.   With the aid of another frigate he could have captured the whole, to the great advantage of Dearborn's military movements ; but the British commander managed his convoy so well that the battalion escaped, and enabled Prevost to strengthen the force at Niagara which threatened and defeated Van Rensselaer.   August 13 the British 20-gun sloop-of-war " Alert " came in sight, bore down within short pistol-shot, and opened fire on the " Essex."   Absurd as the idea seemed, the British captain behaved as though he hoped to capture the American frigate, and not until Porter nearly sunk him with a broadside did

[1] Hamilton to Porter, June 24, 1812; MSS. Navy Department Records.

the Englishman strike his colors. After taking a
number of other prizes, but without further fighting, September 7 Porter brought his ship back to
the Delaware River.

The return of the " Essex " to port, September 7,
brought all the national vessels once more under the
direct control of the Department. Nearly every ship
in the service was then at Boston. The three forty-
fours — the " Constitution," " United States," and
" President " — were all there; two of the thirty-
eights — the " Congress " and " Chesapeake " — were
there, and the " Constellation " was at Washington.
The " Adams," 28, was also at Washington; but the
" Hornet," 18, and " Argus," 16, were with Rodgers
and Decatur at Boston. The " Syren," 16, was at
New Orleans; the " Essex," 32, and the " Wasp," 18,
were in the Delaware.

Carried away by Hull's victory, the Government
could no longer hesitate to give its naval officers
the liberty of action they asked, and which in spite
of orders they had shown the intention to take. A
new arrangement was made. The vessels were to
be divided into three squadrons, each consisting of
one forty-four, one light frigate, and one sloop-of-
war. Rodgers in the " President" was to command
one squadron, Bainbridge in the " Constitution " was
to command another, and Decatur in the " United
States " was to take the third.[1] Their sailing orders,

[1] Hamilton to Rodgers and Decatur, Sept. 9, 1812; MSS.
Navy Department Records.

dated October 2,[1] simply directed the three commodores to proceed to sea : " You are to do your
utmost to annoy the enemy, to afford protection
to our commerce, pursuing that course which to
your best judgment may under all circumstances
appear the best calculated to enable you to accomplish these objects as far as may be in your power,
returning into port as speedily as circumstances
will permit consistently with the great object in
view."

Before continuing the story of the frigates, the fate
of the little " Wasp " needs to be told. Her career
was brief. The " Wasp," a sloop-of-war rated at
eighteen guns, was one of President Jefferson's addi-
tions to the navy to supply the loss of the " Philadelphia ; " she was ship-rigged, and armed with two
long 12-pounders and sixteen 32-pound carronades.
She carried a crew of one hundred and thirty-seven
men, commanded by Captain Jacob Jones, a native
of Delaware, lieutenant in the " Philadelphia " when
lost in the war with Tripoli. The " Wasp " was attached to Rodgers's squadron, and received orders
from the commodore to join him at sea. She sailed
from the Delaware October 13, and when about six
hundred miles east of Norfolk, October 17, she fell
in with the British 18-gun brig " Frolic," convoying
fourteen merchantmen to England. The two vessels
were equal in force, for the " Frolic's " broadside
threw a weight of two hundred and seventy-four

[1] MSS. Navy Department Records.

pounds, while that of the " Wasp " threw some few
pounds less; the "Frolic" measured, by British report,[1] one hundred feet in length, the " Wasp " one
hundred and six; their breadth on deck was the
same; and although the " Wasp's " crew exceeded
that of her enemy, being one hundred and thirty-five
men against one hundred and ten, the British vessel
had all the men she needed, and suffered little from
this inferiority. The action began at half-past eleven
in the morning, the two sloops running parallel, about
sixty yards apart, in a very heavy sea, which caused
both to pitch and roll so that marksmanship had
the most decisive share in victory. The muzzles
of the guns went under water, and clouds of spray
dashed over the crews, while the two vessels ran side
by side for the first fifteen minutes. The British
fire cut the " Wasp's " rigging, while the American
guns played havoc with the " Frolic's " hull and lower
masts. The vessels approached each other so closely
that the rammers of the guns struck the enemy's
side, and at last they fell foul, — the " Wasp " almost
squarely across the " Frolic's " bow. In the heavy
sea boarding was difficult; but as soon as the
" Wasp's " crew could clamber down the " Frolic's "
bowsprit, they found on the deck the British captain and lieutenant, both severely wounded, and one
brave sailor at the wheel. Not twenty of the British
crew were left unhurt, and these had gone below to
escape the American musketry. The " Wasp " had

[1] James, Naval Occurrences, p. 152.

only ten men killed and wounded.   The battle lasted
forty-three minutes.

If the American people had acquired a taste for
blood, the battle of the " Wasp " and " Frolic " gratified it, for the British sloop was desperately defended,
and the battle, won by the better marksmanship of
the Americans, was unusually bloody.   Captain Jones
lost the full satisfaction of his victory, for a few hours
afterward the " Poictiers," a British seventy-four,
came upon the two disabled combatants and carried
both into Bermuda ; but the American people would
have been glad to part with their whole navy on such
terms, and the fight between the " Wasp " and the
" Frolic " roused popular enthusiasm to a point where
no honors seemed to satisfy their gratitude to Captain Jones and his crew.

The " Wasp's " brilliant career closed within a
week from the day she left the Delaware.   A week
afterward another of these ship-duels occurred, which
made a still deeper impression.   Rodgers and Decatur
sailed from Boston October 8, with the " President,"
the " United States," " Congress," and " Argus,"
leaving the " Constitution," " Chesapeake," and " Hornet " in port.   Rodgers in the " President," with the
" Congress," cruised far and wide, but could find no
enemy to fight, and after making prize of a few merchantmen returned to Boston, December 31.   The
" Argus " also made some valuable prizes, but was
chased by a British squadron, and only by excellent
management escaped capture, returning Jan. 3, 1813,

to New York.   Decatur in the " United States," separating from the squadron October 12, sailed eastward to the neighborhood of the Azores, until, October 25, he sighted a sail to windward.   The stranger made chase.   The wind was fresh from south-southeast, with a heavy sea.   Decatur stood toward his enemy, who presently came about, abreast of the " United States " but beyond gunshot, and both ships being then on the same tack approached each other until the action began at long range.   The British ship was the 38-gun frigate " Macedonian " commanded by Captain Carden, and about the same force as the " Guerriere."   At first the " United States " used only her long 24-pounders, of which she carried fifteen on her broadside, while the " Macedonian " worked a broadside of fourteen long 18-pounders.   So unequal a contest could not continue.   Not only was the American metal heavier, but the American fire was quicker and better directed than that of the Englishman ; so that Carden, after a few minutes of this experience, bore down to close.   His manœuvre made matters worse.   The carronades of the " United States " came into play ; the " Macedonian's " mizzen-mast fell, her fore and main top-mast were shot away, and her main-yard ; almost all her rigging was cut to pieces, and most of the guns on her engaged side were dismounted.   She dropped gradually to leeward, and Decatur, tacking and coming up under his enemy's stern, hailed, and received her surrender.

The British ship had no right to expect a victory for the disparity of force was even greater than between the " Constitution " and " Guerriere ; " but in this case the British court-martial subsequently censured Captain Carden for mistakes. The battle lasted longer than that with the " Guerriere," and Decatur apologized for the extra hour because the sea was high and his enemy had the weather-gauge and kept at a distance ; but the apology was not needed. Decatur proved his skill by sparing his ship and crew. His own loss was eleven men killed and wounded ; the " Macedonian's " loss was nine times as great. The " United States " suffered little in her hull, and her spars and rigging suffered no greater injury than could be quickly repaired ; while the " Macedonian " received a hundred shot in her hull, and aloft nothing remained standing but her fore and main masts and her fore-yard.

Decatur saved the " Macedonian," and brought her back to New London, — the only British frigate ever brought as a prize into an American port. The two ships arrived December 4, and from New London the " Macedonian " was taken to New York and received in formal triumph. Captain Jones of the " Wasp " took command of her in reward for his capture of the " Frolic."

Before the year closed, the " Constitution " had time for another cruise. Hull at his own request received command of the Navy Yard at Charlestown, and also took charge of the naval defences in New

York harbor, but did not again serve at sea during
the war. The "Constitution" was given to Captain
Bainbridge, one of the oldest officers in the service.
A native of New Jersey, Bainbridge commanded
the "Philadelphia" when lost in the Tripolitan
war, and was held for eighteen months a prisoner
in Tripoli. In 1812, when he took command of
the "Constitution," though a year older than Hull
and five years older than Decatur, he had not yet
reached his fortieth year, while Ròdgers, born in
1771, had but lately passed it. The difference
in age between these four naval officers and the
four chief generals — Dearborn, Wilkinson, Wade
Hampton, and William Hull — was surprising; for
the average age of the naval commanders amounted
barely to thirty-seven years, while that of the four
generals reached fifty-eight. This difference alone
accounted for much of the difference in their fortune, and perhaps political influence accounted for
the rest.

Bainbridge showed no inferiority to the other
officers of the service, and no one grumbled at
the retirement of Hull. The "Constitution" sailed
from Boston, October 25, with the "Hornet." The
"Essex," then in the Delaware, was ordered to join
the squadron at certain specified ports in the south
Atlantic, and sailed October 28, expecting a very
long cruise. December 13 Bainbridge arrived at San
Salvador, on the coast of Brazil, where he left
the "Hornet" to blockade the "Bonne Citoyenne," a

British 18-gun sloop-of-war bound to England with specie.   Cruising southward, within sight of the Brazilian coast, in latitude 13° 6′ south, Bainbridge sighted the British frigate " Java," a ship of the same tonnage as the " Guerriere," throwing a slightly heavier broadside and carrying a large crew of four hundred and twenty-six men, if the American account was correct.   Bainbridge tacked and made sail off shore, to draw the stranger away from a neutral coast ; the British frigate followed him, until at half-past one o'clock in the afternoon Bainbridge shortened sail, tacked again, and stood for his enemy.   Soon after two o'clock the action began, the two ships being on the same tack, the " Java " to windward and the better sailer, and both fighting their long-range guns.   The British frigate insisted upon keeping at a distance, obliging Bainbridge after half an hour to risk the danger of being raked ; and at twenty minutes before three o'clock the " Constitution " closed within pistol-shot.[1]   At ten minutes before three the ships were foul, the " Java's " jibboom in the " Constitution's " mizzen rigging ; and from that point the battle became slaughter.   In fifteen minutes the " Java's " bowsprit, fore-mast, and main top-mast were cut away, and a few minutes after four o'clock she ceased firing.   Her captain, Lambert, was mortally wounded ; the first lieutenant was wounded ; forty-eight of her officers and crew

[1] Brainbridge's Journal, Report of Jan. 3, 1813 ; Niles, iii. 411.

were dead or dying; one hundred and two were wounded; little more than a hulk filled with wreck and with dead or wounded men floated on the water.

The "Constitution" had but twelve men killed and twenty-two wounded, and repaired damages in an hour. Owing perhaps to the death of Captain Lambert the reports of the battle were more contradictory than usual, but no one disputed that although the "Java" was to windward and outsailed the American frigate, and although her broadside counted as nearly nine against her enemy's ten, — for the "Constitution" on this cruise carried two guns less than in her fight with the "Guerriere," — yet the "Java" inflicted no more damage than she ought to have done had she been only one fourth the size of the American frigate, although she was defended more desperately than either the "Guerriere" or the "Macedonian."

With this battle the year ended. Bainbridge was obliged to blow up his prize, and after landing and paroling his prisoners at San Salvador sailed for Boston, where he arrived in safety, February 27, 1813. During the six months the war had lasted the little United States navy captured three British frigates, besides the 20-gun "Alert" and the 18-gun "Frolic;" privateers by scores had ravaged British commerce, while the immense British force on the ocean had succeeded only in capturing the little "Nautilus," the 12-gun brig "Vixen," and the

" Wasp." The commerce of America had indeed suffered almost total destruction ; but the dispute was to be decided not so much by the loss which England could inflict upon America, as by that which America could inflict upon England.

CHAPTER XVIII.

In such a war the people of the United States had only themselves to fear; but their dangers were all the more formidable. Had the war deeply disturbed the conditions of society, or brought general and immediate distress, government and Union might easily have fallen to pieces; but in the midst of military disaster and in plain sight of the Government's incompetence, the general public neither felt nor had reason to fear much change in the routine of life. Commerce had long accustomed itself to embargoes, confiscations, and blockades, and ample supplies of foreign goods continued to arrive. The people made no serious exertions; among a population exceeding seven millions, not ten thousand men entered the military service. The militia, liable to calls to the limit of one hundred thousand, served for the most part only a few weeks in the autumn, went home in whole regiments when they pleased,[1] and in the East refused to go out at all. The scarcity of men was so great that even among the sea-going

[1] Brigadier-General Tannehill to Brigadier-General Smyth, Dec. 7, 1812; State Papers, Military Affairs, i. 507.

class, for whose rights the war was waged, only with the utmost difficulty and long delays, in spite of bounties and glory, could sailors be found to man half-a-dozen frigates for a three-months cruise, although the number of privateers was never great.

The nation as a whole saw nothing of actual warfare. While scarcely a city in Europe had escaped capture, and hardly a province of that continent was so remote as not to be familiar with invading armies or to have suffered in proportion to its resources, no American city saw or greatly feared an enemy. The rich farms of New York, New Jersey, Pennsylvania, and Virginia produced their usual harvests, and except on exposed parts of the coast the farmers never feared that their crops might be wasted by manœuvring armies, or their cattle, pigs, and poultry be disturbed by marauders. The country was vast, and quiet reigned throughout the whole United States. Except at the little point of Niagara, occupied by a few hundred scattered farmers, and on the extreme outskirts of Ohio and Indiana, the occupations and industries of life followed in the main their daily course.

The country refused to take the war seriously. A rich nation with seven million inhabitants should have easily put one hundred thousand men into the field, and should have found no difficulty in supporting them; but no inducement that the Government dared offer prevailed upon the people to risk life and property on a sufficient scale in 1812. The ranks

of the army were to be filled in one of two ways, —
either by enlistment in the regular service for five
years, with pay at five dollars a month, sixteen
dollars bounty, and on discharge three months pay
and one hundred and sixty acres of land; or by
volunteer organizations to the limit of fifty thousand men in all, officered under State laws, to serve
for one year, with the pay of regular troops but without bounty, clothed, and in case of cavalry corps
mounted, at their own expense. In a society where
the day-laborers' wages were nowhere less than nine
dollars a month,[1] these inducements were not enough
to supply the place of enthusiasm. The patriotic citizen who wished to serve his country without too
much sacrifice, chose a third course, — he volunteered
under the Act. of Congress which authorized the
President to call one hundred thousand State militia
into service for six months; and upon this State militia Dearborn, Hull, Van Rensselaer, and Smyth were
obliged chiefly to depend.

If the war fever burned hotly in any part of the
country Kentucky was the spot. There the whole
male population was eager to prove its earnestness.
When Henry Clay returned to Lexington after the
declaration of war, he wrote to Monroe[2] that he was
almost alarmed at the ardor his State displayed;

[1] Remarks of D. R. Williams, Nov. 20, 1812 ; Annals of Congress, 1812–1813, p. 156.

[2] Clay to Monroe, July 29, 1812; Monroe MSS., State Department Archives.

about four hundred men had been recruited for the regular army, and although no one had volunteered for twelve months, the quota of six-months militia was more than supplied by volunteers.

" Such is the structure of our society, however," continued Clay, " that I doubt whether many can be engaged for a longer term than six months. For that term any force whatever which our population can afford may be obtained. Engaged in agricultural pursuits, you are well aware that from about this time, when the crop is either secured in the barn or laid by in the field until the commencement of the spring, there is leisure for any kind of enterprise."

Clay feared only that these six-months militia corps, which had armed and equipped themselves for instant service, might not be called out. His friends were destined not to be disappointed, for early in August pressing letters arrived from Hull's army at Detroit begging reinforcements, and the governor of Kentucky at once summoned two thousand volunteers to rendezvous, August 20, at Newport, opposite Cincinnati. This reinforcement could not reach Detroit before the middle of September, and the difficulties already developed in Hull's path showed that the war could not be finished in a single campaign of six months; but the Kentuckians were not on that account willing to lengthen their term of service even to one year.

The danger revealed by Hull's position threw a double obstacle in the way of public energy, for where

it did not check, it promised to mislead enthusiasm,
and in either case it shook, if it did not destroy, confidence in the national government.   The leaders of
the war party saw their fears taking shape.   Henry
Clay wrote without reserve to Monroe,[1] —

" Should Hull's army be cut off, the effect on the public
mind would be, especially in this quarter, in the highest
degree injurious. ' Why did he proceed with so inconsiderable a force ? ' was the general inquiry made of me.
I maintained that it was sufficient.   Should he meet with
a disaster, the predictions of those who pronounced his
army incompetent to its object will be fulfilled ; and the
Secretary of War, in whom already there unfortunately
exists no sort of confidence, cannot possibly shield
Mr. Madison from the odium which will attend such
an event."

Clay was right in thinking that Eustis could not
shield Madison ; but from the moment that Eustis
could no longer serve that purpose, Clay had no
choice but to shield the President himself.   When
the threatened disaster took place, victims like Eustis,
Hull, Van Rensselaer, Smyth, were sacrificed ; but the
sacrifice merely prepared new material for other and
perhaps worse disasters of the same kind.   In Kentucky this result was most strongly marked, for in
their irritation at the weakness of the national Government the Kentuckians took the war into their
own hands, appointed William Henry Harrison to the

[1] Clay to Monroe, Aug. 12, 1812 ; Monroe MSS., State Department Archives.

command of their armies, and attempted to conquer
Canada by a campaign that should not be directed
from Washington. August 25 Clay described the
feelings of his State by a comparison suggesting the
greatest military misfortunes known in history: [1]

" If you will carry your recollections back to the age
of the Crusaders and of some of the most distinguished
leaders of those expeditions, you will have a picture of
the enthusiasm existing in this country for the expedition
to Canada and for Harrison as commander."

A week later, September 21, Clay gave another
account, even less assuring, of the manner in which
the popular energy was exhausting itself: —

" The capitulation of Detroit has produced no despair;
it has, on the contrary, awakened new energies and
aroused the whole people of this State. Kentucky has
at this moment from eight to ten thousand men in the
field; it is not practicable to ascertain the precise number. Except our quota of the hundred thousand militia
the residue is chiefly of a miscellaneous character, who
have turned out without pay or supplies of any kind,
carrying with them their own arms and their own sub-
sistence. Parties are daily passing to the theatre of
action; last night seventy lay on my farm; and they
go on, from a solitary individual, to companies of ten,
fifty, one hundred, etc. The only fear I have is that
the savages will, as their custom is, elude them, and
upon their return fall upon our frontiers. They have
already shocked us with some of the most horrid mur-

[1] Clay to Monroe, Aug. 25, 1812; Monroe MSS., State Department Archives.

ders. Within twenty-four miles of Louisville, on the headwaters of Silver Creek, twenty-two were massacred a few days ago."

The adventures of these volunteers made part of the next campaign. Enthusiastic as Kentucky was, few or none of the eight or ten thousand men under arms offered to serve for twelve months. Excessively expensive, wasteful, insubordinate, and unsteady, no general dared to depend on them. No one could be more conscious of the evils of the system than the Government; but the Government was helpless to invent a remedy.

" Proofs multiply daily," wrote Madison to Monroe, September 21,[1] " of the difficulty of obtaining regulars, and of the fluctuating resource in the militia. High bounties and short enlistments, however objectionable, will alone fill the ranks, and then too in a moderate number."

To dislike of prolonged service even the most ardent Western supporters of the war added distrust of the Executive. The war Republicans of the West and South were hardly less vigorous than the Federalists of Massachusetts and Connecticut in their criticisms of the Government at Washington. John Graham, chief clerk of the State Department, who went to Kentucky in September, wrote to Monroe[2] that " great as is the popularity of the President, it

[1] Madison to Monroe, Sept. 21, 1812; Monroe MSS., State Department Archives.

[2] Graham to Monroe, Sept. 27, 1812 ; Monroe MSS., State Department Archives.

is barely able to resist the torrent of public opinion against the Secretary of War, who, so far as I can judge, is universally considered by the people of this country as incompetent to his present situation." Clay's opinion has already been shown; but the angriest of all the war leaders on hearing of Hull's surrender was Senator Crawford of Georgia.

" Such is my want of confidence in the leaders of our forces," he wrote to Monroe,[1] " and their directors, Eustis and Hamilton in the Cabinet, that I am fearful a continuance of the war, unless it should be for several years, will only add to the number of our defeats. The only difficulty I had in declaring war arose from the incompetency of the men to whom the principal management of it was to be confided. A Secretary of War who, instead of forming general and comprehensive arrangements for the organization of his troops and for the successful prosecution of the campaign, consumes his time in reading advertisements of petty retailing merchants to find where he may purchase one hundred shoes or two hundred hats ; and a Secretary of the Navy who, in instructing his naval officers, should make the supply of the heads of departments with pineapples and other tropical fruits through the exertions of these officers, — cannot fail to bring disgrace upon themselves, their immediate employers, and the nation. If Mr. Madison finds it impossible to bring his feelings to consent to the dismission of unfaithful or incompetent officers, he must be content with defeat and disgrace in all his efforts during the war. So far as he may suffer from this course he deserves no

[1] Crawford to Monroe, Sept. 27, 1812 ; Monroe MSS., State Department Archives.

commiseration, but his accountability to the nation will be great indeed!"

Harsh as these comments were, the Secretary of State found no difficulty in listening to them; indeed, no member of the party was more severe than Monroe. He visited Jefferson, and apparently Jefferson agreed with his criticisms : [1] —

" We conferred on the then state of the Departments of War and Navy, and agreed that whatever might be the merit of the gentlemen in them, which was admitted in certain respects, a change in both was indispensable."

Indeed, Monroe did what no northern Democrat liked to do, — he found fault with Dearborn.

" Our military operations," he told Jefferson, " had been unsuccessful. One army had been surrendered under circumstances which impeached the integrity of the commander ; and to the north, in the whole extent of the country, so important and delicately circumstanced as it was, the management had been most wretched. The command at the important post of Niagara had been suffered to fall into State hands, and to be perverted to local and selfish purposes. Van Rensselaer, a weak and incompetent man with high pretensions, took it. It was late in the year before General Dearborn left Boston and repaired to Albany, and had given no impulse to the recruiting business in the Eastern States by passing through them and making appeals to the patriotism of the people ; and when he took the command at Albany it was in a manner to discourage all hope of active opera-

[1] Monroe to Jefferson, June 7, 1813 ; Jefferson MSS., State Department Archives.

tions during the favorable season. The commander
ought to lead every important movement. If intended
to attack Montreal, that being the grand attack, his
station was there. If a smaller blow only could be
given, the feint against Montreal should have been
committed to another, while he commanded in person
where real service was to be performed. It was soon
seen that nothing would be done against Lower Canada;
General Dearborn doubtless saw it on his first arrival at
Albany, if he did not anticipate it before he left Boston.
Niagara was the object next in importance, and had he
taken the command there he might and probably would,
by superseding little people and conducting our military
operations, have prevented the riotous and contentious
scenes exhibited there, saved the country and the Government from the disgraceful defeat of Van Rensselaer,
and the more disgraceful and gasconading discomfiture of
Smyth. The experience of the campaign had excited a
doubt with many, if not with all, whether our military
operations would prosper under General Dearborn; . . .
he was advanced in years, infirm, and had given no proof
of activity or military talent during the year."

The Secretary of State required nothing less than
the retirement of the two of his colleagues in the
Cabinet, and of the general in chief command of
the army. The Secretary of the Treasury, though
less censorious than Clay, Crawford, or Monroe,
shared their opinions. He spoke of Eustis's incompetence as a matter universally admitted, and wrote
to Jefferson that though the three disasters of Hull,
Van Rensselaer, and Smyth could not with justice

be ascribed to the Secretary of War, "yet his incapacity and the total want of confidence in him were
felt through every ramification of the public service." [1]
Jefferson abstained from criticising the chief incom-
petents, but set no bounds to his vindictiveness against
the unfortunate generals. "Hull will of course be
shot for cowardice and treachery," he wrote to Madison; [2] "and will not Van Rensselaer be broke for
incapacity?"

The incapacity of Eustis, Hamilton, Dearborn, Hull,
Van Rensselaer, and Smyth pointed directly to the
responsible source of appointment, — the President
himself; but in face of a general election Republicans could not afford to criticise their President, and
only in private could they assail his Cabinet. The
Federalists, factious, weak, and unpopular as they
were, expressed the secret opinion of the whole country, and could be answered by no facts or arguments
except military success, which Madison was admittedly incompetent to win; but perhaps the failure of
his Cabinet, of his generals, and of his troops gave
the Federalists less advantage than they drew from
the failures of diplomacy in which his genius lay.
With reasons such as few nations ever waited to
collect for an appeal to arms, Madison had been
so unfortunate in making the issue that on his own

[1] Gallatin to Jefferson, Dec. 18, 1812; Adams's Gallatin,
p. 470.

[2] Jefferson to Madison, Nov. 5, 1812; Jefferson MSS. series v.
vol. xv.

showing no sufficient cause of war seemed to exist. His management was so extraordinary that at the moment when Hull surrendered Detroit, Great Britain was able to pose before the world in the attitude of victim to a conspiracy between Napoleon and the United States to destroy the liberties of Europe.   Such inversion of the truth passed ordinary bounds, and so real was Madison's diplomatic mismanagement that it paralyzed one half the energies of the American people.

Largely if not chiefly owing to these mistakes, the New England Federalists were able to convince themselves that Jefferson and Madison were sold to France.   From the moment war was declared, the charge became a source of serious danger.   Only one more step was needed to throw the clerical party of New England into open revolution.   If the majority meant to close their long career by a catastrophe which should leave the Union a wreck, they had but to try the effects of coercion.

For a time the followers and friends of the Essex Junto had some reason to hope that matters would quickly come to this pass, for the declaration of war caused on both sides an outbreak of temper.   In Massachusetts, Governor Strong issued, June 26, a proclamation[1] for a public Fast in consequence of the war just declared " against the nation from which we are descended, and which for many generations has been the bulwark of the religion we profess;" and

[1] Niles, ii. 355.

although such a description of England would in previous times have scandalized the clergy, it was received with general assent.   The returning members
of Congress who had voted for war met a reception
in some cases offensive and insulting, to the point
of actual assault.   Two of the Massachusetts members, Seaver and Widgery, were publicly insulted
and hissed on Change in Boston; while another,
Charles Turner, member for the Plymouth district,
and Chief-Justice of the Court of Sessions for that
county, was seized by a crowd on the evening of August 3, on the main street of Plymouth, and kicked
through the town.[1]   By energetic use of a social machinery still almost irresistible, the Federalists and
the clergy checked or prevented every effort to assist
the war, either by money or enlistments.   The Supreme Court of Massachusetts, with Chief-Justice
Parsons at its head, advised[2] Governor Strong that
not to Congress or to the President, but to the governor, belonged the right to decide when the Constitutional exigency existed which should call the State
militia into the service of the United States; and
Governor Strong decided that neither foreign invasion nor domestic insurrection existed, and that therefore he could not satisfy the President's request for
the quota of the United States militia to defend the
coast.   When, later in the season, the governor called
out three companies for the defence of Eastport and

[1] Judge Turner's Affidavit, Boston Patriot, Aug. 19, 1812.
[2] Opinion, etc. ; State Papers, Military Affairs, i. 324.

Castine, in Maine, the chief-justice privately remonstrated, holding that this act yielded the main point
at issue between the State and National government.[1]

General Dearborn's annoyance at the difficulties
thrown in the way of enlistments was well-founded.
By one favorite device, the creation of fictitious
debts, the person enlisting caused himself to be arrested and bailed. The courts held that while the
suit was pending the man was the property of his
bail, and could not be obliged to resume his military
duties.[2] Many such difficulties were created by the
activity of individuals ; but organized efforts were
made with still more effect in counteracting the
wishes of government. The Federalist members of
Congress issued an Address to their constituents protesting against the action of Congress in suppressing
discussion ; and this address declared the war to be
unnecessary and inexpedient. Immediately after the
declaration, the House of Representatives of Massachusetts issued another Address to the People of the
State,[3] declaring the war to be a wanton sacrifice
of their best interests, and asking their exertions to
thwart it.

" To secure a full effect to your object, it will be necessary that you should meet and consult together for the
common good in your towns and counties. It is in dark

[1] Sumner's East Boston, p. 738.

[2] Speech of E. Bacon, Nov. 20, 1812; Annals of Congress,
1812–1813, pp. 157, 158.

[3] Address, etc., June 26, 1812; Niles, ii. 417.

and trying times that this Constitutional privilege becomes invaluable. Express your sentiments without fear, and let the sound of your disapprobation of this war be loud and deep. Let it be distinctly understood that in support of it your conformity to the requisitions of law will be the result of principle and not of choice. If your sons must be torn from you by conscription, consign them to the care of God; but let there be no volunteers except for defensive war."

The people at once acted upon the recommendation to hold town-meetings and county conventions. Among the earliest was a meeting in Essex County, July 21, Timothy Pickering presiding, which adopted a declaration drawn by him, closing with his favorite proposal of a State Convention, to which the meeting chose delegates. This step — a revival of the old disunion project of 1804 — was received with general favor, and defeated only by the courageous opposition of Samuel Dexter, who, breaking away from his party associates, attacked the scheme so vigorously in Boston town-meeting, August 6 and 7, that though Harrison Gray Otis and other Federalists leaders gave it their public support, and though the motion itself was carried, the plan was abandoned.[1] Thenceforward, while towns and counties continued to adopt addresses, memorials, and resolutions, they avoided committing themselves to expressions or acts for which the time was not ripe. A typical memorial

[1] Pickering to John Lowell, Nov. 7, 1814; New England Federalism, p. 404. The Palladium, Aug. 7, 1812; The Patriot, Aug. 8, 1812.

among many that were showered upon the President was adopted by a convention of electors of the county of Rockingham in New Hampshire, August 5, and was the better worth attention because drawn by Daniel Webster, who made there his first appearance as a party leader : —

" We shrink from the separation of the States as an event fraught with incalculable evils ; and it is among our strongest objections to the present course of measures that they have in our opinion a very dangerous and alarming bearing on such an event. If a separation of the States ever should take place, it will be on some occasion when one portion of the country undertakes to control, to regulate, and to sacrifice the interest of another ; when a small and heated majority in the government, taking counsel of their passions and not of their reason, contemptuously disregarding the interests and perhaps stopping the mouths of a large and respectable minority, shall by hasty, rash, and ruinous measures threaten to destroy essential rights and lay waste the most important interests. It shall be our most fervent supplication to Heaven to avert both the event and the occasion ; and the Government may be assured that the tie that binds us to the Union will never be broken *by us*."

The conduct of England strengthened the Federalists. After the repeal of the Orders in Council became known, Monroe, July 27, authorized Jonathan Russell in London to arrange an armistice, provided the British government would consent to an informal arrangement in regard to impressments and blockades. Hardly had these instructions been sent

to England, when from Albany came news that Sir
George Prevost had proposed an armistice and General Dearborn had accepted it. This act compelled
the President either to stop the war and disorganize
his party, or to disapprove Dearborn's armistice without prejudice to the armistice which Russell was to
negotiate in London, and also without censure to
General Dearborn. To Dearborn the President, as
the story has shown, sent immediate orders for the
renewal of hostilities ; while Monroe, in fresh instructions to Jonathan Russell,[1] explained the disavowal.
The explanations given by Monroe were little likely
to satisfy Federalists that the Government honestly
wished for peace. Monroe alleged that the repeal
of the Orders in Council did not satisfy the United
States, because the repeal still asserted the principle
underlying the orders, which the United States could
not admit ; but he further maintained that any
armistice, made before obtaining redress on the subject of impressments, might be taken as a relinquishment of the claim to redress, and was therefore
inadmissible.

However sound in principle these objections were,
they seemed to declare perpetual war ; for until England should be reduced to the position of Denmark
or Prussia, she would not abandon in express terms
either the right of impressment or that of blockade.
The probable effect of a successful war waged on

[1] Monroe to Jonathan Russell, Aug. 21, 1812 ; State Papers,
iii. 587.

these grounds would give Canada and the Floridas to the United States as the consequence of aiding Napoleon to destroy European and English liberties. The Federalist clergy had little difficulty in convincing their congregations by such evidence that Madison was bound under secret engagements with Napoleon; and while Madison planted himself in the Napoleonic position of forcing war on a yielding people, the British officials in Canada stood on the defensive, avoided irritation, and encouraged trade and commerce. American merchant-vessels carried British passes; and most of them, to the anger of Napoleon, were freighted with supplies for the British army in Portugal and Spain. The attitude of England would have been magnificent in its repose had its dignity not been ruffled by the conduct of Hull, Decatur, and Bainbridge, and by the privateers.

While the New England Federalists, taking the attitude of patriots who strove only to avert impending ruin, made their profit of every new national disaster, and repressed as well as they could the indiscretions of their friends, the war party was not so well disciplined. Democracies in history always suffered from the necessity of uniting with much of the purest and best in human nature a mass of ignorance and brutality lying at the bottom of all societies. Although America was safe for the time from Old World ruin, no political or military error went so far to disgust respectable people with the war and its

support, as an uprising of brutality which occurred
in Baltimore. Within some twenty years this newest
of American cities had gathered nearly fifty thousand inhabitants, among whom were many of the
roughest characters in America, fit only for privateersmen or pirates, and familiar with both careers.
On the other hand, the State of Maryland like the
State of Delaware contained many conservatives, who
showed their strength every four years by depriving
the Republican candidate for the Presidency of some
portion of the State's electoral vote. Under their
patronage a newspaper called " The Federal Republican " was published in Baltimore, edited by Jacob
Wagner, who had been chief clerk of the State Department under Secretary Pickering, and was retained
in that office by Secretary Madison until 1807, when
he resigned the place and made use of his knowledge
to attack Madison in the press. As an editor, Jacob
Wagner belonged to the extreme wing of his party,
and scrupled at nothing in the way of an assertion or
a slander. His opposition to the war was bitter and
unceasing, while the city of Baltimore shared in the
feeling common in the South and West, that, after
the declaration, opposition to the war amounted to
treason and should not be tolerated. June 22, immediately after the declaration, a well-organized mob
deliberately took possession of Wagner's printing
office and destroyed it, pulling down even the walls,
while the citizens looked on and the mayor confined
his exercise of authority to deprecations.

Wagner removed to the District of Columbia, and began to publish his paper in Georgetown, where the Government could be made directly responsible in case of further violence; but his associate, A. C. Hanson, and several of the Baltimore Federalists, were not disposed to tolerate the dictation of a mob; and after discussing the matter a month, some of them determined on an attempt as fool-hardy as it was courageous.[1]   Monday, July 27, the "Federal Republican" was circulated among its subscribers in Baltimore, purporting to be printed at 45 Charles Street, though really printed at Georgetown; while about twenty persons, under the general direction of Henry Lee, — a Virginian distinguished in the Revolutionary War, and in 1791 governor of his State, — fortified themselves in the house and waited attack. The same evening a mob gathered and broke open the door.   The garrison fired, and killed or wounded some of the assailants.   The attacking party brought up a cannon, and a serious battle was about to begin, when the mayor with a small squadron of cavalry intervened, and persuaded Hanson and his friends to submit to the civil authority and go to jail to answer for the blood they had shed.   General Lee, General Lingan, — also a Revolutionary officer, — Hanson, and the other occupants of the house were marched to the jail through an angry and violent mob.   The city was in commotion, the authorities were helpless, the militia when called

[1] Report of Baltimore City Council; Niles, ii. 376, 377.

upon did not appear; and that night the mob, consisting chiefly of low Irish and Germans, entered the jail and took out the prisoners. Some managed to escape in the confusion; the rest were savagely beaten. Eight more or less unconscious victims lay all night and till noon the next day piled on the prison steps, and the crowd, which would not permit their removal, amused itself by cutting and burning the sufferers to ascertain whether they were dead. When at last the rioters permitted them to be removed, General Lingan was in fact dead, General Lee was crippled, and the others were more or less severely injured.

At that moment, and even long after the heat of temper subsided,[1] party feeling tended to favor the rioters rather than the Federalists, who had, as was said, "given aid and comfort to the enemy;" but when the political effects of the massacre showed themselves, the war party became aware that a blunder had been committed more serious than any ordinary crime. The Baltimore massacre recalled the excesses of the French Revolution, still fresh in men's minds; and although Democrats in Pennsylvania and Republicans in Virginia might feel themselves too strong for disorder, in the North and East the murder of Lingan shook the foundation of society. Massachusetts and Connecticut looked to their arms. If their political opinions were to be repressed by such means, they had need to be unanimous on their

[1] Lossing, p. 244.

own side. The town of Boston, August 6, declared
in strongly worded resolutions [1] that the riot was
"the first fruit of the unnatural and dreadful alliance into which we have entered in fact, if not in
form," and ordered the magistrates and citizens to be
ready at a moment's warning, armed and equipped,
to suppress any kind of disorder. Under this excitement, the Federalists at Rockingham, August 5,
talked of disunion, and the rabble of Plymouth
mobbed Turner on the night of August 3. If the
majority alone was to utter opinions, the Republican
party north of Pennsylvania might yet be forced to
practise the virtue of silence. Not all the political
and military disasters of the year harmed the Government and the war more seriously than they were
injured by the Baltimore mob.

Under the influence of such passions the Presidential election approached. Except beyond the mountains the war party was everywhere a social minority,
and perhaps such strength as Madison retained in the
East consisted partly in the popular impression that
he was not a favorite with the authors of the war.
The true sentiment of the people, if capable of expression, was one of fretful discontent; and the sense
of diffused popular restlessness alone explained the
obstinacy of De Witt Clinton in refusing to desist
from his candidacy, and still more the first prominent appearance of Martin Van Buren as manager of
the intrigue for defeating Madison. De Witt Clinton

[1] The Palladium, Aug. 7, 1812.

was classed by most persons as a reckless political gambler, but Martin Van Buren when he intrigued commonly preferred to intrigue upon the strongest side. Yet one feeling was natural to every New York politician, whether a Clinton or a Livingston, Burrite, Federalist, or Republican, — all equally disliked Virginia; and this innate jealousy gave to the career of Martin Van Buren for forty years a bias which perplexed his contemporaries, and stood in singular contradiction to the soft and supple nature he seemed in all else to show.

No canvass for the Presidency was ever less creditable than that of De Witt Clinton in 1812. Seeking war votes for the reason that he favored more vigorous prosecution of the war; asking support from peace Republicans because Madison had plunged the country into war without preparation; bargaining for Federalist votes as the price of bringing about a peace; or coquetting with all parties in the atmosphere of bribery in bank charters, — Clinton strove to make up a majority which had no element of union but himself and money. The Federalists held a conference at New York in September, and in spite of Rufus King, who was said to have denounced Clinton as a dangerous demagogue in almost the words used by Hamilton to denounce Aaron Burr ten years before, after three days debate, largely through the influence of Harrison Gray Otis, the bargain was made which transferred to Clinton the electoral votes of the Federalist States. No one knew what pledges were given by Clinton and his friends; but no man of common-sense who wished to preserve the government and the Union could longer refuse to vote for Madison. Only to that extent could the people be said to have reached any conviction.

CHAPTER XIX.

In the midst of confusion the election took place. Few moments in the national history were less cheerful. In the Northwest the force organized to recapture Detroit, commanded by General Harrison, was still at Franklinton in the centre of Ohio, unable to advance and preparing to disband. At Niagara, Van Rensselaer had failed, and Smyth was in command. At sea, the "Guerriere" and the "Frolic" had been captured, but Decatur's victory over the "Macedonian" was still unknown. Napoleon, though supposed to be dictating peace at Moscow, was actually in full retreat. Every hope of the war party had already proved mistaken. Canada was not in their hands; no army had been enlisted; the people were less united than ever; taxation and debt could no longer be avoided; and military disgrace had been incurred beyond the predictions of John Randolph and Josiah Quincy. All this took place before the country had seen five hundred enemies except its own Indians on its soil, and when it had no reason to fear immediate attack.

Once more the steadiness of Pennsylvania saved the Administration from its worst perils. The election took place, and the electoral votes of New England, except Vermont, were duly thrown for De Witt Clinton, while under the management of Martin Van Buren the Republicans of the New York legislature chose Clinton electors by Federalist aid. New Jersey and Delaware also voted for Clinton. Maryland gave five of her electoral votes to Clinton, six to Madison, and elected a legislature strongly Federalist. A change of twenty electoral votes would have turned the scale. In 1808, under all the disadvantages of the embargo, Madison received one hundred and twenty-two votes in an Electoral College of one hundred and seventy-five; but in 1812 he obtained only one hundred and twenty-eight votes in an Electoral College of two hundred and seventeen, although the three new votes of Louisiana increased his proportion. In Massachusetts the Federalists surprised even themselves by their immense majority of twenty-four thousand, and the peace party swept the Congressional districts throughout New England and New York, doubling Federalist strength in the Thirteenth Congress.

If John Taylor of Caroline was to be believed, the support given by Virginia to the Administration was hardly more flattering than the sweeping condemnation of the North and East. The County of Caroline, south of the Rappahannock on the road to Richmond, was distinguished by no peculiarities from the other seaboard counties in the Southern States, and Colonel Taylor himself did not openly oppose the war; but he saw no enthusiasm for it among his neighbors. November 8 he wrote to Monroe,[1] —

" I think I expressed my opinion to you during the last Congress that the people were not for the war in these parts, though they were attached to Mr. Monroe and Mr. Madison. In that opinion I am confirmed by the apathy in choosing electors. Those respectable and popular men, Colonel James Taylor and Dr. Bankhead, could not, I am told, get more than about one hundred and thirty out of about seven hundred free-holders to attend and vote for Mr. Madison. Among these were the most prominent minority-men."

This apathy extended through the three great States of Pennsylvania, Virginia, and North Carolina. Only along the Indian frontier, west of the Alleghany Mountains, could enthusiasm be said to exist, and even there took rather the form of hostilities against the Indians than against the British.

The effect of these embarrassments and difficulties showed itself in wavering and uncertain judgment in the Government, and especially in its diplomacy. The President and the Cabinet hoped and believed, when the news of Hull's surrender arrived, that it would produce an outburst of patriotism. So strong was Monroe's faith in the people that he talked to Serurier, September 1, as though the nation were alive with his own ardor.[2]

[1] John Taylor to Monroe, Nov. 8, 1812 ; Monroe MSS. State Department Archives.

[2] Serurier to Maret, Sept. 2, 1812; Archives des Aff. Étr. MSS.

" ' We want no armistice for the present,' said Mr. Monroe to me with great energy; ' our resolution is taken. It has been done after long and cool deliberation, and by consent of the whole nation; we shall not easily renounce it. Never, certainly, have we been more determined on war; the disgraceful affront we have lately experienced at Detroit renders its prolongation indispensable until our honor is restored. . . . For myself,' he cried, with indignation altogether military and worthy one of the founders of Independence, ' Secretary of State as I am, if to-morrow a British minister should arrive in Washington to negotiate peace, I would say to him, No; I will not treat with you now! wait till we have given you a better opinion of us! When our honor shall be avenged, when you shall have recrossed the rivers, when our generals shall occupy the best part of your Canada, then I shall be disposed to listen, and to treat of peace.' "

These remarks were made in September. In about six weeks the French minister talked again with the Secretary of State, who assured him, to his astonishment, that peace might be made with England at any moment. Serurier, who took Monroe's pacific temper as seriously as he had taken his warlike expressions, wrote in alarm to his Government,[1] —

" The English want peace with America; they want it at any price; they offer all that America asks, and negotiations are about to open, or rather are continuing, and henceforward openly. Mr. Monroe made me this communication in nearly these terms. . . . ' We did not

[1] Serurier to Maret, Oct. 21, 1812; Archives des Aff. Étr. MSS.

flatter ourselves on obtaining so quickly such important concessions. Mr. Russell had occasion to see Lord Castlereagh. Discussing with this minister the repeal of the Orders in Council, he asked why the repealing Order treated with such vagueness the renunciation of paper blockades, and whether the Ministry had in fact wholly abandoned them. Lord Castlereagh answered: ' They fall to dust of themselves, and we shall think no more of them.' Mr. Russell having noticed the caution with which the Prince Regent seemed to retain the right to restore at any time the abolished Orders, Lord Castlereagh observed that, indeed, something had to be said for the public, but the phrase did no harm.' "

Monroe added that " very certainly the American government would not consent to sign the peace without having obtained from England the renunciation of impressments ; " but Serurier had reason for alarm, for Monroe expected an immediate renewal of negotiations. He had received from Admiral Sir John Borlase Warren at Halifax another offer of armistice and negotiation, dated September 30 ; and soon after the interview with Serurier, Monroe wrote to Admiral Warren a reply, dated October 27,[1] which accepted the armistice on condition that, pending the cessation of hostilities, the practice of impressments should be suspended, while he made the additional offer of negotiating without an armistice if the suspension of impressments should be conceded in principle.

Nothing remained of the refusal to hear England's

[1] Monroe to Admiral Warren, Oct. 27, 1812; State Papers, iii. 596.

advances until " our honor shall be restored and our generals shall occupy the best parts of your Canada." The unexpected indifference to the war which made itself so evident in all the Atlantic States paralyzed the government. Even the Federalists of New England, New York, New Jersey, and Maryland spoke to Monroe in tones hardly more emphatic than those used by his oldest Virginia friend, Colonel Taylor, who wrote: [1] "If the President thinks that defeat has raised the spirit of the nation, and goes on with the war on that ground, he will find himself mistaken." The President clearly came to the same conclusion, for he renewed attempts at negotiation a week before Congress met, and a fortnight before the election of November 8.

Thenceforward, Madison risked the charge of continuing the war only to satisfy himself that England could not be forced into an express renunciation of what she called her right of impressment, — a result which the opposition already knew to be certain. The experiment was worth trying, and after the timidity of the American government in past years was well suited to create national character, if it did not destroy the nation; but it was not the less hazardous in the face of sectional passions such as existed in New England, or in the hands of a party which held power by virtue of Jefferson's principles. That the British government should expressly renounce its

[1] John Taylor to Monroe, Nov. 8, 1812; Monroe MSS., State Department Archives.

claim to impressment was already an idea hardly
worth entertaining ; but if the war could not produce
that result, it might at least develop a government
strong enough to attain the same result at some
future time. If a strong government was desired,
any foreign war, without regard to its object, might
be good policy, if not good morals ; and in that sense
President Madison's war was the boldest and most
successful of all experiments in American statesmanship, though it was also among the most reckless ;
but only with difficulty could history offer a better
example of its processes than when it showed Madison, Gallatin, Macon, Monroe, and Jefferson joining
to create a mercenary army and a great national
debt, for no other attainable object than that which
had guided Alexander Hamilton and the Federalists
toward the establishment of a strong government
fifteen years before.

Unnatural as Madison's position was, that of Monroe was more surprising. Such were the revolutions
of politics that Madison found himself master of the
situation, and Monroe was obliged to forego his
ancient distrust of Executive power in the effort to
prevent his rivals from sharing it. Somewhat to the
amusement of the Federalists, who held no high
opinion of Monroe's abilities, the Secretary of State
was placed before the country in the attitude of
Cromwell. He could no longer follow the path of
ambition in civil life. If he were to maintain his
hold upon the Presidency, he must serve his coun-

try in the field where his services were needed, or
some bolder man would capture Quebec and the
Presidency by a single stroke.

The President himself gave Monroe an early hint
to this effect. After the adjournment of Congress,
July 6, 1812, and some two months before Hull's
surrender was known, Madison suggested[1] to his
Secretary of State the idea of leading the advance
upon Montreal. Fortunately for Monroe, he could
neither out-rank Dearborn, nor serve as a subordinate.
Unable to overcome this objection, Madison laid the
subject aside, and soon afterward, toward the end of
August, left Washington for Montpelier, where he
enjoyed only a few days' rest before the news of
Hull's surrender arrived. The idea that he was
himself in any degree responsible for Hull's disaster,
or for Eustis's or Dearborn's supposed shortcomings,
did not distress the President; but he was anxious
to restore confidence in the military administration,
and Monroe was earnest in the wish to assist him.
September 2, immediately after receiving the news,
Monroe wrote to the President offering to take a volunteer commission, and to assume command of the
fresh force then gathering in Kentucky and Ohio to
recapture Detroit. Madison replied September 5,[2]
balancing the advantages and objections, but lean-

[1] Madison to Monroe, Sept. 5, 1812; Monroe MSS., State
Department Archives.

[2] Madison to Monroe, Sept. 5, 1812; Monroe MSS., State
Department Archives.

ing toward the step.   The next day he wrote more
strongly,[1] urging Monroe to go as a volunteer without
rank, if no sufficient commission could be given him.
Again, September 10,[2] the President wrote, offering
to risk issuing a volunteer commission under a doubt
as to the meaning of the Act: " I see no evil in risking your appointment comparable to that which may
be obviated by it.   The Western country is all in
motion and confusion.   It would be grievous if so
much laudable ardor and effort should not be properly concentrated and directed."   Neither the President nor the Secretary was aware that Governor
William Henry Harrison had taken steps long in
advance for occupying the field on which Monroe's
eyes were fixed.   Monroe actually made his arrangements, sent off cannon to besiege Detroit, and was
himself on the point of starting westward, when
letters arrived which showed that Harrison was not
only the popular idol of the moment in Kentucky and
Ohio, but that he had received from the governor of
Kentucky the commission of major-general.[3]

This double set-back from men so inferior as Dearborn and Harrison irritated Monroe, who could not
command in the North on account of Dearborn, or in
the West without a contest with Harrison and Win-

[1] Madison to Monroe, Sept. 6, 1812; Monroe MSS., State
Department Archives.

[2] Madison to Monroe, Sept. 10, 1812; Monroe MSS., State
Department Archives.

[3] Monroe to Jefferson, June 7, 1813; Jefferson MSS.

chester. Evidently, if he was to take any military position, he must command in chief.

This idea became fixed not only in Monroe's mind, but also in that of the public, particularly among Monroe's personal following. The man who stood closest in his confidence and whose advice weighed most with him in personal matters was his son-in-law, George Hay. September 22 Hay wrote to him from Richmond,[1] —

" It is rumored here that you are to be appointed lieutenant-general. Such an appointment would give, I believe, universal satisfaction. . . . This is indeed a critical moment. Some great effort must be made. Unless something important is done, Mr. Madison may be elected again, but he will not be able to get along. But Mr. Madison ought not to exact any further sacrifices from you. If you go into the army you ought to go with the supreme power in your hand. I would not organize an army for Dearborn or anybody else. Mr. Madison ought not to expect it, and if he did I would flatly and directly reject the proposal. Everybody is looking forward to an event of this kind, and I do not believe that any man calculates that you are to go in a subordinate character. The truth is that Dearborn is laughed at, not by Federalists but by zealous Republicans. I do not give on this subject a reluctant, hesitating opinion. I am clear that if you go into the army (about which I say nothing), you should go as the commander-in-chief."

Monroe also felt no doubt that if he went to the field at all he must go in chief command ; but

[1] Hay to. Monroe, Sept. 22, 1812; Monroe MSS.

he hesitated. As compared with Madison's major-
generals, Monroe was young, being only fifty-four
years old; in the Revolutionary War he had risen to
the rank of captain, and had seen as much service
as made him the military equal of Dearborn or
Pinckney, but he felt no such special fitness for
carrying out a campaign as for planning and super-
intending it. Probably he could reconcile the two
careers only by some expedient, such as by taking
the War Department, and as Secretary of War ac-
companying the general in command; or by accepting the post of lieutenant-general, and from headquarters advising the Secretary of War as to the conduct of the campaign. The former course seemed to
Monroe to imply serious Constitutional difficulties,
and he inclined to the latter.

Secretary Eustis waited until Dearborn returned
from Lake Champlain to Albany, Smyth failed at
Niagara, and Harrison became stationary in Ohio,
then, December 3, sent his resignation to the President. Instantly informed of this event, and having
reason to suppose that the place would be offered to
him, Monroe called his friends to a consultation,[1] the
result of which was narrated in a letter written to
Jefferson six months afterward : [2] —

" I stated [to the President] that if it was thought
necessary to remove me from my present station in the
idea that I had some military experience, and a change

[1] Monroe to Crawford, Dec. 3, 1812; Monroe MSS.

[2] Monroe to Jefferson, June 7, 1813; Jefferson MSS.

in the command of the troops was resolved on, I would prefer it to the Department of War in the persuasion that I might be more useful. In the Department of War a man might form a plan of a campaign and write judicious letters on military operations; but still these were nothing but essays, — everything would depend on the execution. I thought that with the army I should have better control over operations and events, and might even aid, so far as I could give aid at all, the person in the Department of War. I offered to repair instantly to the Northern army, to use my best efforts to form it, to promote the recruiting business in the Eastern States, to conciliate the people to the views of the Government, and unite them so far as it might be possible in the war. The President was of opinion that if I quitted my present station, I ought to take the command of the army. It being necessary to place some one immediately in the Department of War to supply the vacancy made by Mr. Eustis's retreat, the President requested me to take it *pro tempore*, leaving the ultimate decision on the other question open to further consideration. I did so."

Monroe, with only the model of Washington before his eyes, felt aggrieved that the Clintons and Armstrongs of the North thought him greedy of power; but the curious destiny which had already more than once made a sport of Monroe's career promised at last to throw the weight of a continent upon his shoulders. Secretary of State, acting Secretary of War, general-in-chief by a double guarantee, and President thereafter, what more could the witches

promise on the blasted heath of politics that could
tempt ambition? Neither Cromwell nor Napoleon
had, at any single moment, laid a broader claim upon
the favors of Fortune.

Monroe grasped too much, and the prizes which
would have destroyed him slipped through his fingers.
The story that he was to be general-in-chief as well
as Secretary of War, exaggerated by jealousy, roused
a storm of protest. Even the patient Gallatin inter-
posed there, and gave the President to understand
that if Monroe were transferred to the army, he
should himself claim the vacant Department of State;
and Madison admitted the justice of the claim, although the difficulty of filling the Treasury created a
new obstacle to the scheme. A greater difficulty
arose from sectional jealousies. The loss of New
York to the Republican party, due chiefly to dislike
of Virginia and to Monroe's previous promotion, was
too recent and serious to allow further experiments.
The Republican leaders in New York — Governor
Tompkins, Judge Spencer, and their connections —
felt their hopes depend on checking the open dis-
play of Virginia favoritism. Finally, the Federalists made a scandal of the subject. January 5,
Josiah Quincy, in a speech which for literary quality
was one of the best ever delivered in the House,
after giving a keen if not an exact account of the
"Cabinet, little less than despotic, composed, to all
efficient purposes, of two Virginians and a foreigner,
which had for twelve years ruled the nation," rose

to a climax by averring that all the new Cabinet projects — the loan of twenty millions, an army of fifty-five thousand regulars, the scheme of mock negotiation — had no other object than to satiate the ambition of a single man : —

" The army for the conquest of Canada will be raised, — to be commanded by whom? This is the critical question. The answer is in every man's mouth. By a member of the American Cabinet; by one of the three; by one of that trio who at this moment constitute in fact, and who efficiently have always constituted, the whole Cabinet. And the man who is thus intended for the command of the greatest army this New World ever contained, — an army nearly twice as great as was at any time the regular army of our Revolution, — I say the man who is intended for this great trust is the individual who is notoriously the selected candidate for the next Presidency."

In face of these difficulties, Madison could not carry out his scheme. His only object in pushing Monroe forward was to strengthen himself by using what he supposed to be Monroe's popularity; but from the moment it appeared that Monroe, in the War Department or at the head of the Northern army, would be a source of weakness rather than of strength, Madison had no motive to persist; so that Monroe, failing to take a decided step, suddenly found himself — he hardly knew how — in the awkward attitude of a disappointed Cromwell. His rival first withdrew the War Department from his

hands.   He described to Jefferson [1] the way in which
he lost this vantage ground : —

"It was soon found to be improper, at a period of
so much danger and urgency, to keep that Department
in the hands of a temporary occupant; it ought to be
filled by the person who would have to form the plan of
the campaign in every quarter, and be responsible for
it.   It being indispensable to fill it with a prominent
character, and the question remaining undecided relative
to the command of the army, more persons thinking a
change urgent, and the opinion of the President in regard to me being the same, General Armstrong was put
in the Department of War.   Had it been decided to
continue the command of the army under General Dearborn, and the question been with me, 'Would I take
the Department of War, the President and other friends
wishing it?'   I would not have hesitated a moment in
complying; but it never assumed that form."

If Monroe was more jealous of one man than of
another, his antipathies centred upon John Armstrong, the late American minister at Paris.   As
has been already shown, Monroe came into the State
Department expecting rivalry with Armstrong; but
he had no occasion to begin active measures of hostility.   Armstrong's opinions of Madison and Monroe
were known to be the same as those of other New
Yorkers; if he came to the support of the Administration he came not in order to please the

[1] Monroe to Jefferson, June 7, 1813; Jefferson MSS.   Cf.
Monroe to Madison, Feb. 25, 1813; Monroe, MSS., State Department Archives.

Virginians, but to rescue the government from what
he thought Virginian incompetence or narrowness ;
and that Armstrong would shut the door of military
glory in the face of the Secretary of State was as
certain as that the Secretary of State would, sooner
or later, revenge the insult by ejecting Armstrong
from the Cabinet if he could.

No one denied that Monroe had reason for fearing Armstrong, whose abilities were undoubted and
whose scruples were few.   Since his return from
Paris, Armstrong had been known as a discontented
Republican, grumbling without reserve at the manner in which public affairs were conducted ; yet this
was no more than many other Northern Republicans
had done, and Armstrong behaved better than most.
On the declaration of war he avoided the mistakes
of the Clintons, and acted with Governor Tompkins
and Ambrose Spencer in support of the Administration.   July 6, 1812, to the surprise and anger
of the Clinton Republicans, Armstrong accepted the
commission of brigadier-general, and was placed in
command of New York city and its defences.   His
knowledge of the theory and practice of war was
considerable, and his influence as a politician was
likely to be great.   In the chronic chaos of New
York politics, Armstrong stood between De Witt
Clinton, who wished to win the Presidency by intrigue, and Governor Daniel D. Tompkins, who hoped
to become President by regular party promotion.
Ambrose Spencer, who liked neither Clinton nor

Tompkins, preferred Armstrong as the candidate of
New York. The influence of Spencer in the contest with De Witt Clinton became for the moment
absolute ; and the necessity of securing re-election
as governor, in April, 1813, drove Tompkins himself to support Spencer in urging Armstrong's appointment as Secretary of War, although he knew
that the appointment of Armstrong to the Cabinet
opened to him the door to the Presidency.[1]

In spite of Armstrong's services, abilities, and experience, something in his character always created
distrust. He had every advantage of education,
social and political connection, ability and self-confidence ; he was only fifty-four years old, which was
also the age of Monroe ; but he suffered from the
reputation of indolence and intrigue. So strong was
the prejudice against him that he obtained only
eighteen votes against fifteen in the Senate on his
confirmation ; and while the two senators from Virginia did not vote at all, the two from Kentucky
voted in the negative. Under such circumstances,
nothing but military success of the first order could
secure a fair field for Monroe's rival.

The nomination of Armstrong to be Secretary of
War was made Jan. 8, 1813, and was accompanied
by that of William Jones of Pennsylvania to succeed
Paul Hamilton as Secretary of the Navy.

The resignation of Paul Hamilton was supposed
to be made at the President's request, for reasons

[1] Hammond, i. 358, 360, 405, 406.

not given to the public. His successor, William Jones, long a prominent Republican, a member of Congress at the beginning of Jefferson's administration, had been offered the Navy Department in 1801, when that Department was offered to almost every leading Republican before falling into the hands of Robert Smith. Jones then declined the task, and soon retired from Congress to follow his private business as a ship-owner in Philadelphia. His appointment in 1812 was probably as good as the party could supply. He was confirmed by the Senate without opposition ; but he had little to do with the movement of politics or with matters apart from business.

These changes left no one except Gallatin who belonged to the Cabinet of President Jefferson. Attorney-General Rodney had resigned his position a year before, in natural displeasure because the President nominated Gabriel Duval, the Comptroller of the Treasury, to the vacant seat of Justice Chase on the Supreme Bench, thus passing over the Attorney-General in a manner which could be regarded only as a slight. The President, Dec. 10, 1811, nominated William Pinkney, the late minister at London, to succeed Rodney. The influence and activity of the Attorney-General in the Cabinet were at that time less than they subsequently became; and Pinkney, like Rodney, and like William Wirt afterward, had little responsibility beyond the few cases in which the United States were a party before the Courts.

With this reorganization of the Cabinet Madison's first term of Presidency drew toward a close. Only Congress required his attention, and as some compensation for the cares of war, the cares of Congress diminished. After the general election of Nov. 8, 1812, serious opposition or even faction in Congress became impossible. Madison had no reason to fear anything that could happen in the Legislature, provided he had no difficulties with his Cabinet.

President Madison's Annual Message of Nov. 4, 1812, was an interesting paper. Gliding gently over the disasters of the Northern campaign; dilating on British iniquity in using Indians for allies; commenting on the conduct of Massachusetts and Connecticut with disfavor, because it led to the result that the United States were " not one nation for the purpose most of all requiring it;" praising Rodgers and Hull for the results of their skill and bravery, — the Message next touched upon the diplomatic outlook and the future objects of the war in a paragraph which needed and received much study : —

" Anxious to abridge the evils from which a state of war cannot be exempt, I lost no time, after it was declared, in conveying to the British government the terms on which its progress might be arrested without awaiting the delays of a formal and final pacification ; and our *chargé d'affaires* at London was at the same time authorized to agree to an armistice founded upon them. These terms required that the Orders in Council should be repealed as they affected the United States, without a revival of blockades violating acknowledged rules; and that there should be an immediate discharge of American seamen from British ships, and a stop to impressment from American ships, with an understanding that an exclusion of the seamen of each nation from the ships of the other should be stipulated; and that the armistice should be improved into a definite and comprehensive adjustment of depending controversies. Although a repeal of the orders susceptible of explanations meeting the views of this Government had taken place before this pacific advance was communicated to that of Great Britain, the advance [made by us] was declined [by the British government] from an avowed repugnance to a suspension of the practice of impressments during the armistice, and without any intimation that the arrangement proposed with respect to seamen would be accepted. Whether the subsequent communications from this Government, affording an occasion for reconsidering the subject on the part of Great Britain, will be viewed in a more favorable light remains to be known. It would be unwise to relax our measures in any respect on a presumption of such a result."

Not without difficulty could one understand from this statement precisely what prevented the restoration of peace. England had never refused to discharge American seamen on sufficient evidence of wrongful impressment. According to the Message, the President asked only "an immediate discharge of American seamen from British ships, and a stop to impressment from American ships." The demand

of this point seemed to imply that England had
made or would probably make satisfactory concessions on all others.   The Message therefore narrowed
the cause of war to the requirement of a formal suspension of impressments from American ships, though
not of American citizens on shore, pending negotiations, and to be made permanent by treaty.   The demand was proper, and its only fault was to fall short
of full satisfaction ; but considered in its effect upon
the politics of the moment the attitude was new,
unsupported by a precedent, unwarranted by any
previous decision or declaration of President or Congress, and open to the Federalist charge that Madison sought only an excuse for continuing to stake
the national existence on the chance of success in
his alliance with Bonaparte.   The rest of the Message helped to strengthen the impression that a
policy of permanent war was to be fixed upon the
country ; for it recommended higher pay for recruits
and volunteers, an increase in the number of general officers, a reorganization of the general staff
of the army, and an increase of the navy.   The
impression was not weakened by the President's
silence in regard to the financial wants of the government, which left to the Secretary of the Treasury
the unpleasant duty of announcing that the enormous
sum of twenty million dollars must be borrowed for
the coming year.   Every one knew that such a demand was equivalent to admitting the prospect of
immediate bankruptcy.

" I think a loan to that amount to be altogether un-
attainable," Gallatin told Madison in private.[1]   " From
banks we can expect little or nothing, as they have
already lent nearly to the full extent of their faculties.
All that I could obtain this year from individual subscriptions does not exceed three million two hundred
thousand dollars."

The President refrained from presenting this demand to Congress, and not until after the election
was the financial situation made known ; but then
Gallatin's report, sent to the House December 5,
estimated the military expenses at seventeen millions, the naval at nearly five millions, and the civil
at fifteen hundred thousand, besides interest on the
public debt to the amount of three million three
hundred thousand, and reimbursements of loans,
treasury notes, etc., reaching five million two hundred thousand more, — in all, thirty-one million nine
hundred and twenty-five thousand dollars.   This
estimate omitted every expenditure not already
authorized by law, such as the proposed increase
of army and navy.

To meet these obligations, amounting probably to
thirty-three million dollars, Gallatin counted on a revenue of eleven million five hundred thousand dollars
from imports, and half a million from the sale of
lands, — making twelve millions in all ; leaving a sum
of at least twenty millions to be borrowed, with an
increase of debt to the amount of fifteen millions.

[1] Gallatin's Writings, i. 528.

The state of war brought the advantage of compelling the Legislature to act or perish; and although
Congress had seldom if ever been so unanimously
dissatisfied, it was never so docile. For the first
time Madison could recommend a measure with
some certainty that Congress would listen, and with
some confidence that it would act. Faction began
to find its limits, and an Executive order had no
longer to excuse itself; while Congress, on its side,
with shut eyes, broke through the barriers hitherto
set to its powers, and roamed almost at will beyond
the limits which the Republican party assigned to
the Constitution.

CHAPTER XX.

HARDLY had Henry Clay seated himself again in the Speaker's chair and appointed the select committee on military affairs, when the process of reorganizing the government on a new and energetic footing began. November 19, David R. Williams, chairman of the military committee, reported a bill raising the soldiers' pay to eight dollars a month, and exempting them from arrest for debt. At any previous moment in national history such a bill would have aroused paroxysms of alarm, but the Republicans of 1812 were obliged to accept it without a protest, and with grave doubts whether it would prove effective; while the Federalists tried only to strike out the clause which allowed minors above eighteen years of age to enlist without the consent of their parents, guardians, or masters. On this subject Josiah Quincy made a vehement speech, which ruffled the temper of David R. Williams. Quincy was defeated in the House; but the Senate by a vote of twenty-six to four saved the rights of parents, guardians, and masters, without reducing the age of enlistments. The bill became law December 12, and was quickly followed by another bill raising the bounty and organizing the recruiting service.

Before this matter was finished, the naval committee reported a bill for increasing the navy; and the two Houses vied with one another in their enthusiasm for this recently unpopular branch of the public service.   Here and there an old Republican protested that he could not in conscience violate every fixed idea of his political existence by voting for a large naval establishment; but when the House was asked to appropriate money for four ships-of-the-line and six forty-four-gun frigates, although the Federalists were much divided as to the wisdom of building seventy-fours, and debated the subject at great length with contradictory votes, the House closed the discussion, December 23, by passing the bill as it stood.   In the minority of fifty-six were several warm friends of the navy, who thought Congress needlessly extravagant.

" Frigates and seventy-fours," wrote Jefferson,[1] " are a sacrifice we must make, heavy as it is, to the prejudices of a part of our citizens."   No one who saw the quickness of this revolution could doubt that whatever evils war might cause, it was a potent force to sweep nations forward on their destined way of development or decline.   Madison, Monroe, Gallatin, as well as Jefferson and the whole Republican party accepted a highly paid mercenary army, a fleet of ships-of-the-line, a great national debt at high inter-

[1] Jefferson to Monroe, Jan. 1, 1815 ; Works, vi. 400.

est, and a war of conquest in coincidence with the wars of Napoleon, on ground which fifteen years before had been held by them insufficient to warrant resistance to France.

More serious suggestions were offered by the failure of Congress to act its intended part as the controlling branch of government. The founders of the Constitution had not expected the legislative power whose wishes the President was created to carry out, and which was alone responsible for the policy of government, to prove imbecile; yet every one saw that Congress was sinking, or had already sunk, low in efficiency. Before the declaration of war, this condition of the Legislature was concealed by the factiousness which caused it; but the first meeting of Congress during the war disclosed one of the commonplaces of history, — that no merely legislative body could control a single, concentrated Executive, even though it were in hands as little enterprising as those of President Madison. The declaration of war placed Congress in a new position. Although the sessions were unchanged in character, they became suddenly unimportant compared with Executive acts. Congress no longer counteracted directly the Executive will, or refused what the President required; the wishes expressed in his Annual Message were for the first time carried out like orders. On the other hand the country was excited by a reorganization of the Cabinet, and Congress seemed to feel itself superfluous, while the President decided upon the

conflicting claims of politicians to act as channels
for dispensing his power.

The exceptions to the newly-established discipline
were chiefly found among the war leaders themselves,
who had done most to make it necessary. As the
demands of the government became greater, they
interfered with favorite interests or prejudices. This
was particularly the case with the required financial
measures. Gallatin made in his annual report no
direct recommendations ; he contented himself with
a brief statement of receipts and estimates ; but in
a letter to the Committee of Ways and Means, dated
November 18, he suggested a resource which might
to the extent of a few millions relieve the Treasury
from its immediate burden. The resource was accidental. Immediately after the repeal of the British
Orders in Council, British merchandise to a great
amount was shipped to America in reliance on the
Act of Congress of March 2, 1811, which declared
that the repeal of the British Orders, at any time,
should of itself put an end to the American non-
importation. The declaration of war, five days before
the British repeal, rendered inoperative the Act of
March 2, 1811, so that the importers became liable
not only to capture by the public and private armed
vessels of both countries, but also to confiscation of
their property by the government on its arrival in
the United States. Both events occurred. Some
vessels were captured at sea, and sent in ; but these
and all the rest were alike seized on their arrival,

and libelled by the government without distinction. The question then arose, what should be done with them.

Under the law of forfeiture, one half was vested in the custom-house officers or informers, the other half in the United States; and the power to remit, in whole or in part, was vested in the Secretary of the Treasury. No one expected the government to exact the full forfeiture, for the importations had been made in good faith, and the property was chiefly American. As though to protect the owners the courts interfered, and in certain districts compelled the collectors to release the cargoes on receiving bonds to their appraised value. The action of the courts obliged the President to make the rule general. All the cargoes were released, the goods passed into the market, and only bonds to the amount of near eighteen million dollars, besides duties to the amount of five millions, remained in charge of the Treasury. The five millions were safe; but the bonds were by no means as good as the gold.

Gallatin expressed to the Committee of Ways and Means the opinion, that in view of the extraordinary profits of the importers, who had no right to any profit at all, substantial justice would be done by remitting that half of the forfeitures which would otherwise fall to the collectors, and by exacting for the public only an equivalent for unexpected war profits. His plan aimed at placing the importers, as nearly as possible, in the condition they had expected, on the withdrawal of the non-importation, when they ordered the importations to be made.[1]

Gallatin's views were explained more fully in the course of the debate. The importers had been aware of their risk, and had not taken it without much hesitation, after consulting Jonathan Russell, then in charge of the legation at London. The Government held non-importation to be more effective than armies or fleets in bringing England to terms, and the non-importation was still in force as a war measure. Gallatin's orders, which admitted these goods for sale, violated the law and the policy of government; but if the goods had been admitted, as was the case, at least they should not be used to diminish the government's receipts from internal taxation. The duties already levied to the amount of five million dollars did not exceed twenty-five per cent on their cost, while the goods themselves commanded war prices, and no other goods of the same kind were allowed to enter the country. The profits could hardly fail to be great, and no small part of these profits, besides the invested capital, was British. Finally, within the wider questions of equity, law, and policy remained the fact that bankruptcy in one form or another stood directly before the Treasury, and that four or five million dollars might be the means of national salvation.

If objections were to be made, one might have

[1] Gallatin to Cheves, Nov. 23, 1812 ; Annals, 1812–1813, p. 1258.

supposed that Cheves, Clay, and Calhoun would have resisted Gallatin's idea because it offered too much encouragement to mercantile speculation resting on violation of law; but nothing was more uncertain than the moral sensitiveness of a political body. What seemed to one statesman a right and proper act seemed evident dishonesty to another; nor had the science of ethics made sensible progress toward the invention of practical tests. Statesmen who saw nothing improper in the seizure of West Florida, the attacks on East Florida, or the campaign of Tippecanoe; who maintained the doctrine that the admission of Louisiana dissolved the Union, or that Champagny's letters satisfied the demands of government and the Acts of Congress, — war Democrats and Federalists alike, representing the morality and the energy of the country, joined in attacking Gallatin's plan. Langdon Cheves, chairman of the Ways and Means Committee, after reporting from the committee, November 25, a resolution to leave the subject to the Secretary of the Treasury, began a speech, December 4, by declaring that he trembled for the consequences of the measure; it would shake the party to pieces; it would make angels weep.

" I trust in God," cried Cheves, " no man who may be thus consigned by this House to the Secretary of the Treasury to await his decision and to supplicate his clemency, will so far forget what he owes to his own true interests and to his character as a free citizen as to give an equivalent for that sum of money which may be de-

manded as the government's share of the profits. I
would rather see the objects of the war fail, — I would
rather see the seamen of the country impressed on the
ocean and our commerce swept from its bosom, — than
see the long arm of the Treasury indirectly thrust into
the pocket of the citizen through the medium of a penal
law."

Henry Clay admitted and favored total confiscation,
but not the idea of a compromise : —

" The law ought to be enforced or not. He thought
a compromise in the case dangerous and undignified ;
indeed, he felt shocked at the idea of an equivalent.
Already are our laws too openly violated or fraudulently
eluded. Shall we degrade them still further by carrying
them into the market and fixing a price upon their violation? Extend the principle of an equivalent, from cases
of prohibition merely, to instances of moral turpitude, —
to felony and homicide, — and every gentleman will see
its enormity. No, sir! Let us not pollute our hands
with this welt-gild ! "

Calhoun would not allow that the government
could properly act at all : —

" If our merchants are innocent," he said, " they are
welcome to their good fortune ; if guilty, I scorn to par-
ticipate in its profits. I will never consent to make our
penal code the basis of our Ways and Means, or to
establish a partnership between the Treasury and the
violators of the Non-importation Law."

William Lowndes fortified his position by an argument showing that " if the plan of confiscation and
of a rigid execution of the law were dismissed, no

just principles of policy and not even the interests of the Treasury could sanction an exaction which would resolve itself into a tax." Josiah Quincy found himself for once in accord with his chief opponents, and declared that in his opinion highway robbery stood a little higher in point of courage, and was a little less in point of iniquity, than this Treasury attempt to make calumny the basis of plunder. Felix Grundy said : " Gentlemen have assumed a strange, high-minded position in this argument, the force of which, I confess, is beyond my comprehension."

December 11 the House in Committee of the Whole, by a vote of fifty-two to forty-nine, rejected Gallatin's suggestion. December 15 a bill came from the Senate remitting all forfeitures on goods owned by Americans and shipped from England before September 15, when the declaration of war became known there. After a sharp debate this bill passed by a vote of sixty-four to sixty-one, — Calhoun, Cheves, and Lowndes voting with the Federalists and securing its passage. This decision closed one source of revenue for the year.

The course taken by Cheves, Calhoun, and Lowndes was largely due to their dislike of the non-importation system on which the proposed forfeiture rested. They wished to abolish commercial restrictions ; they were anxious to avoid internal taxation, and to supply the Treasury with revenue by admitting British goods under heavy duties. So earnest was Cheves in pursuit of this object that he hardly tolerated any other,

and made no secret of his hope that the failure to
exact these forfeitures and to lay internal taxes
would compel Congress to depend upon imports for
resources.

" How are the exigencies of the government for the
next year to be supplied?" he asked as early as December 4. " Is the deficiency to be derived from [internal]
taxes? No! I will tell gentlemen who are opposed to
them, for their comfort, that there will be no taxes imposed for the next year. It was said last session that
you would have time to lay them for this session, but I
then said it was a mistake. You now find this to be the
fact. By your indecision then, when the country was
convinced they were necessary, you have set the minds
of the people against taxes; but were it otherwise, you
have not time now to lay them for next year."

Calhoun also laid down emphatic principles on this
point, dwelling in strong language on what he held
to be the radical error of Virginia statesmanship.

" At the end of the last session," said Calhoun, December 8, " I recommended high duties as a substitute
for the Non-importation Act. High duties have no per-
nicious effects, and are consistent with the genius of the
people and the institutions of the country. It is thus
we would combine in the highest degree the active resources of the country with the pressure on the manufactures of the enemy. Your army and navy would feel
the animating effect. . . . The non-importation as a redress of wrongs is radically defective. You may meet
commercial restrictions with commercial restrictions, but
you cannot safely confront premeditated insult and in-

jury with commercial restrictions alone. . . . It sinks
the nation in its own estimation; it counts for nothing
what is ultimately connected with our best hopes, — the
Union of these States. Our Union cannot safely stand
on the cold calculation of interest alone; it is too weak
to withstand political convulsions; we cannot without
hazard neglect that which makes man love to be a member of an extensive community, — the love of greatness,
the consciousness of strength."

The three South Carolinians — Calhoun, Cheves,
and Lowndes — had a financial policy of their own,
in which they received some private sympathy, if not
much active support, from the Treasury.   Gallatin, in
his own way, stood in a position almost as solitary as
that of John Randolph; but condemned as he was
to support the burden of a war which Congress had
insisted upon, with only such financial means as Congress left him, he could feel little sympathy with
any financial scheme, for all were more or less clumsy
and inefficient. As far as he could see, nothing but
peace could save the Treasury. In June, at the time
of declaring war, he urged taxation; but the party
feared taxation, and preferred to wait the chances of
military success. In December these expected suc-
cesses turned into disasters; the country showed
an unforeseen hostility to the war. Taxation might
easily be fatal, for the war found little real support
except in Kentucky, Tennessee, and the Southern
States, precisely where internal taxation would excite
deepest resistance. The war leaders would not hear

of laying taxes at such a moment, and they had no great difficulty in carrying their point. Gallatin himself could afford to wait. The accidental importations from England after the repeal of the British orders brought five million dollars into the Treasury, — a sum so much greater than had been expected, and so ample for meeting the interest on old and new loans, that Gallatin could not think himself obliged to exhaust his influence and risk that of his party in order to wring taxes from a timid Congress. The secretary's attitude brought upon him a fair and just rebuke from John Randolph, that he had trifled with the dignity of the House.[1] Had Gallatin been inclined to retort, he would have replied that so far as the Treasury knew, the House had no dignity to trifle with; but Gallatin never lost control of his temper or his tongue, and after having been the readiest and boldest adviser of his party he had become a master in the art of silence. He expressed once more his belief in the necessity of taxation;[2] but this done he let Congress go its own gait.

Cheves aspired to abolish the remains of Jeffersonian statesmanship, — non-importations, embargoes, and restrictions, — and to restore the freedom of commerce; and in support of this scheme he obtained from Gallatin a letter dated Feb. 9, 1813,[3] expressing the

[1] Annals of Congress, 1812–1813, p. 800.

[2] Letters of Gallatin, Feb. 3, 1813, and Feb. 9, 1813; Annals of Congress, 1812–1813, p. 1063.

[3] Annals of Congress, 1812–1813, p. 1063.

decided opinion that Congress must not only impose war taxes, both external and internal, but must also repeal the non-importation, if the increased expenditures authorized by law were to be met. February 15 Cheves introduced a bill carrying out the secretary's opinion so far as to suspend the Non-importation Act in part, though continuing it against articles specially enumerated. Two days afterward the House, by a vote of sixty-nine to forty-seven, instructed the Committee of Ways and Means to report tax-bills, although Cheves complained that the instruction was deceptive, and that no system of taxation could possibly be adopted within the fortnight that remained of the session. Apparently Cheves looked on the motion as a manœuvre to save the Non-importation Act; but he could hardly have been prepared to see the Federalist member, Elisha Potter of Rhode Island, rise, February 20, and declare that his constituents had invested a capital of four or five million dollars in manufactures protected by non-importation, and that Cheves's bill, sacrificing as it did the interests of the manufacturing States, ought not to pass.

Such a change of attitude foreshadowed a revolution. New England had her price. The system which Jefferson forced upon her at the cost of the Southern States had begun to work its intended effect. Under the pressure of Virginia legislation, New England was abandoning commerce and creating manufactures. While every Federalist newspaper in the country denounced the restrictive system without ceasing, nearly every Federalist in the House voted with Potter in its favor. By seventy-nine votes to twenty-four, the Committee of the Whole struck out Cheves's proposed relaxation, and converted his bill into a measure for the stricter enforcement of non-importation. Cheves and Lowndes were then obliged to vote against their own bill, so amended, in a minority of forty-five to sixty-seven.

Nothing remained but to depend upon loans and call an extra session to consider the taxes. The loan bill, passed January 26, authorized the President to borrow sixteen million dollars on any terms he could obtain, provided only that the nominal capital might be repaid at the end of twelve years. Attempts to limit the rates of interest and discount were defeated, and the bill passed by a vote of seventy-five to thirty-eight. Another bill immediately followed, authorizing the issue of treasury notes bearing interest at five and two fifths per cent, to be redeemed in one year. Five millions in such notes were to be issued at all events, and five millions more in case the loan should prove less advantageous than the notes. By these means Congress proposed to supply the needed twenty-one million dollars, although no one could say with confidence how much these millions would cost, or whether they could be obtained at any price.

There ended the financial work of the session. The military and naval results were more considerable. Besides the Act increasing the soldiers' pay to eight dollars a month, Congress authorized the President to raise twenty new regiments of infantry for one year's service, with full pay, bounty of sixteen dollars, and invalid pensions of five dollars a month. Six new major-generals and an equal number of brigadiers were authorized February 24; the departments of the commissary and quartermaster-general were placed on a better footing; the general staff was organized with comparative liberality, — until, March 3, 1813, the last day of Madison's first term, the President, who had begun his career of power in an Administration which in effect abolished army and navy, commanded a regular force consisting by law of fifty-eight thousand men,[1] and was surrounded by major-generals and brigadiers by the dozen, instead of the solitary brigadier Wilkinson who had been left to command the frontier garrisons of 1801, while four ships-of-the-line, six forty-fours, and six sloops-of-war were building to reinforce the six frigates and the rest of the navy actually in service; and in addition to all this, an unlimited order had been issued for flotillas on the lakes.

With each new Act, John Randolph showed how his old friends were giving the lie to their old political professions; but by common consent party consistency was admitted to be no longer capable of defence. The party which had taken power in 1801 to carry out the principle that the hopes of society and the rights of the States must not be risked by

[1] Organization of the Army. Niles, iv. 145.

war for points of pride or profits of commerce, declared with equal energy in 1812 that the country
had no choice but to sacrifice hopes and rights because England would not expressly abandon a point
of pride. Doubtless this momentary position was far
beyond the conscious convictions of the party, but it
made a precedent; and although political parties were
apt to think that precedents could be ignored, history
seldom failed to show that they decided the course of
law. As far as concerned the old Republican party,
the triumph of the national movement was for the
time complete.

Yet the government was not so rigid in its logic,
even in regard to municipal legislation, as it professed to be. If the dispute about impressment was
to be settled, it must be settled by a general consent
to abandon the practice. Whether governments consented expressly or tacitly, by a preliminary agreement, by treaty, by legislation, or by simply ceasing
to impress, was a matter of little concern provided
the practice was stopped. The United States were
not obliged to wage war on England or France
merely because, under old international law, those
governments claimed what they called a right to
seize their subjects on the high seas. Indeed, the
cause of war would not have been removed by an
express surrender of impressment on the high seas,
though it had been accompanied by an equally express surrender of the right of search. The difficulty
lay deeper and extended further than the American

flag had ability to go. Much the larger number of impressments took place on shore or within British waters. Many of the American seamen for whose sake the war continued to be fought were American only in the sense that they carried American papers. They were British-born, in British service, and were impressed in the grog-shops of London or Liverpool. The American government could hardly concede to its seamen the liberty refused to its ships, — of carrying double sets of papers, and appearing as American or British at will; yet if the American protection had legal meaning, it entitled the seaman to complete immunity, no matter where he might be, or might have been in the past, or might intend to be in the future, even though he had never been in the United States in his life. The British officer could not be allowed to disregard the protection, even though such a system would make seamen a privileged class, with double nationality and no allegiance.

Annoyed by this insuperable obstacle to an arrangement, Monroe offered the British government to prohibit by Act of Congress the employment of British seamen in the public or private marine of the United States.[1] The offer was meant as an inducement for England to sacrifice her seamen already naturalized in America, on the chance of recovering those who might not carry American papers; but it bore to England the look of an evasion, and was received by

[1] Monroe to Jonathan Russell, June 26, 1812; State Papers, iii. 585.

Lord Castlereagh in that sense.[1] The subject had reached this stage when it was brought before Congress by the President's Annual Message, and was referred by the House to the Committee of Foreign Relations. January 29 Felix Grundy made a report from the committee,[2] doubtless written in concert with Monroe and intended to support his position, since it approved what the secretary had done and gave authority to his views. The report asserted with emphasis that impressment alone prevented an armistice. More than once, as though this were the weak point of the government's situation, Grundy returned to the theme that impressment "must be provided for in the negotiation; the omission of it in a treaty of peace would not leave it on its former grounds,— it would in effect be an absolute relinquishment."

The danger of thus committing the government to a *sine qua non* which might need to be abandoned was becoming more evident every day, for already Napoleon was known to have suffered some great disaster in Russia, and his power in Spain was evidently threatened with overthrow. After Napoleon should have been routed in Russia and Spain, and the American armies should have abandoned the hope of conquering Canada, the chance of driving England into an express surrender of impressments would vanish. Wisdom dictated caution; but Monroe's letters and

[1] Lord Castlereagh to Jonathan Russell, Aug. 29, 1812; State Papers, iii. 589.

[2] Annals of Congress, 1812–1813, p. 932.

Grundy's report, while committing the government to a *sine qua non* preliminary to negotiation, proposed to escape the inevitable difficulty by an expedient less dignified than the country had a right to expect. Grundy reported a bill to serve as the groundwork for peace.

This bill began by a prospective, reciprocal prohibition, " from and after the termination of a treaty of peace," to employ on any vessel, public or private, any but actual citizens, " or persons who being resident within the United States at the time of such treaty, and having previously declared agreeably to existing laws their intention to become citizens of the United States, shall be admitted as such within five years thereafter in the manner prescribed by law." With these exceptions, Congress was to dismiss all foreign seamen from the American service, and to forbid forever the sea as a livelihood to persons coming into the country with the intention of acquiring citizenship, after the treaty of peace.

The objections to this measure were evident. It seemed tacitly to admit the right of impressment ; it denied to one class of citizens rights in which all others were protected, and its Constitutionality was at least doubtful ; it trenched on Executive functions and the treaty-making power ; it placed American merchants under great disadvantages, depriving them of seamen, and under many circumstances making it impossible for an American ship to return from a distant port. Yet perhaps its worst practical fault consisted in pressing upon England, as an ultimatum, terms of peace which she had again and again rejected and was certain to reject. Indeed, the only argument of weight advanced in favor of the bill was that its rejection by England would heal the divisions of America. Unfortunately, even this argument seemed to have little foundation.

The bill passed the House by a vote of eighty-nine to thirty-three, and February 12 went to the Senate. There Giles took it in hand, and after sharp opposition it was amended and passed, February 27, by a vote of eighteen to twelve. In its adopted form the Act did not contain the clause that roused most opposition, but reached the same result in a less direct way : —

" From and after the termination of the war," ran the new statute, " it shall not be lawful to employ on board any of the public or private vessels of the United States any person or persons except citizens of the United States, or persons of color, natives of the United States. . . . No person who shall arrive in the United States from and after the time when this Act shall take effect shall be admitted to become a citizen of the United States who shall not for the continued term of five years next preceding his admission as aforesaid have resided within the United States, without being at any time within the said five years out of the territory of the United States."

The subject of impressment was so difficult to understand, even in its simpler facts, that the practical workings of this measure could not be foreseen. No one knew how many naturalized British seamen were in the American service, or how many British seamen not naturalized; and there was no sufficient evidence to serve as the foundation for a probable guess as to the number of impressments from American ships, or how they were distributed among the three classes, — (1) native American citizens; (2) naturalized British seamen; and (3) seamen avowedly British subjects. According to a report made from the Department of State, Feb. 18, 1813,[1] the supposed number of seamen registered in the United States since 1796 amounted to about one hundred and forty thousand. The actual number in any one year was unknown. In 1805 Gallatin estimated them, from the registered tonnage, at fifty thousand.[2]

Foreign seamen served chiefly in the foreign trade; and since the registered tonnage in foreign trade increased from 750,000 tons in 1805 to 984,000 tons in 1810, the number of seamen increased proportionately from 45,000 to 60,000 or thereabout. In 1807 Gallatin estimated the increase at five thousand a year, more than half being British sailors.[3] Probably fifteen thousand seamen, or one fourth of the whole number employed in 1810,[4] were of foreign origin, and might or might not carry American papers. If

[1] Annals of Congress, 1812–1813, p. 93.
[2] Gallatin to Jefferson, November, 1805 ; Works, i. 267.
[3] Gallatin to Jefferson, April 16, 1807; Works, i. 335.
[4] Dallas to the Committee of Foreign Relations, Jan. 26, 1816. Annals of Congress, 1815–1816, p. 176.

they did not, the reason could only be that they knew
the worthlessness of such papers.   Genuine American
protections could be bought in any large port for two
dollars apiece, while forged protections were to be
had by the gross.[1]   A large proportion of the British
seamen in American service carried no evidence of
American citizenship.

According to Lord Castlereagh's statement in
Parliament, the number of seamen claiming to be
Americans in the British service amounted to three
thousand five hundred in January, 1811, and to something more than three thousand in February, 1813, at
the time he was speaking.[2]   Of these, he said, only
about one in four, or some eight hundred, could offer
proof of any sort, good or bad, of their citizenship;
the others had no evidence either of birth or of
naturalization in America.   If this was true, and the
closest American calculation seemed rather to favor
Castlereagh's assertion, the new Act of Congress sacrificed much to obtain little; for it authorized the
President to expel from American service five or ten
thousand seamen, and to forbid future employment
or naturalization to all British seamen, if England in
return would cease to employ five or six hundred
impressed Americans.

The concession was immense, not only in its effect

[1] Massachusetts Report on Impressed Seamen, 1813, p. 53.
Speech of James Emott, Jan. 12, 1813; Annals of Congress,
1812–1813, p. 735.

[2] Cobbett's Debates, Feb. 18, 1813.

on legitimate American commerce and shipping, but also on the national character. America possessed certainly the right, which England had always exercised, of naturalizing foreign seamen in her service, and still more of employing such seamen without naturalization. In denying herself the practice she made a sacrifice much greater in material cost, and certainly not less in national character, than she ever made by tolerating impressments under protest. The impressments cost her about five hundred seamen a year, of whom only a fraction were citizens ; of these such as were natives could in most cases obtain release on giving evidence of their citizenship, while five times the number of native British seamen annually deserted the British service for the American. Thus England was much the greater sufferer from the situation ; and America preserved her rights by never for an instant admitting the British doctrine of impressment, and by retaining the ability to enforce at any moment her protest by war. All these advantages were lost by Monroe's new scheme. Under the Act of 1813 America would save her citizens to whatever number they amounted, but she would do so by sacrificing her shipping, by abandoning the practice if not the right of employing and naturalizing British seamen, and by tacitly admitting the right of impressment so far as to surrender the use of undoubted national rights as an equivalent for it.

Numbers of leading Republicans denounced the measure as feeble, mischievous, and unconstitutional.

Only as an electioneering argument against the extreme Federalists, and as a means of satisfying discontented Republicans, was it likely to serve any good purpose ; but the dangers of discord and the general apathy toward the war had become so evident as to make some concession necessary, — and thus it happened that with general approval the law received the President's signature, and the next day the Twelfth Congress expired. With it expired President Madison's first term of office, leaving the country more than ever distracted, and as little able to negotiate as to conquer.

INDEX TO VOLS. I. AND II.

ACT OF CONGRESS, of June 28, 1809, restoring intercourse with Great Britain, i. 80; of June 28, 1809, suspending the recruiting service, 85; of June 28, 1809, reducing the naval establishment, 85; of March 1, 1810, concerning the commercial intercourse between the United States and Great Britain and France, 194–198 (see Non-intercourse); of Feb. 14, 1810, appropriating sixty thousand dollars for the Cumberland Road, 209 ; of March 26, 1810, providing for the Third Census, 209; of March 30, 1810, appropriating five thousand dollars for experiments on the submarine torpedo, 209; of Feb. 20, 1811, admitting the State of Louisiana into the Union, 326 ; of Jan. 15, 1811, authorizing the occupation of East Florida, 327; of March 2, 1811, reviving non-intercourse against Great Britain, 338–354 (see Non-intercourse); of Jan. 11, 1812, to raise an additional military force of twenty-five thousand men, ii. 147, 153; of Feb. 6, 1812, to accept volunteers, 159–161 ; of March 14, 1812, authorizing a loan for eleven million dollars, 169; of April 4, 1812, laying an embargo for ninety days, 201, 202, 203; of April 8, 1812, admitting the State of Louisiana into the Union, 235; of April 10, 1812, authorizing a call for one hundred thousand militia, 204; of June 18, 1812, declaring war against Great Britain, 228, 229; of July 1, 1812, doubling the duties on imports, 235; of Dec. 12, 1812, increasing the pay of the army, 435; of Jan. 20, 1813, increasing the bounty for recruits, 436; of Jan. 2, 1813, for building four seventy-fours and six frigates, 436; of Jan. 5, 1813, remitting fines, forfeitures, etc., 443; of Feb. 8, 1813, authorizing loan of sixteen millions, 448; of Feb. 25, 1813, authorizing the issue of Treasury notes for five millions, 448; of Jan. 29, 1813, for raising twenty regiments for one year, 449; of Feb. 24, 1813, for appointing six major-generals and six brigadiers, 449 ; of March 3, 1813, to provide for the supplies of the army, 449; of March 3, 1813, for the better organization of the general staff, 449; of March 3, 1813, for building six sloops-of-war, 449; of March 3, 1813, for the regulation of seamen on board the public and private vessels of the United States, 453–458.

Act of the territorial legislature of Indiana, permitting the introduction of slaves, ii. 76.

Adams, President, expenditures of his administration, i. 200, 205, 206.

Adams, John Quincy, nominated as minister to Russia, i. 11 ; renominated and confirmed, 86; nominated and confirmed Justice of the Supreme Court, 360; sails for Russia, 408; arrives, 409; his negotiations in 1809, 409, 411; his negotiations in 1810, 412–418; his success, 419, 420, 422.

"Adams," brig, launched at Detroit, ii. 304; captured and recaptured, 347; destroyed, 347.

"Adams," 28-gun frigate, ii. 364.

"Aeolus," case of, ii. 273.

"Aeolus," British frigate, ii. 368.

"Africa," British frigate, ii. 368.

Albany, headquarters of Dearborn, ii. 304, 305, 308, 309, 310.

"Alert," British sloop-of-war, her action with the "Essex," ii. 35, 377.

Alexander, Czar of Russia, with Napoleon at Erfurt, i. 23; his alliance with Napoleon, 134, 257; his approaching rupture with Napoleon, 385, 408–424; interferes for American commerce in Denmark, 410, 411; his reply to Napoleon's demands, 413, 414; gives special orders to release American ships, 415; his attachment to the United States, 415; his ukase on foreign trade, 418.

Amelia Island, i. 165.

Anderson, Joseph, senator from Tennessee, defeats mission to Russia, i. 12; criticises Giles, ii. 150; chairman of committee on declaration of war, 228.

"Argus," sloop-of-war, ii. 363, 364, 378, 381.

Armistice between Dearborn and Prevost, ii. 322, 323, 324, 404; known to Brock, 330; disavowed by Madison, 340, 404; an advantage to Dearborn, 343; proposed by Monroe, 403; proposed by Admiral Warren, 416.

Armstrong, John, minister in Paris, his discontent, i. 28; his relations with Roumanzoff, 29; his complaints in 1809, 39; communicates Non-intercourse Act of March 1, 1809, 135, 235; his comments on the right of search, 145; his interview with King Louis of Holland, 147, 148; his despatch on Fouché and Montalivet, 224; on Napoleon's motives, 225; his minute for a treaty, 228; his recall asked by Napoleon, 228, 229, 252; his remonstrance against the doctrine of retaliation, 233, 234; his report of Jan. 10, 1810, 238; inquires condition of revoking decrees, 251; communicates Non-intercourse Act of May 1, 1810, 252; his reception of Cadore's letter of Aug. 5, 1810, 259, 260; returns to America, 260, 261, 381; declares Napoleon's conditions to be not precedent, 261; silent about indemnity, 260, 296; Virginian jealousy of, 370; on Napoleon's designs on the Baltic, 417; becomes brigadier-general, ii. 427; his attitude towards Monroe and Madison, 426, 427; nominated Secretary of War, 428; his character, 428.

Army, in 1809, i. 169; described by Wilkinson, 170, 171; encamped at Terre aux Bœufs, 171–175; reductions in 1810, 200–207; raised by law to thirty-five thousand men, ii. 148, 151–153; useless, 165; condition of, 289, 292; recruiting for, 294; war establishment in 1812, 295; enlistments in, 337, 390, 391, 401; difficulty of filling, 394; Acts of Congress for filling ranks of, 435, 436; war establishment in 1813, 449. (See Infantry.)

"Asia," American ship, burned by French squadron, ii. 193, 198.

Astor, John Jacob, ii. 301.

Austria, i. 27, 134; fights battles of Essling and Wagram, 106.

BACON, EZEKIEL, member of Congress from Massachusetts, ii. 156; votes against frigates, 164; moves war taxes, 165, 166.

Baen, William C., captain of Fourth U. S. Infantry, killed at Tippecanoe, ii. 104.

Bainbridge, William, captain in U. S. navy, ii. 384; takes command of the "Constitution," 384; captures "Java," 385, 386.

Baltimore, population in 1810, i. 289.

Baltimore riot, July 27, 1812, ii. 406-409.

Bank of the United States, i. 167; bill introduced for rechartering, 207, 208; hostile influence of State Banks, 327, 330, 332, 335, 336; pretexts for opposition to charter of, 328, 329; necessity for, 329; Crawford's bill for rechartering, 332; debate on, 332–336; defeat of, 337.

Banks, popularity of, ii. 208, 209.

Baring, Alexander, ii. 276.

Barlow, Joel, on Robert Smith's appointment, i. 10; on Smith's opposition to Macon's bill, 187; his defence of the President, 299, 301, 378; appointed minister to France, 359; his instructions on revocation of French Decrees, 427; his departure delayed by Monroe, ii. 50; ready to start, 55; order for his departure countermanded, 56; order finally given, 61; his instructions, 66; his want of success, 217; arrives in Paris, Sept. 19, 1811, 245; his negotiation with Bassano,

248-263; his journey to Wilna, 263, 264; his death, 265.

Bassano, Duc de. (See Maret.)

Bassett, Burwell, member of Congress from Virginia, i. 206.

Bathurst, Lord, on the Orders in Council, ii. 275.

Baton Rouge, i. 306.

Bayard, James A., senator from Delaware, ii. 229.

Baynes, Edward, adjutant-general to Sir George Prevost, ii. 323.

Bayonne Decree. (See Decrees.)

Belden, Lieutenant, ii. 32.

"Belvidera," British frigate, blockading New York, ii. 364, 365; escapes from Rodgers' squadron, 366; chases "Constitution," 368, 370.

Bernadotte. (See Sweden.)

Bibb, William A., member of Congress from Georgia, on the annexation of West Florida to Louisiana, i. 324.

Bidwell, Barnabas, i. 359.

Bingham, A. B., captain of the British corvette "Little Belt," his account of his action with the "President," ii. 30, 31, 33–36.

Bleecker, Harmanus, member of Congress from New York, ii. 211.

Blockade, Napoleon's definition of, i. 149, 227, 250; Pinkney's definition of, 287; ii. 10; of April 26, 1809, by England of all ports and places under the government of France, i. 63, 64, 103, 277; of May 16, 1806, (Fox's) 277; Wellesley's conduct regarding, 278-280, 318; withdrawal required by Madison, 318, 383; withdrawal demanded by Pinkney, ii. 4, 5, 17; reply of England to demand of withdrawal, 6, 9, 15, 23; becomes the only apparent *casus belli*, 221; alleged by Madison as the third *casus belli* 222; of Venice, July 27, 1806, i. 279; of New York, ii. 25, 118, 222.

Bloomfield, Joseph, brigadier general, ii. 291; at Plattsburg, 359, 360.

"Bonne Citoyenne," British sloop-of-war, ii. 384.

Boston, reception of F. J. Jackson, in, i. 214, 216; population in 1810, 289.

Boston town-meeting on Baltimore riot, ii. 409.

Boyd, Adam, member of Congress from New Jersey, i. 206.

Boyd, John P., colonel of Fourth U. S. Infantry, ii. 92, 93 ; arrives at Vincennes, 94. (See Infantry.)

Bradley, Stephen R., senator from Vermont, votes against occupying East Florida, ii. 243.

Brazil, i. 46.

Brock, Isaac, governor of Upper Canada, ii. 316; his military precautions, 317; his military force, 317; his civil difficulties, 318, 319; orders expedition to Mackinaw, 320; his proclamation, 320; dismisses his legislature, 320; passes Long Point, 321, 322; arrives at Malden, 329; decides to cross the Detroit River, 330; his march on Detroit, 332; returns to Niagara, 341; his military wishes, 342; distressed by loss of vessels, 347; his force at Niagara, 348; surprised on Queenston Heights, 349; his death, 350.

Broke, P. B. V., captain of British frigate "Shannon," commands squadron, ii. 368, 369; chases "Constitution," 370, 371.

Brougham, Henry, organizes agitation against Orders in Council, ii.

271, 280, 283; his speech of March 3, 1812, 276; obliges ministers to grant a committee of inquiry, 283–285; moves repeal, 285.

Burr, Aaron, his memoir to Napoleon, i. 239.

Burwell, William A., member of Congress from Virginia, on reducing the army and navy in 1810, i. 202.

CABINET. (See Robert Smith, James Monroe, Albert Gallatin, William Eustis, John Armstrong, Paul Hamilton, William Jones, Cæsar A. Rodney, William Pinkney.)

Cadore, Duc de. (See Champagny.)

"Caledonia," 2-gun British brig, captured by Lieutenant Elliott, ii. 347.

Calhoun, John Caldwell, member of Congress from South Carolina, ii. 122; on Committee of Foreign Relations, 124, 123; his war-speech of Dec. 12, 1811, 143, 144; votes for frigates, 164; warns Quincy of the embargo, 201; on the conquest of Canada, 212; his war-report, 226; his bill declaring war, 228; his speech of June 24, 1812, against the restrictive system, 233; favors war-taxation, 235; opposes compromise of forfeitures under Nonimportation Act, 442; favors high import duties, 444.

Campbell, George Washington, member of Congress from Tennessee, his Report reaches Canning, i. 49; not a member of the Eleventh Congress, 76; senator from Tennessee, his criticism of Giles, ii. 150, 151.

Canada, intended conquest of, ii. 136, 141, 142, 145, 146, 150, 212; invasion planned at Washington,

297; ordered by Eustis, 302; conquest attempted by Hull, 296; invaded by Hull, 302; evacuated, 315; difficulties of defending, 316–319; extent of Upper, 316; military force in 1812, 317, 338; Jefferson and Madison on campaign in, 337; invasion of, at Niagara, 344, 345; Van Rensselaer's attack on, 346–353; Smyth's attempts against, 354–358; Dearborn's march to, 360.

Canning, George, his reply to Napoleon and Alexander, i. 23; his notice to Pinkney of possible change in the Orders, 42; his note of Dec. 24, 1808, announcing a change, 43; his anger at Pinkney's reply, 44, 45; his willingness for further relaxations, 45; his discontent with Castlereagh and Perceval, 48, 106; his reception of Erskine's despatches and Campbell's Report, 49, 50, 51; his assertion as to the cause of the embargo, 51; his instructions to Erskine of Jan. 23, 1809, 52–57, 66, 70–73, 90; his character, 56; his influence declining, 57, 58; his speech of March 6, 1809, on the Orders, 61; his remark to Pinkney on the Order of April 26, 64; his disavowal of Erskine's arrangement, 87–95; his statement to the House of Commons, 97, 98; his instructions to F. J. Jackson, July 1, 1809, 98–105; his charge of duplicity against Madison, 99, 100, 114, 125; his resignation, 107; his duel with Castlereagh, 107; his relations with Wellesley, 266, 267; his speech on the renewal of intercourse between the United States and Great Britain, 276; his speech of March 3, 1812, on the Orders in Council and licenses, ii. 277, 278.

Carden, J. S., captain of the British frigate "Macedonian," ii. 382, 383.

Cass, Lewis, colonel of Ohio militia, ii. 298; refuses to abandon Detroit, 315; his discontent with Hull, 326; detached to open an interior road to the river Raisin, 328; ordered to return, 329; included in Hull's capitulation, 334.

Castlereagh, Lord, his supposed failures as Secretary of War, i. 47, 48, 106, 107; retires from the cabinet, 107; his quarrel with Canning, 56, 57; his duel with Canning, 107; becomes foreign Secretary, ii. 216; his instructions to Foster of April 10, 1812, 216, 220; announces suspension of Orders in Council, 286; his statement of number of American seamen in British service, 456.

Caulaincourt, Duc de Vicence, French ambassador in Russia, i. 412; recalled, 418; congratulates Adams, 419.

Census of 1810, i. 289.

Champagny, Duc de Cadore, his instructions to Turreau in defence of the Decrees, Dec. 10, 1808, i. 31; in defence of the Spanish colonies, 33; his remonstrances to Napoleon against severity to the United States, 138, 139; complains of the Non-intercourse Act, 140; his instructions to Hauterive, June 13, 1809, on concessions to the United States, 140; his note on the right of search and blockade, 149, 150, 250; his efforts on behalf of neutral commerce, 222; his interview with Armstrong, Jan. 25, 1810, 229, 230; his note of Feb. 14, 1810, announcing reprisals for the Non-intercourse Act, 232; his letter of August 5, 1810, announcing that the Decrees are revoked, 253–256, 286, 296–302, 383, 414,

415; ii. 7; creates a contract by letter of August 5, i. 342; his report on the Decrees, 348, 349, 382, 388; ii. 8; his phrase *bien entendu*, 387, 388; declares the Decrees revoked on Feb. 2, 1811, 386, 389, 390; removed from office, 401.

Champlain, Lake. (See Plattsburg.)

Chauncey, Isaac, takes command on Lake Ontario, ii. 344.

"Chesapeake Affair," Canning's instructions of Jan. 23, 1809, for settling, i. 52, 53; Erskine's settlement of the, 67, 68; settlement disavowed, 88–90; Canning's instructions of July 1, 1809, for settling, 101; Jackson's offer to settle, 126, 130; untouched by Wellesley, 285; Foster's instructions to settle, ii. 23; American indifference to settlement, 37; its effect on the Indians, 79; settled by Foster, 121, 122, 270.

"Chesapeake," frigate, ii. 29, 36.

Cheves, Langdon, member of Congress from South Carolina, asserts contract with Napoleon, i. 342, 343; in the Twelfth Congress, ii. 122; chairman of naval committee, 124; on Committee on Ways and Means, 124; his opinion on the war-power, 160; his motion to build a navy, 162; his argument in favor of seventy-fours, 163; his hostility to non-importation, 205, 230, 232, 446, 447, 448; favors war-taxation, 235; opposes forfeitures under Non-importation Act, 441; on war-taxes, 444.

Chew, Captain Samuel, deposition of, ii. 193, 196.

Chicago. (See Dearborn, Fort.)

Christie, John, lieut.-colonel of Thirteenth Infantry, ii. 349, 350, 351.

Cintra, convention of, i. 48.

Claiborne, W. C. C., governor of

Orleans Territory, takes possession of West Florida, i. 310–314.

Clay, Henry, senator from Kentucky, his war-speech of Feb. 22, 1810, i. 189; his speech on the occupation of West Florida, 320, 321; his speech on the Bank Charter, 333, 334; elected speaker, ii. 122, 124; favors army of thirty-five thousand men, 151; favors war-power, 161; favors navy, 164; supposed to have coerced Madison to war, 196; urges embargo, 201; suppresses discussion in the House, 227; his vote defeats repeal of non-importation, 234; his account of the military efforts of Kentucky, 390–393; his comments on Hull's surrender, 392, 393; opposes compromise of forfeitures under Non-importation Act, 442.

Clinton, De Witt, nominated for the presidency by New York, ii. 215; his canvass, 409, 410; his electoral vote, 413.

Clinton, George, Vice-President of the United States, i. 76, 190; his vote against the Bank Charter, 337; his political capacity, 363, 364; his death, ii. 214.

Commerce, nature and value of American, i. 290, 291.

Commercial Intercourse, Act of May 1, 1810, regarding. (See Non-intercourse.)

Commercial restrictions, list of measures of, i. 152, 194; Madison's devotion to, 293, 295; Madison's return to, 304.

Congress, first session of Eleventh, meets, May 22, 1809, i. 76; proceedings of, 77–86; adjourns June 28, 86; second session meets, Nov. 27, 1809, 176; proceedings of, 178–209; adjourns, May 2, 1810, 209; character of, 316; election of Twelfth, 316; third session of

Eleventh, 319–358; close of Eleventh, 358; first session of Twelfth, meets Nov. 4, 1811, ii. 118; its composition, 122; chooses Henry Clay speaker, 124; war-debate in, 133–153; proceedings of, 133–175, 201, 202, 204; declares war against England, 228, 229; adjourns, July 6, 1812, 235; decline of influence, 437; second session of Twelfth, 435–458.

"Congress," 38-gun frigate, ii. 363; at Boston, 378; her cruise, 381.

"Constellation," 38-gun frigate, at Washington, ii. 364, 372, 378.

"Constitution," 44-gun frigate, chased by British squadron, ii. 364, 369–372; captures "Guerriere," 373–375; captures "Java," 385, 386.

Cotton, manufacturers of, i. 16; American, prohibited in France, 151.

Craig, Sir James, governor of Lower Canada, i. 86.

Crawford, William H., senator from Georgia, opposes mission to Russia, i. 12; on the message of Jan. 3, 1810, 179; represents the Treasury, 181; votes with Samuel Smith, 191; his character, 331; introduces Bank Charter, 332; his speech on Bank Charter, 332, 333; reports bill for fifty thousand volunteers, 358; party to revolutionizing East Florida, ii. 239; his comments on the conduct of the war, 395.

Creek Indians, Tecumthe visits, ii. 92, 108.

Crillon, Count Edward de, his family, ii. 176; acts as John Henry's agent, 177–179; his social success, 178, 180; his evidence, 183; sails for France, 184; an impostor, 185; an agent of French police, 186.

Croker, John Wilson, Secretary to the Admiralty, i. 58.

Cuba, i. 37, 38.

Cumberland Road, i. 209.

DACRES, J. R., captain of the "Guerriere," ii. 27, 37, 373; his action with the "Constitution," 373–375.

Dalberg, Duc, negotiates with Joel Barlow, ii. 259; his remonstrances to Bassano against Napoleon's treatment of the United States, 262.

Dallas, Alexander James, third lieutenant of the frigate "President," ii. 28, 32.

Daveiss, Joseph H., offers to serve as a volunteer in Harrison's campaign, ii. 94; urges an attack on Tippecanoe, 99, 101; his death, 103, 104, 107.

Dearborn, Fort, at Chicago, murders at, ii. 110; garrison at, 294; evacuated, 334.

Dearborn, Henry, appointed collector at Boston, i. 9; his orders, as Secretary of War, to Wilkinson, Dec. 2, 1808, 169; appointed senior major-general, ii. 289; his plan of campaign, 297, 306, 340, 341; reaches Albany, 304; goes to Boston, 305; his difficulties at Boston, 306, 307, 309; returns to Albany, 310; ignorant that he commands operations at Niagara, 310, 322, 339; sends militia to Niagara, 321; negotiates armistice, 322, 323, 340; effect of armistice, 324, 343; armistice rejected by the President, 340; his opinion of Van Rensselaer, 353; his campaign against Montreal, 360; his reflections on the campaign of 1812, 360, 361; Monroe's criticisms of, 396, 397; George Hay's remark on, 421.

Decatur, Stephen, captain in U. S. navy, commands squadron, ii. 363; his orders, 363, 364, 368; his advice, 364; his first cruise in 1812, 366, 368, 375; his second cruise, 381; captures the "Macedonian," 382, 383; returns to port with prize, 383.

Decrees, French, of 1798, ii. 139.

Decrees of Berlin, Milan, and Bayonne, i. 24, 152, 297; their rigid enforcement, 30; Champagny's argument in defence of, 31, 32; their effect on England, 46; their effect on France, 138; Napoleon drafts, June 10, 1809, decree repealing that of Milan, 139–141; lays aside draft of repealing decree, 141; drafts Vienna decree of August, 1809, retaliating the Nonintercourse Act, 143, 144, 150, 230; Louis's resistance to, 148, 240, 241; Napoleon's condition of repeal, 229, 245, 250, 251; null and void for licensed vessels, 248; declared by Champagny revoked on Nov. 1, 1810, 255; declared revoked by Madison, 304, 317, 347, 348; Russell's reports on the revocation, 381–396; declared revoked by Champagny for Feb. 2, 1811, 386, 389, 390; not revoked, 394, 395; declared fundamental laws by Napoleon, 397, 407; declared successful by Napoleon, 398; considered suspended by Madison, 400, 401; recognized by United States, 402, 403; their revocation doubted by Russell, 395, 400, 406; their revocation affirmed by Russell, 405; enforced on the Baltic, 426, 427; Barlow instructed that they are considered revoked, 427; revocation asserted by Pinkney, ii. 3, 5, 6, 11; evidence of revocation asked by Wellesley, 4; argued by Pinkney, 7, 8; revocation denied by Wellesley, 23; affirmed to be still in force by Foster, 41; affirmed by Monroe to be revoked as far as America has a right to expect, 42; their international and municipal characters, 43; argued by Monroe, 44, 45; their revocation unknown to the President, 56; argued by Serurier, 60; disputed by Madison, 64; their revocation a personal affair with Madison, 65; their effect on the northwestern Indians, 83; declared not repealed by British courts, 118; their repeal doubted by Madison and Monroe, 120, 187–189; repeal asserted in annual message, 125; repeal assumed by House committee, 133, 134; repeal denied by Monroe, 194, 195, 201; repeal assumed by Monroe, 198; Bassano's report on validity of, 216, 253; repeal assumed by Madison, 218, 224; repeal maintained by Monroe till June, 1812, 232; Bassano's instructions on repeal of, 248–249; repeal asserted by Barlow, 252; evidence of repeal required by Barlow, 254; Decree of St. Cloud, dated April 28, 1811, repealing, 255–257, 259; still enforced, 260, 261; revocation unknown to the French authorities, 262, 263.

Decree of Rambouillet, March 23, 1810, sequestering American property in retaliation for the Non-importation Act, i. 236, 242, 274; of July 25, 1810, regarding licenses, 247; of July 22, 1810, confiscating American property in Dutch and Spanish ports, 258; of Aug. 5, 1810, confiscating American property in France, 258.

Decrès, Denis, Duc, Napoleon's minister of marine, i. 142, 143; Marmont's story of, 222.

Delaware Indians, ii. 73.

Denmark, spoliations in, i. 409, 411.

Detroit, military situation of, ii. 293, 295, 301; measures for protection of, 296; Hull's difficulties in defending, 315, 322, 324; Hull besieged in, 325–331; Brock's attack on, 332–334; Hull's surrender of, 334, 393; reinforcements for 391; expedition to recover, to be commanded by Harrison, 392, 393.

Dexter, Samuel, defeats project of State convention in Massachusetts, ii. 402.

Duane, William, editor of the "Aurora," his attacks on Gallatin, i. 361, 364.

Duval, Gabriel, appointed Justice of the Supreme Court, ii. 429.

EEL RIVER Miami Indians, ii. 71, 75.

Elections in 1809, i. 12, 13, 158; in 1810, 215, 316; in Massachusetts in April, 1811, ii. 115; in April, 1812, 204; in May, 1812, 209; in New York, May, 1812, 209; presidential, of 1812, 409, 410, 412–414.

Electoral College in 1808 and 1812, ii. 413.

Elliott, Jesse D., lieutenant U. S. navy, ii. 344; cuts out British vessels at Fort Erie, 347.

Embargo, repeal of, i. 33; Turreau's complaints of repeal, 34, 25, 37; Canning's note on, 42; revocation of orders attributed to, 75, 77; John Taylor's explanation of repeal, 195, 196; approved by Napoleon, 254; causes France to lose her colonies, 254; its effect on the northwestern Indians, ii. 83; for sixty days, recommended by the President, March 31, 1812, 193, 194, 195, 197, 198; Foster's report on, 199; act passed by Congress, 201, 202.

England, financial dangers of, in 1809, i. 46, 47; political decline of, 57, 58; distress of, in 1811, ii. 2; apathy of, upon American questions, 24; change of tone between 1807 and 1812, 225, 270, 286; war declared against, 228, 229; distress of, in 1812, 268; attitude toward the war, 405.

Eppes, John W., member of Congress from Virginia, chairman of Committee of Ways and Means in Eleventh Congress, i. 76; his appropriation bills for 1810, 200; his bill for reviving non-intercourse against Great Britain, 338; maintains doctrine of contract with France, 341; waits arrival of Serurier, 345; amends his non-intercourse bill, 351; quarrels with John Randolph, 352.

Erie, Fort. (See Fort Erie.)

Erie, Lake, armaments on, ii. 296, 304, 317, 344.

Erskine, David Montague, British minister to the United States, i. 34; his report, March 17, 1809, of Turreau's anger at the repeal of embargo, 34, 35; his threatening despatches of November and December, 1808, 49, 50; his instructions of Jan. 23, 1809, 52–57, 66, 70–72, 90, 94, 111; his reasons for exceeding instructions, 67, 70, 94; his settlement of the "Chesapeake affair," 67, 68; "Chesapeake" settlement disavowed by Canning, 88, 89; his settlement of commercial disputes, 70–73; his commercial arrangement received in England, 87; disavowed, 90, 95; his explanation of the order of April 26, 1809, 82, 83; his reply to Canning's criticisms, 94; his recall, 95; effect of his disavowal in the United States, 109; Jackson's opinion of, 119, 120; his farewell audience, 120; effect of his arrangement on Napoleon, 139, 140, 141; comparison between his pledges and those of Champagny, 301.

"Essex," 32-gun frigate, her action with the "Alert," ii. 35, 377; arrives with despatches, 52, 56; sails in July, 1812, 377; returns to port, 378.

Essex county in Massachusetts, declaration of meeting, ii. 402.

Eustis, William, appointed Secretary of War, i. 9: orders Wilkinson not to camp at Terre aux Bœufs, 172, 174; authorizes Harrison to buy Indian land in the Wabash valley, ii. 82; approves Harrison's purchase, 85; orders Harrison to preserve peace with Indians, 88, 93; orders the Fourth Regiment to Indiana, 92, 93; his lost letter of Sept. 18, 1811, to Harrisón, 95; appears before the Committee of Foreign Relations, 129; his supposed incompetence, 168, 206, 392, 395, 396, 397, 398; his duties in 1812, 168; on recruiting, 294; his letters to William Hull, announcing war, 299; and ordering conquests in Canada, 302; his orders to Dearborn to repair to Albany, 306, 308, 309; and to take direction of militia at Niagara, 310, 321, 340; resigns, 422.

Exchange, turn of, against England, in 1808, i. 47.

FAGAN, agent of Fouché, i. 239.

"Federal Republican" newspaper, ii. 406, 407.

Federalist party, deprived of grievances, i. 77; praise Madison, 78; 158; make common cause with Jackson, 158; described by Giles, 180.

Federalists, in Congress, Foster's reports of their conduct and advice, ii. 171–175; their reception of Henry's documents, 183, 184; cease attempts to discuss war, 227, 228; their attitude towards the war, 398, 399; support Clinton for the presidency, 410.

Fenwick, John R., lieut.-colonel of Light Artillery, ii. 352.

Ferdinand VII., proposed kingdom for, in America, i. 239; cedes Florida by treaty of 1819, ii. 159.

Fernandina in East Florida, seized by United States, ii. 240; occupation disavowed and maintained, 242, 243.

Finances in 1809, i. 163, 178; customs-revenue in 1807, 1808, 1809, 1810, 290, 319; military and naval appropriations of the Eleventh Congress, 357; in 1811, ii. 126; Gallatin's estimates for war, 156–159; war-taxes proposed by Gallatin, 166; approved by the House, 166, 167; laid aside, 167, 168; in 1812, 432, 433; in 1813, 438–448. (See Loans.)

Findlay, James, colonel of Ohio volunteers, ii. 298, 315, 326.

Findley, William, member of Congress from Pennsylvania, favors war, ii. 145.

Florida, Napoleon's retention of, i. 32, 33; Napoleon insinuates an idea regarding, 408; Foster instructed to protest against the seizure of, ii. 23; his protest, 37; Monroe's reception of the protest, 38, 39.

Florida, East, Madison asks authority to occupy, i. 326, 327; Congress authorizes occupation of, 327; commissioners sent to take possession of, 327; revolutionized, ii. 237–243; bill for occupation of, 243.

Florida, West, revolution in, i. 307–315; Madison orders occupation of, 310–312, 318; Claiborne takes possession of, 313; organized as part of Orleans Territory, 314; protest of British chargé, 314, 315; Giles's bill for annexing to Orleans Territory, 320; debate on annexation, 320–323; Macon's bill, admitting, as a part of Louisiana, 323, 324; remains a separate territory, 326; divided by act of Congress, ii. 236; ceded by Spain in 1819, 237.

Forfeitures under the Non-importation act, ii. 436–443.

Fort Dearborn, Chicago, ii. 110, 294; garrison massacred, 334.

Fort Erie, ii. 343, 347, 348, 358.

Fort George, ii. 300, 343, 347; Brock's headquarters, 341, 348, 349, 351.

Fort Harrison, ii. 95, 106, 294.

Fort Niagara, bombarded, ii. 355.

Fortifications, appropriation for, in 1809, i. 85; appropriation asked for, in 1810, 319.

Foster, Augustus John, appointed British minister to the United States, ii. 16, 21; F. J. Jackson's opinion of, 22; his instructions, 22, 23; arrives at Washington, 37, 52; protests against the seizure of Florida, 37; reports Monroe's language about Spanish America, 38; protests against the non-importation, 39; narrows the issue to Fox's blockade and the Orders in Council, 40, 41; reports Monroe's language on the revocation of the French decrees, 42; threatens retaliation for the non-importation, 44; reports that the Orders in Council are the single object of irritation, 45; settles the "Chesapeake" affair, 121, 122; his report of executive temper in November, 1811, 131; his report of Gallatin's language about taxes, 156; his report of the conduct of Federalists in Congress, 172–175; receives instructions, March 21, 1812, 191;

communicates them, 192; his report of Monroe's remarks on recent French spoliations, 195, 198; his report of Madison's and Monroe's remarks on the embargo of April, 1812, 199; suggests Madison's re-election, 213.

Fouché, Joseph, Duc d'Otrante, Napoleon's minister of police, i. 222; opposes the commercial system, 224; sends an agent to the British government, 238, 239; disgraced and exiled, 241.

France, alienation between United States and, i. 28–41, 141–151; difficulties of commerce with, 152, 245; value of spoliations in 1809, 1810, 242, 243; contract with, 339, 340; unfriendly language of the annual message toward, ii. 125; Madison's language regarding, 187, 218, 224; theory of contract with, apparently abandoned, 223; Monroe's language regarding, 232. (See Napoleon.)

Fremantle, Colonel, letter on the situation of Parliament, i. 58.

Frigates. (See Navy, "President," "Constitution," "United States," "Chesapeake," "Congress," "Constellation," "Essex," and "Adams.")

"Frolic," British sloop-of-war, ii. 379; her action with the "Wasp," 380.

Fulton's torpedo, i. 209.

GALLATIN, ALBERT, Secretary of the Treasury, his appointment as Secretary of State defeated, i. 4–8; his quarrel with Samuel Smith, 10; his conversation with Turreau about the Floridas, 38, 39; his remarks to Turreau on renewing intercourse with Great Britain, 74; his letters on Erskine's disavowal, 110, 111;

his expectations from Jackson's mission, 110, 116, 117; his feud with Giles, Smith, and Leib, 159; his letter of remonstrance to Jefferson, 160, 161, 164; his enemies, 167; his annual report of 1809, 178; his bill for excluding British and French ships, 183 (see Macon); his remarks on Napoleon's secret confiscations, 259; his remarks to Turreau on revival of non-intercourse against England, 303; gives notice of revival of non-intercourse against England, 304; his annual report of 1810, 319; his dependence on the bank, 329, 335; asks an increase of duties, 357; his letter of resignation, 360–366; Serurier's estimate of, ii. 46; his annual report of November, 1811, 126; attacked by Giles, 148, 149; delays his estimates, 156; his war-taxes, 156–159, 165, 166, 204; reported June 26, 235; his loan of 1812, 206, 207; believed to think war unnecessary, 225; complains of Congress, 234, 235; reports tax-bills to Congress, 235; his instructions at the outbreak of war, 301; his opinion of Eustis, 397, 398; claims department of State, 424; his annual report of Dec. 5, 1812, 433, 438; his views on the forfeiture of merchandise imported in 1812, 439, 440; his attitude toward war-taxation, 446.

Gardenier, Barent, member of Congress from New York, his remarks on Jefferson and Madison, i. 79, 80; supports Macon's bill, 185; cause of changing rule of previous question, 353.

Gaudin, Duc de Gaete, orders of, i. 348.

George III., king of England, becomes insane, i. 288; ii. 2.

George, Prince of Wales, his Whig associations, ii. 3, 4; becomes Prince Regent, Feb. 6, 1811, 14; retains Spencer Perceval's ministry, 14; his audience of leave for William Pinkney, 16, 18–20; his conditional declaration of April 21, 1812, that the Orders in Council should be withdrawn, 254, 282.

Gerry, Elbridge, elected governor of Massachusetts in 1810 and 1811, i. 215; ii. 115; defeated in 1812, 204; nominated for the vice-presidency, 214; elected, 413.

"Gershom," American brig, burned by French squadron, ii. 193, 198.

Gholson, Thomas, member of Congress from Virginia, moves new rule of previous question, i. 353.

Giles, William Branch, senator from Virginia, defeats Gallatin's appointment as Secretary of State i. 4–7; votes for mission to Russia, 11; his report on F. J. Jackson, 178, 179, 182, 183; wishes energy of government, 180, 189; his bill for the annexation of West Florida, 319, 320; his speech on the Bank charter, 333; his political capacity, 363; reports bill for raising twenty-five thousand troops, ii. 147; his speech attacking Gallatin, 148, 149; his factiousness, 150; his admission of errors, 154; his speech on the volunteer bill, 161; votes for war, 229; votes against occupying East Florida, 243; on seamen's bill, 454.

Gore, Christopher, elected governor of Massachusetts in 1809, i. 12; invites F. J. Jackson to Boston, 213; defeated in the election of 1810, 215; and in 1811, ii. 115.

"Grace Ann Greene," American vessel released by Napoleon, i. 391.

Graham, John, his account of public opinion in Kentucky, ii. 394.

Grandpré, Louis, i. 306, 307.

Grenville, Lord, on Canning, i. 49.

Grétry, i. 235.

Grundy, Felix, member of Congress from Tennessee, ii. 122, 137, 196; on Committee of Foreign Relations, 124, 128; his speech in favor of war, 137–141; favors large army, 152 ; opposes war-power, 161 ; against frigates, 164 ; on embargo, 201; on the political effects of war, 213 ; on forfeitures, 443; reports bill for regulation of seamen, 452, 453.

"Guerriere," British frigate, ii. 25; "Little Belt" mistaken for, 26–30; Captain Dacres of, 37; joins Broke's squadron, 368 ; chases "Constitution," 370; captured by "Constitution," 372–375.

Gunboats, i. 168.

HAMILTON, PAUL, appointed Secretary of the Navy, i. 9, 206; his orders to Commodore Rodgers of June 9, 1810, ii. 26; of May 6, 1811, 25; his supposed incompetence, 169, 290, 395, 398; his orders to Rodgers, Decatur, and Hull in June, 1812, 363–365, 368; his orders of September, 1812, 378 ; resigns, 428.

Hammond, George, Under Secretary for Foreign Affairs, i. 45.

Hampton, Wade, brigadier-general in U. S. army, i. 169; takes command at New Orleans, 175; ii. 291.

Hanson, A. C., ii. 407.

Harper, Robert Goodloe, ii. 144.

Harrison, Fort, ii. 95, 106, 294.

Harrison, William Henry, governor of Indiana Territory, ii. 68; his account of Indian affairs, 69–73; his treaties of 1804 and 1805, 75, 77; his influence in the dispute about slavery in Indiana, 75–77; his interview with the Prophet in August, 1808, 80; his treaty of Sept. 30, 1809, 83, 84; his interview with Tecumthe of Aug. 12, 1810, 85–88; his letter to Tecumthe June 24, 1811, 90; his talk with Tecumthe July 27, 1811, 91; instructed to avoid hostilities, 93; raises military forces, 93; sends army up the Wabash valley, 94; constructs Fort Harrison, 95; marches on Tippecanoe, 97; his arrival, 98–100; his camp, 102; attacked, 103; his return to Vincennes, 106; Humphrey Marshall's opinion of, 107; his estimate of the effect of his campaign, 107, 108; appointed by Kentucky to command expedition to recover Detroit, 392, 420; unable to advance, 412.

Hauterive, Alexandre Maurice, Comte d', charged with negotiations with Armstrong, i. 140, 141.

Hawkesbury, Lord. (See Liverpool.)

Hay, George, his advice to Monroe, ii. 421.

Henry, John, secret agent of Sir James Craig, his report on disunion, i. 14; recalled, 86; demands money, ii. 176; comes to Boston, 177; employs Crillon to negotiate with Monroe, 178; obtains fifty thousand dollars, 179 ; sails for Europe, 180; papers of, 182; supposed effect of, in Florida affairs, 241.

Holland, exempted from the nonintercourse, i. 72, 90–92, 112. (See Louis Bonaparte.)

Holland, Lord, ii. 275.

Holstein, Duchy of, i. 413.

"Hornet," sloop-of-war, brings despatches, ii. 215, 217 ; cruises with Rodgers' squadron, 365, 366; at

Boston, 378, 381; her second cruise, 384; blockades the "Bonne Citoyenne," 384.

Howell, Jeremiah B., senator from Rhode Island, votes against occupying West Florida, ii. 243.

Hull, Isaac, captain in U. S. navy, commands "Constitution," ii. 364; his orders, 364; chased by a British squadron, 369-371; captures "Guerriere," 372-375; takes command at New York, 383.

Hull, William, governor of Michigan Territory, ii. 292; appointed brigadier-general, 292, 298; his advice regarding the defence of Detroit, 296; his march to Detroit, 298; his loss of papers, 300; arrives at Detroit, 301; invades Canada, 302, 317; his proclamation, 303; his required campaign, 311; decides to besiege Malden, 312-314; sudden discovery of his danger, 314, 315; evacuates Canada, 315; his situation at Detroit, 322-329; his capitulation, 332, 334; Jefferson's opinion of, 336, 398.

Illinois Territory, population in 1810, i. 289.

Impressment becomes a *casus belli*, ii. 116-118; not expressly mentioned as such by Pinkney, 18; or in the annual message, 125; treated by House Committee of Foreign Relations, 134, 135; mentioned by Grundy, 139; by Madison's war-message, 222; only obstacle to peace, 430-432, 450-452; extent of, 451, 452.

Impressments, i. 74, 292, 351, 352.

India, career of Marquess Wellesley in, i. 266.

Indiana Territory, population in 1810, i. 289; created in 1800, ii. 68; its dispute about the introduction of

slavery, 75; adopts second grade of territorial government, 76.

Indians in 1810, i. 318; in the Northwest, ii. 69; their condition described by Governor Harrison, 69; trespasses on their territory, 70; effects of intoxication upon, 71, 72; murders committed upon, 72, 73; Jefferson's policy toward, 73-75; Harrison's treaties with, in 1804 and 1805, 75; Tecumthe and the Prophet, 78; Jefferson's refusal to recognize them as a confederated body, 79; establishment at Tippecanoe Creek, 79-81; their hostility to cessions of land, 82, 87; their land-cession of Sept. 30, 1809, 83, 84; their outbreak imminent in 1810, 85; outbreak delayed by British influence, 85; their interview with Harrison, Aug. 12, 1810, 86-88; government wishes peace with, 89; of the Six Nations in Upper Canada, wish to remain neutral, 319; their employment in war by the British, 320; murders by, 393, 394.

Infantry, Fourth Regiment of, ordered to Indiana July, 1811, ii. 92, 93; arrives, 94; part of the expedition to Tippecanoe, 96; losses in the battle, 104; its share in the battle, 107; ordered to Detroit, 110; marches to Detroit, 298; at the battle of Maguaga, 325.

Invisibles, the, i. 363.

Jackson, Francis James, his reputation, i. 96; appointed British minister to the United States, 97; his instructions, 99-105; sails for America, 105; Gallatin's expectations from, 111, 117; arrives at Washington, 115, 116; his impressions, 117-120; his negotiation, 120-132; rupture with, 132;

his anger, 154, 155; his complaints, 156 ; his reception in Baltimore and New York, 157 ; discussed before Congress, 176, 178, 179, 182 ; his letters from New York and Boston, 212–218 ; returns to England, 219; his treatment by Wellesley, 218, 219, 269, 271, 272; his influence with the British government, ii. 13 ; his account of Pinkney's "inamicable leave," 20; his opinion of Augustus J. Foster, 22; his death, 22.

Jackson, Mrs. F. J., i. 115, 157.

"Java," British frigate, her action with the "Constitution," ii. 385, 386.

Jefferson, Thomas, Turreau's anger with, i. 34; Gallatin's remarks on, 38, 39 ; the "National Intelligencer" on, 75 ; Randolph's remarks on, 78; Robert Smith's remarks on, 84; intermediates with Monroe, 161, 162; expenditures of his administration, 200, 205, 206; considered too timid by Robert Smith, ii. 48; his Indian policy, 69, 73–75, 78, 79, 81; his opinion of William Hull, 336, 398; his expectation of the conquest of Canada, 337; his opinion of Van Rensselaer, 398.

Jesup, Thomas S., acting adjutant-general at Detroit, ii. 329.

Johnson, Richard Mentor, member of Congress from Kentucky, i. 197, 203; ii. 122; his war speech, 142; on the dangers of a navy, 164; on the treason of opposition, 212.

Jones, Jacob, captain in U. S. navy, commands the "Wasp," ii. 379; his action with the "Frolic," 380; captured, 381; takes command of the "Macedonian," 383.

Jones, Walter, his letter to Jefferson, on dissensions in Madison's Cabinet, i. 188.

Jones, William, appointed Secretary of the Navy, ii. 428, 429.

KENTUCKY, enthusiasm for the war, ii. 390 ; number of men in the field, 391, 393 ; distaste for the regular army, 391, 394.

Key, Philip Barton, member of Congress from Maryland, i. 185.

King, Rufus, his supposed opposition to Clinton, ii. 410.

LABOUCHERE, i. 238, 239.

Lambert, Henry, captain of the British frigate "Java," ii. 385, 386.

Langdon, John, of New Hampshire, nominated for the Vice-Presidency, ii. 214.

Lansdowne, Marquis of, ii. 275.

Lauriston, Marquis de, French ambassador to Russia, i. 418.

Lee, Henry, crippled by Baltimore rioters, ii. 407, 408.

Leib, Michael, senator from Pennsylvania, i. 181, 189, 191; ii. 229, 243; votes against Bank charter, 337; his political capacity, 364.

Licenses of trade, British, i. 59, 64; scandal of, 273; debate on, 274, 275 ; Canning's remarks on; 278, 280 ; Sidmouth's conditions on, 281; Castlereagh proposes to abandon, 221, 282.

Licenses, Napoleon's system of, i. 246–249 ; promised abandonment of, 392, 393 ; continued issue of, 400 ; repudiated by Napoleon, 414, 417, 422 ; municipal character of, ii. 43; their continued issue, 54; extension of, 250.

Lincoln, Levi, declines appointment as justice, i. 359.

Lingan, James Maccubin, killed by Baltimore rioters, ii. 407, 408.

"Little Belt," British sloop-of-war, affair of, i. 25–37, 45, 270.

Livermore, Edward St. Loe, member of Congress from Massachusetts, i. 184.

Liverpool, Lord, on American partiality to France, i. 50; succeeds Castlereagh at the War Department, 263.

Lloyd, James, senator from Massachusetts, ii. 183.

Loan for 1810, i. 178; of 1812, for eleven millions, ii. 169 ; partial failure of, 207; of 1813, for twenty millions, 433, 448.

Long, Charles, joint paymaster-general of the forces, i. 58.

Louis Bonaparte, king of Holland, resists Napoleon's decrees, i. 146; his interview with Armstrong, 147, 148; threatened by Napoleon, 236, 237, 240 ; stipulates seizure of American ships, 240, 274; abdicates, 242.

Louisiana, government offered to Monroe, i. 162 ; proposed as a kingdom for the French Bourbons, 239; admitted into the Union, 323–326; ii. 235.

Lowndes, William, member of Congress from South Carolina, ii. 122, 164; his hostility to non-importation, 205, 234, 445, 448; opposes compromise of forfeitures, 442.

Lyon, Matthew, member of Congress from Kentucky, i. 358.

McArthur, Duncan, colonel of Ohio militia, ii. 298, 326, 328, 332, 334.

"Macedonian," British frigate, capture of, ii. 382, 383.

McKee, John, ii. 237.

Macon, Nathaniel, member of Congress from North Carolina, votes with Federalists, i. 182; his bill for excluding British and French shipping, 183, 184; bill defeated by Senate, 185, 191, 193; Samuel Smith's motives for defeating, 185–188, 192, 193; his bill No. 2, 194, 195; adopted by Congress, 197, 198 ; his remark on manufacturing influence, 197; his speech on reducing the army and navy in 1810, 201 ; his bill admitting the State of Louisiana, with West Florida, into the Union, 323–326; not candidate for speaker, ii. 123, 124; his account of the opinions prevailing at Washington, 129; supports war, 145; his remark on France and England, 196.

Madison, James, inauguration of, i. 1; his inaugural address, 2, 3, 4; offers the Treasury to Robert Smith, 7, 379; appoints Robert Smith Secretary of State, 8 ; his Cabinet, 9, 10; nominates J. Q. Adams to Russia, 11; his letter to Erskine accepting settlement of the "Chesapeake affair," 68–70, 89 ; issues proclamation renewing intercourse with England, 73, 74 ; his views of the change in British policy, 75, 76, 81, 83; his message of May 23, 1809, 76, 77 ; his popularity, 80, 85, 86; on the disavowal of Erskine's arrangement, 112 ; revives non-intercourse against England, 114 ; his negotiation with F. J. Jackson, 117, 122–132; described by Jackson, 120; his message of Nov. 29, 1809, 176, 177; special message of Jan. 3, 1810, asking for volunteers, 179; his opinions of Samuel and Robert Smith, 186; dissensions in his cabinet, 188; remarks on the experiment of unrestricted commerce, 210, 211; his reply to Napoleon's note on the right of search and blockade, 250; his anger at

Napoleon's confiscations, 292 ; his instructions of June 5, 1810, to Armstrong on Champagny's reprisals, 293, 294; his devotion to commercial restrictions, 293, 295; his instructions of July 5, 1810, to Armstrong requiring indemnity, 295, 296, 297, 299 ; his decision to accept the conditions of Champagny's letter of August 5, 296–301 ; revives non-intercourse against Great Britain, 303, 304; takes military possession of West Florida, 308–312, 318; his supposed character, 310; his annual message of Dec. 5, 1810, 314, 317–319; asks authority to take possession of East Florida, 327; appoints commissioners for East Florida, 327 ; decides to enforce the non-intercourse against Great Britain, 347; his doubts regarding Napoleon's folly, 350; his irritation at Smith's proposed inquiry from Serurier, 350, 351 ; offers the State Department to Monroe, 366, 372, 374 ; his parting interview with Robert Smith, 375–377 ; his anger with Smith, 378; his translation of *bien entendu*, 387, 388 ; his success in maintaining his own system in the Cabinet, ii. 61, 62 ; his discontent with Napoleon's conduct, 63, 64, 125, 187, 218, 224; his orders to maintain peace with the northwestern Indians, 88, 93 ; his attitude toward war with England, 118, 125, 129, 131, 175, 196, 197, 213; his annual message of Nov. 5, 1811, 124; entertains Crillon, 179, 185; his message communicating Henry's papers, 181; his embargo message, 193, 198, 199 ; his comments on the conduct of the Senate, 203 ; sustains non-importation, 205; renominated for the presidency, 214 ; perplexed by the French decrees, 218 ; his letter to Barlow threatening war on France, 218, 259 ; his view of the "immediate impulse " to war with England, 220, 226; his war message, 221–226; signs declaration of war, and visits departments, 229; his measures regarding East Florida, 237, 239, 241, 243 ; his remarks on Napoleon's Russian campaign, 265 ; his remarks in August, 1812, on the Canadian campaign, 337; re-elected President, 413 ; wishes Monroe to command western army, 419, 420, 425; his annual message of 1812, 430–433.

Maguaga, battle of, ii. 325.

Malden, British trading post on the Detroit River, ii. 73, 80, 85, 300; to be besieged by Hull, 303, 314 ; British force at, 312, 313.

Manufactures, growth of, in 1809–1810, i. 15–19; political influence of, 197; protection of, 319.

Maret, Hugues Bernard, Duc de Bassano, Napoleon's secretary, i. 143; succeeds Champagny as Minister of Foreign Affairs, 401 ; his report to Napoleon of March 10, 1812, ii. 216, 253; his negotiation with Joel Barlow, 248–263; his instructions to Serurier of October, 1811, on the revocation of the Decrees, 248, 249; communicates Decree of St. Cloud to Barlow and Serurier, 255–257, his instructions to Dalberg, 260 : invites Barlow to Wilna, 263; dismisses his guests, 264.

Marmont, Marshall, his story of Decrès, i. 222.

Marshall, Humphrey, on W. H. Harrison, ii. 107.

Maryland, her electoral vote, ii. 406, 413.

Massa, Duc de, letter from, i. 347.

Massachusetts, election of 1809, i. 12;

tonnage of, 15; manufactures of, 17-19 ; resolutions of legislature regarding F. J. Jackson, 214; election of, 1810, 215; Republican control of, in 1810 and 1811, ii. 115; Federalists recover control of, in 1812, 204 ; gives trouble to Dearborn, 305; refuses to obey call for militia, 309 ; temper of, 397–401, 409; Federalist majority in the Congressional elections of 1812, 413.

Massassinway, council at, ii. 111.

Matthews, George, appointed commissioner to take possession of East Florida, ii. 237; his proceedings, 238-240; disavowed, 240-242.

Mecklenburg, Grand Duchy of, closes its ports to American commerce, i. 413.

"Melampus," British frigate, ii. 25.

Merry, Anthony, i. 118, 119, 120, 121.

Message, first annual of President Madison, May 23, 1809, i. 76; annual, of Nov. 29, 1809, 176–178; special, of Jan. 3, 1810, asking for volunteers, 179 ; annual, of Dec. 5, 1810, 317–319; special, of Feb 19, 1811, on the revocation of the French decrees, 347, 348; annual, of Nov. 5, 1811, ii. 124–126; special, of March 9, 1812, communicating John Henry's papers, 181; special, of April 1, 1812, recommending an embargo for sixty days, 198; of April 24, 1812, asking for two Assistant Secretaries of War, 206 ; of June 1, 1812, recommending a declaration of war with England, 221–226 ; annual, of Nov. 4, 1812, 430–433.

Michigan territory, population in 1810, i. 289.

Michillimackinaw, Island of, ii. 294; captured by British expedition, 314, 320.

Militia, constitutional power of Congress over, ii. 159, 160, 400; Cheves's opinion on the war power, 160 ; act authorizing call for one hundred thousand, 204, 390 ; refuses to cross the frontier, 351, 352, 360 ; of Kentucky, 391, 393.

Miller, James, Lieutenant-Colonel of Fourth U. S. Infantry, at Detroit, ii. 326, 328.

Mitchell, D. B., Governor of Georgia, ii. 242.

Mobile, ii. 236.

Monroe, James, Madison's advances to, i. 159, 161, 162 ; his state of mind, 162 ; offered the State Department, 366; his acceptance and policy, 368–374; takes charge, 380; Secretary of State, April 1, 1811, ii. 50 ; his sensitiveness about the title to West Florida, 38 ; his reply to Foster's protest against the seizure of Florida, 38, 39; blames Jonathan Russell for questioning the revocation of the French decrees, 42; asserts the revocation of the French decrees, 42, 43; abandons task of reconciliation with England, 44; requires revocation of the Orders in Council, 45; delays Barlow's departure, 50; his remonstrances to Serurier about Napoleon's conduct, 51, 54, 188, 189, 194, 195, 200, 217; his remarks on protection accorded to commerce, 58; his acceptance of Madison's policy, 59–61 ; affirms to Foster the repeal of Napoleon's decrees, 65 ; his letter of June 13, 1812, to John Taylor, of Caroline, 66 ; his language to Serurier, in October, 1811, 120; informs Serurier, in November, of executive plan, 129; agrees to assist the independence of Spanish America, 130; negotiates purchase of Henry's papers, 178–180; his remarks to Foster on Wellesley's instructions, 192 ; his conference with House Committee of Foreign Relations, March 31, 1812, 197 ; his remarks on the embargo, 199, 200, 202 ; his relations toward Matthews and the occupation of East Florida, 238, 240, 241, 242; his criticisms on the conduct of the war, 396, 397; assures Serurier he will not negotiate for peace, 415; proposes to negotiate, 416 ; proposes to take a military commission, 419, 420 ; hesitates between civil or military control of the war, 421–423 ; becomes acting Secretary of War, 423; excites jealousy, 424, 425; abandons military career, 425, 426 ; offers to prohibit the employment of foreign seamen, 451.

" Moniteur," The, ii. 253.

Montalivet, Comte de, Napoleon's Minister of the Interior, i. 221; his efforts for American commerce, 223, 224.

Moore, Sir John, his Spanish campaign, i. 26, 47, 48.

Morier, J. P., British chargé at Washington, i. 219 ; his protest against the seizure of West Florida, 315.

Mountmorris, Lord, i. 265.

NAPOLEON, his Spanish campaign, i. 22–28; his severity toward American commerce, 30–32; withholds Florida, 32, 33; his causes for rupture with the United States, 39, 40 ; his war with Austria in 1809, 106, 134; learns the repeal of the embargo and of the British Orders, 136; his first reply to Armstrong's communication, 137 ; drafts Decree withdrawing the Milan Decree, 139 ; cause of his hesitation, 140,

141; lays aside his repealing Decree, 141 ; his draft of Vienna Decree of August 4, 1809, 143, 144, 230, 233, 236; his view of the right of search, 137, 145, 149; quarrels with his brother Louis, 146, 147; his increased severity toward the United States, 150–152, 220; calls a Cabinet council on commerce, Dec. 19, 1809, 220, 221; discussions with Montalivet, 221, 223; his note to Gaudin on American ships, 224; his want of money, 225, 226, 237; calls for a report from Champagny, Jan. 10, 1810, 226, 227; his dislike for Armstrong, 228, 229; his condition for the revocation of his Decrees, 229; his draft of note asserting retaliation on the Non-intercourse Act, 230, 231; his reply to Armstrong's remonstrances, 234, 235; his memory, 235; his decree of Rambouillet, 236; his threats of annexing Holland, 238, 246; his annexation of Holland, 241, 242; his reflections on Macon's act, 244, 245; his license system, 246; his instructions to Champagny ordering announcement that the Decrees will be withdrawn, 253; dictates letter of August 5, 1810, 253; his idea of a trap, 257, 383; his instructions of Dec. 13, 1810, on the non-intercourse and the Floridas, 384; on commercial liberties, 386 ; his address of March 17, 1811, to the deputies of the Hanse Towns, 396, 397; his address of March 24, 1811, to the Paris merchants, 398, 399, 420; appoints Maret in place of Champagny, 401; orders a report on American commerce, 402, 403 ; admits American cargoes, May 4, 1811, 404; his instruction of August 28, 1811, about Spanish America and Florida, 407, 408; his rupture with Russia and Sweden,

408–427; his order of May 4, 1811, opening his ports to American commerce, ii. 44, 59; probable amount of his spoliations, 247; his restrictions on American commerce, 247 ; goes to Holland, Sept. 19, 1811, 248; his interview with Joel Barlow, 249; his extension of the license system in January, 1812, 250; his seizure of Swedish Pomerania, 251, 252; his decree of St. Cloud, April 28, 1811, 255, 256; his departure for Poland, May 9, 1812, 258; enters Russia, 259, 288; his battle at Borodino, Sept. 7, 1812, 263; enters Moscow, Sept. 15, 1812, 263 ; begins his retreat, 264; his passage of the Beresina, 264; his return to Paris, December, 1812, 265.

"National Intelligencer" on renewal of intercourse with Great Britain, i. 75; on Erskine's disavowal, 109, 110; Joel Barlow's letter in, 299.

"Nautilus," sloop-of-war, captured, ii. 369, 386.

Navigation Act, moved by Macon, i. 183.

Navy, in 1809, i. 168, 169; reductions in 1810, 200–207; opposed by Republican party, ii. 162; increase refused by Congress in January, 1812, 164; condition of, in June, 1812, 363, 364; distribution of, in September, 1812, 377, 378; movements and battles of, in 1812, 362–387; increase of, 436, 449. (See "Constitution," "President," "United States," "Constellation," "Chesapeake," "Congress," "Essex," "Adams," "Wasp," "Hornet," "Argus," "Syren," "Nautilus.")

Nelson, Roger, member of Congress from Maryland, i. 202, 203.

New Hampshire, becomes Federalist in 1809, i. 13.

New Orleans, i. 170.

"New Orleans packet," seized under the Berlin and Milan Decrees, ii. 8; by a "municipal operation," 42, 43.

New York city, described by F. J. Jackson, i. 213 ; population in 1810, 289.

New York State, election of 1809, i. 13; banking mania in, ii. 208; election in May, 1812, 209; nominates De Witt Clinton to the presidency, 215; recruiting in, 305.

Niagara, military importance of, ii. 304, 310 ; force at, 311, 320, 341, 344; force raised to six thousand men, 345; Van Rensselaer's campaign at, 346–353 ; Alexander Smyth's campaign at, 353–358 ; sickness of troops at, 359.

Niagara, Fort. (See Fort Niagara.)

Nicholas, Wilson Cary, member of Congress from Virginia, on the appointment of Gallatin as Secretary of State, i. 4, 5, 6; resigns from Congress, 76.

Non-intercourse, list of measures, i. 194.

Non-intercourse Act of March 1, 1809, its effect on commerce, i. 35, 36; English view of, 62 ; affected by Erskine's arrangement, 80, 88, 90; revived by Erskine's disavowal, 111, 114, 115 ; communicated to Napoleon, 135; communication denied by Napoleon, 232, 2 4, 235, 254; Champagny's complaints of, 140; Napoleon's retaliation on, 143, 150, 151, 230, 232, 254, 255 ; its mischievous effects in America, 164, 165, 166, 178, 184 ; about to expire, 183 ; suspended, 195–198, 210 ; revived by proclamation of Nov. 2, 1810, 302, 303, 304.

Non-intercourse Act of May 1, 1810, its passage, i. 194-198, 274 ; its effect on Napoleon, 220, 244, 255 ; its effect in England, 273–276; its condition precedent to reviving non-intercourse, 297; creates a contract, 342, 395, 396.

Non-intercourse Act of March 2, 1811, reviving act of March 1, 1809, moved by Eppes, Jan. 15, 1811, i. 338; decided upon, 347; amended, 351; reported, 352; passed, 354, 391; its effect on Napoleon, 393, 394, 400, 404; Foster's instructions on the, ii. 23; his protest against, 39; his threat of retaliation, 44, 124; not noticed by Napoleon, 56; an intolerable burden to the United States, 140; efforts to suspend, 205, 230–234, 447; not retaliated by England, 270; forfeitures under, 438–443; Calhoun on, 444; bill for stricter enforcement of, 448.

OCAÑA, battle at, i. 268.

Ohio, population in 1810, i. 289.

Olmstead, Gideon, case of, i. 13.

Ontario, Lake, armaments on, ii. 342, 344.

Order in Council, of January, 1807, called Howick's, i. 112, 278; of November, 1807, possible alterations in, 42; Order of Dec. 21, 1808, suspending export duties on foreign produce, 43, 44; further relaxations proposed, 45; their effect on English trade, 46; asserted by Canning not to have caused the embargo, 51; Canning's conditions of repealing, 53, 54, 56, 70–73, 90, 94, 101, 102; Grenville and Sidmouth's language regarding, 59, 60; debate on, March 6, 1809, 60–62; Order of April 26, 1809, establishing a general blockade in place of the Orders of November, 1807, 63, 64, 65, 81, 103, 113, 126, 152; Erskine's arrangement withdrawing, 70–73; disavowal of Erskine's arrangement, 87–95, 109–113; Order of May 24, 1809, repudiating Erskine's arrangement, and protecting vessels sailing under it, 93, 95; Canning's instructions of July 1, 1809, to F. J. Jackson, on, 101–105; issue chosen by Madison and Monroe, ii. 39, 40, 45, 121, 188; conditions of repeal, 124, 220; enforced by British prize-courts, 118, 124, 267; alleged as Madison's fourth complaint, 222; revocation promised by Prince Regent on formal revocation of French decrees, 254, 282; popular agitation against, 271, 281, 283; debate of Feb. 28, 1811, in House of Lords, 275; debate of March 3 in House of Commons, 276; Rose's definition of, 276, 283; Canning's remarks on, 277, 278; Perceval's account of, 279; ministers grant a committee on, 283, 284; suspension of, June 16, 1812, 286, 287, 403; suspension not satisfactory to the President, 404; repeal susceptible of satisfactory explanations, 431.

Otis, Harrison Gray, ii. 402; supports Clinton, 410.

Ouvrard, Gabriel Julien, i. 239.

PAPENBERG, i. 165.

Parliament, debates on the Orders in Council, i. 49–52, 58–62; on the Duke of York, 57, 58; passes the Regency bill, ii. 13, 14; meets Jan. 7, 1812, 270; debates in, 270–280; orders a committee of inquiry into the Orders in Council, 282, 284.

Parsons, Theophilus, chief-justice of Massachusetts, his opinion on the power of a State over its militia, ii. 400.

Pennsylvania, resists mandate of Supreme Court, i. 13; decides

presidential election of 1812, ii.
412.

Perceval, Spencer, Chancellor of the
Exchequer, his relaxations of the
Orders in Council, i. 42, 45, 63;
decline of his authority in 1809,
57, 58, 62, 63; his difficulties with
Canning and Castlereagh, i. 107;
becomes First Lord of the Treasury, 263 ; invites Wellesley into
the Cabinet, 267 ; Wellesley's opinion of, 281, 282, 283 ; prime minister of England, becomes ruler after
the insanity of George III., ii. 2, 3;
retained as prime minister by the
Prince Regent, 14; his indifference
to Wellesley's advice, 268; his remarks on an American war, 271;
his persistence in the system of
commercial restriction, 272; his remarks on licenses, 274; his silence
towards Canning, 280; his bargain
for Sidmouth's support, 281 ; con-
cedes a committee on the Orders
in Council, 283; his assassination,
284.

Petry, M., i. 228, 229.

Philadelphia, population of, in 1810,
i. 289.

Phillimore, Dr. Joseph, his pamphlets on the license system, ii. 274.

Piankeshaw Indians, ii. 71, 75.

Pickering, Timothy, senator from
Massachusetts, his toast at Jackson's dinner, i. 217; his speech on
the occupation of West Florida,
321, 322; loses his seat in the Senate, ii. 116; his attempt to call a
State convention in 1812, 402.

Pinckney, Thomas, appointed major-
general, ii. 290.

Pinkney, William, United States
minister in London, his reply, Dec.
28, 1808, to Canning's first advance, i. 43, 44, 45; his reception
of Canning's further advances, 49,
51, 52; opinion attributed to. by

Canning, 54; his pleasure at the
Order of April 26, 1809, 63, 64; his
opinion of Francis James Jackson,
96 ; his intimacy with Wellesley,
270, 275; his reports of Wellesley's
intentions, 271; inquires whether
Fox's blockade is in force, 277-280;
notifies Wellesley of Champagny's
letter of Aug. 5, 1810, 286; his republican insolence, 287; demands
repeal of the Orders, Nov. 3, 1811,
ii. 3; his argument that the French
Decrees were revoked and that
Fox's blockade was illegal, 5, 6, 7, 9,
10, 11; his definition of blockade,
10; his demand for an audience of
leave, 12, 15; his hesitation, 16;
his note of Feb. 17, 1811, to Wellesley, 17; insists on "an inamicable
leave," 18, 20; his final audience,
19, 20; his character as minister,
20, 21; sails for America, 21; appointed Attorney-General, 429.

Pitkin, Timothy, member of Congress
from Connecticut, votes for war
measures, ii. 147.

Pitt, William, his patronage of young
men, i. 264, 265.

Plattsburg, on Lake Champlain, military force at, ii. 344; Dearborn's
campaign from, 360.

Poland, i. 257.

Population of the United States in
1810, i. 289.

Porter, David, captain in U. S. navy,
commands "Essex," ii. 377; captures "Alert," 377; returns to port,
378; sails again, 384.

Porter, Peter Buell, member of Congress from New York, ii. 122; on
Committee of Foreign Relations,
124, 128; his report favoring war,
133-136; his war speech, 136; favors small army, 151 ; asks for provisional army, 165; introduces embargo bill, 201 ; calls for volunteers,
355; charges General Smyth with

cowardice, 358 ; his duel with Smyth, 358.

Portland, Duke of, his death, i. 107.

Pottawatomies, charged by Tecumthe with bad conduct, ii. 111, 112.

Potter, Elisha, member of Congress from Rhode Island, i. 167; ii. 447.

"President," American 44-gun frigate, ordered to sea, May 6, 1811, ii. 25, 26; chases a British war-vessel, 27; fires into the "Little Belt," 30; at New York, 363, 365; goes to sea, 366; cruise of, 366, 368; returns to Boston, 375, 378; sails again, 381; returns to Boston, Dec. 31, 1812, 381.

Previous question, the rule of, adopted, i. 353–356; denounced by Stanford, ii. 146.

Prevost, Sir George, governor general of Canada, ii. 317; his report on the lukewarm and temporizing spirit in Upper Canada, 318, 319; negotiates armistice with Dearborn, 323; his military superiority in August, 1812, 338, 339.

Prince Regent. (See George, Prince of Wales.)

Proclamation of July 2, 1807, on the "Chesapeake" affair, i. 31; of April 19, 1809, renewing intercourse with Great Britain, 73, 115; of Aug. 9, 1809, reviving the Non-intercourse Act against Great Britain, 114, 115; of Nov. 2, 1810, reviving the non-intercourse against Great Britain, 302, 303, 304, 338, 400; of Oct. 27, 1810, ordering the military occupation of West Florida, 310, 311; of November 2, 1810, announcing the repeal of the French Decrees, ii. 4, 56 ; of William Hull on invading Canada, 303, 320; of Isaac Brock in reply to Hull, 320.

Proctor, Henry, Colonel of the Forty-first British Infantry, arrives at Malden, ii. 314; disapproves Brock's measures, 330.

Prophet, the Shawnee, begins Indian movement at Greenville, ii. 78 ; removes to Tippecanoe Creek, 79 his talk with Gov. Harrison in August, 1808, 80; charged with beginning hostilities, 95 ; sends Indians to Harrison, 97, 100 ; blamed for the affair at Tippecanoe, 108.

Prussia, spoliations by, i. 226; closes ports to American vessels, 413, 416.

QUEENSTON, battle at, ii. 349–352.

Quincy, Josiah, member of Congress from Massachusetts declares the admission of Louisiana a virtual dissolution of the Union, i. 325, 326 ; votes for war-measures, ii. 147, 152; gives warning of embargo, 201; moves that the war-debate be public, 227 ; opposes enlistment of minors, 435; opposes forfeitures, 443.

RAMBOUILLET, decree of. (See Decrees.)

Randolph, John, his remarks on Jefferson, i. 78; on Erskine's arrangement, 79; on Madison's message, 177; his attempt to reduce expenditures in 1810, 199–207; on the incapacity of government, 209 ; on the contract with Napoleon, 344, 345; his quarrel with Eppes, 352; denounces the previous question, 353; his remarks on President and Cabinet, February, 1811, 360, 361; supports the Bank charter, 362; his opinion of "the cabal," 363, 364; his quarrel with Monroe, 367; his report on slavery in Indiana, ii. 76 ; replies to Grundy on war, 142, 145; ridicules army bill, 153; declares war impossible, 202; his comments on Eustis and Hamilton, 206; his remarks on war, 211; criticises Gallatin, 446.

Regiments. (See Army.)

Remusat, Mme. de, i. 235.

Revenue. (See Finances.)

Rhea, John, member of Congress from Tennessee, on the annexation of West Florida to Louisiana, i. 324; asserts contract with Napoleon, 343.

Richardson, Lieutenant of Canadian militia, his account of the capture of Detroit, ii. 332.

Rockingham, in New Hampshire, county meeting of, ii. 403, 409.

Rodgers, John, captain in the United States navy, ordered to sea in the "President," May 6, 1811, ii. 25; chases the "Little Belt," 26, 27; mistakes the "Little Belt" for the "Guerriere," 29, 30; his action with the "Little Belt," 28–36; his orders in June, 1812, 363, 365, 367, 368; chases the "Belvidera," 366; arrives with his squadron at Boston, 375; sails again with squadron, 378, 381; returns, Dec. 31, 1812, 381.

Rodney, Cæsar A., his report on slavery in Indiana, ii. 76; resigns attorney-generalship, 429.

Rose, George, on the Orders in Council, ii. 276, 277, 281, 283; yields to an inquiry, 283.

Rose, George Henry, i. 95, 112–116.

Roumanzoff, Count, Nicholas, chancellor of the Russian empire, his language about Austria, i. 134; declines to interfere in Danish spoliations, 409, 410, 411; declines to release vessels at Archangel, 415; protests against ukase, 418.

Rovigo, Duc de. (See Savary.)

Rule of 1756, Canning's demand for

express recognition of, i. 53, 55, 72, 104.

Rush, Richard, comptroller of the Treasury, ii. 229.

Russell, Jonathan, charged with legation at Paris, i. 260, 380; his reports on the revocation of the Decrees, 381–395; blamed by Monroe for questioning the revocation of the French Decrees, ii. 42; blamed by Serurier for his tone, 53; sent as chargé to the legation at London, 252, 282; asks proofs that the French Decrees are repealed, 252; his reports from London, 283.

Russia, mission to, declared inexpedient, i. 11; minister to, appointed, 86; her rupture with France in 1811, 385, 398, 399, 412–423.

Ryland, Herman W., secretary to Sir James Craig, i. 86.

Sackett's Harbor, military importance of, ii. 342, 343.

Saint Mary's River, i. 165.

Salt duty, repeal of, ii. 149, 150; to be re-enacted, 157, 166, 167.

Sandwich, opposite Detroit, ii. 302.

Savary, Duc de Rovigo, i. 241.

Sawyer, British Vice-admiral, ii. 368.

Sawyer, Lemuel, member of Congress from North Carolina, i. 184.

Scheldt, British expedition to, i. 107.

Schooner, the swiftest sailer in the world, ii. 48.

Scott, Sir William, decides the French Decrees to be still in force, ii. 267.

Scott, Winfield, captain of artillery in 1808, ii. 292; his description of the army, 292; lieutenant-colonel at Queenston Heights, 351; surrenders, 352.

Seamen, foreign, in the American service, ii. 455–457.

Search, right of, as understood by Napoleon, i. 137, 145.

Seaver, Ebenezer, member of Congress from Massachusetts, ii. 400.

Sedition Law, the, ii. 146.

Semonville, Comte de, his official address, i. 382, 388, ii. 8.

Serurier, succeeds Turreau as French minister at Washington, i. 345, 346; his first interview with Robert Smith, 346; reports the government decided to enforce non-intercourse against Great Britain, 347; his estimates of Gallatin and Robert Smith, ii. 46–50; the crisis of his fortune, 52; reports Monroe's anger at Napoleon's conduct, 51, 53, 54, 57; remonstrates at Barlow's delay, 55; his letter of July 19, 1811, on the repeal of Napoleon's Decrees, 60; his report of Monroe's and Madison's remarks on Napoleon's arrangements, July, 1811, 63, 64; his report of Madison's warlike plans in November, 1811, 129, 130; his reports on Crillon and John Henry's papers, 178–181; his report of Madison's language on the French spoliations, 187; his report of Monroe's language regarding the repeal of the French Decrees, 188, 189, 194, 195; his report of Monroe's remarks on the embargo and war, 200; remonstrates against suspension of the Non-importation Act, 205; his remarks on the failure of the loan, 208; his report of angry feeling against France, 217; his report of Monroe's complaints in June, 1812, 231; his report of Monroe's language about the occupation of East Florida, 241; his report of Monroe's language about negotiation for peace, 415, 416.

" Shannon," British frigate, ii. 368; chases " Constitution," 370.

Sheaffe, R. H., Major-General of the British army in Canada, ii. 349, 351.

Sheridan, Richard Brinsley, i. 265.

Shipping, its prosperity in 1809–1810, i. 15, 290 ; protection of, 319.

Short, William, i. 11.

Sidmouth, Lord, speech on the Orders in Council, i. 59 ; his weariness of the Orders, 282, 283 ; enters Cabinet, ii. 281.

Slavery in Indiana, ii. 75–77.

Sloops-of-War, in the U. S. navy, act of Congress for building six, ii. 449. (See " Wasp," " Hornet," " Argus," " Syren," " Nautilus.")

Smilie, John, member of congress from Pennsylvania, i. 204.

Smith, John Spear, chargé in London, ii. 21, 267.

Smith, Robert, offered the Treasury Department, i. 7, 379 ; becomes Secretary of State, 8, 10; his language about war with France, 35; his letter to Erskine accepting settlement of the " Chesapeake Affair," 68, 69, 89 ; his replies to Canning's three conditions, 71–73; his remarks to Turreau on Jefferson's weakness and indiscretions, 84; introduces F. J. Jackson to the president, 120; his interviews with Jackson, 122–124, 126; his incompetence, 159; Madison's resentment of his conduct on Macon's bill, 186, 187; his supposed quarrels in the Cabinet, 188 ; opposed to Madison's course toward France, 296, 297, 366, 374, 375, 378 ; notifies Turreau of the President's intention to revive the non-intercourse against England, 302, 303; explains to Turreau the occupation of West Florida, 313; his first interviews with Serurier, 346, 347; irritates Madison by questioning

Serurier, 350; his abilities, 363, 376; his removal from the State Department, 375–377; his Address to the People, 378; his retort against Madison, 379; Serurier's estimate of, ii. 46–50; his remark about American schooners, 48; his comments on Jefferson, Madison, and Clinton, 48; his pamphlet reveals secrets annoying to Madison, 54.

Smith, Samuel, senator from Maryland, defeats Gallatin's appointment as Secretary of State, i. 4–7; his quarrel with Gallatin, 10, 11; votes for mission to Russia, 11; re-elected to the Senate, 159; his support of Giles, 180; defeats Macon's bill, 185, 192, 193; his motives, 185, 186, 187, 192; reports bill of his own, 197, 198; moves censure of Pickering, 322; his speech on the Bank Charter, 335, 336; his abilities, 363; opposes every financial proposal, 234; votes against occupying East Florida, 243.

Smyth, Alexander, inspector-general of U. S. army, with rank of brigadier, ii. 353; arrives at Buffalo with brigade, 346; his disagreement with Van Rensselaer, 346, 348; ordered to take command, 353; his Niagara campaign, 354–358; dropped from the army-roll, 358.

Snyder, Simon, governor of Pennsylvania, i. 13.

Spain, Napoleon's and Moore's campaigns in, i. 22–28; Wellesley's campaigns in, 268.

Spanish America, Napoleon's policy toward, i. 32, 33, 384, 385, 407; Jefferson's wishes regarding, 37, 38 ; Madison's policy towards, 38, 39, 305–315; Spencer Perceval's policy toward, 269, 283, 284;

movements for independence in, 305.

Specie in the United States in 1810, i. 330.

Spoliations by Napoleon, i. 30, 151, 152, 220, 255; value of, 242, 243; Madison's anger at, 292; Madison's demand for indemnity, 295, 296; their municipal character, 299; their justification as reprisals, 230, 232, 234, 237, 254, 258, 259, 388, 391, 396; in Denmark, 409, 411; not matter of discussion, ii. 54, 125; Madison's language regarding, 187; Monroe's language regarding, 188, 189; new, reported in March, 1812, 193, 224, 251, in June, 231; probable value of, 247.

Stanford, Richard, member of Congress from North Carolina, i. 182; his retort on Calhoun, ii. 144; his speech on war, 146.

Stanley, Lord, ii. 283.

Steamboat, i. 215, 216.

Stephen, James, his speech of March 6, 1809, i. 60, 65; his remarks on Erskine's arrangement, 98; on the Orders, ii. 276; yields to a parliamentary inquiry, 284.

Story, Joseph, retires from Congress, i. 76; obnoxious to Jefferson, 359.

Strong, Caleb, re-elected governor of Massachusetts in April, 1812, ii. 204; his Fast Proclamation, 399; declines to obey call for militia, 400; calls out three companies, 400.

Sumter, Thomas, appointed minister to Brazil, i. 11.

Sweden, Bernadotte, Prince of, i. 424; his rupture with Napoleon, 425, 426; Napoleon declares war on, ii. 251.

Swedish Pomerania, i. 425.

" Syren," sloop-of-war, ii. 378.

TALLEYRAND, Charles Maurice de, his letter of Dec. 21, 1804; on the boundaries of Louisiana, i. 321, 322.

Taxes, war, ii. 157, 165, 166; postponed, 168, 204; reported June 26, 1812, 235; postponed by Congress 235, 444: bill for, 447.

Taylor, John, member of Congress from South Carolina, author of Macon's bill No. 2, i. 194; his speech, 195, 196; introduces Bank charter, 208.

Taylor, John, of Caroline, his advice to Monroe, i. 369, 370; Monroe's letter to, June 13, 1812, ii. 66; his remarks on the presidential election of 1812, 414, 417.

Tazewell, Littleton Waller, i. 161.

Tecumthe, or Tecumseh, his origin, ii. 78; his plan of Indian confederation, 78, 79; establishes himself at Tippecanoe, 79; character of his village, 80; joined by the Wyandots, 83; his conference with Harrison, Aug. 12, 1810, 85-88; seizes salt in June, 1811, 90; his talk at Vincennes, July 27, 1811, 91; starts for the Creek country, 92; his account of the affair at Tippecanoe, 105, 109; returns from the Creek country, 108; his reply to British complaints, 109; his speech of May 16, 1812, 111; joins the British at Malden, 329, 330; routs Ohio militia, 315; at the battle of Maguaga, 325; at the capture of Detroit, 332.

Terre aux Bœufs, encampment at, i. 171-175.

Thiers, Louis Adolphe, on Napoleon, i. 225, 226, 236.

"Times," The London, on the Orders in Council, i. 62; on English apathy towards the United States, ii. 24; on an American war, 287.

Tippecanoe Creek, ii. 68, 79; Indian settlement at, 80; character of, 81; to be a large Indian resort, 91; to be broken up, 92, 94; Harrison's march on, 97; arrival at, 98; camp at, 101; battle of, 103; characterized by Tecumthe, 105, 109, 111; retreat from, 106 ; Harrison's estimate of effect of battle, 107, 108; charged upon England, 140, 143.

Tompkins, D. D., Governor of New York; his prevention of the bank charter, ii. 209.

Toronto. (See York.)

Torpedo, Fulton's, i. 209.

Totten, Joseph G., captain of engineers, ii. 350, 352.

Towson, Nathan, captain of artillery, ii. 347.

Treaty of Feb. 22, 1819, with Spain, ceding Florida, 237.

Treaties, Indian, of Greenville, Aug. 3, 1795, ii. 79; of Aug. 18, 1804, with the Delaware Indians, ceding land, 75; of Aug. 27, 1804, with the Piankeshaw Indians, ceding land, 75, 77; of Aug. 21, 1805, with the Delawares, Pottawatomies, Miamis, Eel River, and Weas, 75; of Nov. 25, 1808, with the Chippewa, Ottawa, Pottawatomy, Wyandot and Shawanee nations, 82; of Sept. 30, 1809, with the Delawares, Pottawatomies, Miamis, and Eel River Miamis, 83, 85, 87.

Troup, George McIntosh, member of Congress from Georgia, i. 185, 202; on admission of West Florida, 324; his war-speech, ii. 144, 145; votes for frigates, 164.

Turner, Charles, member of Congress from Massachusetts, assaulted in Plymouth, ii. 400, 409.

Turreau, French minister to the United States, his anger with the government in the spring of 1809, i. 33-40; his report on the repeal of the embargo, 34; on the non-importation act, 35; on disunion, 36; on the Spanish colonies, 37; his advice on rupture with the United States, 40 ; his report of Gallatin's remarks on renewal of intercourse with Great Britain, 74; his report of Robert Smith's remarks on Jefferson's weakness and indiscretions, 84; his note of June 14, 1809, remonstrating at the unfriendly conduct of the United States, 84; his recall ordered by Napoleon, 226 ; his successor arrives, 345, 346.

UKASE, Imperial, of Dec. 19, 1810, i. 418, 419.

Union, dissolution of, a delicate topic, i. 14; a cause of repealing the embargo, 34 ; discussed by Turreau, 36; discussed in New England, ii. 403, 409.

United States, population in 1810, i. 289.

"United States," 44-gun frigate, ii. 363; first cruise of, in 1812, 366, 375; at Boston, 378; second cruise of, 381; captures the "Macedonian," 382, 383.

University, national, i. 319.

VAN BUREN, MARTIN, his support of De Witt Clinton, ii. 409, 413.

Van Rensselaer, Solomon, colonel of New York militia, commands attack on Queenston, ii. 348.

Van Rensselaer, Stephen, Major-General of New York militia, ordered to take command at Niagara, ii. 321; forwards letter to Hull, 324; his force, Aug. 19, 1812, 341; his alarming position, 342, 343; his force, Sept. 15, 344 ; expected to invade Canada with six thousand

men, 345; his attack on Queenston, 346, 347–353 ; retires from command, 353; Monroe's opinion of, 396 ; Jefferson's comment on, 398.

Varnum, Joseph B., of Massachusetts, re-elected speaker, i. 76; his rulings on the previous question, 353; elected senator, ii. 116.

Vermilion River, Indian boundary, ii. 97, 98.

Vienna, Napoleon's draft for a decree of, i. 143, 144, 150, 152.

Vincennes, territorial capital of Indiana, ii. 68, 71, 79; the Shawnee prophet's talk at, 80; Tecumthe's talks at, 85, 91; citizens' meeting at, 92; Indian deputation at, 108; panic at, 110.

Virginia creates manufactures in New England, i. 19, 20 ; apathy of, toward the war, ii. 413, 414.

"Vixen," sloop-of-war, captured, ii. 386.

WABASH, valley of, ii. 67, 68, 75, 77; Harrison's land purchase in, 83; war imminent in, 85.

Wadsworth, William, Brigadier-General of New York militia, ii. 351 ; surrenders at Queenston, 352.

Wagner, Jacob, editor of the "Federal Republican," ii. 406, 407.

Wales, Prince of.   (See George, Prince of Wales.)

War, declared by Monroe to be nearly decided in November, 1811, ii. 130; recommended by House Committee of Foreign Relations, Nov. 29, 1811, 133–136; its objects explained by Peter B. Porter, 136; its effects discussed by Felix Grundy, 138, 141; Grundy's account of its causes, 139, 140; Macon's view of its object, 145 ; war-taxes (see Finance), war-power (see Militia), department of, its incompetence, 168 (see Eustis ;) Monroe's remarks on, 190; Madison's message recommending, 221–226; expediency of, 223; Madison's recapitulation of causes, 220–223; Calhoun's report on causes, 226; Calhoun's bill for, adopted by the House, 228; by the Senate, 228, 229; and signed by the President, 229; criticisms on the conduct of, 392–399; opposition to, 398–403; apathy towards, 414; only attainable object of, 418; reasons of continuance, 430–432.

Ward, Robert Plumer, ii. 279.

Washington city, F. J. Jackson's impressions of, i. 116–119.

Washington, President, expenditures of his administration, i. 200.

"Wasp," sloop-of-war, ii. 364, 378; her action with the "Frolic," 379, 380.

Wayne, Fort, ii. 294.

Wea Indians, ii. 71, 75, 87.

Webster, Daniel, his Rockingham Resolutions, ii. 403.

Wellesley, Marquess, his character, i. 264, 265, 269; appointed ambassador to the Supreme Junta, 267; becomes Foreign Secretary, 268; his friendship with Pinkney, 270, 275; his promises, 271; his note on Jackson, 272; his remark on American hatred, 273; his procrastination, 277–280, 285; his contempt for his colleagues, 281, 282; resolves to retire, 285; his reply to Champagny's letter of August 5, 286; hopes for a Whig ministry in November, 1811, ii. 4; his controversy with Pinkney over the French Decrees and the law of blockade, 5, 6, 9; abandons hope of a Whig ministry, 14; rejects Pinkney's demands, 14, 15, 18; appoints a minister to Washington, 16; his instructions of April 10, 1811, to the new minister (see Foster), 22, 23; criticises his colleagues for apathy towards America, 24; his instructions to Foster of Jan. 28 1812, 191, 192; settles the "Chesapeake" affair, 121, 122, 270; urges his colleagues to choose a course, 267, 268; resigns from the cabinet, Jan. 16, 1812, 271.

Wellesley, Sir Arthur, i. 266; fights th' battle of Talavera, 106; made a viscount, 264; general-in-chief, 267; retreats, 268.

Wellesley, Henry, i. 264; envoy in Spain, 268; on Perceval's commercial policy, 283, 284.

Westmoreland, Lord Privy Seal, i. 282.

West Point, school at, i. 319.

Whiskey-tax, rejected, ii. 167.

Whitbread, Samuel, member of Parliament, i. 50; ii. 270.

Widgery, William, member of Congress from Massachusetts, ii. 400.

Wilberforce, William, member of Parliament, ii. 273, 280.

Wilkinson, James, brigadier-general, his movements, i. 37; Gallatin's remarks on his character, 38; military court of inquiry on, 169; his influence on the army, 169; ordered to New Orleans, 170; his encampment at Terre aux Bœufs, 171–175; summoned to Washington for investigation, 175; senior brigadier, ii. 291.

Williams, David R., not a member of the Eleventh Congress, i. 76; in the Twelfth Congress, ii. 122; chairman of military committee, 124, 435.

Wilna, in Poland, Barlow's journey to, ii. 263, 264.

Winchester, Joseph, brigadier-general, ii. 291.

Winder, William H., Colonel of Fourteenth Infantry, ii. 357, 359.

Wolcott, Alexander, i. 359, 360.

Wool, John E., Captain of Thirteenth Infantry, gains Queenston Heights, ii. 349, 350.

Woollen manufactures, i. 17.

Wright, Robert, member of Congress from Maryland, his motion on impressments, i. 351, 352 ; opposes Gallatin's taxes, ii. 167; his threats against opposition, 213.

YORK, or Toronto, capital of Upper Canada, ii. 316.

York, Duke of, i. 57, 58, 105.

END OF VOL. II.